INFORMATION TECHNOLOGY IN LIBRARIANSHIP

INFORMATION TECHNOLOGY IN LIBRARIANSHIP

New Critical Approaches

EDITED BY GLORIA J. LECKIE
AND JOHN E. BUSCHMAN

LIBRARIES UNLIMITED
A Member of the Greenwood Publishing Group
Westport, Connecticut • London

Library of Congress Cataloging-in-Publication Data

Information technology in librarianship : new critical approaches / edited by Gloria J. Leckie and John E. Buschman.
p. cm.
Includes bibliographical references and index.
ISBN 978-1-59158-629-6 (alk. paper)
1. Libraries—Information technology. I. Leckie, Gloria J. II. Buschman, John.
Z678.9.I5334 2009
025.00285—dc22 2008030424

British Library Cataloguing in Publication Data is available.

Library of Congress Catalog Card Number: 2008030424
ISBN: 978-1-59158-629-6

First published in 2009

Libraries Unlimited, 88 Post Road West, Westport, CT 06881
A Member of the Greenwood Publishing Group, Inc.
www.lu.com

Printed in the United States of America

The paper used in this book complies with the Permanent Paper Standard issued by the National Information Standards Organization (Z39.48–1984).

10 9 8 7 6 5 4 3 2 1

CONTENTS

2 Applications

INTRODUCTION: INFORMATION TECHNOLOGIES AND LIBRARIES—WHY DO WE NEED NEW CRITICAL APPROACHES?

John E. Buschman and Gloria J. Leckie

WHY AGAIN?

Fifteen years ago one of us edited the first edition of this volume (Buschman, 1993b), and asked in the title of the introductory chapter, "Why do we need a critical approach to information technology in librarianship?" The answer was that, given the enormous changes to libraries that new information technologies had brought about, "if the profession as a whole . . . is to make responsible decisions about libraries, if we seek to fill a central role in debate about information policy in our institutions . . . , if we are to aid and further public and scholarly inquiry, . . . then we must account for and join that established body of theoretical and critical scholarship which has seriously questioned the role that technology has come to play [and has] challenged [its] role . . . as a historical phenomenon in relation to work, power, education, and media; and critically examined the relationship of technology and science" (Buschman, 1993c, pp. 1–2). The contention was that to do otherwise would be to ignore a serious, longstanding, relevant, and informative intellectual debate and would be irresponsible. Librarianship needed to deepen its analysis of technology.

What followed in that volume were relatively straightforward introductions to ideas and scholarship on the nonneutrality of technology (Balabanian, 1993; Slaby, 1993), critiques of technology in education (Carbone, 1993) and communications scholarship (Jansen, 1993), and questions about transformations and control of work (Zuboff, 1993). The approach was to ask, What does discipline or field X do in the way of critiques of technology? The library applications of critical approaches in the second half of the book have proven prescient: technology and censorship/monitoring possibilities in libraries (Buschman, 1993d), the role of libraries in a shrinking civic sphere (Gray, 1993), technology and changing library work (Winter, 1993), the political economy of our new information resources (Haar, 1993), and the downside of entrepreneurial emphases in the field (Buschman, 1993a) are *all* very current concerns. Though the means and speed of information delivery, the pace and scope of development, and the public's expectations of libraries have all been transformed again (and again) in the last 15 years, the underlying critical perspective of all of those contributions remain germane.

Librarianship tended to take up the first volume's themes in a variety of ways. For instance, Crawford and Gorman (1995) vigorously defended print. They cast it as oppositional to what they critiqued as "technolust," serious fiscal imbalances in library investments, and consistently overblown predictions on behalf of technologies and what they would do for libraries and patrons. Gorman (2003) later followed up some of these same themes with his defense of traditional, core library services (e.g., reference and cataloging) in the face of technology and its cheerleaders. Mann (2001, 2007) takes much the same approach, but from an explicit research library perspective, and he is more analytical of the resulting specific intellectual and research problems and highly critical of library leadership in the process. And, ironically enough, F. W. Lancaster (1999)—the early champion of the "paperless library"—now complains that technology has been dehumanizing and that librarians have been "uncritical" and "mesmerized" by the technology. (pp. 806–807) Michael Harris and his coauthors (1993, 1998) linked library technological faddishness with social and economic bandwagons and provided a thoroughgoing critique of Lancaster's (and librarianship's) long-running and shallow appropriation of Daniel Bell's postindustrial thesis. There has been a critical examination of the gentle discursive handling information technology and its science has received (for example see Frohmann, 1992, 1994). Gorman (2006/2007) and Warner (2002) are two notable examples of *critical* (vs. passive) concern over technology and future preservation issues, joining a topic that has made it into the popular media (Grafton, 2007; Stille, 1999). Buschman and Carbone (1991, 1996) linked library technologies to control issues and technocracy, and Buschman (2003, pp. 149–167) further linked new library technological developments to postmodern temporal disjunction. Finally, the journal *Progressive Librarian* has led the way in promoting and publishing scholarship taking a variety of explicitly critical approaches to technology over the years (see, for example, Agre, 1997; Andersen, 2005; Buschman 2007; Darch, 2000; R. Harris, 1995/1996; Hudson, 1999; McDonald, 2004–2005; Schiller, 1990/1991; Sharman, 2001; Tien, 2005/2006; Warner & Buschman, 2000).

So the question is begged, why *new* critical approaches now? First and foremost, while the first edition of this book did its small part in spurring some critical output sampled above, the juggernaut of technology has in no way been halted. Quite the opposite: our investments and our promotional rhetoric have doubled and redoubled. Second, the newer forms of technology have become so saturated into wealthy cultures that their existence has become quite naturalized. As a result, their effects are invisible in new ways (OCLC, 2007) and the demands to accommodate technologized culture (in classrooms or libraries, for instance) is itself considered natural and self-evident. Third, there is a difference between skepticism (the attitude of doubt or even of common complaint about technology's so-called benefits) and critique (involving analysis, estimation, judgment, evidence, theory). Gorman, and Lancaster's late comments noted previously, are prominent examples in the profession of a skeptical, "it ain't necessarily so" approach. Professional eye-rolling and complaint about prominent technology firms and system or product upgrades are now common—no longer taboo. A *critical* approach to information technology in librarianship systematically contrasts the "descriptive 'is' [with] the normative 'ought'" to look past and examine the status quo (Brosio, 1990, p. 69). In more up-to-date theoretical language, by a critical approach we invoke a "hermeneutics of suspicion" (Ricoeur, quoted in White, 2006, p. 317)—a suspicion "that casts into question social structures of inequality [and] power" (White, 2006, p. 317). It is more than mere assertion to say that technologies are prime elements in our social and personal identities and the social structures in which we embed them (see, for example, Bray, 2007; DiMaggio, Hargittai, Neuman, & Robinson, 2001; G. Marx & Muschert, 2007; Zukin & Maguire, 2004). Fourth, new critical approaches are called for in our field because the capital accumulation efforts conducted through new technologies have much more than redoubled. So-called Fast capitalism (Hardt & Negri, 2000), varying surveillance technologies (G. Marx & Muschert, 2007), and the effects of technologies on systems of legal protection (Braman, 2006) are swamping grassroots attempts to harness and shape the technology for democratic purposes (Pyati, 2007) or for children's learning (Large, 2005), for example. Finally, the grounds for critique need renewing, the reasons for critique need reminding, and alternative perspectives on our library technological juggernauts need to be renewed so that they may be an effective part of the discussions over technology in libraries. The first volume did this by sampling relevant disciplines. This volume seeks to highlight a series of broader theoretical approaches and traditions in which many of the old and new critical approaches are rooted.

CRITICAL APPROACHES TO TECHNOLOGY (INFORMATION AND OTHERWISE): SIX TYPES

The types of critical approaches to be reviewed in brief are (adapted from DiMaggio et al., 2001, p. 309, except where noted):

- A focus on capital control of technology for purposes of production, cultural hegemony, and promoting needless consumption.

- An emphasis on the technologies (social, mechanical, informational) of rationalization, control, and monitoring.
- The information revolution viewed as an ideological phenomenon (Slack, 1984).
- Feminist critiques of technology (Bray, 2007).
- The analysis of technological utopianism (Segal, 2005).
- The problem of technology, politics, civil society, and the public sphere.

The usual caveats apply here: these are not pure and distinct divisions—the scholars characterized as taking these approaches very clearly draw from and utilize many sources and critical traditions and so they bleed into one another. That will clearly be seen in even the brief overviews that follow. They have been chosen because their work illustrates one of these types of critical approaches. Second, there are disagreements over characterizations. For example, Marxism contains both critiques of technological developments *and* took technology to be a rather neutral affair with potential for good (Etzkowitz, 1991; Ferre, 1988, pp. 54–57). Third, this can in no way be a thorough accounting of the literatures relating to the six areas—merely a characterization of each.

Capital Control of Technology

Classically, this view is anchored in the work of Karl Marx: "the bourgeoisie cannot exist without constantly revolutionizing the instruments of production . . . and with them the whole relations of society" (K. Marx & Engels, 1955, p. 135). Capitalist "society [is] based upon the production of commodities, in which the producers in general enter into social relations with one another by treating their products as commodities and values, whereby they reduce their individual private labour to the standard of homogeneous human labour"—itself now a commodity (K. Marx, 1955b, p. 151). In turn, science becomes "the analysis and application of mechanical and chemical laws . . . which enables the machine to perform the same labor as that previously performed by the worker." Scientific knowledge and inquiry itself becomes a commodity—"Invention then becomes a business" (K. Marx, quoted in Etzkowitz, 1991, p. 359). And, "One capitalist always kills many. [C]entralisation, or [the] appropriation of many capitalists by few, develops, on an ever extending scale . . . the economizing of all means of production . . ., the entanglement of all peoples in the net of the world-market, and . . . the international character of the capitalistic regime" (K. Marx, 1955a, p. 150).

These basic ideas reached their apotheosis in the pessimism of the Frankfurt School and its analysis of the culture industry via its role in propelling consumerism (via the technologies of communication over long distances and mass communication and the techniques of advertising and marketing) to the fore of individual identity, definitions of the so-called good life, and of democracy (Beniger, 1989; Brosio, 1980, pp. 20–26; Brown, 1991; Kellner, n.d.). Marcuse (1964) called it a "one dimensional" society wherein "Nature, scientifically comprehended and mastered, reappears in the technical apparatus of production . . . which sustains and improves the life of the individuals while subordinating them to the masters of the apparatus" (p. 166). A consumer economy so constructed calls for "social controls [to address] the overwhelming need for the production and consumption of waste" (Marcuse, 1964, p. 7; see also Brown, 1991; Zukin & Maguire, 2004). These basic ideas resurface in current forms in the critiques of the following:

- Media monopolies, the control of information and its distribution and the political effects (Bagdikian, 2004; Bennett, 2004; DiMaggio et al., 2001; McChesney, 1999; Robins & Webster, 2004; Schiller, 1989).
- The technological/media/consumerist construction of identity and its effects on personality development, civic institutions, community, the family, social isolation, political participation and dissent, and so forth (Bennett, 2004; Brown, 1991; DiMaggio et al., 2001; Robins & Webster, 2004; Wilson & Peterson, 2002; Zukin & Maguire, 2004).
- The digital divide between haves and have-nots within wealthier nations, and the global digital divide between wealthier portions of the globe and the poorer portions. There are further lines of critique that note that, since the new technologies are means of communication—our new form of highly concentrated power—they continue to reproduce, market and sell the hegemony of classes within nations and regions within the globe (Bennett, 2004; DiMaggio et al., 2001, Norris, 2004; Wilson & Peterson, 2002).
- The automation, packaging, direction, and control of intellectual work (Noble, 2001; Zuboff, 1993).

Rationalization, Control, Monitoring

Closely related to the critical perspective just outlined, this view is classically associated with the nineteenth-century German sociologist Max Weber. Rationalization was a predominant theme of analysis and investigation in Weber's career. He saw that the Enlightenment (primarily in the form of the development of science and technology) had killed off the "enchanted" religious view of the world, giving rise to the rational worldview. This had a direct effect on the legitimacy of traditional forms of authority (the divine right of monarchs and ecclesiastical authority), and in turn promoted a rationalistic legal form of authority, exercised through bureaucracy—itself a particular form of rationalization of human activity (Glassman, 1991). The stage was thus set for Weber's famous "iron cage": "the modern economic order . . . is now bound to the technical and economic conditions of machine production which to-day determine the lives of all the individuals who are born into this mechanism, not only those directly concerned with economic acquisition, with irresistible force" (Weber, 1958, p. 181). Capitalism depends on and is in turn absorbed into the hyperrationalizing imperatives of bureaucracy to function, increasing authoritarian and antidemocratic tendencies in society both governmentally and economically (Glassman, 1991). There is a correspondence to Marx in the "concentration of the means of administration," which takes on an "unshatterable," "permanent character." It promotes a "rationalist way of life," and, with it, the rise of and dependence on experts. Weber comes to the fatalistic conclusion that we are indeed trapped in the "iron cage" of our own reason: anything that seeks to displace bureaucratic rationalization must be at least as well organized (Weber, 1946, pp. 221, 228, 240).

Perhaps the most famous and persistent proponent of this dark view is Jacques Ellul (1986) who calls it "technique"—essentially a hyperrationalized social organization that sprang (originally) from machines and "mechanics." Technique, he declares, is inescapable: we "cannot choose . . . means any more than . . . ends" (Ellul, 1986, p. 32). It is an all or nothing proposition, and when human needs, human limitations, or human desires of any type (economic, spiritual, physical, emotional, familial, etc.) come up against the autonomy and force of technique, there is no question of which will adapt to which: performance in sports, economic performance, speed performance in transportation, and so forth must all register higher on the scale. Socially and educationally, problems of technique are the only serious problems worth study and research, and to question their basis or worth has become the ultimate in social dysfunction (Ellul, 1986). Less dire but equally unsettling from a somewhat different perspective is Lewis Mumford (1991). He notes that civilization had its beginnings in "theological-technological mass organization," or what he called "technics." What followed were the technological triumphs of that form of rational organization (or, "megamachines"): pyramids and large armies—Roman armies of conquest in particular. It is technics—his version of rationalization—that harnesses technologies to undemocratic ends: "The inventors of nuclear bombs . . . and computers are the pyramid builders of our own age: psychologically inflated by a . . . myth of unqualified power, . . . moved by obsessions and compulsions no less irrational than those of earlier absolute systems: particularly the notion that [they] must be expanded" (Mumford, 1991, p. 17). Though he takes pains to identify democratic (vs. authoritarian) technics, like Weber and Ellul, Mumford argues that this juggernaut of social rationalization threatens democracy and especially our existence. Similarly, Mumford (1991) notes the loss of security and comfort that human beings depended on for millennia forming a bedrock of human identity—family, hearth, tradition, community, faith, connection to one's tools and work product, connection to the people one exchanged goods and coinage with, and so forth—and speculates on this loss and the results for people in a rationalized, technic- and machine-mediated culture. These baseline analyses, which identify instrumental/technical/technological rationalization, lay out core ideas contained in other critiques. For example:

- Joseph Weizenbaum's (1976, p. 259) analysis of the internal functioning of computers and computer programs posits that, in a culture of "technological inevitability," the opaqueness of computer programs to most people who more and more depend on and intertwine their lives with computers and software will embed even further the "imperialism of instrumental reason" (p. 259). When science is understood *as* reason, and yet science and the information science basis of our newest technologies are so little understood, we set ourselves up for such imperialism.
- James Beniger (1989) tracks the "control revolution"—that is, the combination of technological communications inventions and social science that allowed more and more and more social and economic functions to come under rational control: the "purposive influence toward a predetermined goal" (p. 53). Beniger (1989) consciously carries on Weber's analysis in noting the "crisis of control" within the early industrial revolution: the growth of production, consumption, commodity flow, distribution, and the organization of labor had all outstripped the limits of the personal form of organization and management in place at the time. Weber's bureaucratic rationalization was the first answer to this crisis, and it soon coupled with early forms of the "new control technologies" like the steam engine, open loop loom controllers, interchangeable parts, accounting, railroads, and the telegraph to harness, direct, and control in manageable bureaucratic forms the explosion in economic output (pp. 57–61). Beniger in turn traces the bleed-through to social scientific forms of rationalization and control via research in advertising, marketing, and media to stimulate and direct consumption to snap up this production (1989, pp. 61–63).
- It is a short leap from this point to the information society and the dystopian potential of misunderstood trends that dramatically increase the scope and power of control technologies. Panoptical possibilities within the new technological surveillance methods combine with persistent misunderstandings of the technology along with slippage in basic concepts like privacy and security (G. Marx & Muschert, 2007). A further short step is the technologically enhanced social science method to hyperrefine marketing to further consumption (Robins & Webster, 2004; Zukin & Maguire, 2004).

The Information Revolution as Ideology

In an important 1984 article, Jennifer Daryl Slack encapsulated a set of perspectives on the information society concept, identifying the shaping and structuring of it as an ideology. She begins by stating categorically that she is neither arguing that the information revolution is merely false consciousness nor purely ideological (p. 247). Rather, there are "incredibly successful" meanings and articulations now in place that form the "ideological terrain" to the extent that talk of an information revolution or an information society "appeals powerfully to common sense" (Slack, 1984, p. 249). Cast as a "revolution," this phenomenon comes to us as a positive *fait accompli*—"almost nobody criticizes [prior technological] revolutions for having brought us anything significantly undesirable" (p. 251)—and we are thus "encouraged to adapt rather than act" (p. 250). There is a correlative tendency to "collapse all the alternative definitions into a definition of information as a commodity"

(p. 252), and having declared ourselves to be in an information "age, the organizing principle upon which society is based changes" (p. 253). Thus a notion of technology as autonomous is enshrined—that is, technologies are not seen to be guided or produced by social and economic choices and interests (p. 254). Slack was not the first—or only—scholar to identify the ideological and interest-bound nature of the information revolution, its technological basis, and its attendant society. Others have fleshed out the analysis:

- John McDermott (1986) wrote originally over three decades ago of technology as the "opiate of the intellectuals" with an ethos of "*laissez innover*" (p. 99): "Technological innovation exhibits a distinct tendency to work for the general welfare in the long run." Ideologically, this tends to enshrine the interests of a certain class of managers and elites, insulating them and the effects of their decisions from democratic forces that should guide society (pp. 111–121).
- Theodore Roszak (1986) famously noted the "cult of information," in which technological artifacts have been constructed as "objects of veneration"—both a change from the past and an absurdity when one contrasts "information" with other significant technological changes like the light bulb (Roszak, 1993). He excoriates "commercially motivated exaggerations and the opportunistic mystifications of the computer science establishment" (Roszak, 2004, p. 61). David Lyon's (1986, 1995) work has tended to connect Slack's points with Roszak's: there are clearly vested interests, there are contradictions in claims and structures, the phenomenon has been constructed as a natural progression, and it has been the subject of a persistent sales pitch from forecasters and futurists.
- Still others see the ideological sources in the historical design and implementation of machinery (Noble, 1984), and the nature of the technological design process *itself*: "without the existence of certain ideas about the nature of domestic life and the part that appliances might play in it," some of those goods would never have come about in the first place (Forty, quoted in Mackay, 1995, p. 48). This idea is itself closely related to marketing as a shaping force in the development of a technology and vice versa (Mackay, 1995, p. 48).

Feminist Critiques of Technology

An informative entry into the basis of feminist critiques of technology is the work of Dorothy Smith. Though Smith does not focus on technology per se, her theoretical insights are characteristic of the approach and broad impact of feminist critiques of technology. Research, she argues, "operated with a conceptual apparatus that has served to detach the phenomena from the working contexts of the social process constituting the phenomena just named." Thus, "women are outside the frame"—that is, their experiences (work, routines, life organization, daily schedules) do not conform to any models or categories, so they don't "exist" in the traditions of research and their theoretical underpinnings (Smith, 1977, pp. 149–151; see also Bart, 1991, pp. 250–254). Her resulting "institutional ethnography" posits that those outside the frame are not merely "cases," but are rather entry points "into the actual workings of [that] which produce[s] the generalized and abstract character of contemporary societies," and a means "into the multiple forms of coordination which shape the everyday world and tie it into broader forms of social organization" (Grahame, 1998, pp. 353, 356). Concretely for Smith (quoted in Mann and Kelley, 1997), this means the invisibility of the apparatus and structures that shape women's worlds (children, health care, food preparation, laundry, clerical work, and, we would add, all the attendant, interwoven technologies) and "provid[e] for a man's liberation [and] the logistics of his bodily existence. . . . The more successful women are in mediating the world of concrete particulars, the more men do not have to become engaged with (and therefore conscious of) that world" (p. 399).

Like Smith, feminist critiques of technology start with a perspective traditionally outside of the frame, and they take women's experiences with and appropriations of technologies as an entry point into how the technology actually works and what the disconnects are between intent in design, how gender is structured by technologies, and the resulting social shaping of the technologies by women (see for example Morritt, 1997, and Vehvilainen, 1997, who both ground their critiques of technology in the theoretical work of Smith). Technologies are thus inextricably intertwined with questions of gender. They are "firmly coded male," with men having a "natural affinity" for it (Bray, 2007, p. 38). From this has flowed a series of critiques:

- Technical skills and domains are divided between the more valued masculine and the less valued feminine (hunting vs. basket-weaving; tool use and care learned from fathers vs. cooking or managing households or servants learned from mothers; hacking skills [boys] vs. emoticons [girls]; Bray, 2007, p. 38).
- From this view of technology came a series of analyses in the 1970s and 1980s rooting out the "patriarchal nature of technology, and technoscience generally," or uncovering technology as dominating or stereotyping women (Bray, 2007, p. 39; Wajcman, 1991).
- In response, other studies emerged that focused on the ambiguity of then-new technologies, the spaces to market them, and the political economy of domestic goods (Parr, 1999). New technologies (appliances) genuinely did spare women some drudgery (Michelfelder, 2000), and new urban spaces like department stores to market them provided women the reason (shopping) to be in public or to be together without men (Zukin & Maguire, 2004).
- There has been a feminist examination of everyday technologies and appliances, like the telephone, that broke down significant isolating barriers to sociability and contact among women (Frissen, 1995; Michelfelder, 2000; Moyal, 1995). In turn, other studies showed certain appliances as redefining cultural standards, for instance, of what was a clean enough house, intensifying the work to be done at home (Bray, 2007, p. 40; Wajcman, 1991). Or women's needs and desires were consistently ignored by the men designing appliances, houses, and products ostensibly for them (Berg, 1995; Zukin & Maguire, 2004, p. 179).

- Birth control was a significant and controversial technology taken up and promoted by women in the face of considerable opposition (Etzkowitz, 1991), but the struggles over control (Wajcman, 1991) and instituting a genuine scientific focus on women and the physiological effects of these products—and women's health issues generally—remain (Wyer, Barbercheck, Geisman, Ozturk, & Wayne, 2001, pp. 277–280). Presently, feminist analyses have broadened to consider reproductive technologies in general and the legal/bioethical implications of them (Callahan 1995; Ehrenreich, 2008; Ferrell 2006; Inhorn 2007; Lublin 1998).
- Historically, the important role that women have played in technological breakthroughs has often been masked (Bix, 2001; Plant, 2004; Wajcman, 1991, pp. 15–17), and generally "as technology has raised the status of a task, women workers have less access to those positions"—and vice versa (Pritchard, 1993, p. 3; Webster, 1997). If we take the high-tech-equals-cultural-and-economic-clout thesis seriously, a review of research continues to find women and girls seriously underrepresented in computer science, mathematics, and scientific-technological areas generally from primary grades through graduate school (Barker & Aspray, 2006).
- A focus on consumption led to analyses of the variety of ways in which women could interact with, shape, and appropriate technologies and socially construct them via gender identities—cyber, cyborg, and otherwise (Asdal, Brenna, Gulbrandsen, Moser, & Refseth, 1997; Paasonen, 2005; Poster, 1995, 2004), producing a renewed call for a focus on the communities that design and produce technologies and the "specific material effects of technology on perception, communication, and identity" (Bray, 2007, pp. 40–43).
- A strong and ongoing concern with the social relations of technology, starting with the pioneering work by Donna Haraway (1985) on the cyborg and carried on in the sociotechnological analyses of other scholars such as Allucquere Rosanne Stone (1995), Heather Menzies (1996), Sadie Plant (1997), Bonnie Nardi and Vickie O'Day (1999), Judy Wajcman (2004), and Katherine Hayles (1999).
- Of particular interest for this volume has been the recent feminist theorization and critique of information technologies and associated fields such as cybernetics and artificial intelligence. Alison Adam (1998, 2005) and Katherine Hayles (1999) have been at the forefront of this critique.

These varying strands of feminist technology analysis and critique illustrate the emphatically nonmonolithic nature of social experiences and their uses. "[T]hat is in itself one of the signal aspects of feminist theory" and its analyses of technology (Pritchard, 1993, p. 1): to simply label a technology and its provenance a "masculine construct and leave it at that . . . is unnecessarily defeatist. Technology should not be understood as ready-made artefacts whose use is non-negotiable" (Berg, 1995, p. 85).

Technological Utopianism

Though this theme had been raised in a variety of ways before, the name most closely associated with this thesis is Howard Segal through his book *Tech-*

nological Utopianism in American Culture (1985, reprinted and expanded 2005). Historically, Segal (1995) argues, America had "an uncritical faith in technology's ability to solve all problems," and the country was seen as a "potential utopia . . . to be brought about by technological progress" (p. 175). In particular, he (1995, 2005, pp. 172–175) takes futurists and "visionaries" to task for their blithe, sweeping, "pecuniary," and careless predictions: Alvin Toffler, John Naisbitt, Patricia Aburdene, Francis Fukuyama, Samuel Florman, Bill Gates, Nicholas Negroponte, Simon Ramo, and Virginia Postrel, to name a few. Amusingly, he notes that a version of the old flying car prediction is still around: Michael Dertouzos' imagined "histori-copter" to transport us to visit the past (Segal, 2005, p. 173). However, these forecasters are taken seriously by millions of people yet are somehow never accountable for their overstatements and flat out mistakes because they make three simple, appealing claims: "high tech will make [us] healthier, happier, more efficient, more productive, and more democratic than ever before"; these advances "will dwarf in impact all prior technological advances in their extraordinary degree and speed of transformation"; and third, "comparisons with all prior technological revolutions can therefore be ignored, so profoundly different will the future be from the past" (Segal, 2005, p. 173). Segal traces this heady blend of faith and prediction all the way back through the predictions about technology and its instantiations in the form of grand exhibitions from London's Crystal Palace (then about the benefits of the Industrial Revolution), the World's Fairs in New York in 1939–1940 and 1960, and Disney's EPCOT. The real historical record is much, much more complex: industrial and nuclear waste, the sometimes-senseless medical extension of life, and the weaponization of space (to name a few) all cut into the euphoria and should lead us to a healthier ambivalence concerning technological progress—but that seems to come slowly (Segal, 1995, 2005; see also Hershock, 2003).

Others have taken up this theme as well:

- Langdon Winner's work ranges over many of the themes outlined in all six of the types of critical approaches to technology, but he has had a consistent focus on the gap between rhetoric and reality: hyperoptimistic technological visions are "technopornographic"; while "unhindered personal consumption" has flourished, the broad pattern of technological development that made that system possible brought much more centralized control and direction. He notes that the "sanguine" promises of computer scientists about the benefits of our never-ending technological upheavals and shift to an information basis avoid asking "What could go wrong?"—or indeed, asking *any* questions about ends, means, and reasons for or reasons against (Winner, 1986, pp. 13, 93, 100–101). Those who raise such "impertinent questions" are labeled Luddites or antitechnology (Winner, 2004).
- Neil Postman's work also ranges far and wide, but he has persistently pointed out the results of the introduction of technologies, best summed by the aphorism "to a man with a hammer, everything looks like a nail" (Postman, 1985). Our technologies change meanings: "virus" and "worm" begat corollary words to describe

computer and network problems and solutions such as "infected," "virulent," "contagious," "quarantine," and "sterilize." This, he argues, is not localized nor mere "picturesque anthropomorphism" but rather "reflects a profound shift in perception about the relationship of computers to humans"—with many implications for sourceless authority and transfer of human responsibility to an abstract reason or agent (Postman, 1993, pp. 113–114). In particular, Postman (1979, 1993) has focused on the technological and media bias (via the mediums themselves, not their content) that promote a nonliterate culture. The hard work of literacy forms the basis of much of what we value as genuine human achievement, and we are massively subjecting our culture to the influence of audio, visual, and distinctly nonlinear technologies and media.

- Edward Tenner (1996) has cataloged and examined the unintended consequences of everyday technologies: carpal tunnel from overuse of computers and keyboards, stronger viruses due to the overuse of antibiotics, back pain from original, supposedly ergonomic design of office chairs, the encouragement of pests in warm and enclosed homes, and so forth. His lesson is that few—or no—new technologies and so-called benefits emerge as unqualified blessings, and continuing to pretend otherwise invites further disasters, discomfort, and suffering. Similarly and more specifically here, computers (and digitized content generally) have developed in such a manner that there is "disagreement about ways of representing electronic text [so] that any given collection of texts . . . will be a mix of usually incompatible kinds of codes requiring different software and often different hardware to interpret"—and this pattern of rapid development and orphaned formats and reading devices has characterized new media (and old media digital conversions) and their storage means for some time (O'Donnell, 1998, p. 47; see also Cornell University Library, 2003–2007).

Technology, Politics, and the Public Sphere

Jurgen Habermas's (1989) public sphere thesis is a complex one, but in terms of a critique of technology, it can be stated succinctly. The public sphere grew out of the sociability and common interests generated by markets and cities in the late Middle Ages and Renaissance, and it grew into exchanges of opinion and debate over policy—essentially then an extragovernmental form of authority—in the intellectual press of the eighteenth century. This idea—of free exchange and the then quasidemocratic, public accountability of governmental authority—is now thought of as natural, but was at the time novel, even radical. However, the logic of the presses *as* a business (versus their communicative role in rational, democratic public debate over policy) took over in the nineteenth and twentieth centuries, and, in combination with other factors, transformed the public sphere: "the degree of economic concentration and technological-organizational coordination in the newspaper publishing industry seems small in comparison to the new media of the twentieth century" (Habermas, 1989, p. 187). After the role of media in democratic formation was abandoned, the media became a means of *administering* the public sphere—that is, in shaping and directing public opinion via the means of publicity, public relations (these terms have more elaborate historical meanings as used by Habermas, but the common understanding of them conveys enough of the idea), and advertising. The logic of the market—always a partner in the formation of the public sphere—essentially took over. Unlike some of the earlier critiques, we can see that Habermas is not against rationalization per se, but rather the hijacking of rational political will formation by a "technocratic consciousness" that he argues is primarily in service of developing and manipulating markets, not democracy (McCarthy, 1981, pp. 382–382). Habermas (1971) further sees a linking-up of this (redirected) rational trajectory with "scientivism," the ascendancy of "technocratic steering mechanisms and [the] exclu[sion of] rational procedures for the clarification of practical questions" (p. 651). This has strong implications for social practice—particularly democratic decision-making. Like rationalization, it is not that technology is problematic per se, but rather it is a symptom of the vexing problem of bringing "technical control . . . within the range of the consensus of acting and transacting citizens" in a hyperdriven market capitalism (Habermas, quoted in Fleming, 1988, p. 91).

Within this broad perspective, a number of types of critiques sit comfortably:

- Herbert Schiller's work (1981; 1989; 1996) stands as a marker for a critical-scholarly view of technology in this vein. He certainly also falls within a number of these categories of critique (particularly capital control of the means of communication), but it can be convincingly argued that his overarching concern is for the role of technologies of mass communication (and recasting that role) in relationship to democracy (Hudson, 1999). Along the lines of Schiller, globalization has recently become a focus: as fierce competition leads to a swallowing up of smaller (local) media entities, "commercial values invade media systems [and] even passive media consumption tacitly legitimizes the politics and morality of a profit-driven social order" (Bennett, 2004, p. 125).
- John Durham Peters (1993) notes that when we debate self-generated media spectacle and their stupefied audiences, we are talking about democracy "by other means." He argues that it is not necessary to channel the eighteenth century to see the place of rational discourse and political will formation and their current importance to democracy. Conversely, the lack of accountability in huge global media corporations—and their technologically enhanced reach—raises serious concerns about the viability of any kind of localized civic life and civil society (concepts closely related to but not entirely the equivalent of the public sphere; Bennett, 2004, pp. 131–132).
- There is the now-familiar admixture of news and infotainment, and the erosion of public service broadcast standards. Opinion recycled as news, scandal packaged as an item of national import, and the steady erosion of information delivered in the interests of the public and political process are all products of the deregulated neoliberal media environment and its cultural reach and saturation (Bennett, 2004, pp. 137–139; Buschman, 2005).
- Finally, the media-induced equation of the citizen as consumer or audience for such output is aided by media/technological saturation and advertising's manipulative

effects (Bennett, 2004, pp. 139–142; Habermas, 1989). Of particular note here is the alternate positing of the Internet as a dissent-friendly political forum (Bennett, 2004, pp. 142–144) or even as a new form of the public sphere (Poster, 1995). The response to this has been (in the spirit of this vein of critique of technology): the rationalizing and control effects of technology "are not the products of rigid bureaucracies whose authority is sapped by a new postmodern individualism, but of flexible centers of command that are well adapted to the new technologies they have designed and implemented" (Feenberg, quoted in Buschman, 2003, p. 153).

Those then are the six types of critiques of technology that inform much of this volume. They do not cover all variations on the theme—or indeed, even within the theme. But, they can easily be seen throughout this volume, as the following review of the structure of the book and individual chapters will illustrate.

STRUCTURE OF THE BOOK

The book is organized into two distinct yet interrelated parts. In part 1, "Foundations," the chapter authors provide metalevel critical analyses and overviews of technologically related issues of great concern for not only libraries, but other types of institutions, individuals, and society as a whole. Chapter 1 is written by Andrew Feenberg, who provides a general overview of critical theory relating to technology. Feenberg begins by exploring the concept of technical action, and the illusion of transcendence that accompanies it. He points out that the technical actions we take as human beings shape society and, in return, shape us individually, though that fact is often invisible to us. Referring to Heidegger and Marcuse, Feenberg notes that technology is a "two-sided phenomenon" involving both the operator and the object, so that technical action is an "exercise of power." As a way to combine the different conceptualizations of technology as evidenced in philosophy and social studies of technology, Feenberg posits instrumentalization theory as a common framework. Instrumentalization theory examines technology at two levels, the first being the functional relation to reality and the second being design and implementation. The theory aids us in seeing how technologies are reduced to their affordances, simplified, and deworlded, while, at the same time, become incorporated into complex systems or networks as if they were natural elements. However, as Feenberg points out, technical systems and devices have potentialities to be used in many dynamic and different ways, thus necessarily complicating the analysis. He also maintains that, despite its critics, Marxian analysis is still extremely useful in understanding the "penetration of technical mediation into every sphere of social life." Feenberg further notes that technologies are given their meanings and uses through ongoing processes of interpretation, processes that can result in very different combinations that might "privilege either a technocratic model of control or a democratic model of communication."

In chapter 2, Gary Marx takes a close look at surveillance as a set of evolving practices and processes that are intimately bound up with various technological apparatuses. Marx reviews the meaning of the terms *surveillance* and *privacy* and, in so doing, examines the critical distinctions between the two terms. He suggests that while surveillance has always been a widespread form of social control enacted by different agencies and organizations in slightly different ways, we are now seeing a new surveillance that encourages "a general ethos of self-surveillance" among citizens, who willingly and often unwittingly submit to personal surveillance techniques under the guise of social good. The new surveillance is particularly insidious in its low visibility, routinization, and manipulation against direct coercion. Marx also examines the dynamic and fluid processes by which surveillance occurs, and the ways in which various surveillance techniques are resisted and subverted by those who are surveilled. In assessing what to do about surveillance, Marx notes that there are no easy answers, either moral or scientific, to the complexities of surveillance as evidenced in contemporary society. He concludes by providing an overview of the myriad number of complex questions that may provide a compass in our quest to find the best route through the surveillance maze.

In chapter 3, Nick Dyer-Witheford uses the perspective of autonomous Marxism to identify and unpack various elements of techno-capital and its appropriation of the Internet. In considering the traditional struggle between capital and labor, autonomous Marxism postulates that workers are not mindless dupes of the control exerted by capital (through cycles of struggle) but actively seek to circumvent or resist such control (i.e., lines of flight). Dyer-Witheford demonstrates how the two concepts of "cycles of struggle" and "lines of flight" have played out over the history of the Internet, starting with the Cold War struggles and hacker flight, through the Net boom and the dot.com bust, to the browser wars and resistance to the Net as a site for consumption through the work of "immaterial labor" to produce and share free goods. He concludes his chapter by looking at the rise of Web 2.0 and social networking ventures such as Second Life and the implications for libraries.

Technologies, literacies, and systems of education are the topic of chapter 4 by Ross Collin and Michael W. Apple. The authors situate their interests in a study of how "literacies evolve in relation to changes in material systems and processes of schooling." Within this framework, literacy is considered as the dynamic and complex ways in which various social actors, positioned within different fields of power, use the technological and other tools available to them to create socially meaningful work given their values, relationships, and goals. The context for the analysis is the transition in many of the developed nations from welfare state industrial economies to neoliberal state informational economies, which, the authors maintain, is changing the ways in which tools are valued, understood, and used. Collin and Apple provide an overview of the literacies associated with the Fordist Keynesian welfare state (such as the manipulation of technical/administrative knowledge in standardized jobs) and discuss how such literacies evolved through industrial-era schooling. These industrial-era literacies are contrasted to those of the informational economy, which involve mediation and synthesis, using computers and other evolving technologies to "carry out multiple tasks communicated to the workplace team through intrafirm networks" and what the authors refer to as "shareholder capitalism." Collin and Apple point out that public schools, mostly still offering an industrial-era education, are failing to provide students with any of the literacies valued in the new economic reality. Concluding, the authors argue that what is needed is not to bow to the demands of "fast capitalism" but rather to engage in educational reform that stresses multiliteracies and diverse traditions, teaching students to use tools to build communities based on social and economic justice.

The final chapter in part 1 is by Sandra Braman, whose discussion of libraries, the law, and information technologies offers a compelling reason as to why libraries, often mired in the practicalities of the everyday, should care about larger theoretical concerns and perspectives. Braman points out that, at an operational level, libraries must deal with a wide variety of legal issues relating to the use of digital technologies. She notes that such issues have a long history and suggests that what is happening now is that traditional legal dilemmas often are taking on new and more complex dimensions. She suggests, therefore, that libraries must "go beyond addressing single issues reactively and in isolation" by taking a more proactive stance and contributing to the development of more coherent information policies. Accordingly, Braman provides an overview of how libraries sustain the law, contribute to political culture and the public sphere, and are implicated in changes to the law. Furthermore, as Braman points out, the ongoing legal and policy issues experienced by libraries really are an indicator of changing relationships between libraries and national government. Thus, she asserts, library and information science (LIS) as a discipline needs to foster a more theoretical perspective on library-state relations, particularly relations with the evolving "informational state" and its apparatuses. To this end, Braman reviews the theoretical foundations of the informational state, including transformations of the state, forms and phases of power, and state uses of information policy. Braman concludes by noting a number of key elements in the relationship between libraries and the informational state, including a loss of transparency, impairment of democratic practice, replacement of narrative memory with data, and replacement of history with epigenetic knowledge.

In part 2, "Applications," authors examine both macro- and microlevel processes and effects surrounding information technology–library relationships and the implications of those relationships for libraries, librarians, users of libraries, and LIS as a discipline. John M. Budd sets the tone for this part of the book in chapter 6 by exploring longstanding understandings of the term *information technology* that, he argues, are confused and even erroneous. Budd first takes apart the phrase *information technology,* pointing out that while technology can create, transmit, and receive messages as a series of technical acts, it cannot inform. He draws upon Wittgenstein, noting that "the name 'information technology' is part of a language game that creates a certain *kind* of understanding, mainly through acceptance and use." The Wittgensteinian language game also extends to meanings of the word *information,* which has become an abstracted concept within the discipline of LIS. This abstraction has led to a paradigmatic stance that is, in itself, problematic yet continually reproduced in the thinking of the discipline (such as in the belief that "systems design can solve problems of becoming informed"). Budd posits that LIS needs to "transcend the paradigm in order to institute a more critical study of informing" and notes that some researchers are establishing a more dialectical approach that takes into account both the process and the means of becoming informed. Budd further notes that we need greater clarity in our understanding of the differences between technology versus technique and practice versus praxis. Otherwise, he suggests, in LIS, "technology is too often the solution in search of a problem."

Chapter 7 is by Michael F. Winter, who examines the elements of library work within modern capitalism. Winter first draws on Karl Marx and Max Weber to ground his analysis of what is happening to labor processes within libraries. He demonstrates how the work of scholars and librarians began to differentiate, particularly as the rationalization of library collections occurred (i.e., they became larger, more coordinated and managed), so that today, librarians and scholars are relatively alienated from one another within the academy. Winter also uses the work of Harry Braverman, who argued that both alienation and rationalization were the means by which capital gains control over work, in order to deskill it. Deskilling is done by administratively breaking down labor processes into smaller parts, while at the same time applying technology intensively. According to Braverman, these techniques of control extend well beyond manual labor into the realm of office work, as well as the intellectual labor of professionals. Winter then discusses how such processes of control have affected the work of librarians and other library staff, and how libraries have become sites of increasingly administrative roles that may be quite remote from the daily work of most professional librarians. The gender structure of librarianship, too, plays a huge part in the ways in which intensification/deskilling have occurred within the profession. Finally, Winter suggests that as libraries are increasingly required to keep up with the latest round of IT products, the work of librarians and other library staff changes subtly with each new technological introduction, constituting "not only transformation of the labor process, but also a new level of intensification [that is] largely unrecognized."

Following on with some of the same themes as Winter, Roma Harris takes a detailed look at the current intersections among technology, gender, and librarianship in chapter 8. She starts by describing the ways in which librarians have disappeared or gone missing from a number of recent government reports and brochures about various efforts at public information provision. The neglect of the work of librarians and other library staff is particularly galling given the long history that librarians have had in "reconstituting themselves in the face of profound technological change" to provide their users with a level of technologically oriented resources that would have been unimaginable a few decades ago. Harris then poses the key question: "Why aren't librarians recognized for the complex work they perform and their ability to apply sophisticated technologies to the fundamental problems of their discipline?" The answer, she suggests, is bound up with perceptions of gender and technology. Librarianship, as a female-intensive profession, is regarded as women's work, which is perceived generally to be nontechnical and lower-skilled. This perception is compounded by the fact that the public is not particularly aware of the work that librarians actually do, as Harris cites in a study showing that most people incorrectly state who is responsible for choosing the books for public library collections. Taking this further, Harris shows that the work of other occupations that are not particularly well understood by the public (such as IT systems work in banks and airlines) are nonetheless given higher status. Harris relates these public perceptions to the ongoing anxiety within the profession regarding how the profession should be labeled and the struggles for naming that are occurring now within LIS programs. Why should we care about all this, she asks? Because if we do not, librarians and the work that they do will continue to disappear from libraries to the point that other occupations and self-service technologies will be substituted for them, with far less ability to effectively manage a contemporary library and care for its users well. In the face of evidence showing that library users want increased relationships with their information providers, Harris remarks that the complete disappearance of librarians would be tragic both for libraries as institutions and for their users.

Examining an often neglected constituency within the discussion of technology, Andrew Large reviews the literature related to children and technology and offers critical commentary on it in chapter 9. Large notes that while children's encounters with IT started in the 1980s, research interest in children as a specific user community was slow to develop. Nonetheless, there is now a growing body of research that examines children's use and understandings of IT in a variety of situations both in libraries and beyond them. Large begins by reviewing issues related to children's use of IT (including both computers and the Internet) at home and at school. He notes that in the literature about IT in the classroom, there is a certain ambivalence as to the benefits derived and there is no consensus on whether a tool like the Internet is a powerful tool for learning. Large then proceeds to look at studies of children's information-seeking behavior with various IT tools, including CD-ROMs, library catalogs, and Web sites. One of the central concerns of this literature is to see what aspects of IT are useful or problematic for children of varying ages. For instance, at what age can children scroll and use hypertext links? When can they effectively use search engines and Boolean logic? Many of the studies found that children had common difficulties when using the Internet to locate information for school projects, despite their own and their teachers' optimism about their success. Large then turns his attention to studies regarding the design of IT for young users. Some of the findings he notes here are that children's Web sites are frequently more difficult to use than those designed for adults, and that the design of IT for children is often based on erroneous assumptions about them and their abilities. Large concludes by raising a number of important issues surrounding children's use of IT, including the role of IT in teaching and learning, the lack of appropriate content, IT design that is better suited to the needs of young people, and alternatives to conventional search engines. Each and every one of Large's areas of investigation and critique have particular relevance for libraries.

In chapter 10, Ajit Pyati explores the issues surrounding open source software (OSS) and the potential that it holds for libraries. Since the OSS library community is still relatively small but growing, Pyati suggests the time is right to explore the challenges of OSS for libraries and to articulate the more political side of the debate. He notes that OSS represents both a movement and a form of software development, with its "inverted logic of property" whereby value is derived from the freely available nature of the code. Pyati points out that the lower cost, ability to customize, rapid development cycle, and more bug-free software are all advantages of OSS. Furthermore, he remarks that the "largely commercial library automation and vendor market has played a role in pushing libraries to consider open source." OSS may be more appealing to libraries on a symbolic level as a more democratic and grassroots movement and also may fit better with a resource-sharing model. There are challenges, however, particularly the need to have in-house expertise to develop and modify code for local practices, and the need to shift budgetary resources away from commercial vendors to investments in staff. Pyati takes a closer look at three prominent OSS projects, and the lessons that can be learned from them, including the need for visionary leadership, the need to build a broad community base beyond the initial development group, the concern over the financial viability of projects, and the technical expertise that will be required within the profession to move OSS projects forward.

Responding to ongoing concerns about the ability of information seekers to effectively employ library catalogs and Web portals, Gloria Leckie, Lisa Given, and Grant Campbell use regulation theory to examine longstanding information retrieval problems in chapter 11. They address longstanding difficulties with library catalogs (and more recently Web portals). That library catalog (OPAC) and Web-management systems are designed and sold as a "social good" obscures that they are not socially neutral and operate within the capitalist marketplace and framework. They further have real implications for both the character and functionality of such tools. There is, they contend, "no relationship more intimate or integral than that of the library and its automated or integrated library system (or ILS)," which represents a large commitment of money, time, labor, and a wide variety of library functions. The OPAC and Web portal have been revolutionary information technologies in many respects, but despite their benefits, they present intrinsic difficulties: library users find the OPAC difficult to understand and use, with unintelligible descriptors and complex organizational concepts, resulting in confusing search experiences with problematic results; and library Web portals multiply the confusion by integrating resources from numerous sources, creating an illusion of uniform control and access that is not borne out by reality. The authors contend that regulation theory places these issues within a context of larger economic and social activity, and they review cataloging as production, MARC, the management of social relations, Web portals, and the role of information literacy as the solution to these problems, and the chimera of usability studies.

In chapter 12 Dorothy Warner reviews the extensive literature surrounding the topic of digital preservation. The decision process as to whether or not to digitize a "remains a prudent and necessary exercise," she contends. While much research is—and has been—underway, the starting points that digitization is both inevitable and that primary concerns are technical/technological in nature are a given. Many of the crucial problems are aired in the literature, but a critical approach that attempts to assess the overall impact is not present. Digital preservation is a "well-intended response to the proliferation of formats and the radical extension of access that networked technology offers," but she concludes that there are three related overarching problems: no clear standards after years of work; proliferation and obsolescence; and insupportably high costs to libraries. Solutions to the problems of digital archiving "are still years away."

The concluding chapter to the volume is written by John E. Buschman, who uses the work of James O'Donnell as his touchstone to examine the ongoing need for librarianship to be critical of technology. Buschman has chosen to employ O'Donnell's book *Avatars of the Word: From Papyrus to Cyberspace* because of its interwoven themes on historical shifts in the technologies of writing and the role of librarians in such shifts. Buschman maintains that O'Donnell is correct in many respects, particularly in his assertion that the book as a technology is not dead, and that "technologies do not simply supplant their predecessors but rather join an existing ensemble." O'Donnell also provides a very enlightened view of libraries and librarians, including librarians' longstanding adoption and adaptation of technologies to provide access to myriad collections and the role that libraries have played and continue to play as conservers of culture. However, Buschman points out that O'Donnell does get some things wrong, such as his lack of concern over the transience and impermanence of digital texts, coupled with his assertion of the cultural need to preserve and study artifacts of the past. In the process,

Buschman is concerned that O'Donnell comes "very close to casting technologies as neutral and apolitical, whereas any more-than-casual examination indicates they are resolutely not so." Buschman concludes that O'Donnell's work reminds us that to have any hope of a reinvigoration of the public sphere through networked communications demands will not occur without a critical approach to technologies, and that librarianship cannot play a positive role in the "democratic consequences" of IT without that critique.

Thematically, the volume moves from the background provided in this introduction to part 1 in the form of a broad overview of the relationship of critical theory to the critique of technology, through an analysis of the flexibility and suppleness of surveillance, to a serious attempt to reapply Marxist analysis to IT work, the broad arguments over literacy and the control of work, and to the institutional and democratic stakes of law and policy in an age of the information-state. In part 2, these frameworks are adapted and brought to bear on librarianship in the form of an unpacking of the concept of information technology in order to enable a more critical LIS relationship to it, two analyses placing librarianship within broad technology mediated workplace trends, a review of research on children's interactions with the basis of so many library services (computers and new media), a critical analysis of OPACs and Web portals within a social and economic framework using regulation theory, and a look at the deep-seated problems of libraries, archives, and digital preservation. The concluding chapter attempts to establish again the need for a *critical* approach to information technologies in librarianship in the face of the social and economic juggernaut that IT is—both in society and in libraries.

REFERENCES

Adam, A. (1998). *Artificial knowing: Gender and the thinking machine.* London: Routledge.

Adam, A. (2005). *Gender, ethics and information technology.* New York: Palgrave Macmillan.

Agre, P. (1997). The end of information and the future of libraries. *Progressive Librarian, 12/13,* 1–6.

Andersen, J. (2005). Information criticism: Where is it?" *Progressive Librarian, 25,* 12–22.

Asdal, K., Brenna, B., Gulbrandsen, E., Moser, I., & Refseth, N. (1997). A cyborg for change: A presentation of Donna Haraway's perspective on knowledge practices. In B. Berner (Ed.), *Gendered practices: Feminist studies of technology and society* (pp. 269–281). Linkoping, Sweden: Department of Technology and Social Change, Linkoping University.

Bagdikian, B. H. (2004). *The new media monopoly.* Boston: Beacon Press.

Balabanian, N. (1993). The neutrality of technology: A critique of assumptions. In J. Buschman (Ed.), *Critical approaches to information technology in librarianship: Foundations and applications* (pp. 15–40). Westport, CT: Greenwood Press.

Barker, L. J., & Aspray, W. (2006). The state of research on girls and IT. In J. M. Cohoon & W. Aspray (Eds.), *Women and information technology: Research on underrepresentation* (pp. 3–54). Cambridge, MA: MIT Press.

Bart, P. B. (1991). Feminist theories. In H. Etzkowitz & R. M. Glassman (Eds.), *The renascence of sociological theory* (pp. 249–265). Itasca, IL: F. E. Peacock Publishers.

Beniger, J. R. (1989). The evolution of control. In T. Forester (Ed.), *Computers in the human context: Information technology, productivity, and people* (pp. 48–70). Cambridge, MA: MIT Press.

Bennett, W. L. (2004). Global media and politics: Transnational communication regimes and civic cultures. *Annual Review of Political Science, 7,* 125–148.

Berg, A-J. (1995). A gendered socio-technical construction: The smart house. In N. Heap, R. Thomas, G. Einon, R. Mason, & H. Mackay (Eds.), *Information technology and society: A reader* (pp. 74–89). London: Sage/Open University.

Bix, A. S. (2001). History of women in science and technology. In E. L. MacNabb, M. J. Cherry, S. L. Popham, & R. P. Prys (Eds.), *Transforming the disciplines: A women's studies primer* (pp. 193–201). New York: Routledge.

Braman, S. (2006). *Change of state: Information, policy, and power.* Cambridge, MA: MIT Press.

Bray, F. (2007). Gender and technology. *Annual Review of Anthropology, 36,* 37–53.

Brosio, R. A. (1980). *The Frankfurt School: An analysis of the contradictions and crises of liberal capitalist societies.* Monograph number 29. Muncie, IN: Ball State University.

Brosio, R. A. (1990). Teaching and learning for democratic empowerment: A critical evaluation. *Educational Theory, 40,* 69–81.

Brown, M. (1991). New directions in neo-Marxism: A Marxist social psychology. In H. Etzkowitz & R. M. Glassman (Eds.), *The renascence of sociological theory* (pp. 321–333). Itasca, IL: F. E. Peacock Publishers.

Buschman, J. (1993a). Conclusion: Contexts, analogies, and entrepreneurial directions in librarianship. In J. Buschman (Ed.), *Critical approaches to information technology in librarianship: Foundations and applications* (pp. 211–220). Westport, CT: Greenwood Press.

Buschman, J. (Ed.). (1993b). *Critical approaches to information technology in librarianship: Foundations and applications.* Westport, CT: Greenwood Press.

Buschman, J. (1993c). Introduction: Why do we need a critical approach to information technology in librarianship? In J. Buschman (Ed.), *Critical approaches to information technology in librarianship: Foundations and applications* (pp. 1–12). Westport, CT: Greenwood Press.

Buschman, J. (1993d). Issues in censorship and information technology. In J. Buschman (Ed.), *Critical approaches to information technology in librarianship: Foundations and applications* (pp. 125–149). Westport, CT: Greenwood Press.

Buschman, J. (2003). *Dismantling the public sphere: Situating and sustaining librarianship in the age of the new public philosophy.* Westport, CT: Libraries Unlimited/Greenwood.

Buschman, J. (2005). On libraries and the public sphere. *Library Philosophy and Practice, 7*(2). Retrieved Februay 15, 2008, from http://www.webpages.uidaho.edu/~mbolin/buschman.pdf.

Buschman, J. (2007, Summer). Talkin' 'bout my (neoliberal) generation: Three theses. *Progressive Librarian, 29,* 28–40.
Buschman, J., & Carbone, M. (1991). A critical inquiry into librarianship: Applications of "the new sociology of education." *Library Quarterly, 61,* 15–40.
Buschman, J., & Carbone, M. (1996). Technocracy, educational structures, and libraries: Historical notes from the United States. *Journal of Education Policy, 11,* 561–578.
Callahan, J. C. (Ed.) (1995). *Reproduction, ethics and the law: Feminist perspectives.* Bloomington: Indiana University Press.
Carbone, M. (1993). Critical scholarship on computers in education: A summary review. In J. Buschman (Ed.), *Critical approaches to information technology in librarianship: Foundations and applications* (pp. 41–57). Westport, CT: Greenwood Press.
Cornell University Library. (2003–2007). *Digital preservation management: Implementing short-term strategies for long-term problems.* Retrieved December 27, 2007, from http://www.icpsr.umich.edu/dpm/dpm-eng/eng_index.html.
Crawford, W., & Gorman, M. (1995). *Future libraries: Dreams, madness and reality.* Chicago: American Library Association.
Darch, C. (2000, Summer). The unsustainable library: Does the Internet really help us in Africa? *Progressive Librarian, 17,* 35–43.
DiMaggio, P., Hargittai, E., Neuman, W. R., & Robinson, J. P. (2001). Social implications of the internet. *Annual Review of Sociology, 27,* 307–336.
Ehrenreich, N. (Ed.) (2008). *The reproductive rights reader: Law, medicine and the construction of motherhood.* New York: New York University Press.
Ellul, J. (1986). The technological society. In A. H. Teich (Ed.), *Technology and the future* (4th ed., pp. 31–46). New York: St. Martin's Press.
Etzkowitz, H. (1991). Technology and social change: Alternative paths. In H. Etzkowitz & R. M. Glassman (Eds.), *The renascence of sociological theory* (pp. 355–374). Itasca, IL: F. E. Peacock Publishers.
Ferre, F. (1988). *Philosophy of technology.* Englewood Cliffs, NJ: Prentice-Hall.
Ferrell, R. (2006). *Copula: Sexual technologies, reproductive powers.* Albany: State University of New York.
Fleming, M. (1988). Technology and the problem of democratic control: The contribution of Jurgen Habermas. In R. B. Day, R. Beiner, & J. Maciulli (Eds.), *Democratic theory and technological society* (pp. 90–109). Armonk, NY: M. E. Sharpe.
Frissen, V. (1995). Gender is calling: Some reflections on past, present, and future uses of the telephone. In K. Grint & R. Gill (Eds.), *The gender-technology relation: Contemporary theory and research* (pp. 79–94). London: Taylor & Francis.
Frohmann, B. (1992). The power of images: A discourse analysis of the cognitive viewpoint. *Journal of Documentation, 48,* 365–386.
Frohmann, B. (1994). Discourse analysis as a research method in library and information science. *Library and Information Science Research, 16,* 119–138.
Glassman, R. M. (1991). Max Weber, the modern world, and modern sociology. In H. Etzkowitz & R. M. Glassman (Eds.), *The renascence of sociological theory* (pp. 125–147). Itasca, IL: F. E. Peacock Publishers.
Gorman, M. (2003). *The enduring library: Technology, tradition, and the quest for balance.* Chicago: American Library Association.

Gorman, M. (2006/2007, Winter). The wrong path and the right: The role of libraries in access to, and preservation of, cultural heritage. *Progressive Librarian, 28,* 87–99.

Grafton, A. (2007, November 5). Future reading: Digitization and its discontents. *New Yorker,* 50–54.

Grahame, P. R. (1998). Ethnography, institutions, and the problematic of the everyday world. *Human Studies, 21,* 347–360.

Gray, C. (1993). The civic role of libraries. In J. Buschman (Ed.), *Critical approaches to information technology in librarianship: Foundations and applications* (pp. 151–171). Westport, CT: Greenwood Press.

Haar, J. (1993). The politics of electronic information: A reassessment. In J. Buschman (Ed.), *Critical approaches to information technology in librarianship: Foundations and applications* (pp. 197–209). Westport, CT: Greenwood Press.

Habermas, J. (1971). Why more philosophy? *Social Research, 38,* 633–654.

Habermas, J. (1989). *The structural transformation of the public sphere: An inquiry into a category of bourgeois society.* Cambridge, MA: MIT Press.

Haraway, D. (1985). A manifesto for cyborgs: Science, technology and socialist feminism in the 1980s. *Socialist Review, 80,* 65–108.

Hardt, M., & Negri, A. (2000). *Empire.* Cambridge, MA: Harvard University.

Harris, M., & Hannah, S. (1993). *Into the future: The foundations of library and information services in the post-industrial era.* Norwood, NJ: Ablex.

Harris, M., Hannah, S., & Harris, P. (1998). *Into the future: The foundations of library and information services in the post-industrial era* (2nd ed). Greenwich, CT: Ablex.

Harris, R. (1995/1996, Winter). Service undermined by technology: Gender relations, economics, and ideology. *Progressive Librarian, 10/11,* 5–22.

Hayles, N. K. (1999). *How we became posthuman: Virtual bodies in cybernetics, literature, and informatics.* Chicago: University of Chicago Press.

Hershock, P. D. (2003). Turning away from technotopia: Critical precedents for refusing the colonization of consciousness. In P. D. Hershock, M. Stepaniants, & R. T. Ames (Eds.), *Technology and cultural values: On the edge of the third millennium* (pp. 577–599). Honolulu: University of Hawaii Press.

Hudson, M. (1999, Fall). Understanding information media in the age of neoliberalism: The contributions of Herbert Schiller. *Progressive Librarian, 16,* 26–36.

Inhorn, M. C. (Ed.) (2007). *Reproductive disruptions: Gender, technology and biopolitics in the new millennium.* New York: Berghahn Books.

Jansen, S.C. (1993). Censorship, critical theory, and new information technologies: Foundations of critical scholarship in communications. In J. Buschman (Ed.), *Critical approaches to information technology in librarianship: Foundations and applications* (pp. 59–81). Westport, CT: Greenwood Press.

Kellner, D. (n.d.). *The Frankfurt School.* Retrieved December 15, 2007, from http://www.gseis.ucla.edu/faculty/kellner/papers/fs.htm.

Lancaster, F. W. (1999). Afterword—the impact of electronic-based communication. *Library Trends, 47*(4), 806–810.

Large, A. (2005). Children, teenagers, and the Web. *Annual Review of Information Science and Technology, 39,* 347–392.

Lublin, N. (1998). *Pandora's box: Feminism confronts reproductive technology.* Lanham, MD: Rowman & Littlefield.

Lyon, D. (1986). From "post-industrialism" to "information society": A new social transformation? *Sociology, 20,* 577–588.

Lyon, D. (1995). The roots of the information society idea. In N. Heap, R. Thomas, G. Einon, R. Mason, & H. Mackay (Eds.), *Information technology and society: A reader* (pp. 54–73). London: Sage/Open University.

Mackay, H. (1995). Theorising the IT/society relationship. In N. Heap, R. Thomas, G. Einon, R. Mason, & H. Mackay (Eds.), *Information technology and society: A reader* (pp. 41–53). London: Sage/Open University.

Mann, T. (2001). The importance of books, free access, and libraries as places—and the dangerous inadequacy of the information science paradigm. *Journal of Academic Librarianship, 27,* 268–281.

Mann, T. (2007). The research library as place: On the essential importance of collections of books shelved in subject-classified arrangements. In J. Buschman & G. Leckie (Eds.). *The library as place: History, community and culture* (pp. 191–206). Westport, CT: Libraries Unlimited.

Mann, S. A., & Kelley, L. R. (1997). Standing at the crossroads of modernist thought: Collins, Smith, and the new feminist epistemologies. *Gender & Society, 11,* 391–408.

Marcuse, H. (1964). *One-dimensional man: Studies in the ideology of advanced industrial society.* Boston: Beacon Press.

Marx, G. T., & Muschert, G. W. (2007). Personal information, borders, and the new surveillance studies. *Annual Review of Law and Society, 3,* 375–395.

Marx, K., (1955a). Karl Marx: Historical tendency of capitalist accumulation. In S. Hook, *Marx and the Marxists: The ambiguous legacy* (pp. 149–151). Princeton, NJ: D. Van Nostrand.

Marx, K., (1955b). Karl Marx: Religion and economics. In S. Hook, *Marx and the Marxists: The ambiguous legacy* (pp. 151–152). Princeton, NJ: D. Van Nostrand.

Marx, K., & Engels, F. (1955). Marx and Engels: The Communist Manifesto. In S. Hook, *Marx and the Marxists: The ambiguous legacy* (pp. 133–139). Princeton, NJ: D. Van Nostrand.

McCarthy, T. (1981). *The critical theory of Jurgen Habermas.* Cambridge, MA: MIT Press.

McChesney, R. (1999). *Rich media, poor democracy: Communication politics in dubious times.* New York: New Press.

McDermott, J. (1986). Technology: The opiate of the intellectuals. In A. H. Teich (Ed.), *Technology and the future* (4th ed., pp. 95–121). New York: St. Martin's Press.

McDonald, P. (2004–2005, Winter). Rethinking ubiquity: Into a Google world. *Progressive Librarian, 24,* 35–40.

Menzies, H. (1996). *Whose brave new world? The information highway and the new economy.* Toronto: Between the Lines.

Michelfelder, D. P. (2000). Technological effects in a different voice. In E. Higgs, A. Light, & D. Strong (Eds.), *Technology and the good life?* (pp. 219–233). Chicago: University of Chicago Press.

Morritt, H. (1997). *Women and computer based technologies: A feminist perspective.* Lanham, MD: University Press of America.

Moyal, A. (1995). The feminine culture of the telephone: People, patterns, and policy. In N. Heap, R. Thomas, G. Einon, R. Mason, & H. Mackay (Eds.),

Information technology and society: A reader (pp. 284–310). London: Sage/ Open University.

Mumford, L. (1991). Authoritarian and democratic technics. In J. Zerzan & A. Carnes (Eds.), *Questioning technology: Tool, toy, or tyrant?* (pp. 13–21). Philadelphia: New Society Publishers.

Nardi, B., & O'Day, V. L. (1999). *Information ecologies: Using technology with heart.* Cambridge, MA: MIT Press.

Noble, D. (1984). *Forces of production: A social history of industrial automation.* New York: Alfred A. Knopf.

Noble, D. (2001). *Digital diploma mills: The automation of higher education.* New York: Monthly Review Press.

Norris, P. (2004). The digital divide. In F. Webster (Ed.), *The information society reader* (pp. 273–286). New York: Routledge.

OCLC. (2007). *Sharing, privacy and trust in our networked world.* Dublin, OH: Author.

O'Donnell, J. J. (1998). *Avatars of the word: From papyrus to cyberspace.* Cambridge, MA: Harvard University Press.

Paasonen, S. (2005). *Figures of fantasy: Internet, women and cyberdiscourse.* New York: Peter Lang.

Parr, J. (1999). *Domestic goods: The material, the moral and the economic in the postwar years.* Toronto: University of Toronto Press.

Peters, J. D. (1993). Distrust of representation: Habermas on the public sphere. *Media, Culture, and Society, 15,* 541–571.

Plant, S. (1997). *Zeros + ones: Digital women + the new technoculture.* New York: Doubleday.

Plant, S. (2004). The future looms: Weaving women and cybernetics. In F. Webster (Ed.), *The information society reader* (pp. 424–438). New York: Routledge.

Poster, M. (1995). *CyberDemocracy: Internet and public sphere.* Retrieved July 10, 2003, from http://www.hnet.uci.edu/mposter/writings/democ.html.

Poster, M. (2004). The mode of information and postmodernity. In F. Webster (Ed.), *The information society reader* (pp. 398–410). New York: Routledge.

Postman, N. (1979). *Teaching as a conserving activity.* New York: Delta.

Postman, N. (1985, June). The contradictions of freedom of information. *WLA Journal,* 4–19.

Postman, N. (1993). *Technopoly: The surrender of culture to technology.* New York: Vintage.

Pritchard, S. (1993, Fall). Feminist thought and critique of information technology. *Progressive Librarian, 8,* 1–9.

Pyati, A. K. (2007). *Re-envisioning libraries in the information society: A critical theory of library technology.* Unpublished doctoral dissertation, University of California, Los Angeles.

Robins, K., & Webster, F. (2004). The long history of the information revolution. In F. Webster (Ed.), *The information society reader* (pp. 62–80). New York: Routledge.

Roszak, T. (1986). *The cult of information: The folklore of computers and the true art of thinking.* New York: Pantheon.

Roszak, T. (1993, Winter/Spring). The politics of information and the fate of the Earth. *Progressive Librarian, 6/7,* 3–14.

Roszak, T. (2004). The cult of information. In F. Webster (Ed.), *The information society reader* (pp. 55–61). New York: Routledge.

Schiller, H. (1981). *Who knows: Information in the age of the Fortune 500.* Norwood, NJ: Ablex.

Schiller, H. (1989). *Culture, Inc.: The corporate takeover of public expression.* New York: Oxford University Press.

Schiller, H. (1990/1991). The global commercialization of culture. *Progressive Librarian, 2,* 15–22.

Schiller, H. (1996). *Information inequality: The deepening social crisis in America.* New York: Routledge.

Segal, H. P. (1995). The cultural contradictions of high tech: Or the many ironies of contemporary technological optimism. In Y. Ezhrahi, E. Mendelsohn, & H. Segal (Eds.), *Technology, pessimism, and postmodernism* (pp. 175–216). Amherst: University of Massachusetts Press.

Segal, H. P. (2005). *Technological utopianism in American culture* (20th anniversary ed.). Syracuse, NY: Syracuse University Press.

Sharman, D. (2001, Summer). Intellectual property: A historical perspective on the commodification of information. *Progressive Librarian, 18,* 9–17.

Slaby, S. (1993). An engineer's critical perspective on technology. In J. Buschman (Ed.), *Critical approaches to information technology in librarianship: Foundations and applications* (pp. 101–122). Westport, CT: Greenwood Press.

Slack, J. D. (1984). The information revolution as ideology. *Media, Culture and Society, 6,* 247–256.

Smith, D. E. (1977). A sociology for women. In J. A. Sherman & E. T. Beck (Eds.), *The prism of sex: Essays in the sociology of knowledge* (pp. 135–187). Madison: University of Wisconsin Press.

Stille, A. (1999, March 8). Overload. *New Yorker,* 38–44.

Stone, A. R. (1995). *The war of desire and technology at the close of the mechanical age.* Cambridge, MA: MIT Press.

Tenner, D. (1996). *Why things bite back: Technology and the revenge of unintended consequences.* New York: Alfred A. Knopf.

Tien, L. (2005/2006, Winter). Location tracking, RFID and libraries. *Progressive Librarian, 26,* 3–10.

Vehvilainen, M. (1997). Women's groups, standpoints, technical subjectivities, and "ecriture feminine" in technology. In B. Berner (Ed.), *Gendered practices: Feminist studies of technology and society* (pp. 157–186). Linkoping, Sweden: Department of Technology and Social Change, Linkoping University.

Wajcman, J. (1991). *Feminism confronts technology.* University Park: Pennsylvania State University Press.

Wajcman, J. (2004). *TechnoFeminism.* Cambridge: Polity Press.

Warner, D. (2002, Spring) "Why do we need to keep this in print? It's on the Web. . .": A review of electronic archiving issues and problems. *Progressive Librarian, 19/20,* 47–64.

Warner D., & Buschman, J. (2000, Summer). *The Internet and social activism: Savage inequalities revisited. Progressive Librarian, 17,* 44–53.

Weber, M. (1946). *From Max Weber: Essays in sociology* (H. H. Gerth & C. W. Mills, Eds.). New York: Oxford University Press.

Weber, M. (1958). *The Protestant ethic and the spirit of capitalism.* New York: Charles Scribner's Sons.

Webster, J. (1997). Information technology, women and their work. In B. Berner (Ed.), *Gendered practices: Feminist studies of technology and society* (pp. 141–156). Linkoping, Sweden: Department of Technology and Social Change, Linkoping University.

Weizenbaum, J. (1976). *Computer power and human reason: From judgment to calculation.* San Francisco: W. H. Freeman and Company.

White, S. K. (2006). The very idea of a critical social science: a pragmatist turn. In F. Rush (Ed.), *The Cambridge companion to critical theory* (pp. 310–335). New York: Cambridge University Press.

Wilson, S. M., & Peterson, L. C. (2002). The anthropology of online communities. *Annual Review of Anthropology, 31,* 449–467.

Winner, L. (1986). *The whale and the reactor: A search for limits in an age of high technology.* Chicago: University of Chicago Press.

Winner, L. (2004). Sow's ears from silk purses: The strange alchemy of technological visionaries. In M. Sturken, D. Thomas, & S. J. Ball-Rokeach (Eds.), *Technological visions: The hopes and fears that shape new technologies* (pp. 34–47). Philadelphia: Temple University Press.

Winter, M. F. (1993). Librarianship, technology, and the labor process: Theoretical perspectives. In J. Buschman (Ed.), *Critical approaches to information technology in librarianship: Foundations and applications* (pp. 173–195). Westport, CT: Greenwood Press.

Wyer, M., Barbercheck, M., Geisman, D., Ozturk, H. O., & Wayne, M. (2001). Reproducible insights: Women creating knowledge, social policy, and change. In M. Wyer, M. Barbercheck, D. Geisman, H. O. Ozturk, & M. Wayne (Eds.), *Women, science, and technology: A reader in feminist science studies* (pp. 275–84). New York: Routledge.

Zuboff, S. (1993). New worlds of computer-mediated work. In J. Buschman (Ed.), *Critical approaches to information technology in librarianship: Foundations and applications* (pp. 83–100). Westport, CT: Greenwood Press.

Zukin, S., & Maguire, J. S. (2004). Consumers and consumption. *Annual Review of Sociology, 30,* 173–197.

1

FOUNDATIONS

1

CRITICAL THEORY OF TECHNOLOGY: AN OVERVIEW

Andrew Feenberg

TECHNOLOGY AND FINITUDE

What makes technical action different from other relations to reality? This question is often answered in terms of notions such as efficiency or control, which are themselves internal to a technical approach to the world. To judge an action as more or less efficient is already to have determined it to be technical and therefore an appropriate object of such a judgment. Similarly, the concept of control implied in technique is "technical" and so not a distinguishing criterion.

There is tradition in philosophy of technology that resolves this problem by invoking the concept of "impersonal domination" first found in Marx's description of capitalism. This tradition, associated with Heidegger and the Frankfurt School, remains too abstract to satisfy us today but it does identify an extraordinary feature of technical action (Feenberg, 2004a). I formulate this feature in systems theoretic terms, distinguishing the situation of a finite actor from a hypothetical infinite actor capable of a "do from nowhere."[1] The latter can act on its object without reciprocity. God creates the world without suffering any recoil, side effects, or blowback. This is the ultimate practical hierarchy establishing a one-way relation between actor and object. But we are not gods. Human beings can only act on a system to which they themselves belong. This is the practical significance of embodiment. As a consequence, every one of our interventions returns to us in some form as feedback from our objects. This is obvious in everyday communication, where anger usually evokes anger, kindness kindness, and so on.

Technical action represents a partial escape from the human condition. We call an action "technical" when the actor's impact on the object is out of all proportion to the return feedback affecting the actor. We hurtle two tons of metal down the freeway while sitting in comfort listening to Mozart or the Beatles. This typical instance of technical action is purposely framed here to dramatize the independence of actor from object. In the larger scheme of things, the driver on the freeway may be at peace in his car but the city he inhabits, with millions of other drivers, is his life environment and it is shaped by the automobile into a type of place that has major impacts on him. So the technical subject does not escape from the logic of finitude after all. But the reciprocity of finite action is dissipated or deferred in such a way as to create the space of a necessary illusion of transcendence.

Heidegger and Marcuse understand this illusion as the structure of modern experience. According to Heidegger's history of being, the modern "revealing" is biased by a tendency to take every object as a potential raw material for technical action. Objects enter our experience only in so far as we notice their usefulness in the technological system. Release from this form of experience may come from a new mode of revealing, but Heidegger has no idea how revealings come and go.

Like Marcuse, I relate the technological revealing not to the history of being but to the consequences of persisting divisions between classes and between rulers and ruled in technically mediated institutions of all types. Technology can be and is configured in such a way as to reproduce the rule of the few over the many. This is a possibility inscribed in the very structure of technical action, which establishes a one-way direction of cause and effect.

Technology is a two-sided phenomenon: on the one hand the operator, on the other the object. Where both operator and object are human beings, technical action is an exercise of power. Where, further, society is organized around technology, technological power is the principle form of power in the society. It is realized through designs that narrow the range of interests and concerns that can be represented by the normal functioning of the technology and the institutions that depend on it. This narrowing distorts the structure of experience and causes human suffering and damage to the natural environment.

The exercise of technical power evokes resistances of a new type immanent to the one-dimensional technical system. Those excluded from the design process eventually suffer the undesirable consequences of technologies and protest. Opening up technology to a wider range of interests and concerns could lead to its redesign for greater compatibility with the human and natural limits on technical action. A democratic transformation from below can shorten the feedback loops from damaged human lives and nature and guide a radical reform of the technical sphere.

INSTRUMENTALIZATION THEORY

Much philosophy of technology offers very abstract and unhistorical accounts of the essence of technology. These accounts appear painfully thin compared to the rich complexity revealed in social studies of technology. Yet technology has the distinguishing features sketched above and these have normative implications. As Marcuse argued in *One-Dimensional Man,* the choice of a technical rather than a political or moral solution to a social problem is politically and morally significant. The dilemma divides technology studies into two opposed branches. Most essentialist philosophy of technology is critical of modernity, even antimodern, while most empirical research on technologies ignores the larger issue of modernity and thus appears uncritical, even conformist, to social critics (Feenberg, 2003).

I find it difficult to explain my solution to this dilemma because it crosses lines we are used to standing behind. These lines cleanly separate the substantivist critique of technology as we find it in Heidegger from the constructivism of many contemporary historians and sociologists. These two approaches are usually seen as totally opposed. Nevertheless, there is something obviously right in both. I have therefore attempted to combine their insights in a common framework that I call "instrumentalization theory."

Instrumentalization theory holds that technology must be analyzed at two levels, the level of our original functional relation to reality and the level of design and implementation. At the first level, we seek and find affordances that can be mobilized in devices and systems by decontextualizing the objects of experience and reducing them to their useful properties. This involves a process of deworlding in which objects are torn out of their original contexts and exposed to analysis and manipulation while subjects are positioned for distanced control. Modern societies are unique in deworlding human beings in order to subject them to technical action—we call it management—and in prolonging the basic gesture of deworlding theoretically in technical disciplines that become the basis for complex technical networks.

At the second level, we introduce designs that can be integrated with other already existing devices and systems and with various social constraints such as ethical and aesthetic principles. The primary level simplifies objects for incorporation into a device while the secondary level integrates the simplified objects to a natural and social environment. This involves a process that, following Heidegger, we can call "disclosure" or "revealing" of a world. Disclosing involves a complementary process of realization that qualifies the original functionalization by orienting it toward a new world involving those same objects and subjects.

These two levels are analytically distinguished. No matter how abstract the affordances identified at the primary level, they carry social content from the secondary level in the elementary contingencies of a particular approach to the materials. Similarly, secondary instrumentalizations, such as design specifications, presuppose the identification of the affordances to be assembled and concretized. This is an important point. Cutting down a tree to make lumber and building a house with it are *not* the primary and secondary instrumentalizations respectively. Cutting down a tree "decontextualizes" it, but does so in line with various technical, legal, and aesthetic considerations determining what kinds of trees can become lumber of what size and shape and are salable as such. The act of cutting down the tree is thus not simply primary but involves both levels, as one would expect of an analytic distinction.

The theory is complicated, however, by the fact that technical devices and systems are built up from simple elements that have a wide variety of potentialities. The process in which these elements are combined consists in successive impositions of limitations on the materials. The secondary instrumentalizations play an increasingly important role as this process advances. Consider again the example of the tree and the house. Although the output of the logger is constrained to some extent by secondary instrumentalizations, it is far less so than the work of the carpenter who uses the logs after they are turned into boards to build the house. The logger need not know anything about the building codes, family structures, and architectural fashions that will eventually constrain the carpenter's work. Thus there is a dynamic process in which the materials and simpler technical elements are mediated ever more thoroughly.

This dynamic is especially developed in differentiated modern societies. Some of the functions of the secondary instrumentalization get distinguished institutionally in particularly striking ways. Thus the aesthetic function, an important secondary instrumentalization, may be separated out and assigned to a corporate design division. Artists will then work in parallel with engineers. This partial institutional separation of the levels of instrumentalization encourages the belief that they are completely distinct. This obscures the social nature of every technical act, including the work of engineers liberated from aesthetic considerations, if not from many other social influences, by their corporate environment.

Analysis at the first level is inspired by categories introduced by Heidegger and other substantivist critics of technology. However, because I do not ontologize those categories, nor treat them as a full account of the essence of technology, I believe I am able to avoid many of the problems associated with substantivism, particularly its antimodernism. Analysis at the second level is inspired by empirical study of technology in the constructivist vein. I focus especially on the way actors perceive the meanings of the devices and systems they design and use. But again, I am selective in drawing on this tradition. I do not accept its exaggerated and largely rhetorical empiricism and its rejection of the categories of traditional social theory. Instead, I attempt to integrate its methodological insights to a more broadly conceived theory of modernity.

CULTURE

In determinist and instrumentalist accounts of technology, efficiency serves as the unique principle of selection between successful and failed technical initiatives. On these terms technology appears to borrow the virtues generally attributed to scientific rationality. Philosophy of technology demystifies these claims to the necessity and universality of technical decisions. In the 1980s, the constructivist turn in technology studies offered a methodologically fruitful approach to demonstrating this in a wide range of concrete cases.

Constructivists show that many possible configurations of resources can yield a working device capable of efficiently fulfilling its function. The different interests of the various actors involved in design are reflected in subtle differences in function and preferences for one or another design of what is nominally the same device. Social choices intervene in the selection of the problem definition as well as its solution. Efficiency is thus not decisive in explaining the success or failure of alternative designs because several viable options usually compete at the inception of a line of development. Technology is "underdetermined" by the criterion of efficiency and is responsive to the various particular interests and ideologies that select among these options. Technology is not "rational" in the old positivist sense of the term but socially relative; the outcome of technical choices is a world that supports the way of life of one or another influential social group. On these terms the technocratic tendencies of modern societies could be interpreted as an effect of limiting the groups intervening in design to technical experts and the corporate and political elites they serve.

In my formulation of this thesis, I argue that the intervention of interests and ideologies does not necessarily reduce efficiency but biases its achievement according to a broader social program. I have introduced the concept of "technical code" to articulate this relationship between social and technical requirements. A technical code is the realization of an interest or ideology in a technically coherent solution to a problem. Although some technical codes are formulated explicitly by technologists themselves, I am seeking a more general analytic tool that can be applied even in the absence of such formulations. More precisely, then, a technical code is a criterion that selects between alternative feasible technical designs in terms of a social goal. *Feasible* here means technically workable. Goals are "coded" in the sense of ranking items as ethically permitted or forbidden, or aesthetically better or worse, or more or less socially desirable. These types of codes reflect the secondary instrumentalizations of the instrumentalization theory, such as ethical and aesthetic mediations. *Socially desirable* refers not to some universal criterion but to a hegemonic value such as health or the nuclear family. Such values are formulated by the social theorist as technical codes in ideal-typical terms, that is, as a simple rule or criterion. A prime example in the history of technology is the imperative requirement to deskill labor in the course of industrialization rather than preserving or enhancing skills.

Where such codes are reinforced by individuals' perceived self-interest and law, their political import usually passes unnoticed. This is what it means to call a certain way of life culturally secured and a corresponding power hegemonic. Just as political philosophy problematizes cultural formations that have rooted themselves in law, so philosophy of technology problematizes formations that have successfully rooted themselves in technical codes.

OPERATIONAL AUTONOMY

For many critics of technological society, Marx is now irrelevant, an outdated critic of capitalist economics. I disagree. I believe Marx had important insights for philosophy of technology. He focused so exclusively on economics because production was the principal domain of application of technology in his time. With the penetration of technical mediation into every sphere of social life, the contradictions and potentials he identified in technology follow as well.

For Marx the capitalist is ultimately distinguished not so much by ownership of wealth as by control of the conditions of labor. The owner has not merely an economic interest in what goes on within his factory but also a technical interest. By reorganizing the work process, he can increase production and profits. Control of the work process, in turn, leads to new ideas for machinery, and the mechanization of industry follows in short order. This leads over time to the invention of a specific type of machinery that deskills workers and requires management. Management acts technically on persons, extending the hierarchy of technical subject and object into human relations in pursuit of efficiency. Eventually professional managers represent and in some sense replace owners in control of the new industrial organizations. Marx calls this the impersonal domination inherent in capitalism in contradistinction to the personal domination of earlier social formations. It is a domination embodied in the design of tools and the organization of production. In a final stage, which Marx did not anticipate, techniques of management and organization and types of technology first applied to the private sector are exported to the public sector, where they influence fields such as government administration, medicine, and education. The whole life environment of society comes under the rule of technique. In this form the essence of the capitalist system can be transferred to socialist regimes built on the model of the Soviet Union.[2]

The entire development of modern societies is thus marked by the paradigm of unqualified control over the labor process on which capitalist industrialism rests. It is this control that orients technical development toward disempowering workers and the massification of the public. I call this control "operational autonomy," the freedom of the owner or his representative to make independent decisions about how to carry on the business of the organization, regardless of the views or interests of subordinate actors and the surrounding community. The operational autonomy of management and administration positions them in a technical relation to the world, safe from the consequences of their own actions. In addition, it enables them to reproduce the conditions of their own supremacy at each iteration of the technologies they command. Technocracy is an extension of such a system to society as a whole in response to the spread of technology and management to every sector of social life. Technocracy armors itself against public pressures, sacrifices values, and ignores needs incompatible with its own reproduction and the perpetuation of its technical traditions.

The technocratic tendency of modern societies represents one possible path of development, a path that is peculiarly truncated by the demands of power. Technology has other beneficial potentials that are suppressed under the capitalism and state socialism that could emerge along a different developmental path. In subjecting human beings to technical control at the expense of traditional modes of life while sharply restricting participation in design, technocracy perpetuates elite power structures inherited from the past in technically rational forms. In the process it mutilates not just human beings and nature but technology as well. A different power structure would innovate a different technology with different consequences.

Is this just a long detour back to the notion of the neutrality of technology? I do not believe so. Neutrality generally refers to the indifference of a specific means to the range of possible ends it can serve. If we assume that technology as we know it today is indifferent with respect to human ends in general, then indeed we have neutralized it and placed it beyond possible controversy. Alternatively, it might be argued that technology as such is neutral with respect to all the ends that can be technically served. But neither of these positions make sense. There is no such thing as technology as such. Today we employ this specific technology with limitations that are due not only to the state of our knowledge but also to the power structures that bias this knowledge and its applications. This really existing contemporary technology favors specific ends and obstructs others.

The larger implication of this approach has to do with the ethical limits of the technical codes elaborated under the rule of operational autonomy. The very same process in which capitalists and technocrats were freed to make technical decisions without regard for the needs of workers and communities generated a wealth of new values, ethical demands were forced to seek voice discursively. Most fundamentally, democratization of technology is about finding new ways of privileging these excluded values and realizing them in the new technical arrangements.

A fuller realization of technology is possible and necessary. We are more and more frequently alerted to this necessity by the threatening side effects of technological advance. Technology "bites back," as Edward Tenner (1996) reminds us, with fearful consequence as the deferred feedback loops that join technical subject and object become more obtrusive. The very success of our technology in modifying nature insures that these loops will grow shorter as we disturb nature more violently in attempting to control it. In a society such as ours, which is completely organized around technology, the threat to survival is clear.

RESISTANCE

What can be done to reverse the tide? Only the democratization of technology can help. This requires in the first instance shattering the illusion of transcendence by revealing the feedback loops to the technical actor. The spread of knowledge by itself is not enough to accomplish this. For knowledge to be taken seriously, the range of interests represented by the actor must be enlarged so as to make it more difficult to offload feedback from the object onto disempowered groups. But only a democratically constituted alliance of actors, embracing those very groups, is sufficiently exposed to the consequences of its own actions to resist harmful projects and designs at the outset. Such a broadly constituted democratic technical alliance would take into account destructive effects of technology on the natural environment as well as on human beings.

Democratic movements in the technical sphere aim to constitute such alliances. But this implies restoring the agency of those treated as objects of management in the dominant technical code. How to understand this transformation? It will not work to simply multiply the number of managers. Subordinate actors must intervene in a different way from dominant ones.

Michel de Certeau (1980) offers an interesting interpretation of Foucault's theory of power that can be applied to this problem. He distinguishes between the strategies of groups with an institutional base from which to exercise power and the tactics of those subject to that power and who, lacking a base for acting continuously and legitimately, maneuver and improvise micropolitical resistances. Note that de Certeau does not personalize power as a possession of individuals but articulates the Foucauldian correlation of power and resistance. This works remarkably well as a way of thinking about immanent tensions within technically mediated organizations, not surprisingly given Foucault's concern with institutions based on scientific-technical "regimes of truth."

Technological systems impose technical management on human beings. Some manage, while others are managed. These two positions correspond to de Certeau's strategic and tactical standpoints. The world appears quite differently from these two positions. The strategic standpoint privileges considerations of control and efficiency and looks for affordances, precisely what Heidegger criticizes in technology. My most basic complaint about Heidegger is that he himself adopts unthinkingly the strategic standpoint on technology in order to condemn it. He sees it exclusively as a system of control and overlooks its role in the lives of those subordinate to it.

The tactical standpoint of those subordinates is far richer. It is the everyday lifeworld of a modern society in which devices form a nearly total environment. In this environment, individuals identify and pursue meanings. Power is only tangentially at stake in most interactions, and when it becomes an issue, resistance is temporary and limited in scope by the position of the individuals in the system. Yet insofar as masses of individuals are enrolled in technical systems, resistances will inevitably arise and can weigh on the future design and configuration of the systems and their products.

Consider the example of air pollution. So long as those responsible for it could escape the health consequences of their actions to green suburbs, leaving poor urban dwellers to breath filthy air, there was little support for technical solutions to the problem. Pollution controls were seen as costly and unproductive by those with the power to implement them. Eventually, a democratic political process sparked by the spread of the problem and protests by the victims and their advocates legitimated the externalized interests. Only then was it possible to assemble a social subject including both rich and poor able to make the necessary reforms. This subject finally forced a redesign of the automobile and other sources of pollution, taking human health into account. This is an example of a politics of design that will lead ultimately to a more holistic technological system.

An adequate understanding of the substance of our common life cannot ignore technology. How we configure and design cities, transportation systems, communication media, agriculture, and industrial production is a political matter. And we are making more and more choices about health and knowledge in designing the technologies on which medicine and education increasingly rely. Furthermore, the kinds of things it seems plausible to propose as advances or alternatives are to a great extent conditioned by the failures of the existing technologies and the possibilities they suggest. The once controversial claim that technology is political now seems obvious.

RECONTEXTUALIZING STRATEGIES

There was a time not so long ago when general condemnation of technology seemed plausible to many social critics. The attitude lingers and inspires a certain haughty disdain for technology among intellectuals who nevertheless employ it constantly in their daily lives. Increasingly, however, social criticism has turned to the study and advocacy of possible reconfigurations and transformations of technology to accommodate it to values excluded from the original design networks. This approach emerged first in the environmental movement, which was successful in modifying the design of technologies through regulation and litigation. Today the approach continues in proposals for transforming biotechnologies and computing. The instrumentalization theory suggests a general account of the strategies employed in such movements.

The primary instrumentalization involves decontextualization, which shatters preexisting natural arrangements, often of great complexity. Of course no decontextualization can be absolute. The process is always conditioned by secondary instrumentalizations, which offer a partial recontextualization of the object in terms of various technical and social requirements. As in the example of logging and construction discussed previously, in every case where objects are stripped of their natural connections, new technical and social connections are implicit in the very manner of their reduction and simplification for technical employment.

Constructive criticism of technology takes aim precisely at the deficiencies in this recontextualization process, for it is here that the bias of design is introduced. This is particularly clear under capitalism, where successful business strategies often involve breaking free of various social constraints on the pursuit of profits. Thus the favored recontextualizations tend to be minimal and to ignore the values and interests of many of the human beings who are involved in capitalist technical networks, whether they be workers, consumers, or members of a community hosting production facilities. In the case of logging it has been difficult to convince corporations to pay attention to the health of forests and the beauty of nature, goods that may appeal to communities in the vicinity and to environmentalists although neither are invited to participate in the design of logging projects.

Real world ethical controversies involving technology such as this often turn on the supposed opposition of current standards of technical efficiency and values. But this opposition is factitious; current technical methods or standards were once discursively formulated as values and at some time in the past translated into the technical codes we take for granted today. This point is quite important for answering the usual so-called practical objections to ethical arguments for social and technological reform. It seems as though the best way to do the job is compromised by attention to extraneous matters such as health or natural beauty. But the division between what appears as a condition of technical efficiency and what appears as a value external to the technical process is itself a function of social and political decisions biased by unequal power. All technologies incorporate the results of such decisions and thus favor one or another actor's values or in the best of cases combine the values of several actors in clever combinations that achieve multiple goals.

This latter strategy involves technical "concretizations," the multiplication of the functions served by the structure of the technology.[3] In this way, wider or neglected contexts can be brought to bear on technological design without loss of efficiency. A refrigerator equipped to use an ozone-safe refrigerant achieves environmental goals with the same structures that keep the milk cold. What goes for devices may be even more true of living things and human beings enrolled in technical networks. For example, industrial animal husbandry can be reorganized in ways that respect the needs of animals while employing their spontaneous behaviors in an improved environment to protect their health and hence the efficiency of the operation (Bos, 2003; Bos, Koerkamp, & Groenestein, 2003).

TERMINAL SUBJECTS

I want to conclude these reflections with an example with which I am personally familiar, which I hope will illustrate the fruitfulness of my approach. I have been involved with the evolution of communication by computer since the early 1980s both as an active participant in innovation and as a researcher. I came to this technology with a background in modernity theory, specifically Heidegger and Marcuse, but it quickly became apparent that they offered little guidance in understanding computerization. Their theories emphasized the role of technologies in dominating nature and human beings. Heidegger (1998) dismissed the computer as the pure type of modernity's machinery of control. Its deworlding power reaches language itself, which is reduced to the mere position of a switch (p. 140).

But what we were witnessing in the early 1980s was something quite different, the contested emergence of the new communicative practices of online community. Subsequently, we have seen cultural critics inspired by modernity theory recycle the old approach for this new application, denouncing, for example, the supposed degradation of human communication on the Internet. Albert Borgmann (1992) argues that computer networks deworld the person, reducing human beings to a flow of data the "user" can easily control (p. 108). The terminal subject is basically an asocial monster despite the appearance of interaction online. But that critique presupposes that computers are actually a communication medium, if an inferior one, which was precisely the issue 20 years ago. The prior question that must therefore be posed concerns the emergence of the medium itself. Most recently the debate over computerization has touched higher education, where proposals for automated online learning have met determined faculty resistance in the name of human values. Meanwhile, actual online education is emerging as a new kind of communicative practice (Feenberg, 2002, chap. 5).

The pattern of these debates is suggestive. Approaches based on modernity theory are uniformly negative and fail to explain the experience of participants in computer communication. But this experience can be analyzed in terms of instrumentalization theory. The computer simplifies a full blown person into a "user" in order to incorporate him or her into the network. Users are decontextualized in the sense that they are stripped of body and community in front of the terminal and positioned as detached technical subjects. At the same time, a highly simplified world is disclosed to the user as it is open to the initiatives of rational consumers. They are called to exercise choice in this world.

The poverty of this world appears to be a function of the very radical deworlding involved in computing. However, we will see that this is not the correct explanation. Nevertheless, the critique is not entirely artificial; there are types of online activity that confirm it, and certain powerful actors do seek enhanced control through computerization. But most modernity theorists overlook the struggles and innovations of users engaged in appropriating the medium to create online communities or legitimate educational innovations. In ignoring or dismissing these aspects of computerization, they fall back into a more or less disguised determinism.

The posthumanist approach to the computer inspired by commentators in cultural studies suffers from related problems. This approach often leads to a singular focus on the most dehumanizing aspects of computerization, such as anonymous communication, online role playing, and cybersex (Turkle, 1995). Paradoxically, these aspects of the online experience are interpreted in a positive light as the transcendence of the centered self of modernity (Stone, 1995). But such posthumanism is ultimately complicit in the humanistic critique of computerization it pretends to transcend in that it accepts a similar definition of the limits of online interaction. Again, what is missing is any sense of the transformations the technology undergoes at the hands of users animated by more traditional visions than one would suspect from this choice of themes (Feenberg & Barney 2004; Kirkpatrick, 2004).

The effective synthesis of these various approaches would offer a more complete picture of computerization than any one of them alone. In my writings in this field I have tried to accomplish this. I set out not from a hypothesis about the essence of the computer, for example, that it privileges control or communication, humanist or posthumanist values, but rather from an analysis of the way in which such hypotheses influence the actors themselves, shaping design and usage.

The lifeworld of technology is the medium within which the actors engage with the computer. In this lifeworld, processes of interpretation are central. Technical resources are not simply pregiven but acquire their meaning through these processes. As computer networks developed, communication functions were often introduced by users rather than treated as normal affordances of the medium by the originators of the systems. In Latour's language, the "collective" is re-formed around the contested constitution of the computer as this or that type of mediation responsive to this or that actor's program (Latour, 1999). To make sense of this history, the competing visions of designers and users must be introduced as a significant shaping force. The contests between control and communication, and between humanism and posthumanism, must be the focus of the study of innovations such as the Internet.

ONLINE EDUCATION

Consider the case of the current struggle over the future of online education (Feenberg, 2002, chap. 5). In the late 1990s, corporate strategists, state legislators, top university administrators, and so-called futurologists lined up behind a vision of online education based on automation and deskilling. Their goal was to replace (at least for the masses) face-to-face teaching by professional faculty with an industrial product, infinitely reproducible at decreasing unit cost, like CDs, videos, or software. The overhead of education would decline sharply and the education "business" would finally become profitable. This is "modernization" with a vengeance.

In opposition to this vision, faculty mobilized in defense of the human touch. This humanistic opposition to computerization takes two very different forms. There are those who are opposed in principle to any electronic mediation of education. This position has no effect on the quality of computerization but only on its pace. But there are also numerous faculty who favor a model of online education that depends on human interaction on computer networks. On this side of the debate, a very different conception of modernity prevails. In this alternative conception, to be modern is to multiply opportunities for and modes of communication. The meaning of the computer shifts from a coldly rational information source to a communication medium, a support for human development and online community. This alternative can be traced down to the level of technical design, for example, the conception of educational software and the role of asynchronous discussion forums (Hamilton & Feenberg, 2005).

These approaches to online education can be analyzed in terms of the model of deworlding and disclosing introduced above. Educational automation decontextualizes both the learner and the educational "product" by breaking them loose from the existing world of the university. The new world disclosed on this basis confronts the learner as technical subject with menus, exercises, and questionnaires rather than with other human beings engaged in a shared learning process.

The faculty's model of online education involves a much more complex secondary instrumentalization of the computer in the disclosure of a much richer world. The original positioning of the user is similar: the person facing a machine. But the machine is not a window onto an information mall but rather opens up onto a social world that is morally continuous with the social world of the traditional campus. The terminal subject is involved as a person in a new kind of social activity and is not limited by a set of canned menu options to the role of individual consumer. The corresponding software opens the range of the subject's initiative far more widely than an automated design. This is a more democratic conception of networking that engages it across a wider range of human needs.

The analysis of the dispute over educational networking reveals patterns that appear throughout modern society. In the domain of media, these patterns involve playing off primary and secondary instrumentalizations in different combinations that privilege either a technocratic model of control or a democratic model of communication. Characteristically, a technocratic notion of modernity inspires a positioning of the user that sharply restricts potential initiative, while a democratic conception enlarges initiative in more complex virtual worlds. Parallel analyses of production technology, biotechnology, medical technology, and environmental problems would reveal similar patterns that could be clarified by reference to the actors' perspectives in similar ways.

CONCLUSION

Philosophy of technology has come a long way since Heidegger and Marcuse. Inspiring as these thinkers are, we need to devise our own response to the situation in which we find ourselves. Capitalism has survived its various crises and now organizes the entire globe in a fantastic web of connections with contradictory consequences. Manufacturing flows out of the advanced countries to the low wage periphery as diseases flow in. The Internet opens fantastic new opportunities for human communication and is inundated with commercialism. Human rights proves a challenge to regressive customs in some countries while providing alibis for new imperialist ventures in others. Environmental awareness has never been greater, yet nothing much is done to address looming disasters such as global warming. Nuclear proliferation is finally fought with energy in a world in which more and more countries have good reasons for acquiring nuclear weapons.

Building an integrated and unified picture of our world has become far more difficult as technical advances break down the barriers between spheres of activity to which the division between disciplines corresponds. I believe that critical theory of technology offers a platform for reconciling many apparently conflicting strands of reflection on technology. Only through an approach that is both critical and empirically oriented is it possible to make sense of what is going on around us now. The first generation of Critical Theorists called for just such a synthesis of theoretical and empirical approaches.

Critical theory was above all dedicated to interpreting the world in the light of its potentialities. Those potentialities are identified through serious study of what is. Empirical research can thus be more than a mere gathering of facts and can inform an argument with our times. Philosophy of technology can join together the two extremes—potentiality and actuality, that is, norms and facts—in a way no other discipline can rival. It must challenge the disciplinary prejudices that confine research and study in narrow channels and open perspectives on the future.

NOTES

1. The implied reference is to the concept of a godlike "view from nowhere." I could rephrase the point here as a "do from knowhere," that is, action understood as just as indifferent to its objects as detached knowing.

2. How Marx, along with most nineteenth-century radical thinkers, could overlook this possible outcome is discussed in Feenberg (2004b) through a comparison of

Edward Bellamy's utopian novel, *Looking Backward,* and Huxley's famous dystopia, *Brave New World,* which each exemplify a different conception of the boundaries of technique.

3. The concept of concretization was introduced by Gilbert Simondon (1958). For further discussion of this concept see Feenberg (1999, chap. 9).

REFERENCES

Borgmann, A. (1992). *Crossing the postmodern divide.* Chicago: University of Chicago Press.

Bos, B. (2003). *Een kwestie van beheersing* [A question of control]. Amsterdam: Academisch Proefschrift, Vrije Universiteit.

Bos, B., Koerkamp, P., & Groenestein, K. (2003). A novel design approach for livestock housing based on recursive control—with examples to reduce environmental pollution. *Livestock Production Science, 84,* 157–170.

de Certeau, M. (1980). *L'invention du quotidien* [The invention of everyday life]. Paris: UGE.

Feenberg, A. (1999). *Questioning technology.* New York: Routledge.

Feenberg, A. (2002). *Transforming technology: A critical theory revisited.* New York: Oxford.

Feenberg, A. (2003). Modernity theory and technology studies: Reflections on bridging the gap. In T. Misa, P. Brey, & A. Feenberg (Eds.), *Modernity and technology* (pp. 73–104). Cambridge, MA: MIT Press.

Feenberg, A. (2004a). *Heidegger and Marcuse: The catastrophe and redemption of technology.* New York: Routledge.

Feenberg, A. (2004b). Looking forward, looking backward: Reflections on the 20th century. In D. Tabachnick & T. Koivukoski (Eds.), *Globalization, technology and philosophy* (pp. 93–105). Albany, NY: SUNY Press.

Feenberg, A., & Barney, D. (2004). *Community in the digital age.* Lanham, MD: Rowman & Littlefield.

Hamilton, E., & Feenberg, A. (2005). The technical codes of online education. *E-Learning, 2*(2), 104–121.

Heidegger, M. (1998). Traditional language and technological language (W. Gregory, Trans.). *Journal of Philosophical Research, 23,* 129–145.

Kirkpatrick, G. (2004). *Critical technology: A social theory of personal computing.* Aldershot, England: Ashgate.

Latour, B. (1999) . *Politiques de la nature: Comment faire entrer les sciences en démocratie* [Policies of nature: How to enter science in a democracy]. Paris: La Découverte.

Simondon, G. (1958). *Du mode d'existence des objets techniques* [The mode of existence of technical objects]. Paris: Aubier.

Stone, A. R. (1995). *The war of desire and technology at the close of the mechanical age.* Cambridge, MA: MIT Press.

Tenner, E. (1996). *Why things bite back: Technology and the revenge of unintended consequences.* New York: Knopf.

Turkle, S. (1995). *Life on the screen: Identity in the age of the Internet.* New York: Simon & Schuster.

Additional Works Consulted

Feenberg, A. (1991). *Critical theory of technology.* New York: Oxford University Press.

Feenberg, A. (1993). Building a global network: The WBSI experience. In L. Harasim (Ed.), *Global networks: Computerizing the international community* (pp. 185–197). Cambridge, MA: MIT Press.

Feenberg, A. (1995). *Alternative modernity: The technical turn in philosophy and social theory.* Los Angeles: University of California Press.

Marcuse, H. (1964). *One-dimensional man.* Boston: Beacon Press.

Marcuse, H. (1978). Beiträge zu einer phänomenologie des historischen materialismus [Contributions to a Phenomenology of Historical Materialism]. In *Herbert Marcuse schriften: Band I.* Frankfurt: Suhrkamp Verlag.

Ruivenkamp, G. (2003, March). Tailor-made biotechnologies for endogenous developments and the creation of new networks and knowledge means. *Biotechnology and Development Monitor, 50,* 14–16.

2

SURVEILLANCE AND TECHNOLOGY: CONTEXTS AND DISTINCTIONS

Gary T. Marx

Perhaps it is fitting that the topic of surveillance, so shrouded in intrigue, is often ambiguous and misunderstood. One error involves the common tendency to see surveillance as the opposite of privacy. Another is to associate it only with government and law and order activities in particular. Privacy and surveillance can be interwoven. Viewed in social process terms, they are different sides of the same coin. Surveillance may be the means of crossing borders that protect privacy. This is illustrated by strong public concern with the nefarious and multifarious electronic, chemical, and database means of collecting personal information without the individual's knowledge and consent. Yet surveillance can also be the means of protecting privacy. Consider the passwords and audit trails required to use some databases or various defensive measures such as a perimeter video camera to protect the home. Whether we see surveillance or privacy invasion partly depends on the point of view taken.

Considered in the abstract, it is difficult to reach broad conclusions about the appropriateness of either surveillance or privacy. They can be socially desirable, as well as destructive. Surveillance can serve goals of protection, administration, rule compliance, documentation, and strategy, as well as goals involving inappropriate manipulation, restricted life opportunities, social control, and spying. Privacy can be central to an individual's dignity and liberty and to intimacy, honest communication, group borders, and democracy, but it can also hide socially destructive behavior (e.g., abuse within families and white collar crime). With the development of new communication and computer technologies and new ways of living that increasingly rely on non-face-to-face forms of interaction, questions of personal information have taken on new social significance. The microchip and computer are of course central to surveillance developments and in turn reflect broader social forces set in motion with industrialization involving empirical documentation, rationality, bureaucracy, and capitalism. The increased availability of personal information is one strand of the constant expansion in knowledge witnessed in recent centuries, and of the centrality of information to the workings of contemporary society.

The dictionary defines surveillance as, "close observation, especially of a suspected person" (*Oxford American Dictionary of Current English*, 1999) or persons. Consider examples such as an individual suspected of bank robbery who is discretely followed by police and is apprehended after robbing another bank or the discovery that a leader of an antiglobalization protest movement is a police informer. These examples are instances of *traditional surveillance*, and the dictionary definition fits. Yet it is too narrow. The focus of surveillance goes beyond suspects, crime, and national security. To varying degrees surveillance is a property of any social system—from two friends to a workplace to a government. Consider for example a supervisor monitoring an employee's productivity, a doctor assessing the health of a patient, a parent observing a child at play in the park, the driver of a speeding car asked to show a driver's license, or a voyeur. Each of these also involves surveillance.

Information boundaries and contests are found in all societies and, beyond that, in all living systems. Humans are curious and also seek to protect their informational borders, even as they must also reveal their information. To survive, individuals and groups engage in, and guard against, surveillance. Seeking information about others (whether within or beyond one's group) is characteristic of all societies, as are efforts to protect information. However the form, content, and rules about information vary considerably. In the case of surveillance, for example, contrast relying on informers, intercepting smoke signals, taking satellite photographs, gathering information from so-called cookies placed on the computers of Internet users, or mapping the spread of a contagious disease. With respect to communicating information, consider expectations that close friends will share secrets and varied disclosure, notice and freedom of information requirements, as well as expectations of confidentiality and sealed or classified records.

The traditional forms of surveillance contrast in important ways with what can be called the *new surveillance*, a form that became increasingly prominent toward the end of the twentieth century. The new social surveillance can be defined as, scrutiny through the use of technical means to extract or create personal or group data, whether from individuals or contexts. Examples include the following: video cameras; computer matching, profiling, and data mining; work, computer, and electronic location monitoring; DNA analysis; drug tests; brain scans for lie detection; various self-administered tests; and thermal and other forms of imaging to reveal what is behind walls and enclosures. The use of technical means to extract and create the information implies the ability to go beyond what is offered to the unaided senses or what is voluntarily reported. Much new surveillance involves an automated process and extends the senses and cognitive abilities through the use of material artifacts or software.

Using the broader verb *scrutinize* rather than *observe* in the definition calls attention to the fact that contemporary forms often go beyond the visual image to involve sound, smell, motion, numbers, and words. The eyes do contain the vast majority of the body's sense receptors, and the visual is a master metaphor for the other senses (e.g., saying "I see" for understanding). Yet the eye as the major means of direct surveillance is increasingly joined or replaced by other means. The use of multiple senses and sources of data is an important characteristic of much of the new surveillance. Traditionally surveillance involved close observation by a person not a machine. But with contemporary practices surveillance may be carried out from afar, as with satellite images or the remote monitoring of communications and work. Nor need it be close or detailed. Much initial surveillance involves superficial scans looking for patterns of interest to be pursued later in greater detail. Surveillance has become both farther away and closer than it was previously. It occurs with spongelike absorbency and laserlike specificity.

In a striking innovation, surveillance is also applied to contexts (geographical places and spaces, particular time periods, networks, systems, and categories of person), not just to a particular person whose identity is known beforehand. For example, police may focus on so-called hot spots where street crimes most commonly occur or seek to follow a money trail across borders to identify drug smuggling and related criminal networks. The new surveillance technologies are often applied *categorically* (e.g., all employees are drug tested or travelers are searched, rather than those whom there is some reason to suspect). Traditional surveillance often implied a noncooperative relationship and a clear distinction between the object of surveillance and the person carrying it out. In an age of servants listening behind closed doors, binoculars, and telegraph interceptions, that separation made sense. It was easy to distinguish the watcher from the person watched. Yet for the new surveillance, with its expanded forms of self-surveillance and cooperative surveillance, the easy distinction between agent and subject of surveillance can be blurred.

In analyzing the rise of modern forms of social control, the French philosopher Michel Foucault (1977) drew on British legal theorist Jeremy Bentham's idea for the Panopticon. Bentham proposed a highly organized system for managing large populations within physically enclosed structures such as a prison, a factory, or a school, in which authorities could see all but could not be seen. Inmates could never be sure when they were being watched and hence through self-interest and habit it was hoped they would engage in self-discipline. Well-publicized contemporary warnings (e.g., that an area is under video surveillance) reflect this pattern in seeking to create self-restraint. A general ethos of self-surveillance is also encouraged by the availability of products that permit individuals to test themselves (e.g., for alcohol level, blood pressure, or pregnancy).

In related forms subjects may willingly cooperate—submitting to personal surveillance in order to have consumer benefits (e.g., frequent flyer and shopper discounts) or for convenience (e.g., fast track lanes on toll roads in which fees are paid in advance). Implanted chips transmitting identity and location, which were initially offered for pets, are now available for their owners (and others) as well. In some work settings smart badges worn by individuals do the same thing, although not with the same degree of voluntarism. Beyond the individual forms, surveillance at an aggregate level is central to social management. The careful tracking of behavior through computer records (referred to by Roger Clarke, 1988, as "dataveillance") is believed to offer a more rational and efficient approach to social organization and control.

The new surveillance relative to traditional surveillance has low visibility or is invisible. Manipulation against direct coercion has become more prominent. Monitoring may be purposefully disguised, as with a video camera hidden in a teddy bear or a clock. Or it may simply come to be routinized and taken for granted, as when data collection is integrated into everyday activities (e.g., use of a credit card for purchases automatically conveys information about consumption, time, and location). With the trend toward ubiquitous computing, surveillance and sensors in one sense disappear into ordinary activities and objects—cars, cell phones, toilets, buildings, clothes, and even bodies. The relatively labor-intensive bar code on consumer goods, which requires manually scanning, may soon be replaced with inexpensive embedded RFID (radio frequency identification) computer chips, which can be automatically read from short distances. The remote sensing of preferences and behavior offers many advantages such as controlling temperature and lighting in a room or reducing shipping and merchandising costs, while also generating records that can be used for surveillance.

There may be only a short interval between the discovery of the information and the automatic taking of action. The individual as a subject of data collection and analysis may also almost simultaneously become the object of an intervention, whether this involves the triggering of an alarm or the granting (or denial) of some form of access (e.g., to enter through a locked door, use a computer, or make a purchase). The new forms are relatively inexpensive per unit of data collected. Relative to traditional forms, it is easy to combine visual, auditory, text, and numerical data. It is relatively easier to organize, store, retrieve, analyze, send, and receive data. Data are available in real time, and data collection can be continuous and offer information on the past, present, and future (a la statistical predictions). Simulated models of behavior are created. The new surveillance is more comprehensive, intensive, and extensive. The ratio of what the individual knows about him or herself relative to what the surveilling organization knows is lower than in the past, even if objectively much more is known.

One way to think about the topic is to note that many of the kinds of surveillance once found only in high security military and prison settings are seeping into the society at large. Are we moving toward becoming a *maximum security society* where ever more of our behavior is known and subject to control? Some features of the maximum security society are the following: (1) a *dossier* society in which computerized records play a major role, (2) a *sensed* (and perhaps censored) society based on *ubiquitous* and *ambient sensors* softly, invisibly, effortlessly, and continually gathering behavioral, locational, communication, and physiological data, (3) a *transparent* society, in which the boundaries of time, distance, darkness, and physical barriers that traditionally protected information are weakened and pierced, (4) a *networked* society in which diverse kinds of previously unavailable (or if available, disaggregated) personal data are woven together in an ever finer mesh, (5) an *actuarial* and risk-adverse society, in which decisions are increasingly made using such data for predictions about future behavior as a result of membership in, and comparisons to, aggregate statistical categories, (6) a *suspicious* society, in which everyone is assumed to be a possible subject of interest, (7) a *self-monitored* society, in which autosurveillance plays a prominent role, and (8) an *engineered* society, in which choices are increasingly limited and determined by manipulating physical and social environments.

SURVEILLANCE STRUCTURES AND PROCESSES

Surveillance can be analyzed by breaking it into components. These tell us where to look and what to measure. This can help in identifying the variation that is central to explanation, understanding, and evaluation. We can differentiate structures that are fixed at one point in time (like a photograph) from processes that involve interaction and developments over time (like a video). Let us first consider some surveillance structures.

Organizational surveillance is distinct from the *nonorganizational surveillance* carried about by individuals. As James Rule (1974) has noted, modern organizations are the driving forces in the instrumental collection of personal data. As organizations increasingly use personal data for what David Lyon (2003) calls social sorting, the implications for many aspects of life are profound—whether involving work, consumption, health, travel, or liberty. At the organizational level, formal surveillance involves a *constituency*. This term is used broadly to refer to those with some rule-defined relationship or potential connection to the organization. This may involve formal membership or merely contact with the organization as through renting a video or showing a passport at a border. Organizations have varying degrees of internal and external surveillance. Erving Goffman (1961) has identified many kinds of employee or inmate monitoring, such as within "total institutions." These offer examples of the *internal constituency surveillance* found in organizations. Here, individuals belong to the organization in a double sense. First, they belong as members. But they also in a sense are belongings of the organization. They are directly subject to its control in ways that nonmembers are not. We can often see a loose analogy to the ownership of property.

External constituency surveillance is present when those who are watched have some patterned contact with the organization, (e.g., as customers, patients, malefactors, or citizens subject to laws of the state). Those observed do not belong to the organization the way that an employee or inmate does. Credit card companies and banks, for example, monitor client transactions and also seek potential clients by mining and combining data bases. The control activities of a government agency charged with enforcing health and safety regulations is another example. In this case, the organization is responsible for seeing that categories of persons subject to its rules are in compliance, even though they are not members of the organization. The same compliance function can be seen with nongovernmental organizations that audit or grant ratings, licenses, and certifications. In the case of *external non-constituency surveillance,* organizations monitor their broader environment in watching other organizations and social trends. The rapidly growing field of business intelligence seeks information about competitors, social conditions, and trends that may affect an organization. One variant of this is industrial espionage. Organizational planning (whether by government or the private sector) also requires such data, although this is usually treated in the aggregate instead of in personally identifiable form.

Personal surveillance, in which an individual watches another individual (whether for protection, strategic, or prurient reasons) apart from an organizational role, is another major form. It may involve *role relationship surveillance,* as with family members (parents and children, the suspicious spouse) or friends looking out for and looking at each other (e.g., monitoring location through a cell phone). Or it can involve *non–role relationship surveillance*—consider the free-floating activities of the voyeur whose watching is unconnected to a legitimate role. With respect to the roles that are played, we can identify the *surveillance agent* (watcher/observer/seeker). The person about whom information is sought is a *surveillance subject.* All persons of course play both roles, although hardly in the same form or degree. This changes depending on the context and over the life cycle. The roles are sometimes blurred and may overlap. Within the surveillance agent category, the surveillance function may be *central* to the role, as with police, private detectives, spies, work supervisors, and investigative reporters. Or it may simply be a *peripheral* part of a broader role whose main goals are elsewhere. Illustrative of this are check-out clerks who are trained to look for shop lifters, or dentists who are encouraged (or required) to report suspected child abuse when seeing bruises on the face.

A distinction rich with empirical and ethical implications is whether the situation involves those who are a party to the generation and collection of data (*direct participants*) or instead involves *third parties.* Third parties may legitimately obtain personal information through contracting with the surveillance agent (e.g., to carry out drug tests or to purchase consumer preference lists). Or information may be obtained because confidentiality is violated by the agent, or because an outsider illegitimately obtains it (wiretaps, hacking, corrupting those with the information). The presence of third parties raises an important secondary use issue—that is, can data collected for one purpose be used without an individual's permission for unrelated purposes? In Europe the answer generally is "no." In the United States, where a much freer market in personal information exists, there are fewer restrictions. Large organizations warehouse and sell vast amounts of very personal information, without the consent and with no direct benefit to the subject.

Surveillance can also be analyzed with respect to whether it is *nonreciprocal* or *reciprocal.* Surveillance that is reciprocal may be *asymmetrical* or *symmetrical*, and that surveillance itself may be *asymmetrical* or *symmetrical* with respect to means and goals. In a democratic society, citizens and government engage in reciprocal but distinct forms of mutual surveillance. Citizens can watch government through freedom of information requests, open hearings and meetings, and conflict of interest and other disclosures required as a condition for running for office. However, citizens can not legally wiretap, carry out Fourth Amendment searches, or see others' tax returns. In bounded settings such as a protest demonstration, there may be greater equivalence with respect to particular means (e.g., police and demonstrators may videotape each other).

Agent-initiated surveillance, which is particularly characteristic of compliance checks, such as an inspection of a truck or a boat, can be differentiated from *subject-initiated surveillance,* such as submitting one's transcript, undergoing osteoporosis screening, or applying for a job requiring an extensive background investigation. In these cases the individual makes a claim or seeks help and essentially invites, or at least agrees to, scrutiny. With agent-initiated surveillance the goals of the organization are always intended to be served. Yet this need not necessarily conflict with the interests of the subject. Consider, for example, the protection offered by school crossing guards or efficient library service dependent on good circulation records. Public health and medical surveillance have multiple goals, protecting the community as well as the individual. Efficiently run companies provide jobs and services. Providing a limited amount of personal information on a warranty form and having a chip record usage of an appliance, such as a lawn mower or a car, may serve the interest of both consumers and businesses (e.g., being notified if the manufacturer finds a problem or offering proof of correct usage if the device fails).

Subject-initiated surveillance may reflect goals that serve the interests of the initiator but often overlap with the goals of the surveilling organization. Consider some protection services that have the capability to remotely monitor home and business interiors (video, audio, heat, gas, motion detection) or health systems for remotely monitoring the elderly and ill (e.g., an alarm sent if the refrigerator of a person living alone is not opened after 24 hours). As forms more likely to involve informed consent, these are less controversial than secretly generated agent surveillance. What is good for the organization may also be good for the individual, though that is not always the case and of course depends on the context.

Surveillance Processes

Let us briefly consider several surveillance processes. Rather than being static and fixed at one point in time, surveillance can be viewed as a fluid, ongoing process that involves interaction and strategic calculations over time. Part of the fascination of the study of surveillance lies in its dynamic nature, as groups in conflict relationships reciprocally and continuously adjust their tactics to each other. Here we also see the moral ambivalence that infuses the topic as a result of conflicting values and social interests. The *myth of surveillance* involves creating and sustaining the belief through the mass media that a technique is omnipresent and omnipotent. The desire is to have people think that the police are everywhere at all times, knowing everything. When such literal watching (whether real or metaphorical) isn't possible, there is an effort to create uncertainty about whether or not surveillance is present. This is presumed to be a deterrent. Of course, in a complex world of conflicting interests—unexpected developments, technology that breaks—perfect knowledge and control are rarely possible. New conditions may appear, and efforts to resist surveillance are common.

A number of *behavioral techniques of neutralization*—strategic moves by which subjects of surveillance seek to subvert the collection of personal information—can be noted (Marx, 2005). Among these are direct refusal, discovery, avoidance, switching, distorting, countersurveillance, cooperation, blocking and masking. Responses to drug testing illustrate most of these. One type of subversion is *refusal*—just saying "no" or feigning an inability to offer the sample in spite of trying. Social systems often leak, and the date of a supposed random or surprise test or search can sometimes be inferred involving a *discovery* move. Employees may receive notice of a test. Such foreknowledge permits *avoidance* moves involving abstinence, the hiding or destroying of incriminating material, not going to work on that day, or leaving early because one is ill. With *switching*, drug-free urine (whether purchased commercially in liquid or powdered form, or obtained from a friend) replaces the person's own. *Distorting responses* (e.g., diuretics and commercially available detox products) manipulate the surveillance-collection process such that while offering technically valid results, invalid inferences are drawn. Given empathy and the multiplicity of actors and interests in complex organizations, various *cooperative* moves, in which controllers aid those purportedly controlled, may also be seen.

Countersurveillance involves an ironic turning of the tables in which the very technologies used to control others come to be used to advance the interests of those controlled. Thus, facing a urine drug test, employees can first experiment at home, testing themselves with a variety of readily available products like those used in the official test. The wide availability of new tools such as covert audio and video recording offers the surveilled the chance to turn the usual stratification tables. The resulting data can be used defensively or to coerce those in positions of authority. Consider for example the potential for the documentation of unwanted sexual advances and police abuse.

Another set of processes involves decisions about whether or not to surveil, and if so which technique to use, how to apply it, and to whom (e.g., to everyone, randomly, or selectively based on criteria), whether or not the surveilled are informed of and have any say in it, how the data are used, who will have access to it, its degree of security, and how long it will be kept. The social scientist seeks to identify and explain these patterns and their prior correlates. Such decisions have consequences. Subsequent developments can be contingent on the choices made. For example, some techniques that can be narrowly applied, such as DNA for identification purposes, will require the creation of large databases against which a sample can be compared. A decision to watch everyone (categorical suspicion) avoids claims of discrimination in targeting but is more expensive and can lead to a sense of privacy invasion, as there is no predicate for the watching.

Another aspect of the process involves the path or career of surveillance events. In many, perhaps a majority of, cases no action follows from surveillance, as nothing of interest is discovered. The surveillance is intended to serve a scarecrow function or simply to generate a documentary record. Information may be saved until it is needed or a critical amount has been obtained. Or occasionally too much is discovered to act on, or the surveilled can exert counterpressure to prevent action from being taken. Yet techniques, too, have careers. The surveillance appetite can be insatiable and often shows a tendency to expand to new goals, agents, subjects, and forms. Awareness of this requires asking of any new tactic, regardless of how benignly it is presented as both means and ends, "Where might it lead?" The expansion of a technology introduced in a limited fashion can often be seen. Extensions beyond the initial use, whether reflecting *surveillance creep*, or in many cases *surveillance gallop*, are common.

There may be new uses for the data. Consider for example the Social Security number that Congress intended only to be used for tax purposes, which has become a de facto national ID number or the video cameras, once restricted to prisons and high-security areas, which are now found in offices, shopping malls, and homes. New surveillance agents and subjects may appear. A common process is a progression from use on animals to prisoners, criminal suspects, noncitizens, the ill and children, and then throughout the society. Tactics developed by government for defense and law enforcement spread to manufacturing and commercial uses and then to uses in interpersonal relations by friends, family, and others. Consider the expansion of drug testing from the military to sensitive categories such as transportation workers to the workforce at large, and then even to parents testing their children. The patterning of the use of global positioning satellite data is equivalent. Yet expansion is only one path. A technique may be developed but not widely used (for example, the case with handwriting analysis—graphology—in the United States, although not in France). Or, if adopted, a tactic may diffuse slowly rather than rapidly throughout the social order. Television, for example, has been available since the late 1920s. Various adoptive patterns can be seen. We can sometimes note a rarely studied phenomenon of *surveillance contraction*. Widely used tactics may come to be less used as a result of political controversy, the development of regulations and unintended consequences, or as better tactics are developed. For example, congressional legislation in 1988 severely restricted the use of the polygraph for employment purposes.

What Is to Be Done?

Social understanding and moral evaluation require attending to the varied contexts and goals of surveillance. The many settings and forms and processes of surveillance preclude any easy explanations or conclusion. Two broad contrasting views of the new surveillance can be identified. A pessimistic Frankensteinian/Luddite view holds that surveillance technology is inhuman, destructive of liberty, and untrustworthy. In addition, because it develops out of an inequitable social context, it is seen as likely to reinforce the status quo. A more optimistic view places great faith in the power of technology, which is seen to be neutral. More powerful surveillance tools are seen as necessary in today's world, where efficiency is so valued and where there are a multiplicity of dangers and risks. Clearly, surveillance is a sword with multiple edges. The area is fascinating precisely because there are no easy scientific or moral answers.

There are value conflicts and ironic conflicting needs and consequences that make it difficult to take a broad and consistent position in favor of, or against, expanding or restricting surveillance. For example, we value both the individual and the community. We want both liberty and order. We seek privacy and often anonymity, but we also know that secrecy can hide dastardly deeds and that visibility can bring accountability, and we value freedom of expression. But too much visibility may inhibit experimentation, creativity, and risk-taking. As with any value-conflicted and varied-consequence behavior, particularly those that involve conflicting rights and needs, it is essential to keep the tensions ever in mind and to avoid complacency. Occasionally, when wending through competing values the absolutist, uncompromising, don't cross this personal line or always cross it standard is appropriate. But more often compromise (if rarely a simplistic perfect balance) is required. When privacy and civil liberties are negatively affected, it is vital to acknowledge rather than to deny this, as is so often the case. Such honesty can make for more informed decisions and also serves an educational function.

Surveillance practices are shaped by manners, organizational policies, and laws and by available technologies and countertechnologies. These draw on a number of background value principles and tacit assumptions about the empirical world that need to be analyzed. Whatever action is taken there are likely costs, gains, and trade-offs. At best we can hope to find a compass rather than a map and a moving equilibrium rather than a fixed point for decision making. The following questions (based on Marx, 2005) are of help in making those distinctions and decisions:

- Goals—Have the goals been clearly stated, justified, and prioritized?
- Accountable, public, and participatory policy development—Has the decision to apply the technique been developed through an open process and, if appropriate, with participation of those to be surveilled? This involves a transparency principle.
- Law and ethics—Are the means and ends not only legal but also ethical?
- Opening doors—Has adequate thought been given to precedent-creation and long-term consequences?
- Golden rule—Would the watcher be comfortable in being the subject rather than the agent of surveillance if the situation was reversed?
- Informed consent—Are participants fully appraised of the system's presence and the conditions under which it operates? Is consent genuine (i.e., beyond deception or unreasonable seduction) and can participation be refused without dire consequences for the person?
- Truth in use—Where personal and private information is involved, does a principle of unitary usage apply in which information collected for one purpose is not used for another? Are the announced goals the real goals?
- Means-ends relationships—Are the means clearly related to the end sought and proportional in costs and benefits to the goals?
- Can science save us?—Can a strong empirical and logical case be made that a means will in fact have the broad positive consequences its advocates claim (the "does it really work?" question)?
- Competent application—Even if in theory it works, does the system (or operative) using it apply it as intended?
- Human review—Are automated results with significant implications for life chances subject to human review before action is taken?

- Minimization—If risks and harm are associated with the tactic, is it applied to minimize these, showing only the degree of intrusiveness and invasiveness that is absolutely necessary?
- Alternatives—Are alternative solutions available that would meet the same ends with lesser costs and greater benefits (e.g., using a variety of measures not just financial)?
- Inaction as action—Has consideration been given to the "sometimes it is better to do nothing" principle?
- Periodic review—Are there regular efforts to test the system's vulnerability, effectiveness, and fairness and to review policies?
- Discovery and rectification of mistakes, errors, and abuses—Are there clear means for identifying and fixing these (and, in the case of abuse, applying sanctions)?
- Right of inspection—Can individuals see and challenge their own records?
- Reversibility—If evidence suggests that the costs outweigh the benefits, how easily can the surveillance be stopped (e.g., extent of capital expenditures and available alternatives)?
- Unintended consequences—Has adequate consideration been given to undesirable consequences, including possible harm to watchers, the watched, and third parties? Can harm be easily discovered and compensated for?
- Data protection and security—Can those performing surveillance protect the information they collect? Do they follow standard data protection and information rights as expressed in the Code of Fair Information Protection Practices and the expanded European Data Protection Directive?

A central point of much social and legal analysis is to call attention to the contextual nature of behavior. Certainly these questions and the principles implied in them are not of equal weight, and their applicability will vary across time periods depending on need and perceptions of crisis and across contexts (e.g., public order, health and welfare, criminal and national security, commercial, private individuals, families, and the defenseless and dependent) and particular situations within these. Yet common sense and common decency argue for considering them.

REFERENCES

Clarke, R. (1988). Information technology and dataveillance. *Communications of the ACM, 31,* 498–512.

Foucault, M. (1977). *Discipline and punish: The birth of the prison.* New York: Pantheon.

Goffman, E. (1961). *Asylums: Essays in the social situation of mental patients and other inmates.* Garden City, NY: Anchor Books.

Lyon, D. (Ed). (2003). *Surveillance as social sorting.* London: Routledge.

Marx, G. (2005). Seeing hazily (but not darkly) through the lens: Some recent empirical studies of surveillance technologies. *Law and Social Inquiry, 30,* 339–399.

Oxford American dictionary of current English. (1999). New York: Oxford University Press.
Rule, J. (1974). *Private lives and public surveillance: Social control in the computer age.* New York: Schocken Books.

Additional Works Consulted

Allen, A. (2003). *Accountability for private Life.* Lanham, MD: Rowman and Littlefield.
Bennett, C., & Grant, R., (Eds.) (1999). *Visions of privacy.* Toronto: University of Toronto Press.
Brinn, D. (1999). *The transparent society.* New York: Perseus.
Ericson, R., & Haggerty, K. (1997). *Policing the risks society.* Toronto: University of Toronto Press.
Gandy, O. (1993). *The panoptic sort: A political economy of personal information.* Boulder, CO: Westview Press.
Gilliom, J. (2001). *Overseers of the poor.* Chicago: University of Chicago Press.
Lyon, D. (2001). *The electronic eye: The rise of surveillance society.* Cambridge, UK: Polity.
Marguilis, S. T. (2003). Contemporary perspectives on privacy: Social, psychological, political. *Journal of Social Issues, 59,* 243–261.
Marx, G. (2004). *Windows into the soul: Surveillance and society in an age of high technology.* Unpublished manuscript.
McCahill, M. (2002). *The surveillance web.* Devon, England: Wilan.
O'Harrow, R. (2005). *No place to hide.* New York: Free Press.
Regan, P. (1995). *Legislating privacy: Technology, social values, and public policy.* Chapel Hill: University of North Carolina Press.
Solove, D. (2004). *The digital person.* New York: New York University Press.
Staples, W. (2000). *Everyday surveillance: Vigilance and visibility in postmodern life.* Lanham, MD: Rowan and Littlefield.
Tunnell, K. (2004). *Pissing on demand.* New York: New York University Press.
Zureik, E., & Salter, M. (2005). *Global surveillance and policing.* Devon, England: Wilan.

3

CYCLES OF NET STRUGGLE, LINES OF NET FLIGHT

Nick Dyer-Witheford

"Get a (second) life," exhorts a recent article in a library journal (Bell & Peters, 2007, p. 1). The topic is, of course, participation in the virtual world of Second Life, where millions of avatars disport themselves, navigating pixilated islands, flying over open waters, wandering amongst rococo architecture, imbibing at house parties, bending their gender, chatting with friends, attending rock concerts, enjoying erotic encounters, and much else besides. Many librarians see in this world as an exciting opportunity to extend services to online populations (Foster, 2007; Grassian & Trueman, 2007; Hurst-Wahl, 2007), one of a wider field of Web 2.0 applications that seem to offer Internet users extraordinary scope to create and share content (Maness, 2006). Others are skeptical (Annoyed Librarian, 2007; Litwin, 2008). At stake are not only questions around the substantiality or ephemeral nature of virtual interactions, the social mores and ethics of digital worlds, the cost, in time and money of providing online services, but also the dilemma of librarians' relationship to corporate power. For Second Life is owned by a for-profit company, Linden Labs. While basic play is free, Linden makes its money by selling the digital property necessary to conduct most significant forms of activity in its world, including library services. Not only do Second Life libraries pay Linden for being in its world, but, by providing free content for that world, they help build the population base from which Linden gets its revenues. Should public library services contribute to such ventures? The issue, then, is not just the technological merits of Web 2.0 projects such as Second Life but the relation of a particular type of information age worker—the librarian—to techno-capital. This is a problem librarians face on an ongoing basis, in different registers: negotiating with database vendors, dealing with electronic journal monopolists like Reed Elsevier, responding to the philanthropic solicitations of Bill Gates, intervening in intellectual property debates, and in many other ways. Without pretending to engage these cases in detail, this chapter explores the relation of digital-age workers to the power of capital on the Internet, using two concepts—*cycles of struggle* and *lines of flight.*

CYCLES OF STRUGGLE, LINES OF FLIGHT

This theoretical perspective comes from autonomist Marxism (Cleaver, 1977; Dyer-Witheford, 1999). Autonomist analysis stems from Marx's discussion of the conflict between capital and labor. But while much Marxian analysis has charted the deepening grip of corporations on all aspects of daily life, the originality of autonomist thought lies in rediscovering Marx's emphasis on the potential independence, or autonomy, of people, and of the creative energy he called *labor*—"the living, form-giving flame" (Marx, 1973, p. 361). Capital incorporates human subjects as a component in its cycle of value extraction, as a factor of production. This inclusion is, however, always partial and contested: people resist reduction to the status of object. Labor is for capital always an other that must be controlled and subdued, but labor just as persistently circumvents or challenges this command.

Technology, correspondingly, is looked at by autonomists from two perspectives, as a power of capitalist domination but also as a potential force through which that domination can be contested. Marx (1977, p. 563) discussed how industrial capital uses machinery as a weapon against the working class, developing machines to replace or deskill labor that is costly and troublesome. However, workers are not just passive victims of technological change, but challenge capital's attempts at control in a variety of ways. One is sheer refusal. From the days of the Luddites, people have responded to technologies that destroy their jobs and skills by sabotage and noncooperation. Yet workers also use their "invention power" to reappropriate technology (Negri, 1979, p. 99). In its attempt at machine control, capital cannot avoid summoning up new types of technically skilled, scientifically literate workers, who themselves become sources of dissent, putting their skills to subversive use, bending, twisting, and even detaching part of the capitalist process of technological development to move it in different directions.

This emphasis on the possibilities of both refusal *and* reappropriation gives autonomist thought a greater dynamism than outright neo-Luddism. Machines are stamped with social purposes, but not all of them are totally implanted with the dominative logic of capital. Technologies are not neutral but constituted by contending pressures and implanted with contradictory potentialities: which ones are actualized is determined in struggle. If machinery is a weapon, then it can, as Harry Cleaver says, be stolen or captured, "used against us or by us" (1981, p. 264). Or, to use Raniero Panzieri's perhaps richer and less instrumental metaphor, if capital "interweaves" technology and power, then this weaving can be undone, and the threads used to make a different pattern (1976, p. 12).

We can put some historical flesh on these theoretical bones with the concept of *cycles of struggles*. The search for profit, and the fear of subversion, drives capital in a perpetual expansion of territorial space and technological intensity. As it does so, however, the composition and capacities of labor also change, and with it, the strategies and tactics of class struggle. Autonomists trace three turns in this process: the eras of the *craft* worker, the *mass* worker and the *global* worker. In the era of the craft worker—roughly through the late eighteenth and the nineteenth century—capital asserted itself over workers whose power lies in their command of craft skills and subsistence production, throwing them off the land, herding them into factories, and deskilling them with semiautomated machinery. This, however, generated the mass worker of the industrial assembly line, whose powerful trade unions and socialist parties terrified capital with prospects of revolution or wrung from it the concessions of the welfare state. This phase occupied most of the twentieth century. In the 1970s, however, a new capitalist response emerged, involving flexible and globalized production regimes, the aggressive mobilization of state power, and, of particular interest to us here, new digital technologies. This new combination, generally known as neoliberalism, was, from capital's point of view, a great success. It won the Cold War, decimated the mass worker, and devastated an entire culture of left militancy. Indeed, in the war between capital and labor, many see this as a knockout punch, the "end of history" (Fukuyama, 1992).

Autonomists, however, suggest that out of the ashes of this apparent defeat is emerging the subject of a new cycle of struggles—manifest in the wave of anticorporate globalization struggles from Seattle to Genoa, the movements opposing the oil war in Iraq, and the many conflicts over global migration. The naming of this new collective subject varies: some, such as Michael Hardt and Antonio Negri (2000, 2004), refer to it as the "multitude," but for the sake of consistency I will speak of the "global worker" (Dyer-Witheford, 2001). This new globality of labor is in one sense geographical, as countries such as China and India industrialize, and corporations use transport and communication networks to outsource and relocate. The world becomes a factory-planet. Globality is, however, also a question of control over time. The global worker is the subject of an order in which work (production), education and training (reproduction), and leisure (consumption) all become points on a circuit of capitalist activity. In a world where profit has insinuated itself everywhere, there is no central locus of antagonism, such as the industrial factory. Conflict fractally replicates through homes, schools, universities, hospitals, and media, manifesting in the myriad new movements of contingent workers, students, welfare recipients, ecologists, and many others, each of whom have distinct demands, but all of whom at some point come into conflict with the bottom-line imperatives of the world market.

Of special interest from our point of view is the emphasis some autonomists put on the role of "immaterial labor" (Hardt & Negri, 2000, p. 290) in this new cycle of struggle. Immaterial labor is the technical and interpersonal work involved in the communication systems, including media of all sorts, but especially digital systems, that integrate and monitor capital's global system. There is hot debate over the relative importance of immaterial labor, relative to say, immigrant labor performing precarious, poorly paid service work (Dyer-Witheford, 2001; Wright, 2005). But it seems fair to say that labor involving not so much the fabrication of things as the circulation of intellectual, informational, and imaginative commodities is at least *one* major activity of the new global worker. Some theorists suggest that a key feature of the immaterial labor that makes the networks of global capital is an ability to repurpose and redesign these networks for its own autonomous purposes.

To the concept of *cycles of struggle* can be added another, related, idea—that of *lines of flight*. The cycles of struggle language comes from the vocabulary of a highly politicized, adversarial militancy, which is often sharply illuminating. Sometimes, however, techno-conflicts are more diffuse, involving agents who seek not so much to defeat a prevailing order but simply depart from it, go somewhere else, or do something different—a process not so much of overthrow as defection. For example, to jump ahead, many people who use the Internet to download music are not particularly concerned about smashing capitalism but just want to enjoy the obvious plenitude of digital resources, establish communities around shared interests, and explore new forms of subjectivity and culture. The philosophic and political theorists Giles Deleuze and Felix Guattari, whose thought is close to that of autonomists, refer to such efforts at escape or defection as "lines of flight" (1987, p. 204).

Cycles of struggle and lines of flight go together. As Deleuze and Guattari point out, lines of flight often become lines of fight. Deleuze says, "to flee is to produce the real, to create life, to find a weapon" (Deleuze & Parnet, 1977, p. 36). Or, again, Deleuze and Guattari quote George Jackson: "I may be running, but I'm looking for a gun as I go" (1987, p. 204). You may just want to use the Internet to share music with like-minded friends, but when music conglomerates prosecute for piracy you are suddenly in the middle of political struggle. Nonetheless, I will distinguish cycles of struggle and lines of flight, using the former to refer to manifestly political conflicts and the latter to more subtle forms of cultural dissent—even while recognizing that the two intertwine.

In the broadest terms, the introduction of digital networks has been part of the restructuring that decimated the mass worker and inaugurated the era of global worker. Within this overall process there are, however, subcycles of struggle and different lines of flight. Drawing both on my own earlier analysis of Internet politics (Dyer-Witheford, 2002) and on other authors writing from an autonomist perspective (Coté & Pybus, 2007; Halpern, 2006; Kleiner & Wyrick, 2007; Lindenschmidt, 2004), I will argue that the main phases of Internet history, from its noncommercial beginnings through the meteoric rise of the dot-coms to the bursting of the Internet bubble and up to contemporary Web 2.0 excitement, can be understood as a cut and thrust, parry and riposte, between capitalist command and unruly immaterial labor. Capital has sometimes held the advantage but has as often had to play catch-up, trying to capture innovations initiated outside its orbit. It is only by seeing how these cycles of Internet struggle and lines of Internet flight are imprinted in the infrastructures, protocols, and practices of today's global networks that we can understand the contradictions a phenomenon like Second Life presents for librarians.

BEGINNINGS: COLD WAR STRUGGLE, HACKER FLIGHT

The origins of the Internet lie in a cycle of struggles in the bluntest, grimmest sense. It was conceived as a weapon in the Cold War waged between U.S. capital and the state socialism of the USSR. The prototype Internet—ARPANET—was initiated by the Pentagon's Advanced Research Projects Agency in its search for a communications system capable of linking U.S. military bases even during a nuclear exchange. A feature of struggle cycles is the way antagonists frequently appropriate or borrow strategies and innovations from each other. The Internet is no exception: Richard Barbrook (2007) has documented how the U.S. Department of Defense copied the idea of digital networks from the ideas of Soviet computer scientists but then implemented it in a way their opponents were unable to do. It was the quest for a system that could operate even in tatters after nuclear Armageddon that generated the Internet's extraordinarily decentralized architecture and the highly flexible packet-switching mode of delivering messages. The lasting significance of this war-waging genesis is recognized in the aphorism often used to explain the difficulty in censoring Internet traffic: "the Net interprets censorship as damage and routes around it" (quoted in Goldsmith & Wu, 2006, p. 3).

This new communication system very rapidly, however, escaped the intentions of its military sponsors. This loss of control began when ARPANET was used to connect university supercomputing centers vital to Pentagon research, such as those at MIT and Stanford. In an unforeseen turn of events, the techno-scientific workers of the military-academic-industrial complex, mainly university faculty and graduate students, extended the Internet far beyond its original scope to eventually connect almost the entire North American university system and designed successive layers of additional operations connecting into the main backbone. This first generation of immaterial labor—so called hackers in the original sense of the term of enthusiastic, if unauthorized, digital tinkerers—also began using the Internet both for nonmilitary research and for entirely nonutilitarian purposes, from UNSENET news groups to science fiction discussion and online games. The metamorphosis was tolerated, indeed often abetted by systems managers enchanted by the technological sweetness of the results and keen to sustain the costless involvement of brilliant computer science students.

The significance of this line of flight for the long-term shaping of the Internet cannot be overestimated. The "hacker ethic" (Himanen, 2001), with its slogan that "all information should be free" (Levy, 1984, p. 28), was in many ways a digital restatement of academic commitments to open knowledge and cooperative learning. It was this ethos that ensured that the basic TCP/IP protocols, the programming that enabled connection to the Internet regardless of who owned computers or telecommunication links, was freely distributed. This end-to-end architecture was profoundly inimical to proprietary control and lies at the root of many of the difficulties subsequent attempts to commodify the Internet encountered. The hacker tradition of open usage, though later vilified and criminalized, constantly resurfaces in the later history of the Internet, informing, for example, open source software and peer-to-peer traditions; it is a quintessential expression of the autonomous, do-it-yourself invention power of immaterial labor (Wark, 2004).

The hacker culture that liberated the Internet from the Pentagon was, however, a matter not only of technical ingenuity and academic autonomy but also of dissident politics; lines of flight and cycles of struggle ran side by side. John Markoff (2005) has recently shown how deeply many Internet pioneers were involved in the radical social movements of the 1960s and 1970s. Student protest, anti–Vietnam War activism, the Watergate scandals—not to mention serious commitment to consciousness-expanding drugs—all flowed through the university computing centers where the Internet was made. To a greater degree than is usually acknowledged, digital experimentation went alongside demonstrations and draft resistance. The development of decentralized, free networks was conceived by many participants as part of a computers for the people movement understood as part of a wider struggle against imperial, and corporate, power.

While these explicitly political struggles started to wane in the 1970s, their cultural repercussions continued to inform the course of Internet development. Much of the first uptake of the Internet outside of academia was by countercultural groups. Gradually abandoning street protest for lifestyle choices, the so-called net heads saw cyberspace as an escape route of from the normative identities of capitalist America. What we can call—in the phrase of Howard Rheingold (1993), a representative figure—the virtual community phase of Internet growth ran from the late 1970s into the early 1990s. The California WELL (Whole Earth 'Lectronic Link), a BBS (bulletin board system) of phone-in digital connection was the exemplary case. Here early Internet culture was shaped in the sexual, political, and artistic discourse of alt. (alternative) Usenet news groups; by fans of bands such as the Grateful Dead, whose lyricist, John Perry Barlow, became a spokesperson for digital libertarianism; and in the online environmentalism of Stuart Brand's Whole Earth project (Turner, 2006). Much of this experimental energy would, in the next, commercial phase of Internet, be reabsorbed to fuel dot-com ventures with a sickly amalgam of hippie utopianism and free market ideology (Barbrook & Cameron, 1996). This should not, however, obscure the fact that early Internet adoption was shaped in a culture sometimes oppositional and often alternative to the values of an America tilting to Reaganism.

Within a few years, the United States would decisively win the Cold War against the Soviet Union. Yet in the process it had created a technology that defied the capitalist values for which it fought. Less than a decade after the Pentagon's initial network experiments, a bunch of hackers had broken the Internet loose from the military and made it into something beyond its sponsor's dreams—or nightmares. As Peter Childers and Paul Delany (1994, p. 72) put it, "the parasites had taken over the host." In an era that supposedly saw the triumph of the free market, the most technologically advanced medium for planet-wide communication had been created on the basis of state support, open usage, cooperative self-organization, and nonproprietary information circulation.

This de facto situation was gradually given official recognition during the 1980s as administration of the Internet shifted from the Advanced Research Project Agency (ARPA) to the civilian National Science Foundation (NSF), conducted by a small groups of scientists and engineers operating on the basis of "rough consensus and running code" (Goldsmith & Wu, 2006, p. 24).

In many respects, the Internet approached radical dreams of a democratic and participatory communications system. In others, it fell short: hacker culture was very much the domain of a technically educated, mainly affluent, and overwhelmingly male minority—an aristocracy of immaterial labor (Halpern, 2006). This was, however, beginning to change. Since universities and other institutions paid a flat rate for connection and offered large numbers of people access for little or no cost, there was a huge potential for expansion. In 1987 the population of Internet users, which had been growing slowly, doubled in a single year for the first time—and then did so every year thereafter for more than a decade, heading on a trajectory of exponential growth. This was spurred by what was to be the last great gesture of the academic free-knowledge tradition—the public giveaway, sans patent, copyright, or fees, in 1991 by Tim Berners Lee and his fellow scientists at the Swiss physics institute CERN, of the World Wide Web application, whose point-and-click hyper-linking and imagistic displays made the Internet easily accessible to vast populations of cyber-neophytes. But the very success of immaterial labor's experiment in digital autonomy was already beckoning to its nemesis—invasion by cyber-capital.

BOOM: CAPITAL CAPTURES THE INTERNET

Up to this point, the corporate world had shown scant interest in the Internet, and, in turn, Internet culture was specifically and explicitly anti-commercial. NSF policy limited so-called acceptable use to research and education. Small scale trade and barter occurred, but big for-profit enterprise, and its advertising, was absent, and free goods and services proliferated. As Dan Schiller (1999) has pointed out, big corporations had been developing their own internal networks—Intranets—to connect customers with suppliers, improve monitoring of employees, automate jobs, cut travel costs, and gather competitive data, and these were crucial to the neoliberal dissolution of the mass worker and the organization of a new globalized labor force for capital. Nonetheless, net heads of the NSF system had enjoyed a provisional autonomy from capital.

From the 1990s on, however, business became increasingly aware of the growing online population and began to encroach aggressively upon it from a number of directions. The first commercial Internet service providers (ISPs) appeared; at first, these were small mom and pop operations, but they were soon squeezed out by giant corporations such as AOL (America Online) mass-marketing Internet connections. In 1991 the NSF lifted its ban on commerce. The first*.com* domain names for business were created. Demand was so high that in 1993 NSF contracted out the allocation of Internet addresses to Networks Solutions, a private company with links to the CIA, which began charging fees for registration. There were other regulatory changes from a U.S. government keen to assist the private sector. The 1992 Clinton-Gore National Information Infrastructure Initiative, also known as the information superhighway project, trumpeted the social benefits of the Internet but actually ensured that while the expansion of the network would be publicly subsidized, it was corporately constructed, owned, and operated. In 1995 ownership of the high-level backbone of the Internet, to which other parts of the so-called network of networks connected, was privatized; previously it belonged to the NSF, which contracted out operations to telecommunication corporations: now this was reversed, with ownership handed to a cartel of corporate giants from which the NSF purchased services. Such high-level change set the scene for an onrush of commodification cascading through the entire Internet.

Anyone who thinks talk of Internet struggles is melodramatic might consider two incidents illustrating the resistance that commercialization encountered. The first was that of the Phoenix immigration law firm of Laurence Canter and Martha Siegel, the first real spammers. In 1994, they plastered 5,000 Usenet newsgroups with advertisements. So-called Netizens outraged by this violation of noncommercial custom, swamped the offenders' ISP with complaints, burning out its fax machine with protests, and sending sophisticated cancelbots to hunt down and destroy the offending e-missives. Today this seems bizarrely anachronistic, but it shows what a violation of previous norms Internet commodification involved (Grossman, 1997, pp. 18–25). Yet more striking is the story of the short-lived takeover of the Internet by John Postel, a leading member of the loose conclave of techno-experts who informally administered it. In 1998 Postel and some colleagues, concerned about the usurpation of their so-called root authority to allocate e-mail addresses by agencies such as Network Solutions, attempted a digital coup d'état. For a few days, they technically divided the Internet into two separate systems, one running under the new privatized arrangements, the other under the old academic free-knowledge conventions. This feat was accomplished so that everyday users suffered no service disruptions and were unaware of the power-struggle. The implications were, however, clear enough to the U.S. government: Postel was swiftly visited by FBI agents and forced, under threat of prosecution, to capitulate and restore the section of the Internet he had briefly abducted (Goldsmith & Wu, 2006, pp. 43–46).

Even as these battles were being fought, however, the capitalization of the Internet proceeded apace. In 1995 an upstart company, Netscape, offered its shares for sale in an IPO (initial public offering) on the New York Stock Exchange: they doubled in price in a single day. This marked the start of the dot-com boom. Netscape's claim to fame was its ownership of the first easy to use commercial browser to navigate the Web—a technology originally created with public funding at the University of Illinois, which its inventor turned into the basis for a private fortune. Both the technology and the stock market success attracted the attention of industry titans. Microsoft had for 25 years ignored the online world, but in 1995 an alarmed internal memo from Gates warned his company to urgently focus on the "Internet tidal wave" (quoted in Auletta, 2001, p. 55). The fight for hegemony over browser technology, pitting two proprietary products, Microsoft's Explorer and Netscape Navigator, against one another marked the decisive end of the open protocols era. Librarians were drawn in through the philanthropy of the Bill and Melinda Gates Foundation, which offered lavish equipment with Internet capable computers—all loaded with Microsoft's Explorer, bundled with the Windows operating system. Since Microsoft was battling (victoriously) to establish its software as a user-norm, and (unsuccessfully) to clear itself from charges of being a predatory monopolist, it was hard to see this as entirely disinterested (BBC News, 2000).

The so-called browser wars signaled that the Internet had become the new frontier of corporate expansion. The digital gold rush that followed involved an array of different actors. There was the computer sector, producing the software and hardware that constituted the nodes of the network; carrier companies—telephone and cable conglomerates—laying the wired and wireless connections; retail and business-to-business (B2B) sectors, trying to transcend the limits of bricks-and-mortar operations; media companies, racing each other to find digital channels for entertainment and news;

the pornography business, persistently at the leading-edge of e-commerce; early search engines; and companies experimenting with novel forms, such as eBay's online auctions. Vital to many of these was a growing world of e-advertising, which soon bred its own specialized agencies. Layered above this was a world of digital financial transactions, online services from big banks and brokerage houses, day-trading operations, and a host of dubious advice sites, all feeding a mounting frenzy of high-tech stock buying. This so-called new economy transformed the composition of cyberspace. Within a decade, the Internet of the hackers' information wants to be free era seemed like some lost city of Atlantis, submerged by a deluge of banner ads and click-through payments. The foundations of the commodified Internet—a place of online purchases, ubiquitous advertisements, and commercial surveillance—were laid in this period. Some of the companies created at this time, such as Amazon.com, eBay, or Yahoo, are still giants of the Internet economy, but what is remarkable is how many of the dot-com companies are gone. For all the appearance of delirious success, capital's Internet triumph was about to turn into catastrophic commercial carnage—a disaster that was in part a revenge of the very hacker traditions e-capital appeared to so have so decisively defeated.

BUST: REVENGE OF THE DOT-COMMUNISTS

NASDAQ, the high-tech stock market index, increased its value eight-fold between 1996 and 2000, hitting its highest point on March 10, 2000. Then an immense financial bubble burst. Of the myriad of dot-com start ups, most were ill-conceived, many cynical get rich-quick schemes, touting vaporware to make money from stock sales or acquisition by larger corporations. Venture capital had raised high risk money for investment in these enterprises. Shares offered for sale on the stock market were priced on expectation not performance. Consumers, confident in their expanding stock market portfolios, spent lavishly on computers and Internet connections, while businesses, anticipating limitless cyberspatial markets, invested heavily in networks, and telecommunication companies laid miles of fiber cable to wire North America. In a bootstrapping dynamic, stock prices continued to rise, even as most dot-coms showed no trace of profit. While some investors knew stocks were overvalued, they continued to buy, on the so-called greater fool theory, which posited that they could always sell to someone yet more gullible than themselves. Online day-traders and financial advisors at respected institutions, both in blatant conflict of interest situations, promoted worthless stocks in variants of time-honored pump and dump strategies. Rising stock prices supported profit-less development in a virtuous circle.

When dot-com failure to meet financial targets finally hit the limits of investor confidence, however, the cycle went into vicious reverse. Friday, April 14, 2000 saw Wall Street's largest one-day fall in history. Venture capital hesitated on new rounds of funding; consumers stopped buying; IT spending decreased; stocks fell yet further in panic selling; and, as venture capital fled completely, thousands of dot-coms flamed into oblivion. This set off an even larger telecommunication meltdown, as the companies that had invested in millions of miles of fiber cable and Internet equipment found themselves holding vast infrastructure overcapacity, massively indebted, without new customers. In this digital Götterdämmerung, dot-com burnout and telecom meltdown were followed by a third act—corporate crime bust. Companies such as Enron, WorldCom, and Global Crossing covered up losses, hoping to ride out the crisis, or to allow executives to sell stocks while they were still high. The discovery of multimillion-dollar fraud in leading corporations, which also implicated major accounting companies and the dubious dealings of leading investment banks, was too much even for the neoliberal state to ignore. Scandal shattered investor confidence. Between March 11, 2000 and October 9, 2002, NASDAQ lost nearly 80 percent of its value. Internet capital had imploded.

Why did capital's first foray into cyberspace end so catastrophically? Most commentators emphasize the hyperbolic expectations, inexperience, and greed of dot-coms; mainstream corporate ignorance about the digital world; and the "irrational exuberance" of investors (Cassidy, 2002; Munroe, 2004; Shiller, 2000). In this account, the story of the Internet bubble is a morality play in which folly and duplicity meet their nemesis. Yet risky speculation and criminality are common features of markets. Why did they attain such peaks in cyberspace? Other observers note a more basic problem; despite some important exceptions, digital capital as a whole failed to find a reliable business model, a way of extracting profits from the Internet (Abramson, 2005). This is a stronger explanation. The absence of a clear accumulation strategy suggests *why* companies resorted to vaporware, financial overvaluation, and get-out-quick sales. The analysis can, however, be taken deeper. Beneath the dot-coms' inability to make money lay a mass resistance to digital commodification—a concatenation of struggles against and flights from Internet capital.

These took two forms. One—we can call it passive resistance—was a large-scale refusal to buy digital goods or attend to advertisements. The basic problem for the dot-coms was that digital consumers didn't consume—or at least, not enough. Internet use continued to grow, giving rise to expectations of an unlimited online market, but the new cyber-population preferred no- or low-cost activity. The most popular application of the Internet turned out to be e-mail, a service sold cheaply, or, for many, available for free through work, school, or university. Millions certainly browsed the Web, drawn onto it through the commercial portals that became the standard entry points; but what many sought—too many from the point of view of capital—was not purchases but free stuff. As the *Economist* (2001a) observed in a postmortem on the boom, "The real problem, however, appears to be that Internet users have come to expect online services to be free."

Free services were indeed there, in part because the precapitalist legacy of academia and virtual community periods had left a great residue of noncommercial sites and gift-economy practices—but also because capital itself provided them. For there was indeed a business model to handle free media, that of television, radio, and every other media that used content to attract audiences while making revenue from selling eyeballs to advertisers. On this basis, dot-coms threw up content, downloads, and services gratis on sites plastered with pop-up and banner advertisements. E-advertising was the new marketing nirvana. What brought things down to earth with a bump, however, was the discovery that no one was paying attention. A tipping point in the dot-com bust was the discovery of very low click-through rates on banner advertisements, showing that costs for the digital creation of loyal consumers were staggeringly high relative to old media (*Economist,* 2001b). The promise of an online advertising bonanza had sustained thousands of dot-coms through incredible burn-rates of expenditure on improbable projects and insane give-aways. As this dream evaporated, realization dawned that there would be no reverse flow from the tide of red ink, and the bubble burst. Internet capital failed because immaterial labor wasn't buying it.

The other, more active side of resistance to Internet commodification was the continuous production and sharing of free goods by immaterial labor. As the online world was commercialized, the hacker ingenuity that had created the Internet was not extinguished but, on the contrary, extended from the initial aristocracy of immaterial labor to a broader population that continued to experiment with digital potentials, often in ways that disturbed e-capital. Some of this was destructive: identity theft, virus releases, and vandalistic denial-of-service attacks made life miserable for millions of ordinary net users while also impeding digital capital and deterring its customers. Far more complicated was the issue of piracy. The tradition of reproducing and circulating digital content without regard to intellectual property laws, a tradition that stood at the very origins of the Internet, expanded. In the 1990s it hit a mass scale, thanks to the invention—by tinkering college students–of peer-to-peer (P2P) networks, which, dispensing with a central server, were almost impossible to repress. First Napster and, later, Gnutella, Kazaa, and BitTorrent enabled a wave of unauthorized copying, focused initially on MP3 music but also involving games, digitized film, and software of all sorts, which spread out from North American university campuses in what amounted to a mass civil disobedience against copyright. While all of this was stigmatized as piracy by industry groups, the phenomenon was complex. Some was organized crime, some circulation among friends and fans; some so-called free warez networks that hacked software for fun and bragging rights; and some was informed by political dissent against property rights seen as obsolete and repressive in an age of digital abundance (Strangelove, 2005). Protracted court cases produced inconclusive results. As capital commodified the Internet, immaterial labor as energetically decommodified it.

Immaterial labor didn't just copy: it also created—and on a radically different basis from capital. The most striking example was the free and open source software (FOSS) movement. The idea that software for which the source code—the key programming—was made freely available for users to adapt and circulate might result in a product as good or better than commercial development was a direct revival of the hacker traditions. It was also, in the formulations of free software theorists such as Richard Stallman (2004), a challenge to traditional concepts of intellectual property. The appearance of Linux in 1991 and of the associated legal instrument of so-called copyleft or the general public license signaled the emergence in the midst of the dot-com era of counterlogic to that of capital. FOSS was only the expert avant-garde of a far wider range of "peer production" (Benkler, 2006, p. 5), which could range from individuals throwing up Web pages to copyright-defying music mash-ups to creations such as the volunteer digital encyclopedia Wikipedia, whose prototype version appeared in 1999. The eventual emergence of a creative commons campaign, dedicated to relaxing IP laws and creating new legal instruments to legitimize collaborative and sharing activities by cultural producers, was just the formal expression of these myriad free culture activities (Lessig, 2004). By 2000, there were even signs that movements such as FOSS and creative commons were starting to converge with the anti-corporate globalization movement, which was not only mounting massive demonstrations in the streets of Seattle and Genoa, but was also showing an extraordinary facility for using the Internet as a means of digital mobilization, creating an "electronic fabric of struggle" (Cleaver, 1998) that filled the Web with news of Zapatistas in cyberspace.

Even though so-called piracy spread panic through the music industry, and FOSS made Microsoft anxious, none of such peer-to-peer copying and production was in and of itself fatal to Internet capital. Alongside the disappointing performance of Internet marketers and advertisers, however, it contributed to uncertainty about how—or if—money could be made on the Internet. The nemesis of the dot-com boom was not just the venality of venture capitalists and foolishness of investors, though there was plenty of that. At a deeper level, it was undermined by people who declined or even actively struggled against the commodification of the Internet. The millions flocking online were bad subjects of cyber-capital. They didn't buy enough or attend properly to advertisements; they displayed an unwelcome proclivity for free culture, much of which they created themselves; they didn't respect digital property, which they transgressed, defaced, and messed up at every opportunity; they saw what industry deemed theft as access to cultural plenty, and made copyright violation into a generational crusade; and they persisted in coming up with inventions, technological and legal, that struck at the very heart of prospective capital accumulation on the Internet. As Barbrook (2001) observed, in the course of their everyday online activities, North Americans were pragmatically "engaged in the slow process of superseding capitalism" by the circulation of free music, films, games, and information: the dot-coms were not only destroyed by their own greed but also subverted by the dot-communism of immaterial labor.

WEB 2.0: RE-APPROPRIATING IMMATERIAL LABOR

After the bubble burst, in a climate further darkened by 9/11, many thought capital's Internet experiment over. It certainly took time to recover. But reemerge it did, with new strategies. These are most generally recognized under the name *Web 2.0* (O'Reilly, 2005). The key to this second wave of Internet accumulation was the explicit acknowledgement of the collective creativity, aversion to commodification, and pirate spirit that had undone the dot-coms—and their paradoxical reappropriation as a source of profit.

Nowhere is this clearer than in the major motor of e-capital's recovery, Google, whose 2004 IPO marked the resurgence of Internet business (Battelle, 2005). Search engines are parasites on peer production, even if benignly symbiotic ones; they don't create new content, but they enable people to find what others have made. Their popularity depends on the availability of a great common reservoir of Internet resources, many of which are free. Early search engines such as Yahoo, Excite, and Lycos had been part of the dot-com boom, but they were trammeled both by the technical difficulties of search and by the commercialism with which they were deployed, functioning as accessories to advertisement-laden portals and beset by scandals over paid rankings. Google's solution to the technical problem of search, its page rank algorithm, was a quintessential Web 2.0 innovation because it depended on using the linking activities of Internet users—the peer-to-peer pathways of immaterial labor's self-activity—to generate search results. Google also scrupulously avoided the corruption of search results by paid rankings. It ditched the portal approach for a famously clean interface. It developed a precise and targeted advertising strategy, known as Ad Words, which was available to small entrepreneurs as well as large corporations, and avoided the plague of indiscriminate banner and pop-up ads. Google also provided a steady stream of free applications that appealed to the self-generating Internet culture. Google's success was based on indexing the Internet population's own creative self-activity and responding to its manifest aversion to previous e-capital strategies. Google's slogan, "do no evil" was the tribute Internet capital had to pay to cyber-communism. The paradox is, of course, that by this strategy it created the greatest concentrations of privatized power and concentrated wealth yet seen on the Internet.

In the wake of Google came a variety of other Web 2.0 ventures—social networks such as MySpace, Facebook, Orkut, and Flickr, video sites such as YouTube, and virtual worlds like Second Life and There. Some were new; others had dot-com origins but survived the winnowing of the crash. The key to Web 2.0 business is to own an innovation for convening or managing

Internet communities. The owner facilitates the formation of community, assumes (some) responsibility for policing and managing it—and profits from its collective activities. With search engines, the content is the World Wide Web, created by myriad Internet-users world wide. With online auctions such as eBay, the content is the transaction of millions of buyers and sellers. With massively multiplayer online games (MMOGs), such as World of Warcraft or Second Life, while the proprietor provides the initial programmed activity, the content is the interaction of players. In video-sharing sites such as YouTube, the content is the videos made and uploaded by users. In social networks, such as Facebook or MySpace, the content is the identities and relationships of users. In many cases, the key community service is free, at least in its most basic form, though subscriptions may be levied for access or premium rates charged. It is quite possible in this model to include a certain amount of open-source software and creative commons licensing in the mix. Web 2.0 proprietors quite unabashedly celebrate themselves as "liberal communists" Zizek, 2005). The main point is to attract the populations whose digital presence can be sold to advertisers and data miners, even while they at the same time, and for nothing, create the content that draws yet more users. Thus, as Coté and Pybus suggest, these ventures are a way of harnessing "immaterial labour 2.0 . . . the 'free' labour that subjects engage in on a cultural and biopolitical level when they participate on a site such as MySpace" (2007, p. 90).

Web 2.0 capitalism promotes itself as "empowering" and "democratizing" and loudly celebrates "participation, collectivism, virtual communities, amateurism" (Carr, cited in Lovink [2008], p. xi). There is some truth to this. Google would not have attained preeminence if it did not offer good search capabilities. Web 2.0 ventures offer in convenient form capacities previously limited to large corporations. YouTube's video uploads seem like a media activist dream; eBay has opened online trading to a host of small businesses and one-person entrepreneurs; and even if there are plenty of questions to be raised about the truth and sagacity of exchanges in MySpace or Facebook, they nonetheless represent an extraordinary opening-up of a domain that 20 years ago was still the preserve of technocratic, and mainly male, elites. This for-profit digital communality has, however, features that belie its apparent benevolence. Web 2.0 proprietors exercise fearsome powers of surveillance and censorship within and over their platforms, highlighted by the scandals over Google's compliance with Chinese censorship laws (Bataille 2005, pp. 204–10) and Facebook privacy transgressions (Hodgkinson, 2008). Ultimately, they control the very existence of a so-called community: social network participants vest their identity in privately managed world where whose parameters, dispositions, and very existence depend on market fluctuations and corporate logic: as players of several MMOGs have found, your social matrix can be profoundly altered or vanish overnight as owners revise or abolish virtual worlds to meet bottom-line imperatives (Varney, 2007).

Most basic, however, are issues of exploitation. In the Web 2.0 business model the activity of myriad unpaid users becomes free labor fuelling profits for owners and shareholders. As Lovink pithily observes, beneath all the babble about empowerment, the actual message of Web 2.0 owners for those who use their applications is "You poor bugger, fool around with your funky free content, while we make the money with the requirements" (Lovink, 2008, p. 247). At stake here is not just the conversion of volunteer creativity into profit, but, as Lovink points out, the increasing ability of media capital to undercut the paid work of professionals by the substitution of free content. Perhaps because this situation is so blatant, and has attracted so much criticism, some Web 2.0 platforms have moved to allow their content-contributors some prospect of remuneration: in 2008 YouTube began a scheme for users to get a fraction of the ad revenues associated with their videos. Yet the situation remains massively asymmetrical. While Web 2.0 users become individual microcapitalists, most of whom get tiny slivers of payment for their efforts, it is the Web 2.0 macrocapitalists, the owners and shareholders, who cream off the aggregated benefits of collective, cooperative immaterial labor.

Web 2.0's paradoxical juxtaposition of real benefits plus rank exploitation makes sense, I suggest, if it is understood as capital's attempt to cut a deal with autonomous powers of peer-to-peer digital culture. Just as the social contract of collective bargaining with trades unions represented the compromise industrial capital had to make with the mass worker, a compromise that provided workers some real gains, even while continuing their subordination to profit, Web 2.0 is information capital's compromise with immaterial labor, providing it with limited, semiautonomous options for content creation in return for overall subordination. As with all such deals, its real price can only be estimated against the more radical possibilities on which it forecloses. In a trenchant critique, Dmytri Kleiner and Brian Wyrick say that "Private appropriation of community created value is a betrayal of the promise of sharing technology and free cooperation" (2007, p. 4). Noting, as we have, that the key ingredient in Web 2.0 is the "collective intelligence" of the users to which the owners bring "finance hype-generation, marketing and buzz," they go on to remark that it is,

> a venture capitalist's paradise where investors pocket the value produced by unpaid users, ride on the technical innovations of the free software movement and kill off the decentralizing potential of peer-to-peer production. (Kleiner & Wyrick, 2007, p. 4)

The deal that Web 2.0 offers immaterial labor is "ease of access compared to the more technically challenging and expensive undertaking of owning your own means of information production" (Kleiner & Wyrick, 2007, p. 5).

It is in this context that we can return to Second Life. Linden Lab's virtual world is the most recent iteration of an online play tradition that recapitulates the sequence of struggles and flights we have traced for the Internet as a whole. The origins of such games lie in the military simulations of the Pentagon culture from which the Internet grew. When hackers took their line of flight, one of their most important acts was the invention of a just-for-fun version of such simulations, Spacewar, often cited as the first videogame. Early freeware game culture bred the first online virtual worlds, text-based MUDS (multi-user dungeons), self-organized and played for no cost. Only in the 1990s were these worlds commercialized in MMOGs such Ultima, EverQuest and, later, World of Warcraft, which made revenues from the sale of CD disks needed for lavish graphic environments and monthly subscription charges. In fact, these commercial games largely escaped the bust of the Internet bubble, largely because they mobilized the user-made content of player activity to sustain interest and community. In this respect they were forerunners of Web 2.0. However, the close integration of virtual and real markets in digital worlds such as Second Life, with regularized exchange rates between actual and virtual currencies, and the allocation of individual property rights over user-created content represents a genuinely new step in the envelopment of do-it-yourself digital culture by commercial ventures (Herman, Coombe, & Kaye, 2006).

Second Life does allow room for semiautonomous social innovations: I have contributed to one of these experiments (de Peuter & Dyer-Witheford, 2005). Those entering such projects should, however, consider the larger balance of powers on this terrain. Capital owns the high ground: virtual libraries in Second Life have to pay Linden Labs; they get none of the revenues for the game to which they provide services, with little or no control over conditions of privacy and surveillance (Litwin, 2006); and they cater to a population which, while it can play for free, has to pay to have any real fun. While Second Life does offer participants the opportunity to make money by sale of user-owned content to other players (only a tiny handful succeed in a massively unequal economy) this in no way subtracts from the owners' revenues. The real beneficiaries are the venture capitalists who finance Linden Labs. Like other Web 2.0 platforms, Second Life engages the creative, cooperative side on digital culture, in order to build a population that advertisers and marketers—the high value purchasers of digital property—find attractive. To go down this route of building public library services in Second Life is to situate them as an appendix of, or client to, digital capital; we might ask whether the powers of immaterial labor do not offer other directions for those who want to expand the free circulation of knowledge in virtual worlds, a point that we now turn to consider.

CONCLUSION: DON'T MOURN, ORGANIZE

Despite the vast prices paid by major corporations for Web 2.0 platforms—$580 million by News Corporation for MySpace (Coté & Pybus, 2007, p. 88), $1.65 billion in shares by Google for YouTube (BBC News,

2006)—capital's return to the Internet may yet reveal itself as Bubble 2.0 or, even more likely, succumb to the bursting of the more mundane financial bubble of subprime mortgages, as tightening economic conditions reduce advertising budgets. In the meantime, however, the apparent success of the corporate world in reappropriating dissident energies in cyberspace has led to second thoughts among radical theorists and activists about the virtual as a site of defection and resistance. One response has been a disillusioned turn away from Internet politics, now seen as fatally compromised by the co-optive powers of the viral marketers and cyber-monopolists of "communicative capitalism" (Dean, 2005). Yet understandable as this reaction is, ceding contestation over the sociotechnical system that is the central communication resource of the age would be a mistake.

More promising are suggestions by Geert Lovink (2008) and Ned Rossiter (2006; Lovink & Rossiter, 2005) not to give up on Internet struggles, but to organize them better. Affirming the continuing importance of the ideals of open communication affirmed by anarchic and utopian Internet movements, they nevertheless propose that to counter Web 2.0 co-option, these movements need to find more coherent strategies. They posit the need for "organized networks"—"a hybrid formation: part tactical media, part institutional formation" (Lovink & Rossiter, 2005). Organized networks would articulate immaterial labor's creative powers not with the corporate sector but with civil society agencies—with public and democratic, rather than privatized and-for profit, projects. A central mission for organized networks would be "to envision sustainable income sources beyond the current copyright regimes" (Lovink, 2008, p. xiii) for the creators of digital content, providing immaterial labor with alternatives to marketing itself under standard intellectual property contracts, or giving its creations away to be appropriated, for nothing, by Web 2.0 capitalists.

Lovink and Rossiter are somewhat vague about what "new institutional forms" (Rossiter 2006, p. 13) they seek, and they are particularly ambivalent about the degree of state support they envisage. In my own view, this agenda requires nothing short of a reconstitution of the conjunction of hacker know-how and governmental support that brought the Internet into being, only now on a much wider basis, with sponsorship coming not from the warfare state of the Pentagon, but from the welfare activities of the cultural, educative, ecological, and health agencies that neoliberalism has sought to marginalize. One element in this would be the development of more publicly owned and operated platforms for user-created content, but owned and operated out institutions such as universities and libraries. Instead of renting space in Second Life and boosting Linden Labs' market value, librarians could participate in the formation of organized networks by campaigning for new forms of public support for digital authors, funded from the taxation of Internet capital; by adopting open-source, rather than proprietary, software, as an institutional norm for public libraries;

by applying their expertise to the organization of not-for-profit wikis and community informatics (see Stevenson, 2007); and by exploring the possibilities for developing search engines and virtual worlds made and owned autonomously—independently—from capital. Such initiatives by coalitions of digital artists and activists, academics, librarians, and social movements would be a response to Web 2.0 that, rather than forgoing the opportunities of virtual worlds, actualizes them within new public, collective institutions. This would serve to initiate a new cycle of struggles to reappropriate the powers of immaterial labor alienated by Internet capital: it would be, in effect, to reply to the exhortation to "get a second life" by saying, Before that happens, we would like our first life—our capacity for cooperative creativity, free from domination by privatized wealth and power—back, thank you very much.

REFERENCES

Abramson, B. (2005). *Digital phoenix: Why the information economy collapsed and how it will rise again.* Cambridge, MA: MIT Press.

Annoyed Librarian. (2007, Aug. 27). The cult of twopointopia. Entry in Weblog, *Annoyed Librarian.* Retrieved January 31, 2007, from http://annoyedlibrarian.blogspot.com/2007/08/cult-of-twopointopia.html.

Auletta, K. (2001). *World war 3.0: Microsoft and its enemies.* New York: Random House.

Barbrook, R. (2001). *Cyber-communism: How the Americans are superseding capitalism in cyberspace.* Retrieved June 23, 2005, from http://www.hrc.wmin.ac.uk/theory-cybercommunism.html.

Barbrook, R. (2007). *Imaginary futures.* London: Pluto.

Barbrook, R., & Cameron, A. (1996). The Californian ideology. *Science as Culture, 6*(1), 44–72. Retrieved December 28, 2006, from http://www.hrc.wmin.ac.uk/theory-californianideology-main.html.

Battelle, J. (2005). *The search: How Google and its rivals rewrote the rules of business and transformed our culture.* New York: Penguin.

BBC News. (2000, April 3). Microsoft vs. US Justice Department: Extracts from the guilty verdict. *BBC News World Edition.* Retrieved February 5, 2008, from http://news.bbc.co.uk/2/hi/in_depth/business/2000/microsoft/700702.stm.

BBC News. (2006, Oct. 10). Google buys YouTube for $1.65bn. *BBC News World Edition.* Retrieved February 12, 2008, from http://news.bbc.co.uk/2/hi/business/6034577.stm.

Bell, L., & Peters, T. (2007). Get a (second) life! Prospecting for gold in a 3-D world. *Computers in Libraries, 27*(1), 10–14.

Benkler, Y. (2006). *The wealth of networks: How social production transforms markets and freedom.* New Haven, CT: Yale University Press.

Cassidy, J. (2002). *Dot.con: The greatest story ever sold.* New York: Harper Collins.

Childers, P., & Delany, P. (1994). Wired world, virtual campus: Universities and the political economy of cyberspace. *Works and Days, 23*(4), 61–78.

Cleaver, H. (1977). *Reading capital politically.* Brighton, Sussex, England: Harvester.

Cleaver, H. (1981). Technology as political weaponry. In R. Anderson (Ed.), *Science, politics and the agricultural revolution in Asia* (pp. 261–276). Boulder, CO: Westview Press.

Cleaver, H. (1998). The Zapatistas and the electronic fabric of struggle. In J. Holloway & E. Pelaez (Eds.), *Zapatista! Reinventing revolution in Mexico* (pp. 81–103). London: Pluto Press.

Coté, M., & Pybus, J. (2007). Learning to immaterial labour 2.0: MySpace and social networks. *Ephemera: Theory & Politics in Organization, 7* (1), 88–106. Retrieved January 24, 2008, from http://www.ephemeraweb.org/journal/7-1/7-1cote-pybus.pdf.

Dean, J. (2005). Communicative capitalism: Circulation and the foreclosure of politics. *Cultural Politics 1*(1), 51–74.

Deleuze, G., & Guattari, F. (1987). *A thousand plateaus: Capitalism and schizophrenia*. New York: Viking.

Deleuze, G., & Parnet, C. (1977). *Dialogues II*. London: Continuum.

de Peuter, G., & Dyer-Witheford, N. (2005). Games of empire: A transversal media inquiry. *Flack Attack, 1*, 4–21. Retrieved January 24, 2008, from http://www.flackattack.org/Prod/pdf/Flack_Attack_Autonomy.pdf.

Dyer-Witheford, N. (1999). *Cyber-Marx: Cycles and circuits of struggle in high-technology capitalism*. Urbana, IL: University of Illinois.

Dyer-Witheford, N. (2001). Empire, immaterial labor, the new combinations, and the global worker. *Rethinking Marxism, 13*(3–4), 70–80.

Dyer-Witheford, N. (2002). E-Capital and the many-headed hydra. In G. Elmer (Ed.), *Critical perspectives on the Internet* (pp. 129–164). Lanham, MD: Rowman & Littlefield.

Economist. (2001a, Apr. 12). *Easy.com, easy.go*. Retrieved January 31, 2008, from http://www.economist.com/business/displaystory.cfm?story_id=E1_VGJRPV.

Economist. (2001b, Feb. 22). *Internet advertising's woes.* Retrieved January 31, 2008, from http://www.economist.com/business/displaystory.cfm?story_id=513117.

Foster, A. (2007). Professor avatar. *Information Chronicle, 54*(4), 24.

Fukuyama, F. (1992). *The end of history and the last man*. New York: Macmillan.

Goldsmith, J., & Wu, T. (2006). *Who controls the Internet?: Illusions of a borderless world*. Oxford: Oxford University Press.

Grassian, E., & Trueman, R. B. (2007). Stumbling, bumbling, teleporting and flying . . . librarian avatars in Second Life. *Reference Services Review, 30*(1), 84–89.

Grossman, W. M. (1997). *Net.Wars*. New York: New York University Press.

Halpern, H. (2006, April 30). *Digital sovereignty: The immaterial aristocracy of the World Wide Web*. Paper presented at Immaterial Labour and New Social Subjects: Class Composition in Cognitive Capitalism, University of Cambridge. Retrieved November 19, 2006, http://www.geocities.com/immateriallabour/halpinpaper2006.html.

Hardt, M., & Negri, A. (2000). *Empire*. Cambridge, MA: Harvard University Press.

Hardt, M., & Negri, A. (2004). *Multitude: War and Democracy in the age of empire*. New York: Penguin.

Herman, A., Coombe, R. J., Kaye, L. (2006). Your second life?: Goodwill and the performativity of intellectual property in online digital gaming. *Cultural Studies, 20*(2/3), 184–210.

Himanen, P. (2001). *The hacker ethic and the spirit of the information age*. New York: Random House.
Hodgkinson, T. (2008, Jan. 14). With friends like these. . . . *The Guardian*. Retrieved January 20, 2008, from http://www.guardian.co.uk/technology/2008/jan/14/facebook.
Hurst-Wahl, J. (2007, June). Librarians and Second Life. *Information Outlook*. Retrieved January 21, 2008, from http://findarticles.com/p/articles/mi_m0FWE/is_6_11/ai_n19311772.
Kleiner, D., & Wyrick, B. (2007). InfoEnclosure 2:0. *Mute*, *2*(4), 2–7.
Lessig, L. (2004). *Free culture: How big media uses technology and the law to lock down culture and control creativity*. New York: Penguin.
Levy, S. (1984). *Hackers: Unsung heroes of the computer revolution*. Garden City, NJ: Anchor Press/Doubleday.
Lindenschmidt, J. (2004). From virtual commons to virtual enclosures: Revolution and counter-revolution in the information age. *The Commoner: A Web Journal for Other Values*. Retrieved January 5, 2006, from http://www.commoner.org.uk/09lindenschmidt.pdf.
Litwin, R. (2006, May 22). The central problem of library 2.0. *Library Juice*. Retrieved February 1, 2008, from http://libraryjuicepress.com/blog/?p=68.
Litwin, R. (2008, January 6). Annotated list of things not to forget (in the 2.0 craze) . . . *Library Juice*. Retrieved February 1, 2008, from http://libraryjuicepress.com/blog/index.php?s=Web+2.0&submit=Search.
Lovink, G. (2008). *Zero comments: Blogging and critical internet culture*. New York: Routledge.
Lovink, G., & Rossiter, N. (2005). Dawn of the organized networks. *Fibreculture, 5*. Retrieved January 31, 2008, from http://journal.fibreculture.org/issue5/lovink_rossiter.html#5.
Maness, J. M. (2006). Library 2.0 theory: Web 2.0 and its implications for libraries. *Webology, 3*(2). Retrieved January 31, 2007, from http://www.webology.ir/2006/v3n2/a25.html.
Markoff, J. (2005). *What the dormouse said: How the sixties counterculture shaped the personal computer industry*. New York: Viking.
Marx, K. (1973). *Grundrisse: Foundations of a critique of political economy*. Harmondsworth, West Drayton, England: Penguin.
Marx, K. (1977). *Capital* (vol. 1). London: Vintage.
Munroe, T. (2004). *Dot-com to dot-bomb: Understanding the dot-com boom, bust and resurgence*. New York: Moraga.
Negri, A. (1979). Domination and sabotage. In Red Notes Collective (Ed.), *Working class autonomy and the crisis* (pp. 93–138). London: Red Notes.
O'Reilly, T. (2005, Sep. 30). *What is Web 2.0?: Design patterns and business models for the next generation of software*. Retrieved January 31, 2008, from http://www.oreilly.com/pub/a/oreilly/tim/news/2005/09/30/what-is-web-20.html.
Panzieri, R. (1976) Surplus value and planning: Notes on the reading of capital. In Conference of Socialist Economics (Ed.), *The labour process and class strategies* (pp. 4–25). London: Conference of Socialist Economics.
Rheingold, H. (1993). *The virtual community*. Reading, MA: Addison-Wesley.
Rossiter, N. (2006). *Organized networks: Media theory, creative labour, new institutions*. Rotterdam, Netherlands: Nai Publishers.

Schiller, D. (1999). *Digital capitalism: Networking the global market system.* Cambridge, MA: MIT Press.

Shiller, R. J. (2000). *Irrational exuberance.* Princeton, NJ: Princeton University Press.

Stallman, R. M. (2004). *Free software, free society.* Thrissur, Kerala, India: Altermedia.

Stevenson, S. (2007). Public libraries, public access computing, FOSS and CI: There are alternatives to private philanthropy. *First Monday, 12*(5). Retrieved January 31, 2008, from http://www.uic.edu/htbin/cgiwrap/bin/ojs/index.php/fm/article/view/1833.

Strangelove, M. (2005). *The empire of mind: Digital piracy and the anti-capitalist movement.* Toronto: University of Toronto Press.

Turner, F. (2006). *From counterculture to cyberculture: Stewart Brand, the Whole Earth Network, and the rise of digital utopianism.* Chicago: University of Chicago Press.

Varney, A. (2007). Blowing up galaxies. *The Escapist, 101.* Retrieved February 11, 2008, from http://www.escapistmagazine.com/articles/view/issues/issue_101/560-Blowing-Up-Galaxies.

Wark, M. (2004). *A hacker manifesto.* Cambridge, MA: Harvard University Press.

Wright, S. (2005). Reality check: Are we living in an immaterial world. *Mute, 2*(1). Retrieved January 31, 2008, from http://www.metamute.org/node/417.

Zizek, S. (2005, Apr. 5) Nobody has to be vile. *London Review of Books.* Retrieved January 25, 2008, http://www.lrb.co.uk/v28/n07/print/zize01_.html.

4

A QUICK DIGITAL FIX? CHANGING SCHOOLS, CHANGING LITERACIES, PERSISTENT INEQUALITIES: A CRITICAL, CONTEXTUAL ANALYSIS

Ross Collin and Michael W. Apple

Education has always been buffeted by ideological and economic forces. In the early years of the twentieth century, for example, business interests called for schools to be run like factories and for educational practices to be reformed in accordance with Taylorist principles (Kliebard, 2004). More recently, there have been calls for schools to return to their so-called real function of preparing the next generation of workers. Accompanying these calls has been a focus on upgrading students' skills, in general, and their technological skills, in particular (Brown & Lauder, 2001). One popular solution to the (supposed) problem of U.S. students' low skills is the technological upgrading of the nation's public schools. Machines, combined with an emphasis on technical knowledge, are to be our saviors (Cuban, 2001).

In an earlier set of studies, one of us critically examined the relationship between these kinds of ideologies and policies and what actually happens in schools (Apple, 1982, 1986, 1995, 1999, 2000). The results have been less than satisfactory, to say the least. In this chapter, we are equally critical. We concentrate our attention on transformations occurring outside of education that are having profound effects on the kinds of knowledge, skills,

Acknowledgments. We would like to thank Scot Barnett for his work on the initial draft of this chapter. We would also like to thank the Friday Seminar at the University of Wisconsin–Madison, as well as Deborah Brandt, for their comments on earlier drafts of this piece. A briefer analysis of the issues we treat here can be found in Bernardo Gallegos, Steven Tozer, and Annette Henry, eds., *Handbook on Social Foundations Research* (Mahwah, NJ: Lawrence Erlbaum, in press).

and dispositions valued inside education. In this study, issues of technology, literacy, and technical and scientific knowledge are of great importance—but not in the ways most analysts assume.

In order to accomplish what we have set out to do in this chapter, we ask for the reader's patience, for we have to do some heavy theoretical and historical lifting. Moreover, we have to look behind many of the arguments directing educators and those working in other cultural fields to turn over their institutions to the technical and administrative needs of the business world. And though we find much to criticize, we conclude this chapter by analyzing promising trends in schools. But let us begin with a story of computers.

LET THEM BUY COMPUTERS

It was on November 8, 1994, the date of the national midterm elections, that the Republican Revolutionaries captured their Winter Palace, taking control of both the Senate and, for the first time in four decades, the House of Representatives. Under the banner of their Contract with America, victorious Republicans marked for final destruction the remaining pillars of the welfare state and made official their plans for the construction of a competitive state driven by a small, strong government that cultivates the entrepreneurialism and so-called traditional values of individual citizens. The day after being sworn in as the new Speaker of the House, however, small government advocate Newt Gingrich proposed one acceptable form of governmental assistance to disadvantaged citizens: tax credits for poor Americans who buy laptop computers.

Although Gingrich later described his idea as more of a thought experiment than a serious policy proposal, a quick analysis of the plan reveals much about the technotopian impulses in certain neoliberal and neoconservative projects. Indeed, underlying Gingrich's idea is the assumption that in an order stripped of many of the social and economic safeguards established in part through the collective efforts of marginalized citizens, basic fairness may be achieved simply by equipping all competitors with some of the same tools (e.g., laptop computers). Occluded in this vision, however, is the fact that mere possession of tools means little for individuals situated in real social, political, and economic systems. While questions of resource availability and distribution remain of great importance, they must be posed alongside other critical questions, including: How are tools used? For what purposes? In what social, political, and economic contexts? How are diverse actors' uses of tools valued in different ways in different systems? What kinds of identities are enacted through specific forms of tool use?

Mindful of the importance of addressing this larger set of questions, we situate the following analysis of the potentialities and limitations of new tools within a broader study of how literacies evolve in relation to changes in material systems and processes of schooling. As we explain below, contemporary theories of literacy provide ways of conceiving of how different actors, positioned in multiple fields of power, utilize tools in specific ways so as to carry out socially meaningful work as particular kinds of people with certain values, relationships, and goals (Brandt, 2001, 2005; Gee, Hull, & Lankshear, 1996; New London Group, 2000). Moreover, contemporary theories of literacy, in conjunction with lines of analysis developed within critical studies of education (Apple, 1995, 2006; Gee, 1996; Robertson, 2000), offer ways of understanding how different modes of tool use (aspects of particular literate practices) change, compete, and increase and decrease in value with shifts in material systems. Indeed, as emerging socioeconomic orders in the United States and similar nations are powered more and more by the generation, assessment, and application of new knowledge (see Apple, 1995; Carnoy, 2000; Castells, 1996; Hardt & Negri, 2000; Reich, 1991), workers' literate skills, as well as their training within educational institutions, grow in importance both for individual workers and for the larger communities of which they are members.

In the following analysis of transformations of literate practices, then, we take as our basic context the ongoing and conflict-ridden shift in the United States and similar nations from welfare state industrial economies to neoliberal state informational economies. By *informational economy,* we do not mean a state of affairs wherein agricultural and industrial labor have disappeared and all workers employ cutting-edge technologies to engage in intellectually challenging endeavors. Rather, we refer to an economy in which value is added in labor processes increasingly through the manipulation of new knowledge and disparate aspects of production are reorganized accordingly (see Apple, 1995; Carnoy, 2000; Castells, 1996; Hardt & Negri, 2000; Reich, 1991). Though in the interest of specificity we focus on developments within the United States and similar capitalist economies, we must emphasize that in the emerging informational economy, both the processes and components of production, consumption, and circulation are organized more or less directly in networks that are global in scope. To cite but one implication of these arrangements, laborers are pressured both to undercut the wages of all other workers around the world and to offer capital full access to their resources (material, intellectual, and spiritual), lest their regions be switched off from worldwide networks of power and transformed into economic black holes, such as the *favelas* around Sao Paulo, the slums of Kolkata, or the South Side of Chicago (see Apple, 1996; Castells, 1996; Davis, 2006). Thus, when we examine how educators and employers produce workers and literacies necessary for the currently constituted global economy, we must see this production as bound up with—*indeed, dependent on*—the exploitation of billions of women, men, and children around the world. Seen in this light, nonsolutions to national and global inequalities such as Newt Gingrich's scheme to offer laptops (and little else) to the poor reveal themselves to be less absurd and amusing than dishonest and outright cruel.

LITERACIES, TOOLS, AND SPONSORS

To cast our analysis of the potentialities and limitations of new tools in terms of sociocultural theories of literacy (Barton, 1994; Heath, 1983; Scollon & Scollon, 1981; Scribner & Cole, 1981; Street, 1984), we draw on Gee's (1996) argument that literacy is the control of a secondary (non–home-based) discourse. Gee (1996) defines discourses as

> ways of being in the world, or forms of life which integrate words, acts, values, beliefs, attitudes, and social identities, as well as gestures, glances, body positions, and clothes. A Discourse is a sort of identity kit which comes complete with the appropriate costume and instructions on how to act, talk, and often write, so as to take on a particular social role that others will recognize. (p. 127)

Extending Gee's definition, we note that central to many discourses are particular modes of tool use. Indeed, for any action involving a given tool (e.g., using a computer to sign an online petition), we must ask what discourses are in play and what identities are being enacted. Thus, bearing in mind that every tool is shaped in part by its historical designs and uses (e.g., the Internet privileges users of English) and has certain perceived affordances (e.g., networked computers may, for particular users, facilitate communication that is text based, many-to-many, fast paced, and time- and place-independent), we argue that the ways in which and the purposes for which tools are used depend to a considerable extent on how tools' designs, uses, and perceived affordances align with the discourses, or forms of life, embodied by actors in specific material contexts (see Warschauer, 1999).

Furthermore, integrating into our argument Brandt's (2001) work on literacy sponsorship, we observe that literacies "exis[t] only as part of larger material systems, systems that on the one hand enable acts of reading or writing"—or, as per Gee's definition of literacy, performances of particular discourses—"and on the other hand confer their value. Changes in these systems change the meaning and the status of individual literacy" (p. 1). Thus, Brandt (2001) writes:

> To treat literacy this way is to understand not only why individuals labor to attain literacy but also to appreciate why, as with any resource of value, organized economic and political interests work so persistently to conscript and ration the powers of literacy for their own competitive advantage. (p. 5)

Crucial to such efforts at conscripting or rationing the powers of literacy is the provision or withholding of the tools of literacy. As Brandt (2001) argues, literacy sponsors such as public schools and private corporations that control many tools of literacy require apprentices (students and employees) to use these tools in proper literate fashion.

Synthesizing the arguments of Brandt and Gee, then, we may note that in shifting material systems, performances of different discourses are valued in different and evolving ways. Indeed, in the emerging fast capitalist system of the United States, the United Kingdom, and elsewhere, competing interests struggle ceaselessly in workplaces,[1] schools, and other sites to sponsor and engage in the development of newer and more valuable[2] forms of life and thereby gain social, political, and economic advantage. Disconcertingly, however, the market values of particular forms of life are determined in part by their potential for exploitation by capital, rendering less valuable the discourses of those who resist the demands of the market or those with access to few high-value resources (Apple, 2006; Apple & Buras, 2006).

Drawing together these lines of analysis, we conclude that many of the literacies and patterns of literacy sponsorship valued in welfare state industrial economies are being reshaped and repositioned as new forms of life and new systems of literacy sponsorship rise in value with the emergence of neoliberal state informational economies (even as changes in literacy practices reshape the social, political, and economic contexts in which they occur). This is not, however, a neutral process. Powerful fast capitalist and neoliberal interests operating in such economies recruit forms of life and endorse patterns of literacy sponsorship that are in many ways antithetical to principles of social justice and strong democracy (Barber, 2003). In opposition to this, we argue that citizens can and should seek out opportunities for intervention in and across nation states and should work together through disparate channels to help each other shape and adapt to the new realities of the emerging socioeconomic order. A crucial step in this process is the widening of opportunity within and across educational institutions for diverse learners to collaborate in developing powerful literacies necessary both for securing productive, rewarding labor in fast-moving informational economies and for reshaping socioeconomic orders according to principles of justice and strong democracy. The prospects for such collaboration, unfortunately, have narrowed over the past few decades because of radical transformations in the relationships among globalizing processes, states, schooling, and economies.

LITERACIES AND THE FORDIST KEYNESIAN WELFARE STATE SETTLEMENT

To understand how kinds of literacies—the control of certain forms of life—are valued in the emerging socioeconomic order and the difficulties students and workers face in acquiring, reshaping, or challenging them, we must investigate the changes in both the material systems that enable and confer value and the social settlements of which these material systems are parts. First, the Fordist Keynesian welfare state settlement of the industrial age is understood as the moment in capitalist development in which profit was ultimately realized by firms through the provision of large quantities of standardized goods and services to more or less stable markets, not through the manipulation of new knowledge. We will then turn to a discussion of the emerging settlement of the neoliberal state informational economy, focusing on the ways particular literacies are recruited, put to work, and traded on.

In the Fordist Keynesian welfare state settlement of the post-WWII era, notes Gary Teeple, the state strengthened its hand in arranging "social policy, programs, standards and regulations in order to mitigate class conflict and to provide for, answer or accommodate certain social needs for which the capitalist mode of production in itself has no solution or makes no provision" (as quoted in Robertson, 2000, p. 95). In return for social and worksite protections (e.g., relatively stable employment for considerable portions of the white male workforce) and access to affordable consumer goods, many laborers accepted jobs in workplaces run on the command-and-control model in which: orders flowed from a small top to a wider base (pyramidal logic); departments within companies were clearly marked off from one another; new projects were generated, refined, and executed in-house by full-time employees; much work was highly routinized; management exhibited low trust of workers' decision-making abilities; and the amount of higher-order thinking required in work decreased the further one moved down the chain of command (see Brown & Lauder, 2001; Carnoy, 2000; Castells, 1996; Gee, 2004; Hardt & Negri, 2000; Reich, 1991; Taylor, 2001).

Relative to the forms of life recruited by capital in the informational era, then, the forms of life sponsored among workers in the industrial age were prescribed, bounded, stable, and less-consuming. Explaining this state of affairs, Hardt and Negri (2000) argue that the industrial era was driven primarily by disciplinary forms of power that

> fixed individuals in institutions but did not succeed in consuming them completely in the rhythm of productive practices and productive socialization; it did not reach the point of permeating entirely the consciousnesses and bodies of individuals, the point of treating and organizing them in the totality of their activities. (p. 24)

Thus, while industrial-era workers may have struggled to control particular literacies, the extent to which they internalized and could reconfigure and draw on new forms of life was of less consequence than it would be for workers in the informational era of fast capitalism.

Furthermore, because of a range of factors, including the modicum of power won by organized labor in the welfare state settlement, some full-time workers (especially white males) were provided within-firm training to help them acquire valuable literacies. Public sponsorship of literacy development also expanded with the growth of the welfare state as organized groups of citizens (e.g., the African American Civil Rights Movement and the Women's Movement) worked collectively in the widened public sphere to press their demands for better and more inclusive public education.

These popular calls for better provision of literacy training through more equitable public schooling interacted with other demands made on the welfare state, in general, and on public schools, in particular, by powerful business interests and by conservative social groups (see Apple, 2006). The state, seeking to "integrate many of the interests of allied and even opposing groups under its banner" (Apple, 1995, p. 26–27), struggled continuously through its educational apparatus to engage certain of these groups and meet certain of their needs. Thus, while the state responded to popular pressure and made limited efforts to equalize participation in public schooling, it also endeavored, as it had since the late nineteenth century, to meet the needs of industry by moving high-cost and high-risk research and worker-training processes into the educational apparatus (this included colleges and universities; see Althusser, 1971). Public schools came to play central roles in the production of both high-status technical/administrative knowledge and the workers who manipulated this knowledge in more-or-less routinized ways for the corporate interests of the industrial economy. Through this and other processes, the state also (re)created (in part) and won the active consent of a white middle class whose children's schools could filter to the top of their classes (in part) by virtue of their possession of and orientation toward dominant groups' valuable literacies (including the workplace literacies of their parents, many of whose jobs involved the manipulation of technical/administrative knowledge; Apple, 1995). The literacy characteristics of the industrial-era public schools were a view of knowledge as stable, standard, decontextualized, bounded, and situated in clear hierarchies that privilege the "official knowledge" of dominant groups (Apple, 2000). Furthermore, they advanced a conceptualization of work as involving deraced, declassed, and degendered individuals laboring alone to carry out the more-or-less routinized tasks handed down to them by authorities.

These features were strengthened by and helped strengthen the institutional structures and practices of industrial-era schools, including: rigid departmentalization; individual (vs. collaborative) teaching; adherence to local and state standards; use of uniform, mass-marketed textbooks and prepackaged curricula; grading of individual students; tracking; standardized testing; 30-to-1 student-to-teacher ratios; and factorylike time management (Apple, 1995). Thus, while allowing that they are complicated institutions shaped by myriad forces, industrial-era public schools are characterized by both good sense and bad sense (Apple, 2000), developed standardized work processes, gridlike organizational forms, and white, middle-class institutional cultures that served, at least partially, to reproduce through struggle both a stratified labor force (privileging the white middle class) and the disparate literacies supposedly necessary for the functioning of the industrial economy (see Apple, 1995; Tyack, 1974; Willis, 1977).

These structures, practices, and processes of literacy sponsorship worked well enough to help reproduce the technical/administrative knowledge and the differently literate and differently oriented workers necessary for the U.S. industrial economy of the twentieth century. However, Gee (2004) argues that industrial-era literacies and literacy sponsors (e.g., standard public schools) are becoming more and more outmoded as *parts* of the economies of the United States, the United Kingdom, and many other nations come to be powered in important ways by nonstandard knowledge, so-called learning to learn, flexibility, diversity, networking, teamwork, and total commitment. It is to an analysis of this emerging order that we now turn.

LITERACIES AND THE NEW SETTLEMENT: THE EMERGENCE OF THE INFORMATIONAL ECONOMY

While many firms and state institutions established in or reconstituted for the industrial era remain prominent in these nations, there are underway profound changes in the social, political, and economic arenas in which these organizations are situated. So dramatic are these changes, in fact, that the Fordist Keynesian welfare state settlement and its accompanying institutions and systems of literacy sponsorship have arguably been strained to the breaking point, and certain fractions of capital, labor, and the state are struggling to establish a new settlement, new institutions, and new systems of literacy sponsorship appropriate for the informational era.[3]

In his analysis of the emergence of global knowledge economies and network societies, Castells (1996) observes that with advances in both information technology and transportation and with the global diffusion of sophisticated manufacturing instruments, greater numbers of firms around the world have become able to provide services and produce large volumes of inexpensive, high-quality goods for international markets. Given both the number of new firms in global competition and the remarkable diversity of emerging international markets, many companies may no longer plan to realize profit simply by providing standardized services and producing large numbers of standardized goods. Instead, these companies now work to engage (and, in part, form) niche markets of customers through the design and provision of competitively priced products and services that are both innovative and customized for particular lifestyles—distinct from all the other inexpensive, high-quality services provided and goods produced around the world. In part to facilitate the generation, processing, and application of new knowledge, including "the continuous discovery of new linkages between solutions and needs" (Reich, 1991, p. 85), ideal fast capitalist firms operating in the United States and other advanced capitalist economies have flattened out parts of their old industrial-model hierarchies and reorganized certain of their operations according to network logic.

Many laborers in networked firms, then, are afforded by employers the (bounded) freedom to generate, process, and apply new knowledge by reworking and mobilizing their literacies in such ways as to forge or strengthen connections within and between firms' shifting networks and between networked firms and evolving niche markets. Thus, as Hardt and Negri (2000) write, in the informational economy, "life is made to work for production and production is made to work for life" (p. 32) and "productivity, wealth, and the creation of social surpluses takes the form of cooperative interactivity through linguistic, communicational, and affective networks" (p. 294). More specifically, they argue, workers in fast capitalist firms perform one or more of the three types of labor that drive the informational economy:

The first is involved in an industrial production that has been informationalized and has incorporated communication technologies in a way that transforms the production process itself. Manufacturing is regarded as a service, and the material labor of the production of durable goods mixes with and tends toward immaterial labor. Second is the immaterial labor of analytical and symbolic tasks, which itself breaks down into creative and intelligent manipulation on the one hand and routine symbolic tasks on the other. Finally, a third type of immaterial labor involves the production and manipulation of affect and requires (virtual or actual) human contact, labor in the bodily mode. (Hardt & Negri, 2000, p. 293)

While there exist significant differences between types of labor in the informational economies of advanced capitalist nations, we may nonetheless identify some common features characteristic of work in each of Hardt and Negri's three categories of labor. Indeed, more so than many industrial-era laborers, workers involved in each of these forms of labor[4] must be willing and able to: commit heart, mind, and body to the vision of the firm employing them at the moment; develop and perform new and constantly evolving literate practices (see Brandt, 2001, and Carnoy, 2000, for discussions of rising standards of literacy for many forms of labor in the United States); work as part of a team; manage their affect in such ways as to facilitate teamwork and, for some workers, evoke in customers a sense of well-being; and utilize computers and other cutting-edge instruments to carry out multiple tasks communicated to the workplace team through intrafirm networks (these tasks are more or less predetermined, depending on the worker's position within a firm's network). Moreover, these workers are expected to invest their hearts and minds in their labors and, oftentimes through writing, feed information about the work process back into the network for the consideration of symbolic analysts who ultimately set the routes for work (see Carnoy, 2000; Castells, 1996; Reich, 1991).

In her study of writing in knowledge economy workplaces, Brandt (2005) discusses how laborers situated in particular positions within their organizations' networks carry out the crucial work of mediation and synthesis by reshaping and enlisting their hearts and minds:

Mediation and synthesis refer to the ways that writers serve as tools of production, transforming complex organizational histories and interests, needs, and constraints into textual form and smelting their awareness of specialized knowledge, regulation, and multiple audiences, constituencies, and competitors into their work processes and products. . . . Workplace writers can be likened to complex pieces of machinery that turn raw materials (both concrete and abstract) into functional, transactional, and valuable form, often with great expenditures of emotional, psychological, and technical effort. As securities dealer George Carlisle observed in answer to a question about whether he used boilerplate formats in his writing, "you better write with your heart and your brain if you expect to win." (p. 176)

A central and multilayered concern of workers who engage in mediation and synthesis, Brandt (2005) writes, is the matter of integrity: the integrity of the multiple interests they represent and address, the integrity of the heteroglot texts they produce, and their own personal integrity. Literacy theorists Suzanne and Ron Scollon (1981) might discuss this matter of integrity by noting that to the extent that the values endorsed by the entities they represent and address in their writing conflict with their own personal values, writers may find it difficult to commit their hearts and minds to the mediation and synthesis of those disparate views. Thus, workers whose values and beliefs align most closely with those of capital (often workers from dominant social groups) may be more comfortable than other workers (often workers from marginalized groups) with investing themselves fully in mediating and synthesizing on behalf of capital (Bernstein, 1990). Moreover, new conflicts may arise again and again for workers in the fast capitalist economy as companies seek constantly to link up with new firms and constitute and engage new niche markets.

These observations cast light on one of the most troubling aspects of unfairly regulated informational economies. With literacies and identities so central to all aspects of production and without progressive laws regulating hiring and labor practices, only those workers possessing what capital considers the right literacies stand to be hired on for rewarding work by fast capitalist firms that demand from their workers total commitment in exchange for short-term employment. Gee et al. (1996) note:

> Work in the old capitalism was alienating. Workers were forced to sell their labor, but often with little mental, emotional, or social investment in the business. Today they are asked to invest their hearts, minds, and bodies fully in their work. They are asked to think and act critically, reflectively, and creatively. While this offers a less alienating view of work and labor, in practice it can also amount to a form of mind control and high-tech, but indirect coercion. (p. 7)

Moreover, because the ideal lean and mean fast capitalist firm (supposedly) operates with flattened hierarchies, *all* workers must commit themselves fully to the enterprise and to their projects. *All* workers must draw upon the so-called right literacies for their jobs.

LITERACIES AND THE NEW SETTLEMENT: THE CONTESTED FORMATION OF THE NEOLIBERAL STATE

While more and more companies around the world, mindful of transformations in the global informational economy, are reorganizing themselves so as to make greater use of their workers' literacies, the particular organizational forms and practices companies adopt—and thus the channels through which workers develop particular literacies—will always be determined in part by the cultures and politicolegal structures of the nations in which they operate. Indeed, argue Carnoy (2000) and Castells (1996), in the global economy, states, through their economic and educational policies, play critical roles in the transformation of corporations operating in their territories and, therefore, they also play critical related roles in the sponsorship of citizens' literacies.

In the United States, ascendant neoliberal politicians, like their counterparts in the United Kingdom, Australia, and New Zealand, have endeavored since the late 1970s to dismantle the welfare state and its modes of literacy sponsorship and to construct a competitive state that would work to create economic, political, and social environments in which shareholder capitalism could flourish. In this form of capitalism, note Brown, Green, and Lauder (2001), executives are pressured to generate substantial short-term profits, often "through takeovers, mergers, and buyouts, rather than through value added production" or long-term investment in the development of workers' literate skills (p. 232). Neoliberals in many nations argued that welfare state settlements had run their course and that government-directed social service providers such as public schools had become financial drains and had grown overly bureaucratic and unresponsive to the needs of disparate citizens. Moreover, working to shift supposedly commonsense understandings of equity, neoliberals insisted that because the missions of welfare state public service providers are determined in part through the collective deliberations of the citizenry, the needs of minority groups were going unmet (Apple, 2006).[5] A more equitable solution, they posited, is a market system in which individual consumers select from a range of private service providers that suit their particular needs. Furthermore, contended neoliberals, the state's provision of welfare services, concessions to labor, and limited support for off-market hiring of minority workers inhibited citizens' entrepreneurship and fostered cultures of dependency. Also, as economic globalization proceeded throughout the 1980s and 1990s, neoliberals argued that because corporations could move production sites and jobs from nations that taxed firms at levels necessary for the maintenance of welfare states, there was no alternative but to cut or privatize programs that soaked up excessive public funding (Greider, 1997).

The cure for these ills, neoliberals insisted, was the building of a competitive state that would place the nation and its workers at the forefront of the global informational economy through the pursuit of policies based on selective deregulation, competition, and privatization (Robertson, 2000). Many services once provided by public agencies would be offered by private companies. Remaining public agencies providing off-market services would provide only the basics, lest they waste taxpayer money and encourage among citizens dependency on the state.[6] Citizens, for their part, would no longer work collectively through government to shape the work of the public agencies that served the nation as a whole but would act as individual consumers selecting the services (e.g., education and training) that place them in favorable positions in a range of markets where they compete against other individuals. Responsibility for the receipt of poor services, then, would rest with citizens who chose poorly, not with the state. And despite talk of getting government off the backs of its people, neoliberals envisioned for the competitive state an active role in arranging and overseeing markets through auditing the performances of both service providers and citizens. In this respect, writes Mark Olssen, the competitive state may be understood as a regulatory state that sees to it that citizens are "perpetually responsive" to key markets and are making "continual enterprises of [them]selves" (as cited in Apple, 2001, p. 72).

Insofar as the neoliberal project of deregulation, competition, and privatization removes certain governmental and union interferences from the economy and subjects individual citizens more directly to the demands of markets, it facilitates the production of workers and citizens necessary for the fast capitalist era. That is, the competitive state under construction in these nations works in certain ways to create forms of life that may be exploited by fast capitalist interests. Indeed, the competitive state's project of requiring individual citizens to make "continual enterprises of themselves" by shopping around for services that fit their shifting lifestyles helps create niche markets for fast capitalist firms perpetually seeking new kinds of consumers. Furthermore, individual citizens' efforts to purchase newer and better services so as to occupy more favorable positions in different markets play to the strategies of fast capitalist companies that call on workers to labor constantly to develop newer and more powerful literacies that can help firms win competitive advantages in important and emerging markets.[7]

Though neoliberals in the advanced capitalist nations have come to dominate many areas of policymaking over the past 25 years (see Apple, 2006), they have been unable (and in certain cases unwilling) to marketize *all* sectors of the state. For instance, there remain tens of thousands of government-run K–12 public schools in the United States, though they are involved more and more in private sector initiatives and are increasingly subject to market forces (see Apple, 2006). Despite the lack of total success of their project, however, neoliberals have, through their advocacy for selectively deregulated markets, shareholder capitalism, a reduced and privatized public sector, and a small, strong competitive state, helped create in a growing number of countries what Brown et al. (2001) call a "high skills/low skills" informational economy. This model of informational economy, they write,

> bases competitiveness on high levels of innovation and productivity in some hi-tech and innovation-led manufacturing and service sectors as well as on flexible labor

markets and capital productivity. The skills formation system which articulates this generates a polarized combination of low skills and high skills elites, typically mirrored by high levels of income inequality. (Brown et al., 2001, p. 143)

Indeed, in the "high skills/low skills" informational economy of the United States, for example, particular versions of Hardt and Negri's (2000) three forms of labor are compensated at different rates, depending in part on the extent to which they can be performed by minimally expensive workers or in minimally regulated areas in the United States or around the world. Thus, workers face a situation in which: a small number of creative symbolic analysts enjoy relatively steady work and high compensation (Brown and Lauder, 2006, note, though, that this may change as more and more low cost students and workers in developing nations such as India and China acquire the literacies and credentials to perform symbolic-analytic work); a small percentage of skilled laborers engage in steady-paying work in informationalized manufacturing (a form of manufacturing that compromises managers' abilities to produce large short-term gains through labor flexibility, thereby making this form of production ill-suited to the shareholder capitalism of the United States [Brown et al., 2001]); many workers perform routine symbolic tasks, though their numbers, pay, and job security are diminishing as advances in communications technologies make it possible for this work to be performed by minimally expensive laborers in developing economies; large numbers of laborers compete with one another for increasingly unsteady work in the low-paying routine service sector; and considerable numbers of citizens are unemployed or incarcerated.[8]

Turning our attention to how this system is created and sustained, we may note that while one of the widely accepted functions of public schools is to help students acquire the literacies necessary for securing steady employment, contemporary public schools run on the industrial model of individuated and standardized work fail to prepare students for employment in *any* level of the informational economy. Indeed, even in the low skills routine service sector, employees are called on to work in shifting teams and to commit their hearts and minds to performing the affective labor that helps firms engage niche markets of customers.

Ironically, perhaps, many of the school reforms proposed and implemented by business-friendly figures in the neoliberal state, including high-stakes standardized testing, school choice programs, and slowed growth in governmental spending on K–12 public education, may work to create situations in which *less* emphasis is placed by the school on fostering the kinds of powerful, nonstandard literacies valued in the new economy and *increased* attention is given by the school to improving its students' test scores (and thus its market position) through standard, traditional instruction and through the use of basic curricula aligned with high-stakes tests (see Apple, 2006; Lipman, 2004; Valenzuela, 2005; Whitty, Power, & Halpin, 1998). Furthermore, evidence suggests that the expansion of school choice programs and educational markets correlates with increased segregation of schools by race and class and thereby works against the development in students of understandings of how to collaborate with diverse coworkers in the production of new knowledge (see Apple, 2006; Lauder & Hughes, 1999).

This partial disarticulation of the public school system with important sectors of national and international economies becomes more understandable when we recall that the state, through its apparatuses, must continuously "integrate many of the interests of allied and even opposing groups under its banner" and must engage in an ongoing "process of compromise, conflict, and active struggle to maintain hegemony" (Apple, 1995, pp. 26–27). In this case, state-run schools are pulled in (somewhat) different directions by groups including certain fast capitalist interests that want flexible, creative, and cooperative workers and white middle-class parents who support the reestablishment of systems that privilege their children and allow for social closure.[9] These parents may support a national education system in which, on the one hand, schools or tracks serving mostly working-class students of color emphasize the standardized knowledge measured on high-stakes tests and, on the other hand, schools or tracks serving mostly white middle-class students stress abstraction, system thinking, experimentation, and collaboration, what Reich (1991) calls the new "basic skills" of the informational economy. Moreover, white middle-class parents know that even when their students' off-market public schools provide only the basics, more-affluent families can use their economic, social, and cultural capital to help their children enjoy the experiences, attain the credentials, and develop the literacies and identities valued in the higher education market and the small high skills labor market of the United States, Britain, and elsewhere (see Apple, 2006; Ball, 2003; Power, Edwards, Whitty, & Wigfall, 2003). Finally, research indicates that in expanded systems of school choice (proposed by neoliberal politicians in many nations), white middle-class parents tend to deploy their economic, social, and cultural capital and tap into *informal* networks to secure for their children positions in schools that cultivate images of prestige in part through the selection of student bodies that are predominantly white and affluent (see Apple, 2006; Gewirtz, Ball & Bowe, 1995; Lauder & Hughes, 1999). Again, while systems of educational markets and high-stakes standardized testing may recreate for white middle-class students environments in which they can maintain their privileges and close out students from marginalized groups, such systems interfere in certain ways with the production of the new literacies that drive the informational economy.

WHAT IS TO BE DONE?

Though they overstate the case slightly, Gee et al. (1996) are correct to argue that certain fast capitalist interests, concerned with the growing disarticulation between public schools and the needs of the informational economy, will heighten their call for schools to adopt "progressive" practices such as fostering diverse communities of practice and encouraging the development of new, nonstandard literacies. They write:

> In its attempts to create new kinds of workers/partners, the new capitalism will put pressure on other learning-centered Discourses to help produce such kinds of people. In particular, the new capitalism will progressively recruit schools to produce suitable "subjects" or "citizens" for new-capitalist Discourse in general and its manifestations in specific Discourses. (p. 22)

Some progressive educators may see real potential for strengthening social justice in reforms that aim to increase economic growth by leaving intact current economic structures and fostering among *each individual student and worker* the development of the literacies most valued in fast capitalist markets. Brown and Lauder (2006) warn, however, that such efforts lead to dead ends. They note that this so-called magnet economy approach of leaving untouched economic structures while training every student and worker for employment in the high skills sector is based on a number of faulty assumptions, including both overestimations of the number of high-paying knowledge jobs available in presently constituted labor markets and underestimations of the abilities of employers to weaken knowledge workers' labor power through the routinization of knowledge work. Furthermore, by developing students' and workers' creative capacities in accordance with market demands, educators reify the present economic system, forbidding meaningful critique of capitalist relations and engaging in what Gee et al. (1996) consider "mind control and high-tech, but indirect coercion" (p. 7).

Rather than beginning with the question of what skills and literacies the informational economy requires or what practices new tools necessitate, argue Brown and Lauder (2001), we must ground our analyses and efforts in a vision of a society that is egalitarian, just, and within reach. With this in mind, they write,

> Marx suggested that in the womb of the old there is the germination of something new, but at this moment in history it is not the overthrow of capitalism, but the potential for a new form of post-industrial cooperation which reflects the growing importance of human collaboration, knowledge, skills and talents in raising economic productivity, enhancing democracy and improving the quality of life. (Brown & Lauder, 2001, p. 205)

Indeed, although possibilities for creating new forms of social organization are not opened solely through shifts in the economy, capital's growing need for intellectual and affective laborers creates opportunities (fraught with conflict) for people to work together in recreating forms of life and recreating societies. A focus on the entire person and on the person as a *social* being can lead to new and progressive possibilities.

Continuing, Brown and Lauder (2001) argue that a new social settlement and new structures and institutions can and should be formed on the basis of collective intelligence, the

> empowerment through the *development and pooling of intelligence* to attain common goals or resolve common problems. It is inspired by a spirit of cooperation rather than a Darwinian survival of the fittest. In a society that eulogizes the virtues of competition, self-interest and acquisitiveness, rather than cooperation, common interests and the quality of life, it is difficult to maximize human potential or to coordinate opportunities for intelligent action in an efficient manner. The struggle for collective intelligence therefore involves more than a democratization of intelligence, it involves making a virtue of our mutual dependence and sociability which we will need to make a dominant feature of post-industrial society based on information, knowledge and lifelong learning. (pp. 218–219, italics in the original)

Although it is at least somewhat difficult to imagine in this era of market individualism, the formation of a social settlement based on collective intelligence may help solve the problems of key interests: workers in need of evolving, nonstandard literacies; citizens requiring means for addressing problems that require collective efforts (e.g., environmental crises); employers looking for workers who can reconstitute themselves for shifting modes of labor; and governments in need of new strategies for strengthening their workforces.

Critical to the progress of a society organized around knowledge and lifelong learning are institutions such as reconfigured public schools that provide spaces for diverse citizens of all ages to work together in creating strong, inclusive communities and rich social networks that help workers from traditionally marginalized groups find employment and training opportunities (see Carnoy, 2000). Moreover, in these spaces, citizens can collaborate in developing the nonstandard literacies that will stand them in good stead in knowledge economy labor markets and, more importantly, enable critical analyses of how social, political, and economic spheres function and how they might be changed. Drawing on theories of design that center humans' creative, socially situated constructions of environments and practices, the literacy scholars of the New London Group (2000) argue that such information age schools must embrace a reflexive, four-part "pedagogy of multiliteracies" consisting of:

> Situated Practice based on the world of learners' Designed and Designing experiences; Overt Instruction through which students shape for themselves an explicit metalanguage of Design; Critical Framing, which relates meanings to their social contexts and purposes; and Transformed Practice in which students transfer and re-create Designs of meaning from one context to another. (p. 31)

Thus, as opposed to the *market-driven* pedagogy endorsed by certain fast capitalist interests that we discussed previously, the New London Group's pedagogy of multiliteracies bases education on *human* experiences and needs and takes as central components of education the critique and purposeful transformation of social, political, and economic relations.

Finally, educators working in public schools, citing both the existence of problems that require the collective efforts of all citizens and the informational economy's emphasis on the creation of diverse forms of life through what has been called biopolitical production, may claim a strong mandate for centering in curricula the experiences and epistemologies of diverse social groups. While the most powerful case for public schools engaging the traditions of different groups will always be based on ethical arguments—it is most ethical for public institutions to engage all social groups openly and respectfully—educators mindful of large-scale socioeconomic transformations may argue with greater emphasis that an education based in engagement with diverse traditions is becoming more of an economic, political, and social necessity for every citizen. Indeed, as the scholars of the New London Group (2000) argue,

> cultural and linguistic diversity is a classroom resource just as powerfully as it is a social resource in the formation of new civic spaces and new notions of citizenship. This is not just so that educators can provide a better "service" to "minorities." Rather, such a pedagogical orientation will produce benefits for all. For example, there will be a cognitive benefit to all children in a pedagogy of linguistic and cultural pluralism, including for "mainstream" children. When learners juxtapose different languages, discourses, styles, and approaches, they gain substantively in metacognitive and metalinguistic abilities and in their ability to reflect critically on complex systems and their interactions. (p. 15; see also Carnoy, 2000)

While such a pedagogy of multiliteracies runs counter to the dominant logics of traditional schooling and neoliberal reform, educators committed to providing opportunities for students to develop literacies necessary for social, political, and economic engagement in our new times need not start with empty drawing boards. Indeed, critical educators may find workable models for powerful, forward-looking education in existing initiatives such as those pursued in the Citizen Schools of Porto Alegre, Brazil and in the classrooms of teachers throughout the world working in the democratic schools movement (Apple & Beane, 2007). While such forward-looking education *may* involve the use of computers and other digital tools, cutting-edge instruments are not absolutely necessary for the development of powerful literacies or for the mobilization of communities around issues of social justice.

Consistent in many ways with the recommendations of the New London Group (2000), students in democratic schools and classrooms develop powerful literacies in part through identifying and responding to the real concerns of their communities. In Porto Alegre's Citizen Schools, for instance, students carried out action research in their communities and determined that poverty should be their object of study and cause for social action (see Apple & Gandin, 2002; Apple et al., 2003). Similarly, students and educators working in Chicago's underfunded Richard E. Byrd Community Academy banded together and engaged in widely noted counterhegemonic mobilizations to challenge the realities of their daily experiences and to change the material conditions in their school (see Schultz, 2007). Once they identified community concerns to address, students in Citizen Schools and at the Byrd Academy worked in shifting networks of educators, community members, political figures, media workers, and other learners to engage both local and dominant ways of knowing in order to generate, assess, and apply knowledge relevant to the interests of their communities. Through these processes, students: utilized a range of tools and technologies (while students at Byrd Academy used computers, students in Citizen Schools carried out their work using paper, pencils, and other basic resources); shifted between identities valued in myriad contexts (e.g., community worker, good student, lobbyist, concerned citizen, etc.); employed Reich's (1991) new basic skills of abstraction, system thinking, experimentation, and collaboration; developed facility with a range of discourses and genres (including high status discourses of city planning and high status genres of political testimony); and strengthened their understandings of how discourses and genres work differently for actors positioned in disparate locations in fields of power.

Although such activity, powered by the production of new identities and characterized by flexibility and multimodality, resonates in some ways with the fast capitalist pedagogy described above by Gee et al. (1996), work carried out in Porto Alegre's Citizen Schools and in democratic classrooms throughout the world is fundamentally different from fast capitalist work because it subordinates profits to people and builds capacity in communities for mobilizations around issues of social and economic justice. Indeed, to appropriate the words of Porto Alegre's Municipal Secretariat of Education, educators working in Citizen Schools and democratic classrooms insist that, contra the neoliberal definition of democracy as individual consumer choice,

> to democratize is to construct, with participation, a project of education that has social quality, is liberating and transformative, where the school is a laboratory of practice, exercise and achievement of rights, of formation of autonomous, critical and creative historic subjects, full citizens, identified with ethical values, willing to construct a social project that has as a center of attention the practice of justice, of freedom, of respect and fraternal relationship among men and women and a harmonic relationship with nature. (quoted in Apple & Gandin, 2002, pp. 263–264)

Such democratic visions, along with depictions of progressive educational practice (see Apple & Beane, 2007; Apple & Gandin, 2002) and precise delineations of the spaces open for struggle in our new times (see Brown et al., 2001; Castells, 1996; Hardt & Negri, 2000), show us that even amidst the dangers of emerging global orders, ideals of democracy persist and real victories in campaigns for social and economic justice are still possible. Moreover, these stories and analyses make clear that while we may utilize computers and other cutting-edge instruments for human purposes, we should not become so enamored of new tools that we come to view them as indispensable elements for progressive change. And although we cannot ensure that such change will be brought about through the development (computer-aided or not) among students of critical literacies and the dispositions and values that accompany them, we can be certain that without struggling to build and defend movements for social and economic justice, capital in its multiple forms will press on, with predictable effects on the lives and hopes of billions of people throughout the world. We cannot afford to let this happen.

NOTES

1. Throughout this chapter, we describe the structures and performance of *ideal* industrial and fast capitalist enterprises doing business in advanced industrial nations. The structures and performance of *actual* firms, of course, are always shaped through interactions of dominant, residual, and emergent organizational forms.

2. Such forms of life are not *inherently* valuable but are valuable because they can be exploited for profit by capital. That is, as we argue later, valuable forms of life—the control of which may be considered valuable literacies—are those forms of life that help workers generate new, profitable knowledge and engage in cooperative labor with other employees and with customers.

3. Although in the following analysis of these changes and struggles we discuss first economic transformations, we do not argue that changes in the economy *wholly determine* changes in social and political spheres (nor vice versa). Rather, we argue that activity in each of these spheres has relative autonomy from, yet interacts with, activity in other spheres.

4. These analyses, argue Hardt and Negri (2000), apply to a range of workers in the informational economy: symbolic analysts collaborating in ad hoc teams and mining and synthesizing information from disparate semiotic domains to create and design new products for new niche markets; laborers engaged in informationalized manufacturing who work in shifting teams with diverse colleagues to produce and to refine processes for making customized goods; and service workers embodying the so-called official values and interests of their companies so as to create senses of well-being in customers from particular niche markets.

5. There is some truth to the argument that welfare state public service providers were not/are not responsive to the needs of marginalized groups. Indeed, neoliberals have achieved success in the political realm in part through speaking to citizens' real concerns (e.g., the unresponsiveness of welfare state public service providers to marginalized groups) and providing seemingly practical solutions (e.g., the privatization of public services). We argue that progressives must interrupt such rightist discourses and must provide alternate solutions that are both practical and consistent with principles of strong democracy (see Apple, 2006).

6. Certain neoliberals are "willing to spend more state and/or private money on schools, if and only if schools meet the needs expressed by capital. Thus, resources are

made available for 'reforms' and policies that further connect the education system to the project of making our economy more competitive" (Apple, 2001, p. 41). See the final section of this chapter for a discussion of school reform proposals premised on enhancing competitiveness in the emerging informational economy.

7. These trends within the neoliberal state informational economy are consistent with Anthony Giddens's (1991) observations that in late modernity, citizens in postindustrial and posttraditional states are called on more and more to engage in reflexive life planning. Giddens (1991) argues that "because of the 'openness' of social life today, the pluralization of contexts of action and the diversity of 'authorities', lifestyle choice is increasingly important in the constitution of self-identity and daily activity. Reflexively organized life-planning, which normally presumes consideration of risks as filtered through contact with expert knowledge, becomes a central feature of the structuring of self-identity" (p. 5; see also Gee, 2004).

8. Walmsley (2005) notes in the World Prison Population List for 2005 that in the United States, 714 out of every 100,000 citizens are imprisoned. This gives the United States the highest imprisonment rate in the world.

9. Also involved in the struggle over public schools' endorsement of nonstandard knowledge and practice are groups on the Right, including: neoliberals in favor of constructing a competitive regulatory state that audits schools through measuring students' control of standardized knowledge; social conservatives and authoritarian populists who endeavor to standardize in public schools' curricula and instructional processes their own (and at least slightly different) forms of supposedly traditional knowledge, values, and habits; and managerial workers with professional commitments to measuring disparate work practices.

We wish to emphasize here the importance of analyzing the actions of multiple groups working in the political sphere (as well as other spheres) to shape processes of schooling. Too much of the educational literature on fast capitalism, we argue, fails to theorize the role of the state as a set of institutions serving in part to mediate social and economic dynamics. Indeed, much of this work neglects to take up the important matter of how the occupation of particular positions within the state by actors of certain classes helps (re)create official networks of sponsorship for certain classed modes of identity formation and literate practice (see Apple, 2006).

REFERENCES

Althusser, L. (1971). Ideology and ideological state apparatuses. In *Lenin and philosophy, and other essays* (pp. 127–186). London: New Left.

Apple, M. W. (Ed.). (1982). *Cultural and economic reproduction in education: Essays on class, ideology and the state.* London: Routledge & Kegan Paul.

Apple, M. W. (1986). *Teachers and texts: A political economy of class and gender in education.* New York: Routledge.

Apple, M. W. (1995). *Education and power.* New York: Routledge.

Apple, M. W. (1996). *Cultural politics and education.* New York: Teachers College.

Apple, M. W. (1999). *Power, meaning, and identity.* New York: Peter Lang.

Apple, M. W. (2000). *Official knowledge: Democratic education in a conservative age* (2nd ed.). New York: Routledge.

Apple, M. W. (2001). *Educating the "right" way: Markets, standards, god and inequality.* New York: RoutledgeFalmer.

Apple, M. W. (2006). *Educating the "right" way: Markets, standards, god and inequality.* (2nd ed.). New York: Routledge.

Apple, M. W., Aasen, P., Cho, M. K., Gandin, L. A., Oliver, A., Sung, Y-K., et. al. (2003). *The state and the politics of knowledge.* New York: Routledge.

Apple, M. W., & Beane, J. A. (Eds.) (2007). *Democratic schools* (2nd ed.). Portsmouth, NH: Heinemann.

Apple, M. W., & Buras, K. L. (Eds.) (2006). *The subaltern speak: Curriculum, power, and educational struggles.* New York: Routledge.

Apple, M. W., & Gandin, L. A. (2002). Challenging neo-liberalism, building democracy: Creating the Citizen School in Porto Alegre, Brazil. *Journal of Education Policy, 17*(2), 259–279.

Ball, S. (2003). *Class strategies and the education market.* London: RoutledgeFalmer.

Barber, B. R. (2003). *Strong democracy: Participatory politics for a new age.* Berkeley: University of California.

Barton, D. (1994). *Literacy: An introduction to the ecology of written language.* Oxford: Blackwell.

Bernstein, B. (1990). *The structuring of pedagogic discourse.* New York: Routledge.

Brandt, D. (2001). *Literacy in American lives.* New York: Cambridge University.

Brandt, D. (2005). Writing for a living: Literacy and the knowledge economy. *Written Communication, 22*(2), 166–197.

Brown, P., Green, A., & Lauder, H. (2001). *High skills: Globalization, competitiveness, and skill formation.* Oxford: Oxford University.

Brown, P., & Lauder, H. (2001). *Capitalism and social progress: The future of society in a global economy.* New York: Palgrave.

Brown, P., & Lauder, H. (2006). Globalization, knowledge and the myth of the magnet economy. *Globalization, societies and education, 4*(1), 25–57.

Carnoy, M. (2000). *Sustaining the new economy: Work, family, and community in the information age.* Cambridge, MA: Harvard University.

Castells, M. (1996). *The rise of the network society. Vol. 1: The information age: economy, society and culture.* Malden, MA: Blackwell.

Cuban, L. (2001). *Oversold and underused: computers in the classroom.* Cambridge, MA: Harvard University Press.

Davis, M. (2006). *Planet of slums.* London: Verso.

Gee, J. P. (1996). *Social linguistics and literacies: Ideology in discourse.* Philadelphia: Falmer.

Gee, J. P. (2004). *Situated language and learning: A critique of traditional schooling.* New York: Routledge.

Gee, J. P., Hull, G., & Lankshear, C. (1996). *The new work order: Behind the language of the new capitalism.* Boulder, CO: Westview.

Gewirtz, S., Ball, S. J., & Bowe, R. (1995). *Markets, choice and equity in education.* Buckingham, UK: Open University.

Giddens, A. (1991). *Modernity and self-identity: Self and society in the late modern age.* Stanford, CA: Stanford University.

Greider, W. (1997). *One world, ready or not.* New York: Simon and Schuster.

Hardt, M., & Negri, A. (2000). *Empire.* Cambridge: Harvard University.

Heath, S. B. (1983). *Ways with words: Language, life and work in communities and classrooms.* Cambridge, UK: Cambridge University.

Kliebard, H. M. (2004). *The struggle for the American curriculum* (3rd ed.). New York: RoutledgeFalmer.

Lauder, H., & Hughes, D. (1999). *Trading in futures: Why markets in education don't work.* Philadelphia: Open University.

Lipman, P. (2004). *High stakes education: Inequality, globalization, and urban school reform.* New York: RoutledgeFalmer.

New London Group. (2000). A pedagogy of multiliteracies: Designing social futures. In B. Cope & M. Kalantzis (Eds.), *Multiliteracies: Literacy learning and the design of social futures* (pp. 9–37). Routledge: New York.

Power, S., Edwards, T., Whitty, G., & Wigfall, V. (2003). *Education and the middle class.* Philadelphia: Open University Press.

Reich, R. (1991). *The work of nations.* Knopf: New York.

Robertson, S. L. (2000). *A class act: Changing teachers' work, the state, and globalization.* New York: Falmer.

Schultz, B. D. (2007). "Feelin' what they feelin'": Democracy and curriculum in Cabrini Green. In M. W. Apple & J. A. Beane (Eds.), *Democratic schools* (2nd ed., pp. 81–105). Portsmouth, NH: Heinemann.

Scollon, R., & Scollon, S. W. (1981). *Narrative, literacy, and face in interethnic communication.* Norwood, NJ: Ablex.

Scribner, S., & Cole, M. (1981). *The psychology of literacy.* Cambridge, MA: Harvard University.

Street, B. (1984). *Literacy in theory and practice.* Cambridge, UK: Cambridge University.

Taylor, M. C. (2001). *The moment of complexity: Emerging network culture.* Chicago: University of Chicago.

Tyack, D. (1974). *The one best system: A history of American education.* Cambridge, MA: Harvard University.

Valenzuela, A. (Ed.). (2005). *Leaving children behind: How "Texas-style" accountability fails Latino youth.* Albany: State University of New York.

Walmsley, R. (2005). *World prison population list* (6th ed.). London: International Centre for Prison Studies. Retrieved July 25, 2006, from http://www.kcl.ac.uk/depsta/rel/icps/world-prison-population-list-2005.pdf.

Warschauer, M. (1999). *Electronic literacies: Language, culture, and power in online education.* Mahwah, NJ: L. Erlbaum Associates.

Whitty, G., Power, S., & Halpin, D. (1998). *Devolution and choice in education: The school, the state, and the market.* Philadelphia: Open University.

Willis, P. (1977). *Learning to labor.* Farnborough, UK: Saxon House.

5

THEORIZING THE IMPACT OF IT ON LIBRARY-STATE RELATIONS

Sandra Braman

Pragmatically, libraries and the library community must solve the myriad legal problems generated by the use of digital technologies at the operational level. These can seem so overwhelming that, as the old saw warns, we can miss the forest for the trees. Viewed together at a more abstract level, these issues are manifestations of changing relations between libraries and national governments. The responsibilities and effects of library-state relations, of course, run in both directions: the legal environment created by states creates the context within which libraries must operate, while the informational and communicative functions of libraries in turn shape, contribute to the sustenance of, and in some cases enable the state and political practices. Details vary from country to country, but there are overarching similarities across nations in twenty-first century library-state relations that betray the shared experience of the transition from the bureaucratic welfare state to the informational state. Because informational power now dominates and has changed the nature of power in its instrumental, structural, and symbolic forms (Braman, 2006a), the information policy issues that so confound libraries today simultaneously offer tools that governments and other entities can also use in the exercise of power.

To fully understand and cope with daily legal struggles, therefore, libraries must go beyond addressing single issues reactively and in isolation. Development of a more proactive stance and coherent overall information policies in an environment permeated with information technologies (IT) requires going further. Given the centrality of libraries to the information society, it is time for those in information science to develop a theory of library-state relations. Doing so would provide a conceptual ground from which to approach specific policy issues as well as support for arguments in the face of what may be political or legal opposition. Libraries would not be the first information sector to undertake this task; scholars have been examining media-state relations since the close of World War II[1] because of keen appreciation for the political ramifications of mass communication.

This is not the only intellectual challenge facing the library sector. Some argue that new theories may be needed to understand how to respond to interactions between socioeconomic class and informational class in the digital environment (Hendrix, 2005). Existing theoretical perspectives from others of the social sciences are being used in the study of interactions between libraries and politics, as in the Gramscian analysis of Raber (2003) and the Rawlsian work of Hendrix (2005). Political theory is being brought to bear on subjects such as archives (Manoff, 2004). There are studies of the specific responsibilities of libraries vis-à-vis digital divide policies (e.g., Aabo, 2005), research on cross-national differences in conceptualizing the societal role of libraries (Shachaf, 2005), and calls for a critical information studies to examine the political economy and cultural effects of libraries (Vaidhyanathan, 2006). This conversation has become more intense since heightened concern about national security issues has changed the roles of information in many contexts (Jaeger & Burnett, 2005). Indeed, Hartman (2007) claims there has been a dramatic shift in how libraries are perceived by both members of the public and by policy makers because of the war on terrorism. However, explicit debate over library-state relations began during the Vietnam War era (Raber, 2007). Libraries all over the world face the same questions, though in ways that may differ in response to the specifics of local ideological contexts (Andersson, 2006).

In this chapter's discussion of libraries, the law, and IT, the state is understood as an organizational and cultural form that is a complex adaptive system (Braman, 1994, 2004). *Information policy* serves as an umbrella term to refer to all laws and regulations that apply to information creation, processing, flows, and use. Using this definition, fundamental information policy principles include far more than free speech and access to information. Twenty information policy principles can be found, for example, in the U.S. Constitution (see the Appendix for a listing). Because policy analysis, at root, is an effort to answer the question "What are we doing to ourselves?," the chapter takes an interdisciplinary approach that combines the use of contemporary social theory, what we have learned from empirical social science research, and legal analysis. In addition to analysis of specific issues, there is attention to policy precession, a policy analysis concept that refers to the interaction of multiple policies with each other in ways that affect the impact of each.

A theory of library-state relations—and of the impact of IT on those relations—must incorporate attention to the legal issues through which libraries and national governments become involved, identification of the various dimensions of library-state relations, articulation of a theory of the state, and analysis of current trends. A first pass at each of these is offered here, in hopes of triggering communal discussion about and theorization of library-state relations.

IT POLICY AND LIBRARIES

Libraries and librarians engage in library-state relations affected by IT when they confront the legal and regulatory problems experienced in an IT-imbued library environment. In the midst of negotiations over who will have access to what under which conditions, however, it is often forgotten that these problems have long histories. Within a decade of the Federal Communications Commission (FCC) confrontation with issues raised by the convergence of computing and communication technologies in the 1950s (Pool, 1983), libraries began to experience legal challenges to their practices and commitments. The first tranche included debates over the use of photocopy machines under copyright law (Lazowska, 1968), concerns that new means of storing scientific information would make it more difficult to fulfill the library mandate (Sophar, 1968), and recognition that networking made it possible to reconsider the local and autonomous nature of libraries (Kochen & Deutsch, 1973). The transformation of seemingly every information exchange into an opportunity for an economic transaction forced reconsideration of the library business model, whether public or private (Mosco, 1988), leading to ongoing training issues (Flatten, 1997). As in other areas of social activity, IT has even brought about changes in the structure of the production of scholarship; the fact that scholarly journals now themselves exhibit firmlike behavior (Havemann, Heinz, & Wagner-Döbler, 2005) has generated its own set of legal problems. Each innovation stimulates experiments that can affect the legal context for libraries in critical ways.

Today the menu of policy problems involving IT is vast (Braman, 2004). Digital technologies—informational metatechnologies—are so problematic from a legal perspective because they are qualitatively different from industrial technologies and preindustrial tools in the degrees of freedom enabled with which information can be created, processed, distributed, stored, and used (Braman, 2006a). Additional factors include jurisdictional issues raised by globalized networks when most law continues to reside at the national or regional levels, growing numbers of rules and regulations from international organizations that apply to libraries (Rikowski, 2005), and the likelihood that any single policy issue in this domain may be claimed within the portfolio of multiple regulators (Braman, 2006a). As is always the case, conflicts among policy principles must also be resolved. IT-related policy issues libraries face can be categorized according to the following typology.[2]

- *Traditional issues in traditional forms:* Not everything happens in the digital environment, and even when it does there may be no significant change in how policy principles are operationalized, interpreted, and applied. An example of an issue in this category would be the need for libraries to protect the privacy of user data irrespective of the medium in which it is stored or the medium through which usage has taken place (Sturges et al., 2003; Swartz, 2005).

- *Traditional issues in new forms:* Often traditional policy problems take on new dimensions, require reinterpretation of the law, or trigger adaptation or replacement of the law when they appear in the digital context because shifts in scale, the relative ease of certain activities, speed, and/or the capacity to engage in new types of activities so change the social processes involved that they are perceived and experienced as qualitatively new. Some privacy issues fall into this category (Regan, 2004). Many copying and first sale issues do as well, since digitization changes the scale, ease, and distributional reach of both. The longstanding library practice of sharing a list of references generated in response to a user query with that user has had to be reconsidered in light of contemporary copyright law (Seadle, 1999). Disagreements over acquisitions profiles, for example, have long been rife but become yet more difficult when access to materials takes place via the Internet and software filters are among the tools being considered as a positive means of exclusion.[3] Even the basic concept of lending has been challenged conceptually, operationally, and legally by the introduction of e-books (Craig, 2003).
- *New types of policy issues:* The distinct characteristics of informational metatechnologies are also generating quite new types of policy issues for libraries. Developing information architectures has long been a specialist responsibility of librarians, but today metadata systems serving users with changing needs from across multiple disciplines depend on input from knowledge producers as well for their development (Elings & Waibel, 2007). The shift away from purchase and towards licensing has involved librarians in struggles over contract law to protect fair use (Johnson, 2007). Issue-specific legal analyses are rife, but scholarly attention to these overarching trends has been sparse.

LIBRARIES AND THE STATE

Irrespective of what type of IT-related policy problem libraries are facing in a specific decision-making context, resolution of the issue will either contribute to reification of some dimension of library-state relations or reconfigure an aspect of the relationship. Though to my knowledge there are no extant explicit theories of library-state relations, there are references to political sources, uses, and effects of libraries and archives by national governments in the literature on the histories of the state and of democracy.

Novelist and cultural critic Umberto Eco describes the library as the central institution of Western culture (Pieterse, 1997), and Richards (1993) identifies the library impulse as perhaps the most successful element of the imperial drive. Library-state relations have been viewed as crucial since the origins of democratic culture (Zaret, 1999). The contemporary concept of libraries as a medium between local communities and the state, however, is a product of the bureaucratic welfare state. This particular type of state took shape and diffused over the course of the nineteenth century, dominating the developed world from about 1870 until observers began to note its decline in the 1970s. Indeed, as Murdock and Golding (1990) note, the concept of social rights as part of the bundle of citizenship rights—including the idea that there should be universal access to information and communication facilities that include public libraries—was largely a twentieth-century phenomenon. As welfare state functions began to decline in the 1970s, however, the burden on libraries to increase their contribution to the delivery of social services went up (Golding & Murdock, 1986).

There may be no more vivid evidence of the importance of libraries to politics and governance than their use as a site for ideological battles. Forgacs (1990) provides a particularly rich case study of this in his history of the political use of libraries during the first half of the twentieth century by both Italian Fascists and by those who opposed them. In a contemporary example, aggressive French right-wing political groups target libraries as a venue through which to promote their views (Kibbee, 2003). Portrayals of libraries in the case law of three U.S. states picture them not only as social and physical places with community as well as informational functions, but also as elements of political and economic structures in ways not predicted by the library literature (Burke & Martin, 2004).

Here, we look at the role of libraries in sustenance of the law, the production and reproduction of political culture, library functions vis-à-vis the public sphere, and new roles for libraries that are appearing as a result of changing library-state relations.

Sustenance of the Law

Libraries fill a number of functions that support the law and contribute to its implementation that are reflected in the curricula of professional schools in both areas: law schools are required to have libraries (Bearden & Esworthy, 2007), and librarians and information scientists take courses in the law (Arundale, 2002; Ellis & Oppenheim, 1993). Libraries are believed to be necessary to the implementation of a variety of types of laws and regulations, including those directed at economic development (Black, 2007), social policy (Black, 2005), and achievement of the goals of foreign relations (Maymi-Sugranes, 2002). While many of the legal functions of libraries are general, such as facilitating literacy, in some cases library programs are designed to serve very specific policy objectives. Examples of the latter include incorporating libraries into a Utah campaign to get rid of Mormon polygamy (Stauffer, 2005) and the United Kingdom's use of libraries to promote that country's agenda of regionalization (Hobbs, 2003).

Another way in which libraries help to uphold the law is by contributing to governmental transparency (Ranson, 2003), though the political and economic future of depository libraries is currently threatened (Shuler, 2005).

At least in the United States, however, this particular function has been seriously damaged by twenty-first-century demands from the White House that materials held by such libraries deemed to threaten homeland security be destroyed. Technical issues also undercut the ability of libraries to fulfill this role fully, for there is still uncertainty about both how to preserve critical digital information and what to preserve (Martin, 2004).

There are times when explicit library support for the law serves library, rather than governmental, objectives. In an influential Santa Monica, California, experiment of the early 1990s, librarians believed that offering those who were homeless access to the Internet would provide resources that would help them get off of the streets. Software supplied to libraries by the county government was intended to facilitate access to government services—but the librarians found that the same software could be used to support e-mail for the homeless. When the government objected to this application, the library response was that there was nothing they could do to prevent this use because they had no way of altering the software to bar such activity (Dutton & Guthrie, 1991).

The law is of course neither perceived nor implemented uniformly. In some political contexts, librarians may believe they are upholding basic legal principles even if they do so in abeyance of contemporary laws or regulations. A historical example: Southern libraries in the United States after the Civil War provided support for those who disliked federal government intrusion into regional affairs (Carmichael, 2005). And a contemporary example: For many years librarian refusal to release book withdrawal records in order to protect patron privacy stood on solid legal ground. Changes in the law in the twenty-first century, however, require librarians to take the additional step of insisting on constitutional (or constitution-like) principles as a justification for resistance even though statutory or regulatory law may provide law enforcement officials with grounds for requesting the information. Though library responses to the war on terrorism have not been uniform (Ross & Caidi, 2005), many individuals and institutions have been leaders in the battle for protection of civil liberties in the post-9/11 environment (Wheeler, 2005).

Political Culture

Library-state relations contribute to political culture via their role in the formation and sustenance of national identity (von Merveldt, 2007). Conflicts over the treatment of rare books during war (Genieva, 2003) and over access to research collections (Niessen, 2006) highlight the cultural centrality of libraries from the perspective of nationhood. During times of radical political change or trauma, libraries critically can provide the cultural memory with which national identity is associated and on which it rests (Chodorow, 2006; von Merveldt, 2007).

Libraries also play a role in the production and reproduction of attitudes towards and expectations of political processes. Caidi (2006) uses the phrase "civilization competence" to describe the contributions of libraries to the building of civic culture in transitional societies such as those of Eastern and Central Europe, and the same interactions are at play for societies such as Scotland in which the political changes are less radical (Guy, 2003). Analysis of national union catalog development in seven countries provides additional detail on ways in which political factors interact with social and technical forces during the building of the catalogs (Caidi, 2004). Even standard selection guides can reveal and reproduce ideological biases (Dilevko & Gottlieb, 2003).

As South African history has shown, however, there is no guarantee that movements towards democratic culture will inevitably be exhibited by libraries; such contributions can be stymied by politics or a lack of resources (Brown, 2004). Today, collection development has again emerged as an explicit site of political conflict. Legislation is now regularly proposed in the United States that would require those building research collections for academic libraries to ensure that they are doing so in a politically neutral manner that involves no advocacy (Highby, 2004).

Finally, libraries are important as sources of information about the shared matters of public concern addressed by policy makers. Content of political importance includes not just newspapers, histories, and statistical works; poetry and novels, too, are important to the development of the intellectual skills necessary for decision making about public affairs (Nussbaum, 1995), and even mundane aspects of daily activities and popular culture play important roles in political socialization (Merelman, 1998).

Libraries as a Public Sphere

Like institutions of higher education (Braman, 2000), libraries are venues within which the public sphere operates, offering opportunities for community discussion of political developments. This aspect of library-state relations is currently receiving scrutiny because of the perceived need to reconsider library design and practices for this purpose (Buschman, 2003; Dean, 2001). A recent study comparing libraries with library-like bookstores that invite prolonged visits with sitting areas and coffee shops found that libraries continue to serve many public sphere functions not found in purely commercial outlets (McKechnie et al., 2004).

Some believe that innovations in practice, materials, and organizational form are the best way to protect the public sphere and other politically important functions of the library in a national security–oriented environment, while others argue that continuing to protect the library as a place to read and find books is more likely to serve the same goal in the long run (Hartman, 2007). In an interesting example of the importance of policy precession, continuing to protect patron privacy is critical to the library's public sphere function.

Changes to the Legal System

There is a long history of changes in the ways in which legal information is created, used, distributed, stored, and made accessible to others as a result of technological innovation (Grossman, 1994). Katsh (1989) cataloged the first wave of effects of computerization on the law. These include the ability to store vast amounts of information, which was particularly important because the multiplication of documentation that was a part of the bureaucratic welfare state was becoming unsustainable in terms of storage of print records. The nature of precedent, so critical to legal thought, has changed significantly because digital search capacities greatly expand the flexibility with which innovative legal arguments can be developed. Digitization has also sped up the processes by which court opinions are distributed, and—of particular interest to librarians—eroded the historical separation of law libraries from other libraries. This shift greatly expands the amount of nonlegal material readily available to lawyers and should encourage those engaged in legal analysis to draw on all of the social science and other pertinent disciplines.

There are at least five ways in which digitization has affected the nature of the law and legal processes in ways that implicate libraries. The area of copyright is the best known but far from the only arena in which technologies themselves (e.g., digital rights management [DRM] systems) are being used to control behavior, complementing or superseding legal and regulatory approaches (Fernandez-Molina, 2004a, 2004b). Now that it is less time-consuming and easier to access library materials at any time and from anywhere, judges are increasingly turning to libraries for scientific information they feel will help them understand cases being litigated, though some question the constitutionality of such activities because of their impact on due process (Marlow, 1998). Internet filtering and related requirements can be viewed as, among other things, efforts by governments to deputize institutions; that is, organizations such as libraries that are not a part of the law enforcement establishment are being asked to serve law enforcement functions (Zittrain, 2004). Requirements that libraries filter Internet access by children can also be understood as an effort to use libraries as the "camel's nose" for an effort to develop wide-reaching controls on Internet content (Miltner, 2005).[4] And in some countries, libraries are also being used as test beds for a variety of e-government efforts, as when the United Kingdom experimented with the use of libraries as venues within which to promote interactive engagement with the government's Web sites (Marcella, Baxter, & Moore, 2002).

THE INFORMATIONAL STATE

Any theory of library-state relations must rest on a theory of the state itself. While it is tempting to think about the nature of the state itself as stable and unproblematic, there have been numerous transformations of political and legal forms since the appearance of the modern state over 500 years ago.

Since the 1970s, the bureaucratic welfare state form that had dominated for a century has been giving away to a new form, the informational state, which has come to dominate in the early twenty-first century.

Transformations of the State

Any given political form, with its institutions, policies, and practices, represents but a moment of stability within a much wider, more diffuse, and constantly shifting policy field. This broad field from which particular legal systems derive and into which they disappear includes ethical and behavioral norms, discourse habits, cultural practices, knowledge structures, organizational forms, private sector and individual decision making, and technologies themselves as well as the formal laws and regulations of officially recognized governments. The information policy field therefore includes *government* (formal institutions of the law); *governance* (decision making with constitutive [structural] effect whether it takes place within the public or private sectors, and formally or informally); and *governmentality* (cultural predispositions and practices that produce and reproduce the conditions that make particular forms of governance and government possible).

Beginning in the 1970s, political scientists and commentators began to suggest that the power of the state relative to that of multinational and transnational corporations was on the wane, perhaps to become relatively insignificant or wither away altogether (e.g., Wallerstein, 1980). Though Marxists had long expected the state to go into decline, appreciation of the changes taking place in the nature of the state throughout most of the developed world appeared across ideological and theoretical spectra. Rather than disappearing, however, the state instead changed its form. With the transition from the bureaucratic welfare state to the informational state we have seen three trends of importance to libraries and library-state relations. First, national governments are learning to master the same types of informational power that corporations and other non-state actors have been successfully using in their challenges to the strength of geopolitical entities. Second, states are developing techniques for extending the use of private sector entities as regulatory agents, turning private centers of power to state purposes; public sector entities (including libraries) are being asked to take on functions never originally intended. Third, the state—like the firm—is increasingly characterized as networked because of the multiplicity of fundamental ways in which governments are intertwined with each other and with non-state actors. (Other theories of the state appearing in response to the decline of the bureaucratic welfare state, such as the notion of a social investment state, also demand reconceptualizations of the roles of libraries [Newman & McKee, 2005].)

Among the ways in which diverse types of states differ from each other is in the form of power that dominates. Heavy use of informational power is a defining characteristic of the informational state.

Forms and Phases of Power

In the digital environment, the ability to use informational power has dramatically increased, and power in its virtual phase has become a site of conflict in its own right.

Informational Power

Analyses of power have typically distinguished among three forms (e.g., Lukes, 2005). *Instrumental power* shapes human behaviors by manipulating the material world via physical force. This type of power has been so important that political theory classically defines a state as the political entity that exercises physical control over a specified geographic space. Library collections are affected by the exercise of instrumental power during times of war. *Structural power* shapes human behaviors by manipulating the social world via rules and institutions that limit degrees of freedom, determine how specific activities will be undertaken, and reduce uncertainty. Laws, treaties, and political processes themselves are all ways in which states exercise structural power. Several of the functions libraries fill for the state support the exercise of structural power. *Symbolic power* shapes human behaviors by manipulating the material, social, and symbolic worlds via ideas, words, and images.[5] Symbolic power also has ancient roots; in modern forms, the exercise of symbolic power has included propaganda, public diplomacy, campaigns, efforts to influence public opinion, and the education system. As discussed previously, libraries are also involved in the exercise of symbolic power.

The informatization of society has made a fourth form of power evident. *Informational power* shapes human behaviors through the many uses of information beyond the message content that is the stuff of symbolic power. This form of power is exercised through manipulation of the informational bases of instrumental, structural, and symbolic power. Today's smart weapons, which can identify a target and direct themselves to it without human intervention, are examples of the effect of informational power on the exercise of instrumental power. The ability to monitor compliance with intellectual property rights law through surveillance of Internet use is an example of the influence of informational power on the exercise of structural power. The ability to tailor Web-based messages to the individual who is surfing is an example of the impact of informational power on the exercise of symbolic power.

Informational power can also be exercised through entirely new techniques; data mining vast quantities of information in diverse forms using pattern recognition is an example of a qualitatively new technique for exercising power. Just as it is possible to qualitatively distinguish the information society as an era despite the ancient importance of information to society on the basis of Engels' law (quantitative change can yield qualitative change), so informational power has existed for a very long time but today it is more evident because it dominates over other forms of power.

Power in Its Virtual Phase

Political scientists also distinguished between power in its actual phase (as it is being exercised) and in a potential phase (power that is claimed, but not currently being used). *Actual power* is potential power in use, as when guns are firing, laws are being implemented, and persuasive campaigns affect the vote. *Potential power* becomes actual only through specific practices. Information processing, distribution, and use are often necessary for the transformation of power from potential to actual. The number of tanks owned by an army that could be brought into use, laws on the books that aren't currently being acted on, and ideas for communication campaigns are all examples of power in its potential phase.

In today's information-intense environment, it is now also possible to recognize power in a virtual phase. Following economist Roberto Scazzieri's (1993) definition of virtual production processes, *virtual power* involves techniques of power that are not currently extant but that can be brought into existence using available resources and knowledge. It includes power that can be acquired or developed through transfers of power, use of resources, or shifts in internal or external conditions. Knowledge is so central to power in its virtual phase that every expansion of the knowledge base of a nation-state concomitantly causes a growth in the realm of power available. An example of power in its virtual phase is government control over the development of encryption techniques and of scientific research in areas believed to be of value for national security purposes, for in such instances the actual techniques or inventions do not yet exist. Power in its virtual phase is so important to national competitiveness and the ability to protect national security in the twenty-first century that research and development (R&D) are now considered key resources for the informational state.

Evaluations of the validity of claims to power in its potential and virtual phases are difficult, for they involve what political scientists refer to as capacity. Elements of capacity include the financial resources, knowledge of how to use those resources, political will, sovereign integrity, stability of administrative control, loyalty and skill among officials, infrastructure, and industrial base that are required to actually put the resources and techniques of potential and virtual power to use.

Information Policy in the Informational State

In the informational state, information policy has two faces. Each law or regulation does address its purported subject, whether that is privacy or access to information. At the same time, however, such policies are tools of power for the state and other entities. Information policy is thus key both to understanding just how the transformation from a bureaucratic welfare state to an informational state has come about and to understanding how the informational state exercises power. Information policy is the proprioceptive organ of the state—the means by which it senses itself—and, therefore, the medium through which all other decision making, public or private, takes place. All informational and communicative issues are of constitutional (or constitutional-like) stature because they define social categories and the processes to be permitted within and between them, while other areas of the law deal with existing categories and processes (Tribe, 1985).

LIBRARY-STATE RELATIONS AND THE INFORMATIONAL STATE: KEY TRENDS

The uses of information policy to exercise state power internationally was evident a decade ago (Braman, 1995a).[6] More recently, a study was undertaken of the domestic uses of information policy as a tool of power using U.S. law as the case. Quite diverse policy issues were examined, ranging from the unavoidably important (intellectual property law and privacy), to very traditional areas of the law in which change has been more radical than might be expected (libel law, and the role of information in maintaining or protecting borders), to those that are new as policy issues in today's technological environment (metadata and global sensing technologies). A synthesis of what is learned by looking at the impact on society of these technology-related information policy developments yields a number of broad trends that are critical to contemporary library-state relations. There is insufficient space to explore all of these here, but a few of particular importance include a decline in the mutual transparency between the state and citizens; impairment of democratic practice; the replacement of narrative memory with memory in visual, sensory, and data forms; and the replacement of state knowledge of its own history (genetic knowledge) with contemporary data about processes unfolding across the globe (epigenetic knowledge). The challenges that each presents to theorization of library-state relations and to library practice are briefly introduced here; for details of the empirical developments and the in-depth analyses that support these generalizations, see Braman (2006a).

Loss of Transparency

The informational state knows more and more about individuals, while individuals know less and less about the state. For most countries, the constitutional or constitutional-like model involves mutual transparency: as has been true since the beginning of the modern state, governments need to know about their citizens at least as much as is needed to provide the services necessary and citizens need to know about government in order to participate in decision making. Today, however, state knowledge of citizens is growing by orders of magnitude while citizen knowledge of state activities is declining. While there is no doubt that, on the surface, the amount of information available from most governments has grown as a result of a variety of e-government practices, the issue of access involves quality and substance from the perspective of materiality for decision making.

Since libraries have long been a site through which citizens can gain access to government information, this issue presents the institutions with a dilemma. At the level of mission definition, libraries must reconsider the extent to which they can continue to fulfill the role of government information repositories, taking into account that the need for them to do so may now be more pressing than ever before. At the level of operationalization, some innovations may be necessary, perhaps learned from those involved in social movements.[7]

Impairment of Democratic Practice

We are now several decades into debates over whether or not the use of digital technologies will increase the possibilities of meaningful participatory democracy. In addition to the much-discussed question of the extent to which the digital divide undermines the positive contributions to democratic practice offered by the Internet, developments in other areas of information policy point to other dimensions of concern. Historically, for example, print literacy was considered necessary for classical political participation as support for contributions to and evaluations of public discourse as well as inputs into individual decision making on candidates and issues. Today, however, mathematical skills and technical knowledge are also politically necessary. The challenges to election legitimacy by electronic voting machines provide one example. Despite the significant amounts of rigorous empirical research available on ways in which the voting results produced by these machines can be falsified—and the number of elections in which this has demonstrably already happened—it has been very difficult to elicit voter concern and effective responses to this issue because of its technical nature. Election official claims that machines are now safe because they have been wrapped around with a piece of yellow tape, and vendor assertions that there are no alternative ways of producing such machines are accepted without question by those who lack the technical knowledge to understand why statements like this hold no water. The result has been a serious undermining of the electoral process and the possibility that in many locations candidates who did not legitimately win elections are in public office.

Since library-state relations include library responsibility for supporting legal processes and political culture, these types of issues present challenges. Should libraries become places where citizens can acquire technological and informational literacy in addition to exercising and deepening their print literacy? If so, how might this best be accomplished? How would incorporating such goals in the library mission affect responses to other policy issues, such as protecting patron privacy and use of Internet filtering when necessary, at the operational level?

Replacement of Narrative Memory with Data

Activities instigated by a wide variety of laws and regulations come together via policy precession to yield the state's knowledge of itself. Such knowledge is acquired not only through the development of national archives but also through the census, satellite surveillance, real-time data from a variety of types of sensors ubiquitously embedded in the environment, access to government-mandated collections of digital data, and government-funded empirical research on state-related matters from social processes to natural resources to pollution. Among these techniques, national archives are particularly weak; record collection is haphazard, organization and access are inadequate or non-existent, documents are often left in ephemeral conditions, and both collection and preservation are fragile in the face of political will. Archival records, however, are particularly important for the ability to develop narratives that can in turn inform decision making and enable political action—we act when we see ourselves as agents within stories. We can pursue answers to specific questions of data that come in other forms, but data in themselves do not tell stories. Thus while we may have more information than ever before, there is less ability to use that information effectively for political purposes.

In a theory of library-state relations, is there room for libraries as a place where data can be turned into stories for political use by citizens—and by policy makers? If so, what new practices would be needed to accomplish this?

Replacement of History with Epigenetic Knowledge of the State

Complex adaptive systems theory distinguishes between *genetic processes* that unfold across time and *epigenetic processes* that unfold across space; globalization processes are often an example of the latter, while historical causation as studied by the social sciences is a premiere example of the former. A corollary of the predominance of data over narrative in the state's knowledge of itself is that today at least the most developed governments, such as those of North American and European states, have better epigenetic knowledge than they have genetic knowledge. This, too, undermines the quality of decision making, for it impedes the ability to learn from experience.

In addition to being loci of knowledge storage, should libraries be sites of knowledge production to ensure that local histories, at the very least, are captured and made accessible? How would doing so affect a theory of library-state relations? What would it mean for organizational design and practice?

CONCLUSIONS

Theories of media-state relations make clear that there is a wide range of possible ways in which libraries, too, can relate to their national governments. Support for the law need not be unquestioning, information provision can be proactive as well as reactive, the need for venues for public debate about public issues rises as the diversity of mass media content decreases, and the public's memory may not be the same as the memory of the state. Checking functions, insistence on governmental transparency, and active knowledge production about the affairs of the state may all be elements of a theory of library-state relations.

This is a period during which libraries must necessarily redefine their roles in response to qualitative changes in the ways that the polity seeks, accesses, and uses information because of rapid and continuous innovations in IT. As a theory of library-state relations develops it should focus most importantly on the population whom the government serves. Such a theory must be cast in such a way that it will continue to be useful even as the nature of society continues to change or it will not have utility as a framework for the comprehensive resolution of IT-related policy issues.

A number of elements of library-state relations that currently exist or that have been experimented with in the past are identified here, along with key dimensions of those relationships and current trends. This is just the beginning, however, of the development of a theory of library-state relations for the informational state of the twenty-first century.

NOTES

1. The classic and highly influential work was *Four Theories of the Press* by Siebert, Peterson, and Schramm (1956). A succinct synthesis of critiques of this work that begins but does not end with the expression of Cold War attitudes in *Four Theories of the Press* can be found in the work *Last Rights* by Nerone et al. (1995). Recent work by Hallin and Mancini (2004) provides a more contemporary typology of media-state relations.

2. Libraries are, of course, not only victims of technological change; at times they are also innovators themselves. The popularity of circulating libraries in London during the nineteenth century in turn affected the nature of the book industry as well as notions of ways in which libraries could serve civic culture (Smith, 1973), and a variety of approaches to information storage have long been critical to the development of a shared imagination that is necessary for the identity of a nation (Anderson, 1991). Libraries have been key to the development of digital archives, libraries, and preprints that are all now centrally critical to knowledge production (Bohlin, 2004); these approaches quickly outran the development of project-specific data collections as a means of disseminating information in support of knowledge production (Finholt, 2002), although many of these are still in play for specialized research communities. The U.S. Library of Congress is playing a lead role in the development of techniques for preserving information when the technologies of access themselves keep changing (National Science Board, 2005), and a number of libraries are doing the same for indexing and accessing what is being referred to as the deep web, meaning data and text buried within documents found through regular browsing software (Lewandowski & Mayr, 2006). Librarians are using file-sharing software to exchange government documents. Research on human-computer interaction now informs

study and practice in indexing (Bates, 1998). Many of these innovative activities create situations that challenge existing frameworks. So, too, do users, as when historians began using digital cameras to photograph archival materials (Carlson, 2004).

3. For contrasting views on filtering and collection development, see Miltner (2005) and Nadel (2000).

4. The folkloric Middle Eastern warning that one should not allow a camel's nose into a tent even though it is so small and disturbs nothing because soon the entire camel will be inside the tent is often used in legal discourse to refer to an act that is believed to lead to a slippery slope of much larger consequences than initially claimed or intended.

5. Symbolic power is also sometimes referred to as consensual or soft power.

6. A special issue of the *Journal of Communication* introduced by the Braman (1995a) article cited here also included a number of case studies dealing with these practices as exercised by countries as diverse as the Philippines (Sussman, 1995), India (McDowell, 1995), and Ireland (Bell, 1995).

7. An introduction to some of these techniques can be found in Braman (2006b).

REFERENCES

Aabo, V. (2005). The role and value of public libraries in the age of digital technologies. *Journal of Librarianship and Information Science, 37*(4), 205–211.

Anderson, P. (1991). *The printed image and the transformation of popular culture, 1790–1860.* New York: Clarendon Press.

Andersson, J. (2006). The people's library and the electronic workshop: Comparing Swedish and British social democracy. *Politics & Society, 34*(3), 431–460.

Arundale, J. (2002). How much law should librarians know? *New Library World, 103*(10), 376–384.

Bates, M. J. (1998). Indexing and access for digital libraries and the Internet: Human, database, and domain factors. *Journal of the American Society for Information Science, 49*(13), 1185–1206.

Bearden, D. M., & Esworthy, R. (2007). *Restructuring EPA's libraries: Background and issues for Congress.* Washington, DC: Congressional Research Service.

Bell, D. (1995). Communications, corporatism, and dependent development in Ireland. *Journal of Communication, 45*(4), 70–89.

Black, A. (2005). The library as clinic: A Foucauldian interpretation of British public library attitudes to social and physical disease, ca. 1850–1950. *Libraries & Culture, 40*(3), 416–434.

Black, A. (2007). "Arsenals of scientific and technical information": Public technical libraries in Britain during and immediately after World War I. *Library Trends, 55*(3), 474–489.

Bohlin, I. (2004). Communication regimes in competition: The current transition in scholarly communication seen through the lens of the sociology of technology. *Social Studies of Science, 34*(3), 365–392.

Braman, S. (1994). The autopoietic state: Communication and democratic potential in the Net. *Journal of the American Society of Information Science, 45*(6), 358–368.

Braman, S. (1995). Horizons of the state: Information policy and power. *Journal of Communication, 45*(4), 4–24.

Braman, S. (2000). The constitutional context: Universities, new information technologies, and the US Supreme Court. *Information, Communication & Society, 3*(4), 526–545.
Braman, S. (2004). Where has media policy gone? Defining the field in the 21st century. *Communication Law and Policy, 9*(2), 153–182.
Braman, S. (2006a). *Change of state: Information, policy, and power.* Cambridge, MA: MIT Press.
Braman, S. (2006b). Tactical memory: The politics of openness in the construction of memory. *First Monday, 11*(7), firstmonday.org/issues/issue11_7/braman/index.html.
Brown, N. E. (2004). The shift from apartheid to democracy: Issues and impacts on public libraries in Cape Town, South Africa. *Libri, 54*(3), 169–178.
Burke, S. K., & Martin, E. (2004). Libraries in communities: Expected and unexpected portrayals in state case law. *Libraries & Culture, 39*(4), 405–428.
Buschman, J. E. (2003). *Dismantling the public sphere: Situation and sustaining librarianship in the age of the new public philosophy.* Westport, CT: Libraries Unlimited.
Caidi, N. (2004). The politics of library artifacts: The national union catalog. *Library Quarterly, 74*(3), 337–369.
Caidi, N. (2006). Building "civilisation competence": A new role for libraries? *Journal of Documentation, 62*(2), 194–212.
Carlson, S. (2004). Scholars take notes by the megapixel, but some librarians object. *The Chronicle of Higher Education, 51*(17), A39.
Carmichael, J. V. (2005). Southern librarianship and the culture of resentment. *Libraries & Culture, 40*(3), 324–352.
Chodorow, S. (2006). To represent us truly: The job and context of preserving the cultural record. *Libraries & the Cultural Record, 41*(3), 372–380.
Craig, C. E. (2003). "Lending" institutions: The impact of the e-book on the American library system. *University of Illinois Law Review, 4,* 1087–1113.
Dean, J. (2001). Cybersalons and civil society: Rethinking the public sphere in transnational technoculture. *Public Culture, 13*(2), 243–266.
Dilevko, J., & Gottlieb, L. (2003). The politics of standard selection guides: The case of the Public Library Catalog. *Library Quarterly, 73*(3), 289–337.
Dutton, W. H., & Guthrie, K. (1991). An ecology of games: The political construction of Santa Monica's public electronic network. *Informatization and the Public Sector, 1,* 279–301.
Elings, M. W., & Waibel, G. (2007). Metadata for all: Descriptive standards and metadata sharing across libraries, archives and museums. *First Monday, 12*(3), http://www.firstmonday.org/issues/issue12_3/elings/index.html.
Ellis, S., & Oppenheim, C. (1993). Legal issues for information professionals: Data protection and the media. *Journal of Information Science, 19*(2), 85–98.
Fernandez-Molina, J. C. (2004a). Contractual and technological approaches for protecting digital works: Their relationship with copyright limitations. *Online Information Review, 28*(2), 148–157.
Fernandez-Molina, J. C. (2004b). Licensing agreements for information resources and copyright limitations and exceptions. *Journal of Information Science, 30*(4), 337–346.
Finholt, T. A. (2002). Collaboratories. *Annual Review of Information Science and Technology, 36,* 73–107.

Flatten, K. (1997). Training librarians and information specialists to support academic staff using networks. *Librarian Career Development, 5*(1), 23–29.

Forgacs, D. (1990). *Italian culture in the industrial era, 1880–1980.* New York: Manchester University Press.

Genieva, E. (2003). The role of displaced book collections in culture. *Library Trends, 52*(1), 151–156.

Golding, P., & Murdock, G. (1986). Unequal information: Access and exclusion in the new communications marketplace. In M. Ferguson (Ed.), *New communication technologies and the public interest: Comparative perspectives on policy and research* (pp. 71–83). Beverly Hills, CA: Sage Publications.

Grossman, G. S. (1994). *Legal research: Historical foundations of the electronic age.* New York: Oxford University Press.

Guy, F. (2003). Developing services in an evolving technological and political era. *Electronic Library, 21*(6), 538–545.

Hallin, D. C., & Mancini, P. (2004). *Comparing media systems: Three models of media and politics.* Cambridge, UK: Cambridge University Press.

Hartman, T. (2007). The changing definition of US libraries. *Libri, 57*(1), 1–8.

Havemann, F., Heinz, M., & Wagner-Döbler, R. (2005). Firm-like behavior of journals? Scaling properties of their output and impact growth dynamics. *Journal of the American Society for Information Science and Technology, 56*(1), 3–12.

Hendrix, E. (2005). Permanent injustice: Rawls' theory of justice and the digital divide. *Educational Technology & Society, 8*(1), 63–68.

Highby, W. (2004). The ethics of academic collection development in a politically contentious era. *Library Collections, Acquisitions, & Technical Services, 28*(4), 465–572.

Hobbs, T. (2003). Libraries and the regional agenda. *Journal of Librarianship and Information Science, 35*(4), 215–217.

Jaeger, P. T., & Burnett, G. (2005). Information access and exchange among small worlds in a democratic society: The role of policy in shaping information behavior in the post-9/11 United States. *Library Quarterly, 75*(4), 464–495.

Johnson, R. K. (2007). In Google's broad wake: Taking responsibility for shaping the global digital library. *Association of Research Libraries, 250,* 1–15.

Katsh, M. E. (1989). *The electronic media and the transformation of the law.* New York: Oxford University Press.

Kibbee, J. (2003). Aux armes citoyens! Confronting the extreme right in French public libraries. *Libri, 53*(4), 227–236.

Kochen, M., & Deutsch, K. W. (1973). Decentralization by function and location. *Management Science, 19*(8), 841–857.

Lazowska, E. S. (1968). Photocopying, copyright, and the librarian. *American Documentation, 19*(2), 123–131.

Lewandowski, D., & Mayr, P. (2006). Exploring the academic invisible web. *Library Hi Tech, 24*(4), 529.

Lukes, S. (2005). *Power: A radical view* (2nd ed.). Basingstoke, UK: Palgrave Macmillan.

Manoff, M. (2004). Theories of the archive from across the disciplines. *Portal: Libraries and the Academy, 4*(1), 9–25.

Marcella, R., Baxter, G., & Moore, N. (2002). An exploration of the effectiveness for the citizen of Web-based systems of communicating UK parliamentary and devolved assembly information. *Journal of Government Information, 29*(6), 371–391.

Marlow, G. D. (1998). From black robes to white lab coats: The ethical implications of a judge's *sua ponte, ex patre* acquisition of social and other scientific evidence during the decision-making process. *St. John's Law Review, 72*(2), 291–335.

Martin, K. E. (2004). Publishing trends within state government: The situation in North Carolina. *Journal of Government Information, 30*(5–6), 620–636.

Maymi-Sugranes, H. J. (2002). The American Library Association in Latin America: American librarianship as a "modern" model during the Good Neighbor Policy era. *Libraries & Culture, 37*(4), 307–338.

McDowell, S. (1995). The decline of the license Raj: Indian software export policies. *Journal of Communication, 45*(4), 25–51.

McKechnie, L., French, P. K., Goodall, G. R., Kipp, M., Paquette D. L., & Pecoskie, J. L. (2004). Covered beverages now allowed: Public libraries and book superstores. *Canadian Journal of Information and Library Science, 28*(3), 39–51.

Merelman, R. M. (1998). The mundane experience of political culture. *Political Communication, 15*(4), 515–535.

Miltner, K. A. (2005). Discriminatory filtering: CIPA's effect on our nation's youth and why the Supreme Court erred in upholding the constitutionality of the Children's Internet Protection Act. *Federal Communications Law Journal, 57*(3), 555–578.

Mosco, V. (1988). Whose computer revolution is it? *Information Technology and Libraries, 7*(4), 341–349.

Murdock, G., & Golding, P. (1990). Information poverty and political inequality: Citizenship in the age of privatized communications. *Journal of Communication, 39*(3), 180–195.

Nadel, M. S. (2000). The First Amendment's limitations on the use of internet filtering in public and school libraries: What content can librarians exclude? *Texas Law Review, 78*(5), 1117–1157.

National Science Board. (2005). *Long-lived data collections: Enabling research and education in the 21st century.* Washington, DC: National Science Foundation.

Nerone, J. (Ed.), Berry, W. E., Braman, S., Christians, C., Guback, T. G., Helle, S. J., et al. (1995). *Last rights: Revisiting four theories of the press.* Champaign: University of Illinois Press.

Newman, J., & McKee, B. (2005). Beyond the new public management? Public services and the social investment state. *Policy and Politics, 33*(4), 657–673.

Niessen, J. P. (2006). Museums, nationality, and public research libraries in nineteenth-century Transylvania. *Libraries & the Cultural Record, 41*(3), 298–336.

Nussbaum, M. C. (1995). *Poetic justice: The literary imagination and public life.* Boston, MA: Beacon Press.

Pieterse, J. N. (1997). Multiculturalism and museums: Discourse about others in the age of globalization. *Theory, Culture, & Society, 14*(4), 123–146.

Pool, I. de S. (1983). *Technologies of freedom.* Cambridge, MA: Belknap Press.

Raber, D. (2003). Librarians as organic intellectuals: A Gramscian approach to blind spots and tunnel vision. *Library Quarterly, 73*(1), 33–53.

Raber, D. (2007). ACONDA and ANACONDA: Social change, social responsibility, and librarianship. *Library Trends, 55*(3), 675–697.

Ranson, S. (2003). Public accountability in the age of neo-liberal governance. *Journal of Education Policy, 18*(5), 459–480.

Regan, P. M. (2004). Old issues, new context: Privacy, information collection, and homeland security. *Government Information Quarterly, 21*(4), 481–497.

Richards, T. (1993). *The imperial archive: Knowledge and the fantasy of empire.* New York: Verso.

Rikowski, R. (2005). *Globalisation, information and libraries: The implications of the World Trade Organization's GATS and TRIPS agreements.* Oxford, UK: Chandos Publishing.

Ross, A., & Caidi, N. (2005). Action and reaction: Libraries in the post-9/11 environment. *Library & Information Science Research, 27*(1), 97–114.

Scazzieri, R. (1993). *A theory of production: Tasks, processes, and technical practices.* Oxford, UK: Clarendon Press.

Seadle, M. (1999). E-mail attachments. *Library Hi Tech, 17*(2), 217–221.

Shachaf, P. (2005). A global perspective on library association codes of ethics, *Library & Information Science Research, 27*(4), 513–533.

Shuler, J. (2005). The political and economic future of federal depository libraries. *Journal of Academic Librarianship, 31*(4), 377–382.

Siebert, F. S., Peterson, T., & Schramm, W. (1956). *Four theories of the press: The authoritarian, libertarian, social responsibility and Soviet Communist concepts of what the press should be and do.* Champaign: University of Illinois Press.

Smith, A. (1973). *The shadow in the cave: The broadcaster, his audience, and the state.* Urbana: University of Illinois Press.

Sophar, G. J. (1968). The determination of legal facts and economic guideposts with respect to the dissemination of scientific and educational information as it is affected by copyright: A status report. *American Documentation, 19*(3), 317–322.

Stauffer, S. M. (2005). Polygamy and the public library: The establishment of public libraries in Utah before 1910. *Library Quarterly, 75*(3), 346–370.

Sturges, P., Davies, E., Dearnley, J., Iliffe, U., Oppenheim, C., & Hardy, R. (2003). User privacy in the digital library environment: An investigation of policies and preparedness. *Library Management, 24* (1/2), 44–50.

Sussman, G. (1995). Transnational communications and the dependent-integrated state. *Journal of Communication, 45*(4), 89–107.

Swartz, N. (2005). ALA: Government asks about patrons. *Information Management Journal, 39*(5), 8.

Tribe, L. H. (1985). Constitutional calculus: Equal justice or economic efficiency? *Harvard Law Review, 98,* 592–621.

Vaidhyanathan, S. (2006). Critical information studies: A bibliographic manifesto. *Cultural Studies, 20*(2–3), 292–315.

von Merveldt, N. (2007). Books cannot be killed by fire: The German freedom library and the American library of Nazi-banned books as agents of cultural memory. *Library Trends, 55*(3), 523–535.

Wallerstein, I. (1980). "The withering away of the states." *International Journal of the Sociology of Law, 8,* 369–378.

Wheeler, M. B. (2005). The politics of access: Libraries and the fight for civil liberties in post-9/11 America. *Radical History Review, 93*(fall), 79–95.

Zaret, D. (1999). *Origins of democratic culture: Printings, petitions, and the public sphere in early-modern England.* Princeton, NJ: Princeton University Press.

Zittrain, J. (2004). Internet points of control. In S. Braman (Ed.), *The emergent global information policy regime* (pp. 203–227). Houndsmills, UK: Palgrave Macmillan.

APPENDIX: INFORMATION POLICY PRINCIPLES IN THE US CONSTITUTION

Principle	Location
Government right to collect information about citizens	Art. 1, Sec. 2
Right of access to information about the government	Art. 1, Sec. 5; Art. 2, Sec. 3
Those within government have free speech	Art. 1, Sec. 6
Federal government controls currency (including in digital form)	Art. 1, Sec. 8
Universal access to an information distribution system	Art. 1, Sec. 8,Cl. 7
Intellectual property rights	Art. 1, Sec. 8, Cl. 8
Restriction of civil liberties during time of war	Art. 1, Sec. 9, Cl. 2
Treasonous communications are illegal	Art. 3, Sec. 3
Freedom of opinion	1st Am.
Freedom of speech	1st Am.
Freedom of the press	1st Am.
Freedom of assembly and association	1st Am.
Freedom to petition the government for change	1st Am.
Right to privacy	1st Am.; 4th Am.
Right to receive information	Art. 1, Sec. 8, Cl. 7; 1st Am.
Protection against unlawful search	4th Am.
Protection against self-incrimination	5th Am.
Right to due process	5th Am.
Rights beyond those enumerated	9th Am.
Incorporation of federal constitution into state constitutions	14th Am.

2

APPLICATIONS

6

THE PROSPECTS FOR AN INFORMATION SCIENCE: THE CURRENT ABSENCE OF A CRITICAL PERSPECTIVE

John M. Budd

Let's begin with some radical propositions. (1) *Information technology* is not only inelegant, it is erroneous and misleading as a name. The technology handles the creation of messages (in a limited sense of coding), the transmission of messages, and the reception of coded messages. In short, what is named *information technology* is the technical application of Claude Shannon's mathematics of communication. This is a vital and complex task, and it encompasses processing data according to computational rules (including semantic rules) and presenting the output by means of textual and graphic design protocols. What I mean by this proposition is that, as powerful as the technology is and as enabling as it can be, it does not inform. In fact, following Shannon, it is not concerned with meaning. I fully realize that this proposition will go nowhere; people will continue to refer to information technology. Following Wittgenstein (1958), to a point, the name *information technology* is part of a language game that creates a certain *kind* of understanding, mainly through acceptance and use. The *kind* of understanding is, simultaneously, a *kind* of misunderstanding. The game applies also to information science. What follows in this chapter is an exploration of the confusion that much of *information science* as a name has created. The confusion is bound between the Scylla of a Habermasian need for discourse ethics as a normative stricture on speech and the Charybdis of language games as they function in the tense *space* of rationality and ideology.

To elaborate a bit on language games, Wittgenstein suggests that a social group (or a working group, or some other kind of communicating group) establishes certain rules for operation. An example he gives in *Philosophical Investigations* is the game of chess. The rules establish the structure of the board, the number of pieces each player has, the movements the pieces make, and the definition of winning. It is when the rules are established and understood that pieces and moves (including strategies and tactics) are named. It is then that the names can be used metaphorically in instances other than playing the game of chess. The technology that has been designed and developed uses a set of logical rules according to programming languages and applications. For some years *computers* and *computing* were preferred names, as was *computer science*. The names were used to designate the hardware, software, and educational and research endeavors. *Computer,* however, has limited linguistic utility; it tends to be associated with a specific object and lacks abstraction that might be applied more broadly and in multiple environments. For example, a computer science department in a university would have a curriculum that was connected to the object. Departments in many universities have dropped *computer* and have replaced it with *information*. As we will shortly see, *information* affords academic departments and other organizations and entities a flexibility to employ language games in ways otherwise impossible.

The foregoing leads to the second radical proposition: (2) Information science is indeed based on a paradigm in one of the ways Thomas Kuhn meant in *The Structure of Scientific Revolutions* (1970). While Kuhn's book has contributed to disputes about the nature of science and has itself been the source of confusion, information science is a socially constrained way of thinking that creates the incommensurability that its adherents experience (consciously or not) when faced with other ways of thinking. (Actually, characterizing information according to Kuhn's terminology is itself an application of a language game; *paradigm* is used so frequently that it carries an array of images. A better descriptive word for information science's dominant way of thinking would be *habitus*. Pierre Bourdieu repeatedly used the word to refer to a group's ecological ties—questions, methods, work in general. Kuhn's word, being much more familiar to people, will be used here.) Kuhn, one of the most cited and most confused writers of the last half century, stated many contradictory things in his work. He denied that he was a relativist, but he said that scientists operating according to one paradigm live in a different world from other scientists. Some commentators have recognized that Kuhn's stance is an extraordinarily strong antirealist one. This means that his observations of the practices of scientists are only loosely connected to the natural world that is the putative focus of their investigations. Some of the rhetoric of information science is likewise strongly antirealist in the same way that Kuhn is. Regardless of the microsubstance of information science thinking, the macrosubstance is that *information* is an abstraction. Effectively, it does not exist. Given that dilemma, a number of information scientists have tried to define the field. Patrick Wilson (1995) is just one who has spoken of the difficulty of nailing down just what information science is; his observations can be taken as somewhat indicative of the ways people have tackled definition: "on the one hand, we occupy a field of engineering research and development. On the other, we occupy a field of social, behavioral and humanistic studies" (p. 277). Michael Buckland (1991) avoided information science as a discipline or field and cut straight to three ways to conceive of information: as knowledge, as process, and as thing. One need not be an essentialist to see that there is something missing from each of the three conceptions.

Defining information in terms of knowledge is somewhat disingenuous (and Buckland did not settle on that definition). The study of knowledge has a nearly 2,500-year history; there is considerable agreement among epistemologists as to what knowledge is. If we accept that knowledge is (at least) justified true belief that is not accidental, we immediately see the difficulty of placing information in that definition. If information is not entirely mapped onto the definition of knowledge, then is it truth, belief, or justification? Information is, in fact, none of these things, although becoming informed can contribute to all three. A number of philosophers, Richard Rorty perhaps the foremost among them, deny that knowledge is even possible, asserting instead that claims that can be corroborated or are practically workable are all we can hope for. If such an idea is correct, then there is no such thing as information (defined as knowledge) either. Information as process leads at the very least to a grammatical problem. The idea of process is attractive in many ways, but one challenge is determining the discreet elements of the process that would constitute informing. I use the word *constitute* intentionally here; the definition of informing as process should include that parts that identify informing as unique, as distinct from other processes. Information as thing is the simplest definition, but it is full of problems also. The physicality of information does not allow for semantic, syntactical, or metaphysical significance (which is why Shannon was drawn to the physical in attempting to solve engineering problems), although it can include semiotic significance of a limited sort. The advantage of defining information as thing, especially for a field like information science, is that the management of transmission of objects can be studied. The potential for meaningful insight, however, is not very great because the physicality of information is itself bereft of meaning in terms of the communication of thoughts, concepts, images, or a host of speech acts. According to any of the three definitions, *information* is abstract.

The abstraction inherent in information science's use of *information* is critical to the academic positioning of the field. From a practical standpoint the abstraction, and a kind of flexibility that goes with it, allows information science to appropriate a number of subjects. The appropriation can enhance a department's abilities to apply for and secure external funding, to present an appearance of breadth that might be attractive to academic administrators, and to attract students to a seemingly inclusive curriculum. The practical aims, which have been topics of conversation in education for librarianship, have resulted in some curious statements. The conversation has, by and large, been an intramural one conducted among programs that have self-identified a so-called I-School movement. A group of programs at several universities have formed a kind of coalition and have convened some conferences. At the I-Schools Project's Web site the purpose is stated:

> The I-School Project consists of schools interested in the relationship between information, technology, and people. This is characterized by a commitment to learning and understanding the role of information in human endeavors. The I-Schools take it as given that expertise in all forms of information is required for progress in science, business, education, and culture. (I-Schools Project, 2008)

The stated purpose confirms the abstraction mentioned above. There is scarcely a subject or an academic department that does not fit into the description of intent. The I-Schools, however, are a self-selected group; only certain programs have been involved in the founding and activities of the I-School Project.

To return to definitions of information, it becomes evident through Buckland's definitions that information science is not paradigmatic in one of the (other) senses that Kuhn meant. Information science does not have a single constellation of beliefs, questions, and problems that unifies practitioners. It is impossible for a field like information science to rally around one such unifying constellation, just as it is impossible for all of physics to be so defined. Nonetheless, the paradigm of information science is a socially unifying structure. The social unification is not based on one single definition of information (and, following the definition, a coherent research program), but on a *belief* that a single definition is possible. Towards the end of unification, individuals, just as Buckland did, suggest definitions. At the heart of many definitions is the objective that Shannon had in developing a mathematical theory of communication. That is, the objective is the management and control of certain kinds of flows. For Shannon this meant the transmission of a message over a high-fidelity path. In information science the mathematical gauntlet was picked up by several people. B. C. Brookes (1974) posited an equation: $\Delta I + (S) \rightarrow (S + \Delta S)$. An existing knowledge structure (S) is transformed by the introduction of information inputs (ΔI) to result in a new knowledge structure ($S + \Delta S$). Shannon was aiming to improve technologically assisted communication (primarily telephony). Information scientists have a similar but considerably less well-defined aim—technological management of all communication. In order to accomplish this aim (as we will see), a particular conception of information has to be imposed.

Brookes's equation is problematic, both semiotically and metaphysically (it presents difficulties as a set of signs and as a representation of reality). While he used symbols that are not uncommon to mathematical representation, the symbols are too simple to signify something as complex as a knowledge structure. Questions arise, such as: Does the symbol signify a subject's entire knowledge base, or only one aspect of the knowledge base? Does the symbol represent a universal structure, or an individualist structure? Peter

Ingwersen (1995) commented on Brookes's equation and observed that Brookes intended ΔI to signify structured information but that the effects of the structured information will be different for different knowledge structures (p. 95). Both information and knowledge are wholes that interact. In other words, they are explicit, definable states existing in time, and the introduction of information to knowledge results in a transformation of the physical state. This error has been repeated by Belkin, Oddy, and Brooks (1982) in their modeling of anomalous states of knowledge (ASK). Douglas Raber (2003), in a thorough and cogent critique of metaphors employed in information science, said that in the ASK model, "in order to be truly effective, information retrieval systems must be constructed in such a way as to account for and represent a user's ASK to the system" (p. 166). Raber put his finger on an essential difficulty—a system must be not only sentient but must be able to know what inquirers do not know.

The paradigm, the way of thinking, in information science is centered on a presumption that systems design can solve problems of becoming informed. Of course not everyone working in the field of information science succumbs to such a deterministic siren song, but the literature in information science is rife with affirmations. Chaim Zins (2006) has written, "Meaning, in the objective domain 'data' are sets of symbols, which represent empirical stimuli or perceptions. 'Information' is a set of symbols, which represent empirical knowledge. 'Knowledge' is a set of symbols, which represent the meaning (or the content) of thoughts that the individual justifiably believes that they are true" (p. 454). If the starting point is the design of a system that is able to produce output that is deemed to be symbolically, semantically, logically relevant, then an assumption that follows will be that knowledge and information are objective. An implication of the assumption is that there is not only an epistemological element of systems design (and information science in general) but also an ontological element. Zins (2006) stated further, "One might claim that information science is focused on the subjective domain. If this is the case, then we are required to formulate a clear distinction between the foci of cognitive sciences and neurosciences and the foci of information science. Clearly, information science has different foci. While cognitive psychology and neurosciences are focused on the subjective domain, by exploring thinking and learning, information science concentrates on the objective domain" (p. 454). Zins effectively and completely dismisses information retrieval's concern with such things as relevance judgments, and human information behavior completely.

Determinism has been frowned upon in information science by a few people. Some of those who have found fault with deterministic information science have focused on the transformation of informing. More than 30 years ago Belkin and Robertson (1976) maintained that the communicative action of informing should be at the heart of information science. They suggested that information science deals with a particular set of phenomena:

I. The text and its structure (the information).
II. The image-structure of the recipient and the changes in that structure.
III. The image-structure of the sender and structuring of the text. (p. 202)

They then suggested that the third part of the phenomena is potentially fertile ground for research. On the positive side, Belkin and Robertson understood that informing is much more than propagandizing and that there is a social aspect of informing. While their suggestions have merit, they then turn to a systems design that makes use of individuals' images. At an earlier time Victor Rosenberg (1974) illustrated deterministic, physicalist tendencies in information science work. At that time he offered an articulate and powerful criticism of the problem:

I would argue that the development of automated systems has inhibited this fundamental understanding [of the nature of information]. . . . When we apply the knowledge derived from the scientific study of information we find a situation that does not fit solutions to problems so much as it fits problems to solutions. (pp. 266, 267)

His point is that what informs people (and this is a metaphysical matter) is not reducible to aggregating and manipulating data. Rosenberg's point is extremely important; we will revisit it later.

BACK TO THE PARADIGM

One thing becomes clear upon pondering *paradigm* (in the Kuhnian sense identified here). The social constraints/social choices lead to some insularity; the group either chooses to focus internally or is balkanized by competing social groups. More likely some combination of the two forces are at work as the group turns inward. The problem is evident in the present state of education for librarianship, especially between the preparation of beginning professional librarians and the study of information writ large. Some commentators state that the formative ideas in information science have been influenced by other fields (communication, computer science, linguistics, cognitive science, and others). These commentators, and others, usually then say that information science has achieved, or must achieve, intellectual and operational autonomy. Jennifer Rowley (1998) is one who paid a bit of homage to other disciplines and spoke to the purpose of information science:

individuals are concerned with the role that information can play in a process such as decision making, learning or innovation whereas information professionals and information system designers, the professionals concerned with information, need to be able to impose structure on information to gather it into their systems and need therefore to treat information as an object and to create a systems view of information. (p. 252)

Her observation encapsulates two important aspects of information science. (1) More often than not, concentration is on the individual's actions, so a degree of atomism hinders expansion of the applicability of information science's ways of thinking. (2) A systems approach, which usually (but not always) involves technical systems, necessitates treating information as an object. The first of these aspects is evident in one of Brian Vickery's (1997) elements on information science metatheory: "A personal knowledge structure (PKS) reflects the life experience of the person, and each is unique" (p. 472).

Each of the two observations is profoundly limiting, so the task is to transcend the paradigm in order to institute a more critical study of informing. The information science paradigm is grounded in control of a certain type—control of the so-called natural object that is information, so that it can be *used* by individuals according to their preferences. Toward the end of this goal, researchers in information science examine the control of flows, the control of human behaviors, and the control of objects by means of technology. Apropos of this goal, information science frequently omits librarianship as a component of the discipline (again, the I-School Project is an example of the phenomenon). This, also, is a rather sweeping statement; of course some people do speak of library and information science as something both broad and unifying. S. D. Neill (1992) wrote of many problems inherent in the study of information and added some responses to the problems in librarianship. Neill cited other writers who have said that librarianship's familial relationship with information science has been manifest in the technical, the manipulable, and the quantifiable. He also cites Leon Brillouin (1962), who built on Shannon's work:

> The methods of this theory can be successfully applied to all technical problems concerning information: coding, telecommunications, mechanical computers, etc. In all of these problems we are actually processing information or transmitting it from one place to another, and the present theory is extremely useful in setting up rules and stating exact limits for what can and cannot be done. But we are in no position to investigate the processes of thought, and we cannot, for the moment, introduce into our theory any element involving the human value of information. (pp. x–xi)

Neill's foremost service to subsequent work revolving around information has been to delineate aporias (conflicts that cannot seem to be resolved) explicitly and, implicitly, to suggest a dialectic: "Information is a social construct, and communication is a social event. . . . Many information scientists began as natural scientists interested in controlling science information. They brought with them the scientist's attitude that problems could be solved by breaking them down into workable (researchable and measurable) parts" (Neill, 1992, pp. 140, 148). The dialectical challenge is to examine and understand the means of informing and becoming informed by resolving the varying natures of the act—some tangible communicative acts are performed;

what is communicated is concrete, metaphorical, or some combination of the two; the act of informing is both individual and social; and meaning is implied and inferred in all informative acts.

SCIENCE AS RHETORICAL DEVICE

The word "science" tends to command respect, even though the public perception of science may have been tarnished in recent years. The cache that the term *science* has in people's minds is an example of an exoteric appreciation for the representation of rigor, sound method, and thorough scrutiny. (Julian Warner, 2001, examined the exoteric and esoteric in information science.) A somewhat different exoteric appreciation of science is characteristic of many academic administrators. Elsewhere in this volume the insidious force of neoliberalism is illuminated; suffice it to say here that higher education is itself a burgeoning locus for neoliberal policies and actions. Administrators have eyes on the bottom line, and things that can be cloaked within supposedly scientific garb are valued because they are deemed to have value. By *value* I mean price tag. A presumption is that scientific work can attract external funding from federal agencies and other entities. The academic units that do attract such funding tend to fare better in the arenas of the campuses. Administrators, as an exoteric audience, may not care at all about the esoteric matters within departments; they do care about nonintellectual matters, though. Given that potential funders of research and instruction constitute another audience (a mix of the exoteric and esoteric), academic administrators act upon a very particular set of perceptions. So academic administrators are also operating according to a paradigm in the sense used here.

Exoteric audiences undoubtedly affect paradigmatic groups. In library and information science (LIS) we can turn to Lloyd Houser and Alvin Schrader (1978) for the most blatant bow to exoteric audiences. In urging a transforming of educational programs Houser and Schrader claimed that the state of research by faculty in the programs was primitive and, at best, prescientific. They stated that research and education should follow strict models of the natural sciences. Moreover, they said that progress would be evident when a Kuhnian paradigm would be identified. The fundamental error that Houser and Schrader made is putting the cart before the horse. A field's desire to be a science is akin to a politician who wants to *hold an office*. The soundest objective for a politician to have is to make the best use of the office to effect actions that will bring all citizens closer to the good life. The soundest objective for an information science researcher, a professional librarian, or an educator is to seek the most effective ways to help people learn, discover, and grow—individually and collectively—through the conscious incorporation of what other people say, write, and show.

The objective just described does not ignore technology, but it does not valorize it. Rowley (1998) commented on Peter Ingwersen's idea of the cognitive viewpoint: "He argues that both the reception and the generation of information are acts of information processing, and therefore, the way that this processing is carried out is dependent on the world model of the actor, whether human or machine. *The important point here is that the machine or system may also act as a recipient applying its own world model*" (p. 250, emphasis added). The information-processing model is severely limiting, though. If a machine and a human proceed according to precisely the same paths, using precisely the same mechanisms, many things would never have been created. Einstein, for example, was not a first-rate mathematician, but he was able to imagine and see the universe in ways that did not simply amalgamate independent (or even dependent) concepts that existed at the time. In the somewhat more quotidian sense, information and technology—being both of human origin—are involved in a rich dialectic that precludes straightforward cause-and-effect analysis. As Raber (2003) said, "Interpretation is an act of negotiation. My need for information may be grounded in my experience, but it emerges from a negotiation I must conduct with reality. I cannot will reality to conform to my wishes" (p. 199).

THE PROPOSITIONS

So we can return to the radical propositions. *Information technology* is a misnomer; the technology has a decided effect on people's actions, but it may misshape one's thought. An example from the educational setting may help clarify this point. A student is told to write a short paper on a particular topic. The student may have an incomplete, or even flawed, understanding of the topic. The student may turn to technological mediation; in practical terms the student may search Google first. As the student enters terms that arise from the incomplete understanding, the search engine carries out information-processing tasks (albeit in quite a sophisticated way). Some of the terms are likely to be present in combinations specified by the student, so a set of items is retrieved. The student, working from incomplete understanding or misunderstanding, may be turned in a particular direction by the items retrieved. The direction may not be the one that the teacher intended, though, so the student receives a poor grade. There is a good chance that the student learns very little from the exercise. Suppose that, instead of using Google, the student searches a database recommended by the teacher. The incomplete understanding can still lead to a set of retrieved items that point the student in the wrong direction. The student, having proceeded according to the prescribed path, may be frustrated and may conclude that it is the teacher who is in error. Would information science be able to diagnose the problem and suggest a remedy? The paradigm, defined here as the dominant way of thinking, suggests that it could do neither well. An information scientist might be able to work backwards from the texts (broadly speaking) to optimal search strategies and posit a search that the student could have executed.

Two distinctions must be made here as part of a correction to the name *information technology* and the paradigm of information science. The first is between technology and technique. Technology can be seen as a particular kind of human creation that is intended to assist human action. Industrial and agricultural technologies have been intended to produce more, of higher quality, at lower cost. The technologies may or may not achieve all of these ends. The printed book, as technology, has been intended to transmit texts to a larger number of people, with a relatively high degree of fidelity to the original text, at an affordable price. Technologies, of course, can have unintended consequences. Some of the consequences (intended or unintended) affect what can be called technique. *Technique* refers to the array of procedures or other instrumental actions that can become reified through usage. *Technique,* as used by critics, is limited to the narrowly rational (that is, rationality aimed at material action) efficiency; the efficiency includes ignorance of purpose, or telos. The most strident critic to date of the transformation of technique has been Jacques Ellul. Ellul's polemic, *The Technological Society* (1964), has been read in a number of ways, including as a rationale for the crimes committed by Ted Kaczynski, the Unabomber. Ellul's principal point can be fairly simply stated, and was succinctly summarized by Robert K. Merton: "[Ours] is a civilization committed to the quest for continually improved means to carelessly examined ends. Indeed, technique transforms ends into means. What was once prized in its own right now becomes worthwhile only if it helps achieve something else. And, conversely, technique turns means into ends" (Merton, 1964, p. x). Ellul (1964) applied his warnings about technique to science: "To the degree that science is taking on a more and more technical aspect, these discoveries are made everywhere at the same time—a further indication that scientific discoveries are, in reality, governed by technique" (p. 86).

The information science paradigm appears to be immersed in technique. Information retrieval is taken to be an end by many who work in information science, but it is actually a means to intellectual growth, learning, and discovery, as well as many practical purposes (such as repairing an automobile). When people in information science reduce problems and questions to matters of systems design they are applying technique in a particular, and particularly constrained, manner. Technique is quite powerful as a human action. In librarianship it can be manifest as rules—explicit or tacit—that shift attention to such things as minutiae of bibliographic records or services that focus in the structures of databases. Without doubt, such applications of technique are not universal. Ian Cornelius (1996), for one, argued persuasively for transcending technique by developing a richer interpretive theory. Technique does tend to be influential, though, in part because the tasks that form much of the route to becoming informed are more readily identified and examined. The analysis of tasks is valuable and necessary, but it is not sufficient. The genuine ends, if omitted from analysis, can be forgotten in the application of technique.

The second distinction I will make here is that between practice and praxis. This distinction may seem much more subtle than the previous one. The distinction may be evident to many professionals; *practice*, for the present purpose, is defined as the day-to-day actions that address such things as organizational maintenance, routine tasks, internally rational operations (that include some components of cataloging and reference services), and competency with technique. Practice is not to be denigrated; the actions related to practice are necessary. Rules, for example, are vital to practice inasmuch as they contribute to efficiency (and possibly some degree of effectiveness). Practice is not unconscious; there is critical thought that accompanies and guides action. Rules, to continue the example, are applied critically within the framework of the internal rationality. Practice, however, is distinct from praxis. *Praxis* is defined in part in Aristotelian terms; it refers to the thoughts and actions within the ethical and political lives of people. Praxis is different from theory, but there is a strong relationship between the two. Jürgen Habermas (1973) has described the relationship best:

> The mediation of theory and praxis can only be clarified if to begin with we distinguish three functions, which are measured in terms of different criteria: the formation and extension of critical theorems, which can stand up to scientific discourse; the organization of processes of enlightenment, in which such theorems are applied and can be tested in a unique manner by the initiation of processes of reflection carried on within certain groups toward which these processes have been directed; and the selection of appropriate strategies, the solution of tactical questions, and the conduct of the political struggle. On the first level, the aim is true statements, on the second, authentic insights, and on the third, prudent decisions. (p. 32)

I will offer a very crude synthesis of the foregoing discussion: technique and practice tend to be connected (not logically, but actually), and technology and praxis tend to be connected. I have claimed that much of the work in information science, and indeed the information science paradigm, is bound to technique, especially by means of control. There is work in information science that is not so constrained, work that is aimed at praxis. Some of the latter work takes into account research from the discipline of communication that emphasizes some of the social, political, and economic (as well as cognitive) elements of speech acts. The less technique-driven work, to some extent, achieves the Aristotelian ideal of setting informing within an ethical and political framework. The present way of thinking in information science militates against praxis, though—not consciously, but effectively. I must emphasize that the limitation is due to the way of thinking in information science; it is not a consequence of the *existence* of an information science. That is, I am not denying that an information science is possible, but in its present state and with its present paradigm, it is not addressing the most important questions associated with becoming informed. A symptom of the limitation is that information science, in seeking to emulate some natural sciences, objectifies information. Buckland articulates his proclivity to conceive of information as a thing. Vickery (1997) also places the objective notion squarely in his elements of metatheory: "4. A message there has knowledge content. . . . 6. The stock of (recorded) messages may be called public knowledge. . . . 28. Information is thus derived from the knowledge content of the message, and is of the same nature as knowledge" (p. 472).

Many writers invoke that name of Karl Popper when speaking of the objective nature of information. In his book, *Objective Knowledge*, Popper (1983) posited a world 3, a world of the recorded speech acts of humankind. He argued that this world 3 is essential to human living; it is the tangible expression of what humans take to exist. While Popper offered many insights over the course of his long and productive life, his concept of objective knowledge is easily the most problematic. He (1994) has written, "We cannot understand world 2, that is, the world inhabited by our own mental states, without understanding that its main function is to *produce* world 3 objects, and to be *acted upon* by world 3 objects. For world 2 interacts not only with world 1 [the world as it is], as Descartes thought, but also with world 3" (p. 7, emphasis in original). I do not mean to dismiss Popper's idea of objective knowledge completely; the artifacts (physical and virtual) that humans create serve both to communicate with others and to provide a means for expressing frequently complicated thoughts. World 3 objects, though, are means, not ends. That is the message that information science (and librarianship) needs to attend to. Reifying information includes the danger of reducing what people say, write, and show to commodities that are components of a political economy in which there are likely to be winners and losers.

LANGUAGE GAMES REDUX

Earlier I mentioned that information science applies language games—a group of people employ language in particular ways, assuming a collective meaning sharing based on the usage of words. Wittgenstein (1958) examined where truth lies in the playing of language games (pp. 52–52, § 136). He stated that *true* and *false* are determined by the rules of the game as it is played. If the group holds that *true* and *false* have the meaning of *this is the ways things are* and *this is not the way things are,* then the group usually applies those meanings within the game. The words *true* and *false* are seldom mentioned explicitly in information science, but I will assume that the meanings mentioned here obtain for information scientists. A consequence of operating according to this assumption, for information science, is that it advances by asserting propositions and then testing them according to their truthfulness or falsity. There is an old joke; one version is,

Three people are stranded on a small island. One is a physicist, one is a circus strongman, and one is an economist. After a few days of surviving on fruit, they discover a cache of canned food, and they have to decide how to open it. The physicist says to the strongman, "Why don't you climb that tree, and smash the cans down on the rocks, and burst them open?" The strongman says, "No, that would spatter the stuff all over. I can open the cans with my teeth!" The economist says "First, we must assume that we have a can opener."

The present paradigm in information science might not hold the foregoing to be a joke; the operating dictum of the paradigm does not include testing propositions.

In the interest of asserting and testing propositions, the second radical proposition stated at the outset of this chapter is tested discursively here. I would suggest that the proposition describes the ways things are in information science. In 2000, when the American Society for Information Science added "Technology" to its name (ASIS&T), the change signified a coalescing of the way of thinking. In particular, it concretized the goal of control by means of technique. Apparently blind to irony, members of ASIS&T have forgotten Martin Heidegger's (1977) two-pronged response to the question of what technology is: "One says: Technology is a means to an end. The other says: Technology is a human activity. The two definitions belong together. . . . Technology is itself a contrivance, or, in Latin, an *instrumentum*" (pp. 4–5). Heidegger's observation brings home what Rosenberg meant in saying that the appropriate investigative order is beginning with problems and then seeking solutions. In information science technology is too often the solution in search of a problem. The examination here leads to a subsequent proposition: Information science's paradigm precludes substantive analysis insofar as it avoids defining *information* in a meaningful way and does not admit to the variability in human cognition and action. Testing that proposition will have to wait until a later date.

REFERENCES

Belkin, N. J., Oddy, R. N., & Brooks, H. M. (1982). ASK for information retrieval: Part 1: Background and theory. *Journal of Documentation, 38,* 61–71.

Belkin, N. J., & Robertson, S. E. (1976). Information science and the phenomenon of information. *Journal of the American Society for Information Science, 27,* 197–204.

Brillouin, L. (1962). *Science and information theory* (2nd ed.). New York: Academic Press.

Brookes, B. C. (1974). Robert Fairthorne and the scope of information science. *Journal of Documentation, 30,* 139–152.

Buckland, M. K. (1991). Information as thing. *Journal of the American Society for Information Science, 42,* 351–360.

Cornelius, I. (1996). *Meaning and method in information studies.* Norwood, NJ: Ablex Publishing Corp.

Ellul, J. (1964). *The technological society* (J. Wilkinson, Trans.). New York: Vintage Books.

Habermas, J. (1973). *Theory and practice* (J. Viertel, Trans.). Boston: Beacon Press.

Heidegger, M. (1977). *The question concerning technology and other essays* (W. Lovitt, Trans.). New York: Harper & Row.

Houser, L., & Schrader, A. (1978). *The search for a scientific profession*. Metuchen, NJ: Scarecrow Press.

Ingwersen, P. (1995). Information and information science in context. In J. Olaisen, E. Munch-Petersen, & P. Wilson (Eds.), *Information science: From the development of the discipline to social interaction* (pp. 69–111). Oslo: Scandinavian University Press.

I-Schools Project. (2008). Information: The power to transform the world. Retrieved July 2008 from http://www.ischools.org.

Kuhn, T. S. (1970). *The structure of scientific revolutions* (2nd ed). Chicago: University of Chicago Press.

Merton, R. K. (1964). Introduction. In J. Ellul, *The technological society*. New York: Vintage Books.

Neill, S. D. (1992). *Dilemmas in the study of information: Exploring the boundaries of information science*. Westport, CT: Greenwood Press.

Popper, K. R. (1983). *Objective knowledge* (Rev. ed.). Oxford: Clarendon Press.

Popper, K. R. (1994). *Knowledge and the mind-body problem*. London: Routledge.

Raber, D. (2003). *The problem of information: An introduction to information science*. Lanham, MD: Scarecrow Press.

Rosenberg, V. (1974). The scientific premises of information science. *Journal of The Society for Information Science, 25*, 263–269.

Rowley, J. (1998). What is information? *Information Services & Use, 18*, 243–254.

Vickery, B. (1997). Metatheory and information science. *Journal of Documentation, 53*, 457–76.

Warner, J. (2001). W(h)ither information science?/! *Library Quarterly, 71*, 243–255.

Wilson, P. (1995). The future of research in our field. In J. Olaisen, E. Munch-Petersen, & P. Wilson (Eds.), *Information science: From the development of the discipline to social interaction* (pp. 277–291). Oslo: Scandinavian University Press.

Wittgenstein, L. (1958). *Philosophical investigations* (3rd ed., G. E. M. Anscombe, Trans.). Englewood Cliffs, NJ: Prentice-Hall.

Zins, C. (2006). Redefining information science: From "information science" to "knowledge science." *Journal of Documentation, 62*, 447–461.

7

LIBRARIANSHIP AND THE LABOR PROCESS: ASPECTS OF THE RATIONALIZATION, RESTRUCTURING, AND INTENSIFICATION OF INTELLECTUAL WORK

Michael F. Winter

WORK IN CAPITALIST MODERNITY: THE EXPANSION OF CONTROL

Librarianship today, like so many other kinds of work, particularly those based on that mix of intellectual and applied expertise initially acquired at universities and tested in work settings, is situated in large and complex, hierarchical organizations requiring the allocation, management, control, and expenditure of considerable resources. Like the larger social structures enveloping them, these organizations typically show the multiple specializations common to an advanced division of labor. In many libraries today, library and information professionals work alongside library technicians or paraprofessionals, clerical and support staff (receptionists, mailroom workers, security personnel, and office managers), systems analysts, programmers, software and interface designers, maintenance and facilities workers, accounting personnel, purchasing specialists, and sometimes graphic artists. These workers and their various specializations are in turn managed by a smaller group of supervisors, who in turn report to an even smaller cadre of administrators exercising authority over the library's major functions; the two top levels in the organization are drawn mostly from the librarian ranks. At both the managerial and the administrative levels, ranges of responsibility are broader, and commitments to specialized areas recede. In smaller or so-called special libraries embedded in nonlibrary organizations, the situation is somewhat different, but the pattern of a complex, specialized division of labor with managerial and administrative oversight nonetheless persists. Today, library administrators emphasize the exploitation of new information and communication technologies (ICTs), a fact having distinct consequences as we shall see in this chapter, for librarians, and indeed for everyone currently working in libraries.

In the early twenty-first century, it is easy enough to regard this situation as natural or inevitable, but it is, historically speaking, a relatively recent development. It is an offshoot of the coming of late eighteenth- and nineteenth-century capitalist modernity. With its strategic and dynamic investment and reinvestment of resources, capitalist modernity fueled large-scale social and historical change (population increases and urbanization being two of the more notable changes), rapid development of technologies, concentration of power and resources in the hands of a progressively smaller number of owners and their representative managers and administrators, and a major transformation of work. In the time before the rise of capitalism, particularly in its industrial phase, much human labor was organized very differently. For present purposes, we may say that the prevailing precapitalist models of skilled work were variant forms of craft labor (Day, 1997): locally and regionally rooted, largely guild-controlled, with masters supervising novices and journeymen and either individually or cooperatively owning many if not all of the key tools of their trades. With the spread of capitalism, this model became increasingly endangered and substantially marginalized. Although it has not disappeared entirely, it has been largely replaced by large, bureaucratically structured work organizations whose leaders exercise considerable control over the routine work originally concentrated in the occupation itself.

Several theorists of modernity are of direct concern here. Two early figures of special interest are Karl Marx (1818–1883) and Max Weber (1864–1920); their perspectives on the development of capitalism provide essential background for virtually any discussion of work in advanced industrial societies. Marx pioneered the analysis of the alienation or deformation of the labor process in capitalist societies, while Weber provided an essential larger context for the analysis with his umbrella concept of rationalization and his crucial identification of bureaucracy as its principal organizational form. Marx's key discussions of the labor process were much later revisited in Harry Braverman's controversial and essential (1974) reexamination of the labor process in capitalist societies after World War II. In the conclusion of this chapter, I turn to the early work of Jean Baudrillard (1929–2007), another recent representative theorist of capitalist modernity, to provide additional framework for understanding the evolution of combined effects of technology and the consumer society on the work of librarians.

MARX'S ANALYSIS OF THE LABOR PROCESS: THE CHAPTER IN *CAPITAL*

The key passages where Marx defines and analyzes the labor process in capitalism are found in the seventh chapter of the first volume of *Capital* (Marx, 1936, pp. 197–206), where he offers a useful summary statement: "The labour process, resolved as above into its simple elementary factors, is human action with a view to the production of use values, appropriation of natural substances to human requirements. . . . It is the everlasting Nature-imposed condition of human existence and therefore is independent of every social phase of that existence" (pp. 204–205). One of the principal reasons why modern capitalism represents a revolutionary development in European history is precisely because it definitively alters this "Nature-imposed condition" of the use of free, creative labor in the production of the means of subsistence. With the aid of an obedient legal system that redefines previously communally or publicly owned natural resources into the private property of the entrepreneur and the owner of capital, capitalists are able to exploit the resulting inequality of resource distribution by reducing free, productive labor to labor power, a commodity exchanged by the worker on the labor market for a living wage. From an at least nominally free and independent producer of use values, in other words, the worker becomes a producer of goods destined to be exchanged, a source of profit for the owner of capital, and at the same time a producer of the wages he will receive from the capitalist in order to subsist well enough to be able to return the following day for another round of exploitation.

WEBER ON RATIONALIZED SCHOLARSHIP AND THE LIBRARY AS MEANS OF INTELLECTUAL PRODUCTION

Commentators have emphasized that Weber's concept of rationalization is multidimensional and includes the three basic themes of knowledge, impersonality, and control (Brubaker, 1984, pp. 30–32; Brubaker, 2003, p. 557). Since rational action is based on knowledge, where this means warranted belief and, more narrowly and by logical extension, authenticated expertise, it has an obvious relevance for professional work in general, and for scholarship and librarianship in particular, occupations particularly preoccupied with the management of knowledge. Its impersonal side is shown by its predilection for rule-governed processes, and by its affinity with bureaucratic routine. Much less welcome, however, but just as inevitably, it also fosters the extension of a society-wide form of technical control that favors the larger private and public administrative hierarchies. "Here the central focus is the technical rationalization of social relationships, their reduction to aspects of scientific, industrial, or administrative processes" (Waters, 1994, p. 181). While Weber accepted Marx's critical perspective on the worker's gradual loss of control over the labor process, he extended it well beyond the classic Marxian focus on economic production. Weber situates the Marxian problematic of control over work in the embedding institution of the evolving capitalist market and uses it to understand a wider range of social phenomena, from politics, military affairs, and status groups to general patterns of bureaucratic social organization, and even beyond this into artistic and intellectual work (Weber, 1946, p. 51). In theory, serving the broader interests of a guiding substantive and reflective rationality infused with purpose and meaning, instrumental or goal-directed reason becomes its own end, perpetuating itself endlessly in all spheres of activity, entrapping social action in a cul-de-sac of purely formal rationality. Nothing, in Weber's famous dark phrase, can escape the iron cage of formal reason, whose concrete social form is the bureaucratic organization. (The iron cage imagery chosen by Talcott Parsons in the first English translation of Weber's classic study of the rise of capitalism [Weber, 1930, p. 181] has been replaced in Stephen Kalberg's new translation [Weber, 2001, pp. 123, 245] by "steel-hard cage." Had Max Weber lived to get a foretaste of the digital age, one suspects that he might well have dropped the allusions to heavy metals and referred darkly to something like "the silicon cage," [Winter, 1998].) In his discussion of the development of the German university and the rationalization of scholarly work, Weber tries to understand how scholarship, and the older relation of the scholar to the library, has responded to the force of rationalization (Weber, 1946, p. 131). Writing at the end of World War I in a notably Marxian idiom, he locates a pivotal point in the development of higher learning—the alienation of the scholar from the process and instruments of intellectual production—and compares this separation to the situation of the worker in industrial society:

> The large institutes of medicine or natural science are "state capitalist" enterprises, which cannot be managed without very considerable funds. Here we encounter the same condition that is found wherever capitalist enterprise comes into operation: the "separation of the worker from his means of production." The worker, that is the assistant, is dependent upon the implements that the state puts at his disposal; hence he is just as dependent upon the head of the institute as is the employee in a factory upon the management. . . . This development, I am convinced, will engulf those disciplines in which the craftsman personally owns the tools, essentially the library, as is still the case to a large extent in my own field. This development corresponds entirely to what happened to the artisan of the past and is now fully under way. (Weber, 1946, p. 131)

Note here Weber's reference to the library as the scholar's means of production. Here he alludes to the passing of the craft-friendly age in which the scholar worked often from a private library, frequently his own or perhaps that of an influential patron. In the era Weber identifies as disappearing, a significant part of the total output of publication might well be owned by the well-to-do of the seventeenth, eighteenth, and nineteenth centuries. John Locke (1632–1704) and Thomas Jefferson (1743–1826), and later figures like Hubert Howe Bancroft (1832–1918)—or, perhaps it would be better to say, like Bancroft and his so-called assistants, who may well have actually authored significant parts of his famous historical studies (Caughey, 1946; Clark, 1973)—come to mind as examples of scholars as craftsmen whose control over the intellectual labor process is reflected in this direct ownership of the primary means of scholarly production (Harrison & Laslett, 1971). Samuel Johnson's observation about turning over an entire library just to make one book (Boswell, 1787/1934) also comes to mind. This observation would not make much sense if—unconsciously projecting backward from our own experience in the early twenty-first century—we were thinking of the British Library, the Bibliothèque Nationale, the Library of Congress, the German national library system (Olson, 1996), or even smaller but still formidable research collections like those housed in court and cathedral libraries all over Europe and the great urban public research libraries of the late nineteenth century United States: they are far too large to make this even thinkable. But in the age of Johnson, one can imagine a much smaller frame of reference, where a few thousand volumes could set the general framework for research. The increase of publication output during and after this period eventually rendered that model of scholarship quaint and obsolete, and ushered in an age of collections so large that they can only be developed and maintained by the largest private fortunes, court societies, regional governments, and powerful nation-states. In this, one can see a clear shift from privately or independently held resources to collections of materials occupying a central place, along with newspapers, magazines, books, and other print resources destined for a growing literate audience of educated readers, in the then-emerging but now declining public sphere (Buschman, 2003; Habermas, 1989; Winter, 2002). The loss was also a gain. Scholarship and librarianship, after a substantial period of relatively close collaboration, began to develop in different, more specialized directions, as the expansionist processes linking them in new ways on a deeper level drove them further and further apart on the surface. This development has some critical consequences. One is the increasing rift between the scholar and her resources (what Marx would call alienation) and the increases of size and organizational complexity in collections that presuppose and demand large-scale coordination, planning, budgetary calculation, forecasting, and bureaucratization (precisely those rationalization processes identified by Max Weber). Weber does not address the issue, but given the closer connection between scholars and librarians in premodern times, presumably the librarian also became estranged from the collection along with the scholar. Another is the emergence of the rationally administered collection providing a kind of public good that forms part of the infrastructure of modern scholarship. Still another is the more or less permanent separation of the role of the scholar from that of the librarian, who becomes a new kind of manager or collection administrator. It would, no doubt, be an oversimplification to suggest that all librarians before the emergence of rational capitalism at the end of Europe's feudal period were themselves scholars, but there is no doubt that until the emergence of modern capitalism at the end of the European Middle Ages, there was often a greater overlap between scholarship and librarianship than there has been at any time since. The splitting of the two branches originally more closely joined on the same parent stem appears as an example of how rationalization processes work along with an increasingly complex division of labor (Franklin, 1993; Winter, 1993, 1996).

ENTER BRAVERMAN: DEGRADATION AND DESKILLING OF WORK IN THE TWENTIETH CENTURY

Almost a century after Marx's death, and a little over a half-century after Weber's, the academically unaffiliated socialist writer and editor Harry Braverman (1920–1976) reexamined the fate of the labor process under a later phase of capitalist development (Braverman, 1974). For Braverman, alienation and rationalization are the broad frameworks that support and reinforce the success of capital in gaining control over work in order to deskill it or, as he puts it in the subtitle of his controversial and influential book, "degrade" it. Deskilling increases administrative control over work, lowers labor costs generally, provides an increased yield in the value extracted from labor, and at the same time displaces workers to lower-skill sectors of the economy, where capital seeks to expand its activities.

Two general themes—difficult to distinguish in practice—emerge. On the one hand there is an interventionist managerial strategy that continuously redefines work by dividing and subdividing the labor process as much as possible. This approach has heavy overtones of paternalism and was and is widely resented by most workers. On the other there is an increased not to say constant reliance on strategic adoption of new technologies, based on a cost-benefit approach to control that redefines the labor process in a less intrusive way (Braverman, 1974, p. 85). This nicely avoids the paternalism issue: "The time and motion study person stands before the worker as a blatant symbol of worker oppression by capital. The machine, however, is a mystified oppressor, often taken to be a neutral artifact of technological society" (Zimbalist, 1979, p. xiii). While Marx, Weber, and other earlier theorists were well aware of the effects of technological innovation in either altering or eliminating certain kinds of work, they only glimpsed the phenomenon in its earlier stages.

Aside from helping to break down the labor process into segments requiring less skill and thus lowering costs, introducing new technologies has one very different kind of consequence perhaps best called *intensification*. Here the impersonality of technological innovation, which helps to conceal the activity of the manager behind a seemingly anonymous process, at the same time masks the widespread extent of the process, as the increasingly rapid introduction of new techniques and equipment place the worker in an environment of perpetual speedup (Larson, 1980, p. 163). While this has a global impact on all work, it also has a special importance for professionalized occupations, where intensification not only decreases the significance and the impact of specialized expertise but also functions as a drag on worker autonomy, the exercise of judgment, independence from external control, and erodes social relationships among coworkers (Larson, 1980, p. 167).

In reality, the breaking down of the labor process and the use of technologies to take the analysis further while masking it are often employed at the same time. As succinctly expressed in an important formulation, "technological innovation functions as the engine of change and capitalist enterprise functions as the engineer" (Day, 1997). One of the earlier attempts at such radical restructuring, called Taylorism after its founder Frederick Winslow Taylor (1856–1915), though often dismissed by contemporary management experts, has nonetheless left an enduring legacy (Larson, 1980, p. 166). Its long shadow in library work can be detected as early as the early twentieth century, when Melvil Dewey grasped and implemented its potential (Day, 1997), and as late as the 1980s, where it made certain inroads into library administration, as can be seen in two highly detailed studies of how much of library work is amenable to Taylorist analysis (Dougherty & Heinritz, 1966, 1982; see also Day, 1997). In these studies, led by Richard Dougherty, a prominent library director, influential library educator, and editor, it is shown that much of the routine work in libraries—with the convenient exception, of course, of administrative and managerial functions—is fragmented and decomposed into the smallest possible operations, eliminating the need for any creativity or judgment in the process.

CONCEPTION, EXECUTION, AND THE DEHUMANIZATITON OF WORK

Capitalism thus breaks down the work process in two ways: administrative restructuring, on the one side, and strategic adoption of new technologies, on the other. While this is customarily justified on the basis of short-range gains in efficiency, it also has a most unfortunate social consequence: it separates conception from execution and relocates the former outside the labor process. In theory, the distinctive feature of human work, for critical social theorists such as Marx, Weber, and Braverman, is the fusion of a guiding conceptual activity, which animates, plans, controls, and finds meaning and a sense of accomplishment, with those executive actions mobilizing energy in order to realize the entertained goal. But this play of opposing forces is not wired into the human organism, and because human work is not reducible to the biological pattern found in many animal species, it is always possible for the more powerful to separate, reorient, and rearrange the phases of the labor process. It is possible, in other words, to separate the conscious or conceptual element from the physical activity:

> Thus in humans, as distinguished from animals, the unity between the motive force of labor and the labor itself is not inviolable. The unity of conception and execution may be dissolved. The conception must still precede and govern execution, but the idea as conceived by one may be executed by another. The driving force of human labor remains consciousness, but the unity between the two may be broken in the individual and reasserted in the group, the workshop, the community, the society as a whole. (Braverman, 1974, p. 51)

Figuratively this distinction can be expressed by analogizing conception to the brain and execution to the rest of the body. Thus: "The production units operate like a hand, watched, corrected, and controlled by a distant brain" (Braverman, 1974, p. 125). The worker's hand is directed by the administrator's brain. This dissociates the labor process from the skills of workers (Braverman, 1974, pp. 113, 118) and allows an administrative monopoly over skill and knowledge to control labor processes. Ironically, the very nature of work in humans, which under different circumstances would lead to the creative development of the worker, leads instead to the dehumanization of work and the subjection of the labor process to the control of administrative forces.

CLERICAL AND OFFICE WORK: ANALOGUES TO WORK IN LIBRARIES

The deskilling and degrading that accompany the separation of conception from execution do not, according to Braverman, stop with work in which energy is transformed into durable goods, the typical focus of nineteenth-century thinkers. Such deskilling and degrading extend as well to office work and into other kinds of intellectual labor, including professional activity. Initially they can be found in any kind of activity generating enough of a profit margin to offer a return on a capital investment, but they are also found in nonprofit enterprises, which tend in market economies to follow the lead of profit-based firms. (Just how far they extend in this direction, and just what kind of effect they have, are however open questions, depending on the scale of the activity and the potentiality for the increase of rationalized profit and control.) One reason why deskilling extends beyond production work is that certain types of work almost invite it. Clerical tasks, at least until about the early 1970s, were mostly conducted on paper, and "paper is far easier than industrial products to rearrange, move from station to station, combine and recombine according to the needs of the process" (Braverman, 1974, p. 315). While Braverman appeared on the scene and died too early to see the importance of the computerization of office communication, his basic point is presumably only more applicable than ever in the age of the networked or virtual office.

THE DIVISION OF LABOR IN LIBRARIES

A troubling question raised by Braverman's extension of labor process analysis to clerical and office work is how far the deskilling and degrading of work can be taken in those occupations where the work is largely intellectual and calls for the exercise of expert judgment—that is to say, in those cases where the occupation is organized along professional lines. Like clerical and office work, professional labor processes do not always and inevitably produce goods for distribution. But unlike clerical work, entry into professional work typically requires documented evidence of appropriate academic preparation in a college or university, and advanced postgraduate study in the professional specialty. In examining the uses of labor process theory to understand professional work, these factors must be taken into account. Do these aspects of professional work enable the worker to resist the encroachments of external control? With their invitingly open and well-lit reading and study spaces, their often rich and diverse collections, their expensive ICTs, and their democratic philosophies of service, libraries may appear to be oases of utopian enlightenment relieving vast arid expanses of materialism. And perhaps they are, when looked at in a certain way. At the same time they show, in their division of labor into administrative, professional, support, and clerical work routines—with conception concentrated largely in the first two levels, and various forms of execution in the last two—many of the patterns that Braverman describes in his analysis of contemporary production and office work. Of course this is much truer of larger libraries and libraries embedded in large complex organizations, but at the same time it should be borne in mind that smaller libraries increasingly seek economies of scale through affiliation with larger networks and resource-sharing consortia. When we look at these networks, the patterns are not much different from the larger research collections; the small unaffiliated library, while not precisely extinct, increasingly resembles, in the modern information landscape, a relic of a former age, like the independent corner grocery. The basic distinction between conception and execution is seen at two levels: first in the differentiation and task division between the librarian and the library assistant, and second in the differentiation between the administrative and the professional levels. Indeed, a considerable part of the intellectual nature of the librarian's work, insofar as this work is clearly professional in nature, comes from the fact that contemporary librarians, even though largely removed from and in this way estranged from the actual work routines of scholarly inquiry, have successfully defined the labor process mostly in terms of the purely conceptual side, leaving the physical side to other groups of workers, most notably library assistants, clerical support workers, and, in the larger university research libraries, to student workers. Thus professional work in libraries, like selection, reference, instruction, and original cataloging—as opposed to paraprofessional jobs like bibliographic searching, collection maintenance, or copy cataloging—though quite different from each other on a technical level, all involve autonomous decision making rather than carrying out decisions that someone else makes. This distinction parallels similar distinctions between teachers and teachers' assistants, nurses and nursing assistants, lawyers and paralegals, physicians and physicians' assistants, and so forth. At the same time there has been a significant growth in the administrative ranks of libraries, and here the distinction between conception and execution is a different matter altogether. Since the 1960s library directors have been joined by deputy directors and, beginning in the 1970s and the 1980s, by assistant directors specialized by function (public services, technical services, collections, specializations based on broad and loosely defined subject, language, or geographical collecting areas, building operations and equipment, and human relations), who have largely taken over the process of planning, budgeting, fiscal management, the most general conceptual aspects of articulating the institutional mission, coordinating the library with other significant nonlibrary agencies, and keeping up with developments on the national and international library scenes. As these functions become more exclusively associated with administrative work, librarians find them remote from their own routines. At the same time librarians appear to gain a stronger hold on more purely professional as opposed to paraprofessional tasks. Between administrators and professionals there is in larger libraries a group of middle managers, who are much closer to professional workers than to administrators, and who perform the functions of supervision, performance evaluation, coordination of the delivery of services, outreach planning, and a variety of communicative tasks. Among the more important of these is carrying messages from administrative circles to professionals, paraprofessionals, or clerical workers. While not directly involved in the higher levels of administrative policy making, managers frequently play an advisory role that is combined with representing the views of other workers to senior administrators.

LIBRARIANSHIP AND THE RATIONALIZATION OF PROFESSIONAL WORK: LIBRARIANS AND THE RISE OF NEW WORKING CLASS

Like Marx and other nineteenth-century theorists, Braverman and the first wave of labor process theorists showed a natural paradigmatic interest in production workers. But unlike these earlier writers they had also to account for the vast pools of proletarianized office workers that swelled the ranks of labor in market societies. Nonetheless, the proletarianization trend is clearer in marginally skilled office work than in professionalized or professionalizing occupations. Some major issues are profitability, scale, and the other economic interests of capitalist accumulation. These are, perhaps, the major fault lines: where potential profit margins are low, there must be economies of considerable scale. Medicine, engineering, architecture, and law all offer relatively high profit margins and largeness of scale.

For much of its history, librarianship showed a minimal potential for capital accumulation; its economic significance was mainly limited to print publishing. But in more recent times, with the advent of computerized database searching and the mass digitization of scientific periodical literature, and librarianship's growing affinity with information science and other quantitative approaches to the control of knowledge records, libraries and librarians have clearly become gateways to extraordinary opportunities for corporate profit, as is clearly demonstrated by the runaway inflation patterns of the last 30 years and the ubiquitous presence of global publishing conglomerates (Springer, Reed-Elsevier, Bertelsmann) on the conference circuit. A different example of the phenomenon of increasing corporate control over information work can be found of course in teaching, because of the strategic investment importance of the textbook and the immense mass market for textbook sales (Apple, 1986). Aside from these considerations, there is also the apparent indivisibility of the labor process in professional work. Braverman argued as we have seen that one of the preconditions of deskilled work is the separation of conception from execution. But sometimes conception and execution cannot be easily separated, and these forms of work cannot be as easily degraded or deskilled for that reason. From a different angle, it has been suggested that in professional work the limit on outside control of the work process is provided by types of work where the work process is itself identical with the outcome (Stehr, 1994, p. 184). For example, in helping a patron find literature on a topic, a reference librarian may conceive of and design a strategy of retrieval and present that very conception to the user. In this case, the conception is the execution. What both of these cases have in common is that the work is relatively seamless and thus resists the kind of analysis that is required in order to assign different phases of the work process to different groups of workers. And of course professionalized work in addition to these factors enjoys the so-called labor market shelter (Larson, 1980, pp. 143, 151) created by university-based specialized training.

But this does not mean that professional work is impervious to the force of rationalization, though it does say that it is more difficult to definitively deskill or degrade than other forms of labor. Only a little work on librarianship sheds light on this question, but what is available is quite interesting. In a study of librarianship as a female-intensive occupation, Roma Harris (1992), for example, argues that bibliography and bibliographic control, broadly conceived and properly supplemented with other kinds of authenticated expertise, provide solid foundation material for professional practice. Yet she also observes that in fact much of this expertise has been systematically eroded.

Once clear of the obligations of their professional education, many librarians find themselves deskilled in practice and, instead of applying their hard-won expertise, continually test-marketing the latest products and services of corporate information providers (Crosby, 1993; Estabrook, 1981).

BRINGING (BOTH) GENDER(S) IN: RATIONALIZATION, INTENSIFICATION, AND THE DISTRIBUTION OF CULTURE

So much has been written about gender in librarianship that it may seem that there could not possibly be anything left to say. This is perhaps one reason why looking at parallels in neighboring occupations can be instructive. For example, some writers on education have argued that teaching is being definitively altered in ways that strongly resemble the process of rationalization outlined here, "because of the encroachment of technical control procedures into the curriculum" (Apple, 1986, p. 32; Connell, Ashenden, Kessler, & Dowsett, 1985). More specifically it is argued that "The integration . . . of management systems, reductive behaviorally-based curricula, pre-specified teaching 'competencies' and procedures . . . was leading to a loss of control and a separation of conception from execution" (Apple, 1986, p. 32). Here we can recognize both the Weberian interest in rationalization and the more Marxian focus on alienation in the form of rationally planned deskilling and degradation. Like librarianship, teaching is female-intensive, and so the attempt to understand the political economy of work in these areas requires special reference to gender. This is not because gender is irrelevant to male-intensive work—as we will soon see, quite the opposite, in fact, is true, since gender-based stratification of necessity involves both groups—but because this deskilling, proletarianizing, or, in broader terms, alienating and rationalizing process, is more characteristic of female-intensive occupations like teaching, social work, nursing, and librarianship than it is of male strongholds like financial analysis, surgery, engineering, or corporate law. Yet no one would suggest that technology, particularly high technology, is somehow less relevant to the pursuits of these very lucrative, highly-paying male specialties than it is in more traditionally female occupations. This is one very important reason why it is unacceptable to attribute major changes in labor processes to technology alone, as if machines were capable by themselves of shaping or forming the complex social relations that characterize work in contemporary societies. If this were the case, then presumably all occupations would be similarly affected. Gender is one of the major reasons why this is not always so. But if technology by itself provides no skeleton key, specific technologies do nonetheless mesh with the underlying gender order in specific ways, and these relationships provide clues for understanding the intersection between work and gender. For example, theorizing changes in the gender order is necessary to fully understand the gradual obsolescence of the traditional personalistic, paternalistic domination that once prevailed in many organizations—schools, libraries, social service agencies, and offices are some of the more obvious examples—and the newer, more impersonal, rationalized forms of technical control that come in with advances in computerization. These newer forms of control partly replace the overtly sexist character of traditional types of control (Apple, 1986, p. 39), recalling the way in which computerization provides a more socially-acceptable alternative to the indignities of the close supervision and relentless analysis of the labor process found in Taylorism. Because the gender order already reflects a strong link between hegemonic masculinity and the forms of technical reason found in modern societies, computerization and many other types of automation also multiply existing gender-based inequalities, reinforcing a work atmosphere more favorable to the advancement of men than women (Dilevko & Harris, 1997; Winter & Robert, 1980). Here we can see a clear example of intensification, that aspect of rationalization found particularly in the more knowledge-based form of work that trades on the fact that the outcome of the labor process is relatively open and intangible and can thus be more or less indefinitely expanded (Connell et al., 1985, pp. 70–71). This expandable horizon of knowledge work is not confined to women's work but affects law, medicine, and perhaps a wide range of consulting occupations. It is acutely present in university teaching and research. At the same time, this form of exploitation seems to have a special form in teaching, where it means greater dependence on pre-established, administratively screened, and approved goals and objectives in work. The relation between intensification and deskilling is clearly complex, and so it is important to note that intensification may in fact be accompanied by an actual reskilling process, as the worker acquires a broader range of skills, yet is prevented from mastering any of them because of increased pressure from above (Apple, 1986, pp. 42–43). Thus deskilling and reskilling—perhaps contrary to Braverman and the earlier wave of labor process writers, who seem to view deskilling as an irreversible loss—are not necessarily contradictory (Harris, Hannah, & Harris, 1998, p. 113). When accompanied by intensification, some of the loss of control actually comes from an attempt to master too many complex routines. Most important, intensification tends to reduce quality, thus overall devaluing the service rendered and reducing the occupational group's ability to compete on the labor market and maintain a high profile among users. These aspects of intensified work are familiar to most librarians. Thus for many professionalized workers, including librarians, intensification, rather than deskilling or degradation, is the actual outcome of the alienation and rationalization of the labor process. Teachers and librarians share yet another very important overlap in their work, and that is in their relation to texts and other types of intellectual products and services. Apple (1986, p. 86) focuses on teachers in relation to classroom texts, and since many libraries don't collect these materials, this overlap and analogy provides some significant parallels rather than direct insights. In particular, book publishing shows a highly gender-typed division of labor. Even though females outnumber males, the decision-making process in publishing is largely male dominated. Since this tends to be generally true in publishing, librarianship is roughly parallel to teaching in at least this respect: both the librarian and the teacher work with cultural commodities that are produced by male-dominated groups. Surprisingly, despite considerable attention to gender and its importance not only in work, but to everything else in the social world, virtually all the emphasis on gender has fallen on women. Yet it is clear that in the long run, rationalization processes in modern societies strongly support and reinforce clearly dominant forms of masculinity (Connell, 1995, pp. 172–173; 2005; Dilevko & Harris, 1997; Harris, 1992, pp. 142–143; Winter & Robert, 1980). Thus Vicki Smith's (1994, p. 409) observation that not only Braverman's initial formulation of the labor process concept but a number of other important subsequent contributions virtually ignored gender, except where the discussions touched on the obvious feminization of clerical and office work, is very much to the point. It took a later group of writers to show how the gender order inherently rather than accidentally shapes managerial attempts to control the labor process (Smith, 1994, p. 410). Of special interest are those who have broadened the discussion beyond female gender typing in work and have focused specifically on masculinity and its significance in the rationalization of work (Collinson, 1992, and others writers cited by Smith, 1994, p. 411).

LIBRARIANS AS INTELLECTUALS: THE KNOWLEDGE WORKERS

The use of the word *intellectual* always creates difficulties, perhaps since the term is so commonly used with both positive and negative slants, sometimes even in the same breath. One the one hand, intellectuals are exalted beings and cultural elites who deal in complex specialized ideas that the average person cannot understand; on the other, they are seen as people ill-suited for action. A greater barrier, however, is the persistent mythical and ideologically charged notion of the intellectual as an isolated individual figure—a person (or, to speak more precisely, a male person), as the Australian sociologist R. W. Connell suggests, who dresses in tweed and expensive leather, drops into an armchair, sends up clouds of smoke, thinking only the deepest of thoughts (Connell, 1983, p. 245). The reality, however, is that most intellectual workers—librarians, archives managers, museum curators, documentation specialists, teachers, journalists, and others making substantial use of research and writing skills in their jobs—are found in much humbler, bureaucratically organized work settings. Since I am following Connell here and using the term in a sociological sense (for a sense of the many other uses, not to mention some entertaining polemics, see Collini, 2006, pp. 46, 156–157), some clarification is in order to dispel some of this mystique. Intellectuals, viewed sociologically, are usually workers possessing certification of intellectual skill and expertise, and their work shows a rationally managed, "planned subdivided labour process" (Connell, 1983, p. 235). Contemporary intellectual work is thus rooted in the highly rationalized intellectual bureaucracies that provide the certification—schools, universities, and institutes—and specialized openness to problem solving based on learned expertise and exposure to academic cultures of inquiry. First seen in industrial work, where a so-called new working class of specialized scientists, engineers, and other technical specialists has emerged (Mallet, 1975), this development later spread outside that original context, eventually enveloping librarianship, information science, archives management, teaching, perhaps journalism, and a number of other occupations that are centered on knowledge and its distribution or application (Connell, 1983, p. 237). In economic terms, these workers are generally neither primary producers nor consumers of intellectual products but act as proxies between those two poles. They handle, treat, distribute, sometimes create, or otherwise process cultural records and frequently make claims to add value along the way. In an essay on the proletarianization of the educated worker in capitalist societies, Larson (1980, p. 140) points out that Braverman's 1974 book influenced writers associated with the new working class thesis who had appeared initially in the revolutionary unrest in France of the 1960s (Mallet, 1975). Despite the obvious surface differences, she points to a major convergence between productive labor, clerical work, and professional work: all three are increasingly sited largely in modern, private, or state-managed complex bureaucratic organizations and thus are subjected to much the same forces of alienation and rationalization. The only factor clearly differentiating them is that the work of the highly educated comes equipped with its own ideology of "free professionalism" (Larson, 1980, p. 140), an Anglo-Saxon concept closely related to the German *freie Berufe*. The labor process of the educated worker reflects a division of labor continually subdivided, a delegation of routine or menial tasks to newer groups of lower-level workers, a lateral multiplication of specialties, and the ubiquitous specter of intensification. "Intensification," Larson wrote, "represents one of the most tangible ways in which the work privileges of educated workers are eroded" (1980, pp. 166–167). A broader social context of knowledge work can be supplied by looking to something like Seymour Martin Lipset's definition of intellectuals as those who "create, distribute, and apply *culture*, that is, the symbolic world . . . including art, science, and religion" (Lipset, 1981, p. 333, italics his). In this three-part classification, Lipset goes on to say, there are two groups at the core. The first of these contains "creators," such as scholars, artists, philosophers, authors, some editors, and some journalists (Lipset, 1981, p. 333; see also Kadushin, 1975). In the second of the core groups are "distributors," including "performers in the various arts, most teachers, and most reporters" (Lipset, 1981, p. 333). (Like the true adopted son of the upper bourgeoisie that he became,

Lipset, originally of much humbler origins, ignores the less typically female-intensive and less visible occupations like librarianship, but it seems obvious that they belong here.)

SUMMARY AND CONCLUSIONS: LIBRARIES, INTELLECTUAL WORK, AND THE RISE OF CONSUMERIZED MODERNITY

Among the more notable socioeconomic changes occurring in the twentieth century is the initially gradual and then much more rapid shift from primary extractive and productive industries toward services. The rise of the service sector is particularly striking and inspired the work of Daniel Bell (1973/1999). Somewhat more narrowly, but just as important, and closer to the present concern with work in libraries, others focused on the rise of knowledge and information industries, and the service economies accompanying them (e.g., Machlup, 1962). Both of these broad strains in the study of postwar capitalism exercised a strong influence on the work of a generation of library and information science scholars (e.g., Wilson, 1983). What has not had nearly as much influence on library and information science thinking, however, and which therefore needs to be addressed, is the rise and steady expansion of a consumer society in the post–World War II period, particularly since the 1960s. While the consumption of goods and services has long had a varying economic impact, a qualitative change in modernity occurs in the mid- and late-twentieth century, as consumption becomes, in the expression of French sociologist Jean Baudrillard, an entire way of life in which not only vast quantities of products and services are created, but as much or even more energy is focused on the creation and maintenance of the consumer demand needed to sustain this way of life (Baudrillard, 2001, p. 41). "We have reached the point," he argued prophetically in 1970, "where 'consumption' has grasped the whole of life" (Baudrillard, 2001, p. 36). We can actually see the beginnings of an awareness of the coming of a kind of consumerized capitalist modernity as far back as Max Weber's fragmentary theory of social class in late nineteenth-century industrial Europe, in his recognition of the continuing importance of social standing or prestige in human societies and the form this takes in modernity. The concept of social class developed by Marx and Engels strongly emphasized one's relation to the means of production. From a perspective of a later generation, and with the benefit of an extremely rapid period of industrialization in late nineteenth-century German society, Weber noted what previous writers would not have been able to see: the growth of a variety of different kinds of capitalist markets offering new opportunities, for those positioned to take advantage of them, in the "possession of goods and opportunities for income" (Weber, 1946, p. 181). Marx and Engels tended to downplay the importance of prestige, regarding social standing largely as a monetized commodity or as rapidly on the way to becoming one. Weber, on the other hand, rightly understood that however true this might be in the long run, the relation between class and standing was more complex, and the latter could not be reduced to the former. Thus he argued that alongside and interwoven with market relations were persistent communities based on shared notions of honor—positive and negative (Weber, 1946, p. 186). Precisely this combination of market factors and status communities provided a critical step in understanding the evolution of consumerized modernity in the late twentieth and early twenty-first centuries. In capitalist societies, the effect of this fusion is to redefine consumption radically: from a process largely focused on use and exchange, in later capitalist modernity consumer goods and services acquire a luminous glow of signification, as they take on the role of acting as signs or markers of success in status competition in market societies (Baudrillard, 1969, 2001, p. 49). Or, as a contemporary American economic historian puts it, "symbolism, as much as function, determines choices" (Schor, 1998, pp. 33–34). (In fact, Baudrillard, 2000, pp. 57–60, makes a distinction between the symbol as carrier of meaning and the sign as marker of social position, but we must bypass this for the present discussion.)

We have discussed how work in libraries has undergone various shifts in response to technological innovation, changes in managerial style, and the pressures of intensification typical in an inherently dynamic and expanding market system. These familiar aspects of the landscape of capitalist modernity are thus now joined by a different kind of pressure altogether, as library workers and libraries find themselves locked in a struggle to compete with one another and with other significant players in the dissemination and distribution of culture and information. Within libraries, status difference markers signify the major groups: administrators (segregated points of entry to the workplace, private office spaces, separate bathrooms, expensive furniture, art objects or—to draw on the mystique of a French signifier, objets d'art), professionals (cubicles for offices, sometimes referred to as veal pens or cube farms, cheap furniture with a patented bargain barn appearance, etc.), and support workers (desks arranged in large, open, brightly lit spaces facilitating a constant supervisory surveillance) and various elaborate forms of behavioral control (Kelley, 1990). On the outside, the major players are much more affluent commercial information providers and conglomerate media cultural content distributors. But just as critical to library work today, if not more so, is the highly status-conscious and rapidly expanding sphere of retail trade, where lifestyle-oriented designer signs and brands have usurped the more prosaic functions of utility, and of buying and selling. Thus while the latest database acquisition does indeed show a logic of use, and is subject to the market forces of the logic of exchange, it also has a powerful sign value, or a logic of signification (Baudrillard, 2000), since it signifies the social location and social standing of the institution in an increasingly market-dominated world. A recent issue of a leading library trade journal spotlighting promising professional talent puts this quite clearly: "A devoted shopper, Jennifer Duvernay loves Nordstrom because of its outstanding customer service. As science reference librarian at Arizona State University (ASU), she wants to make the information shopping experience just as satisfying" (Duvernay, 2005).

As the society around them has changed from a predominantly production and service environment into a landscape fringed with an endless horizon of beckoning consumable signifiers, and individuals struggle to acquire, possess, and, above all, *display* more and more goods and services as signs of their social standing, libraries have experienced an institutionalized version of similar pressures. Where individuals in consumerized modernity increasingly spend much of their time either working to achieve the means to acquire consumer goods, and expending large amounts of the socially necessary labor required to evaluate the great number and wide range of products, libraries and other information-intensive workplaces increasingly spend more and more of their own energies keeping up with the output of the ICT industries. Because libraries and other information providers play the role of proxies for end users, their expert workers are called on to perform two relatively new functions: first, to provide the evaluation and analysis required by administrative groups; second, to elicit and coordinate the responses of end users via surveys, focus groups, and usability studies. Much of this is driven by interinstitutional competition to endlessly acquire, abandon, and reacquire the latest information and communication technologies, and it reflects the specter of late twentieth- and early twenty-first-century advanced industrial civilization referred to by British sociologist Anthony Giddens (1990) as the "juggernaut of modernity"(p. 139; see also Kellner, 2006). Initially the emphasis fell on office automation, bibliographic databases, and the eventual integration of these databases into larger networks. But more recently the focus has expanded to include networked digitized text collections of many different kinds (periodicals, reference works, sound files, visual images, maps, and many more), and even more recently the ICTs of social networking, collaboration, gaming, and simulation. Given the constant expansion in these industries, it is not surprising to find that not only the labor processes but also the essential task domains of work in libraries has shifted to meet this need for a new type of socially necessary labor. Here we can see that the distinction between administrative conception and expert execution is itself rooted in a larger dynamic involving the harnessing of expert, uncompensated labor in the ICT field. Many of the past roles in services played by librarians will, Harris (1992) noted, be done in the future by paraprofessionals and clerical workers (for a review of the relevant literature see Harris, 1992, pp. 126–128, 134, 142). Much of what we see in their place, increasingly, are these newer roles of product tester, as libraries work to keep current with an ever-spiraling output of products and services. These ICT proxy consumers thus assume a role in the dissemination of information that professional testers have already performed for some time in the beverage, food, clothing, cosmetics, motor vehicle, toy, and entertainment industries. However, since the products in question are highly specialized, a tester with an appropriate level of specialized expertise is required. Thus ICT companies today regularly employ significant numbers of workers trained as librarians and information specialists, with previous experience working in libraries, to design and market their products; these workers, of course, are also key players in the recruitment of the socially necessary labor of testing that can only be found in the organizations inhabiting the target market. (The present writer kept an informal record of this activity covering a recent three-month period. In that time he received 10 solicitations, all referred by library administrators as assignments to librarians, to examine and evaluate on a trial basis more than 16 packages of full text resources from five different companies. Extrapolating and annualizing these informally gathered data would produce 40 solicitations, 64 packages, and 20 companies! If Harris and others are correct in their observations that many core areas of practice have been shifted to paraprofessional workers, it isn't that difficult to understand why.) This change is fundamental and constitutes not only transformation of the labor process but also a new level of intensification. It is also largely unrecognized. If library users are increasingly defined as consumers in the expanded sense of that term used here, so also are the librarians who serve them.

REFERENCES

Apple, M. W. (1986). *Teachers and texts: A political economy of class and gender relations in education*. New York: Routledge & Kegan Paul.

Baudrillard, J. (1969). La morale des objets: fonction-signe et logique de classe [The morality of objects: Function-signs and the logic of class]. *Communications, 13,* 23–50.

Baudrillard, J. (2000). The ideological genesis of needs. In J. Schor and D. Holt (Eds.), *The consumer society reader* (pp. 57–80). New York: The New Press. (Originally published in J. Baudrillard, *Pour une economie politique du signe*. Paris: Gallimard, 1972. Eng. Trans. and intro. by Charles Levin, *For a political economy of the sign*. St. Louis MO: Telos Press, 1979.)

Baudrillard, J. (2001). *Selected writings*. (2nd ed., revised and expanded). Stanford, CA: Stanford University Press.

Bell, D. (1999). *The coming of post-industrial society: A venture in social forecasting* (special anniversary ed.). New York: Basic Books. (Originally published 1973).

Boswell, J. (1934). *Boswell's life of Johnson*. Oxford: Clarendon Press. (Originally published 1787).

Braverman, H. (1974). *Labor and monopoly capital: The degradation of work in the twentieth century*. New York: Monthly Review Press.

Brubaker, R. (1984). *The limits of rationality: An essay on the social and moral thought of Max Weber*. London: Allen & Unwin.

Brubaker, R. (2003). Rationalization. In W. Outhwaite (Ed.), *Blackwell dictionary of modern social thought* (pp. 557–558, 2nd ed.). Malden, MA: Blackwell Publishers.

Buschman, J. (2003). *Dismantling the public sphere: Situating and sustaining librarianship in the age of the new public philosophy.* Westport, CT: Libraries Unlimited, 2003.

Caughey, J. W. (1946). *Hubert Howe Bancroft, historian of the west.* Berkeley: University of California Press.

Clark, H. (1973). *A venture in history: The production, publication, and sale of the works of Hubert Howe Bancroft.* Berkeley: University of California Press.

Collini, S. (2006). *Absent minds: Intellectuals in Britain.* Oxford: Oxford University Press.

Collinson, D. (1992). *Managing the shopfloor: Subjectivity, masculinity, and workplace culture.* Berlin: Walter de Gruyter.

Connell, R. W. (1983). Intellectuals and intellectual work. In *Which way is up?: Essays on sex, class, and culture* (pp. 231–254). Sydney, Australia: Allen & Unwin.

Connell, R. W. (1995). *Masculinities.* Berkeley: University of California Press.

Connell, R. W. (2005). *Masculinities.* 2nd edition. Berkeley: University of California Press.

Connell, R. W., Ashenden, D. J., Kessler, S., & Dowsett, G. W. (1985). *Teachers' work.* Sydney, Australia: Allen & Unwin.

Crosby, E. (1993). [Review of the book *Librarianship: The erosion of a woman's profession*]. *RQ, 33*(1), 147.

Day, M. T. (1997, April 13). *Challenges to the professional control of knowledge work in academic libraries: A proposed agenda for organizational research and action.* Paper presented at 8th National Conference of the Association for College and Research Libraries. Nashville, TN. Retrieved January 4, 2008, from http://www.ala.org/ala/acrlbucket/nashville1997pap/day.cfm.

Dilevko, J., & Harris, R. (1997). Information technology and social relations: Portrayals of gender roles in high tech product advertisements. *Journal of the American Society for Information Science, 48*(8), 718–727.

Dougherty, R. M., & Heinritz, F. (1966). *Scientific management of library operations.* Metuchen, NJ: Scarecrow Press.

Dougherty, R. M., & Heinritz, F. (1982). *Scientific management of library operations* (2nd. ed.). Metuchen, NJ: Scarecrow Press.

Duvernay, J. (2005, March 15). A Nordstrom experience. *Library Journal* (Supp.), 7.

Estabrook, L. (1981). Productivity, profit, and libraries. *Library Journal, 106*(13), 1377–1380.

Franklin, P. (1993). Scholars, librarians, and the future of primary records. *College and Research Libraries, 54*(4), 397–406.

Giddens, A. (1990). *The consequences of modernity.* Stanford, CA: Stanford University Press

Habermas, J. (1989). *The structural transformation of the public sphere: An inquiry into a category of bourgeois society* (T. Burger & F. Lawrence, Trans.). Cambridge, MA: MIT Press. (Originally published in 1962.)

Harris, R. (1992). *Libarianship: The erosion of a woman's profession.* Norwood, NJ: Ablex.

Harris, M. H., Hannah, S. A., & Harris, P. C. (1998). *Into the future: The foundations of library and information services in the post-industrial era.* Norwood, NJ: Ablex.

Harrison, J., & Laslett, P. (1971). *The library of John Locke* (2nd ed.). Oxford: Clarendon Press.

Kadushin, C. (1975). *The American intellectual elite.* Boston: Little, Brown.
Kelley, R. (1990, May 20). The library sweatshop: A view from the bottom. *Los Angeles Times Book Review,* p. 15.
Kellner, D. (2006). New technologies and alienation. In *The Evolution of alienation: trauma, promise, and the millennium* (pp. 47–67). Lanham, MD: Rowman & Littlefield.
Larson, M. S. (1980). Proletarianization and educated labor. *Theory and Society, 9*(1), 131–175.
Lipset, S. M. (1981). *Political man* (2nd ed.). Baltimore, MD: Johns Hopkins University Press.
Machlup, F. (1962). *The production and distribution of knowledge in the United States.* Princeton, NJ: Princeton University Press.
Mallet, S. (1975). *Essays on the new working class.* (D. Howard & D. Savage, Trans. & Ed.). St. Louis: Telos Press.
Marx, K. (1936). *Capital: A critique of political economy. Vol. 1. The process of capitalist production* (Translated from the 3rd German ed. by S. Moore & E. Aveling, and edited by F. Engels. Revised and amplified according to the 4th German ed. by E. Untermann). New York: The Modern Library. (Original published in 1901).
Olson, M. (1996). *The odyssey of a German national library: A short history of the Bayerische Staatsbibliothek, the Staatsbibliothek zu Berlin, the Deutsche Bücherei, and the Deutsche Bibliothek.* Wiesbaden, Germany: Harrassowitz.
Schor, J. (1998). *The overspent American: Upscaling, downshifting, and the new consumer.* New York: Basic Books.
Smith, V. (1994). Braverman's legacy: The labor process tradition at 20. *Work and Occupations, 21*(4), 403–421.
Stehr, N. (1994). *Knowledge societies.* London: Sage.
Waters, M. (1994). *Modern sociological theory.* London: Sage.
Weber, M. (1930). *The Protestant ethic and the spirit of capitalism* (T. Parsons, Trans.). With a foreword by R. H. Tawney. New York: Charles Scribners' Sons.
Weber, M. (1946). *From Max Weber: Essays in sociology* (H. H. Gerth & C. W. Mills, Trans. and Ed.). New York: Oxford University Press.
Weber, M. (2001). *The Protestant ethic and the spirit of capitalism* (Stephen Kalberg, Trans.). Chicago: Fitzroy Dearborn.
Wilson, P. (1983). Bibliographical r&d. In F. Machlup & U. Mansfield (Eds.), *The study of information: Interdisciplinary messages* (pp. 289–397) New York: Wiley.
Winter, M. F. (1993). Librarianship, technology, and the labor process. In J. Buschman (Ed.) *Critical approaches to information technology in librarianship: Foundations and applications* (pp. 173–195). Westport CT: Greenwood Press.
Winter, M. F. (1996). Specialization, territoriality, and jurisdiction: Librarianship and the political economy of knowledge. *Library Trends, 45*(2), 343–363.
Winter, M. F. (1998, August 22). *In the silicon cage: Scholarship, the electronic library, and the intellectual commons.* Presentation for Libraries in the Electronic Society: Dinosaurs or Gateways to Cyberspace? American Sociological Association Annual Meeting. San Francisco, CA.
Winter, M. F. (2002, October 11). *Bibliotheken und die wandel der öffentlichkeit: aufstieg der individualiserte bibliothek.* [*Libraries and the change in the public sphere: The rise of the individualized library*]. Presentation for the Social Role of

Libraries, International Center for Information and Content Management at the Frankfurt Book Fair. Frankfurt, Germany. Retrieved from http://libdev2.ucdavis.edu/prodev/mfw/Bibliotheken.ppt.

Winter, M. F., & Robert, E. R. (1980). Male dominance, late capitalism, and the growth of instrumental reason. *Berkeley Journal of Sociology, 24/25*, 249–280.

Zimbalist, A. (Ed.) (1979). *Case studies on the labor process.* New York: Monthly Review Press.

8

"THEIR LITTLE BIT OF GROUND SLOWLY SQUASHED INTO NOTHING": TECHNOLOGY, GENDER, AND THE VANISHING LIBRARIAN

Roma Harris

There is little doubt that new(er) information and communications technologies (ICTs) have had a profound impact on libraries and library services. At the same time, however, these ICTs have vastly increased the prominence of information as an important commodity and the significance of the information services sector in the economy. In view of the heightened importance now attached to the term *information*, public uncertainty about the value of librarians' work seems ironic given that librarianship is *the* original information profession.

In a recent study, my colleagues and I surveyed visitors to a British public library about how they used the library to search for health information (Harris, Henwood, Burdett, & Marshall, 2007). We found that while many patrons have a high level of trust in the library as in institution, some were uncertain about what to expect from the staff, in part because of the changing positioning of technology in the library's service. As one woman said of the librarians, "I think they're quite depressed, really. . . . I feel they've lost their role and maybe they feel that they're not needed because there's so many other things going on in the library, like the computers, the videos downstairs, the DVDs" (Harris et al., 2007). What should we make of her comment? Do librarians have reason to be depressed and have they really lost their role to technology? In this chapter I try to make sense of the sometimes paradoxical relations between technology, gender, and work to understand why librarians seem to have gone missing among those who populate the rich occupational turf afforded by the information sector.

THE DISAPPEARING LIBRARIAN

Librarians and the profession of librarianship suffer from a lack of visibility in the new information world, and what visibility they do have is often positioned in troubling juxtaposition to technology. In policy documents about the repositioning of libraries in relation to these technologies, librarians and the tasks they perform are often overlooked or absent. For example, the Alberta Library, a consortium of libraries in Canada, aims to provide, with the aid of ICTs, "universal, barrier-free access for all Albertans to the information and ideas through Alberta's diverse libraries" (The Alberta Library, 2007). This is laudable goal, but, in the promotional material for the project, the librarians whose work will produce these desirable effects are not mentioned. Similarly, a report on the state of public libraries in the United Kingdom has a lot to say about technology but is largely silent about the role of library staff (House of Commons, Culture, Media and Sport Committee, 2005). The report's authors argue that "the explosion of relevant new technologies has to be embraced by [public libraries] but this should be done in the context of their key function to gather, order, present and disseminate, challenging, as well as relevant, material and information for their community" (p. 18). Again, however, little mention is made of the librarians who will presumably do the gathering, ordering, presentation, and dissemination of these materials, other than when they are chided for their inadequacies. According to the authors of the U.K. report, "library leaders of the future need skills, including management skills, beyond those that come with a professional librarianship qualification" (p. 45), and they suggest looking outside the library profession for expertise in areas such as "book procurement" (p. 34), a recommendation that is a rather astonishing example of taking coals to Newcastle. Surely librarians lead the way among sophisticated procurement agents? One need only consider the success of academic library consortia in managing relationships with publishers through initiatives such as the Ontario Library Consortium, a cooperative of libraries formed in the mid-1980s to collectively purchase computer products and services; or the Ontario Council of University Libraries' widely touted Scholar's Portal, a cooperative project that enables researchers, through a single search interface, to connect with and retrieve items from a vast range of resources including more than 8,000,000 articles and a rapid access document retrieval system that is connected to libraries around the world (Ontario Council of University Libraries, 2005); or the remarkable history of the world's largest library consortium, the Online Computer Library Center (OCLC) "a non-profit, membership, computer library service and research organization" through which "more than 57,000 libraries in 112 countries and territories around the world" are able to "locate, acquire, catalog, lend and preserve library materials" (Online Computer Library Center, 2008).

Academic libraries have been particularly successful in reconstituting themselves in the face of profound technological change by refocusing their collecting activities to provide users with access to a myriad of (often leased) electronic resources (along with maintaining print materials and special collections) and by intensifying their user education programs, especially those directed at students, to improve users' information search skills and assist them in becoming more critical consumers of information. The librarians who work in and lead academic libraries have been central to these institutions' processes of renewal and adaptation, and they remain key service providers in university environments. In fact, their success has been lauded by two nonlibrarians who write, "the real heroes of the digital revolution in higher education are librarians: they are the people who have seen the farthest, done the most, accepted the hardest challenges, and demonstrated most clearly the benefits of digital information. In the process, they have turned their own field upside down and have revolutionized their own professional training" (Ayers & Grisham, 2003, p. 43). According to Ayers and Grisham, "*It is a testimony to [librarians'] success that we take their achievement for granted*" (p. 43, emphasis mine), but is it? I wonder if the lack of awareness of academic librarians' contributions to the digitized world of information has less to do with taking their successes for granted than with a more insidious lack of respect for librarians' skills that renders their achievements either invisible or attributes them to workers in other occupations.

SOCIAL RELATIONS OF GENDER, TECHNOLOGY, AND WORK

Why aren't librarians recognized for the complex work they perform and their ability to apply sophisticated technologies to the fundamental problems of their discipline? Some, like Audunson (2007), argue that "in the wake of technological developments, new and specialized vocations develop, e.g., community moderator, information architect, knowledge manager, information manger, information specialist, and so on" and that these new occupations "challenge librarianship" while those within what he calls "library-oriented traditions" have been slow to adapt. I would argue, however, that rather than an actual failure to adapt to technology, librarians are *perceived* to have failed as a result of the complex and intertwined social relationships that exist between technology, gender, and work (p. 101). An illustration of these relationships emerged in a study I did with Margaret Ann Wilkinson in which we explored perceptions of the work world with more than 2,000 undergraduate students (Harris & Wilkinson, 2004). In the students' responses to questions we posed about various types of health and information work we found that "the presence of women in an occupation generally served as a negative indicator of its perceived status, the salary it attracts, the level of education of those who enter it, and the degree of computing knowledge it requires" (Harris & Wilkinson,

2004, p. 81). Among the 12 occupations we included in the study, librarianship was viewed most negatively and seen as the field least likely to offer future employment, in contrast, for example, with the job title "internet researcher," a career destination claimed for graduates of Syracuse's School of Information Studies, which was regarded by the students to possess higher status, attract better compensation, involve greater computing skill, offer greater opportunity for future employment, and, coincidentally, to employ far more men than women. The students' responses reflect the importance of the perceived connections between technology, gender, skill, and the value assigned to different types of work and those who perform it. As Gill and Grint (1995) explain, "the technical has been defined in such a way as to exclude both those technologies which women invented and those which are primarily used by women" (p. 4). In other words, women's work is regarded to be not technical and, therefore, occupations that are performed largely by women are not perceived to involve any significant level of technical skill. When faced with what amounts to a fundamental contradiction, that is, evidence of highly technical so-called women's work, such as that performed by librarians in academic libraries, the work and the workers who carry it out are essentially disappeared in the minds of onlookers, as though invisible hands have created something that others take for granted.

Nilsen and McKechnie (2002) described the same phenomenon in a study in which they asked library users about who decides what books are on the shelves in the library. Sixty percent of their respondents did not identify library staff as responsible for this key aspect of the professional practice of librarianship—so-called collection development—and attributed this work instead to library boards, government agencies, the library's customers, or some automatic process. Nilsen and McKechnie do not account for their findings in terms of gender relations, suggesting instead that librarians' work is invisible because members of the profession are reluctant to "claim expert knowledge" vis-à-vis those they serve (p. 317). They believe that the field's image would improve if "patrons knew something of the hidden intellectual work of librarians" (p. 318) and encourage libraries and library associations to undertake promotional campaigns to showcase librarians' work and increase public awareness of the profession. These are welcome suggestions and, to some extent, organizations such as the American Library Association have taken up this challenge, albeit only recently.

Increasing public awareness of librarians' work, however, may not be the only hurdle that needs to be overcome if their efforts are to be not only recognized, but valued. For instance, there are many other professionals whose work, while not particularly visible, is respected nonetheless. If one were to inquire of the public who maintains the complex computing systems in IT-intensive environments such as banks, airlines, or the stock exchange, it is likely that systems experts, database managers, or computer scientists would be mentioned. In other words, the work involved, even though it occurs outside public view and is not well understood, would nevertheless be attributed to real people (probably men) who possess sophisticated skills to do their jobs. As I noted earlier, even in documents produced by bodies specifically concerned with the governance of libraries, librarians' contributions often go unmentioned. Their absence is quite striking, for example, on Web sites describing libraries' resources where one sees impressive lists of collections, electronic journals, and various finding aids but seldom any mention of the librarians who are not only responsible for creating this rich cache but, presumably, are themselves important resources for prospective library users (see, for example, University of Washington Libraries, 2008). This contrasts sharply with the ways in which professionals in other service organizations are described by their governing bodies. For example, in reports about institutions such as hospitals or universities it is difficult to imagine leaving out any mention of the contributions made by members of the health professions or the professors who work in them. Visits to hospital Web sites feature prominently the achievements of physicians and other expert staff (see, for example, Detroit Medical Centre [2008] and Mayo Clinic [2008]), and university planning documents invariably highlight the importance of attracting the best possible faculty members in order to achieve their institutional ambitions (see, for example, Ohio State University [2008]).

Not only are librarians absent from the documents that assess and position the organizations they operate so successfully, but they are often bypassed when it comes to significant leadership positions in the library world, such as the Librarian of Congress in the United States. This practice would be almost unthinkable in other disciplines. For example, it is difficult to imagine that the position of Surgeon General in the United States would be held by someone other than a physician. Even the Chief Executive of the prestigious British Library, librarian Lynne Brindley, is described on the Library's Web site, not only as "the first woman," but "the first informational professional to have held the post" (British Library, 2008). One wonders why one of the world's greatest and most respected libraries would describe its top-ranking officer as an information professional rather than as librarian, unless there is something lesser or suspect about the label.

TECHNOLOGY, CHANGE, AND THE LABEL PROBLEM

Given the prominence of information in the current economy, opportunities for employment in the information sector have never been better and one might imagine that, as the original information practice, librarianship would not only be visible but seen to be a leading profession in this sector. However, rather than emerging as a dominant force, librarians' star appears to have fallen, in spite of their successes in incorporating new technologies into their work practices. The experience in librarianship is unlike that of other professions which, as technologies have changed their environments, have not only engaged with but actually appropriated new occupational turf. Accountants, for instance, have also had to adapt to technologies that have absorbed some of their traditional work, but they now lay claim to expertise that goes well beyond bookkeeping. In a recent media release to introduce a new logo for their professional organization, the president of the Chartered Accountants of Canada announced that "CAs play leadership roles in all segments of Canadian and international business, providing financial expertise, strategic thinking and business insight. . . . This powerful new logo visually unifies our profession and graphically symbolizes the value provided by CAs" (Chartered Accountants of Canada, 2007). Engineers, too, are eager to claim new territories of work and expertise, and their associations are prepared to do battle with competing groups, especially those who might make use of their occupation's title, as was the case when the Canadian Council of Professional Engineers sued a university for trademark infringement when its computer science department tried to offer a program in software engineering (University Affairs, 2001). Beyond the blatant self-promotion strategies that these occupations employ, one of the other obvious contrasts with librarianship that these examples bring to light is that when groups like the engineers attempt to hold onto their territory or colonize new ground, they do not change their names (despite occupational stereotypes that have not been entirely flattering).[1] Rather, they boldly add new workspaces to those they already occupy, much to the benefit of their members. In librarianship, on the other hand, we find continual anxiety about the future of the profession and its work, along with an apparently endless energy on the part of influential nonlibrarians or those who wish to abandon their identities as librarians to find occupational titles from which the terms *library* and *librarian* can be dropped.

The label problem in librarianship is perhaps nowhere more clearly expressed than in the discourses that position the educational programs through which students are prepared for professional practice in the information sector. For instance, I read recently that yet another North American library school has changed its name to the School of Information Studies to join the ranks of the so-called I-schools. The decision to make such a name change is isn't entirely surprising because the administrators who head these schools often face real or perceived pressures from colleagues within their departments and from others elsewhere in the academy who see little value in having a library school in their university, no matter how good a school it might be or how venerable its provenance. The motivation behind such name changes appears to be quite similar to the ambitions of the engineering and accounting professions, that is, a desire to claim new territories of expertise and to increase the status of the field and its practitioners. The justification for jettisoning *librarianship* or *library science* in favor of *information studies* in the names of academic departments is that the library label fails to convey the wide array of information problems and work opportunities that have emerged as a result of technological change and with which these schools concern themselves. According to the I-Schools Project Web site (I-Schools Project, 2008), participating schools are "interested in the relationship between information, technology and people" and "take it as given that expertise in all forms of information is required for progress in science, business, education, and culture." Apparently, "this expertise must include understanding of the uses and users of information, as well as information technologies and their applications." To me, this argument seems a bit contrived because librarians are also interested in information, technology, and people, possess demonstrable expertise in managing different forms of information, and are already employed in myriad science, business, education, and cultural settings (libraries and otherwise). Furthermore, it isn't clear why new educational programs are required to produce information workers, that is, nonlibrarians, rather than updating existing library education programs to prepare librarians who are prepared to take on additional or changing roles. Indeed, one of the ironies in this latest naming convention is that while the newly minted I-schools try to bury the expression *library,* many of them continue to prepare librarians for practice. Furthermore, the students who pursue library studies or who intend to work in libraries generally comprise the largest enrollment base of these schools.

The graduate degrees offered in the I-schools are variously named and present a confusing array to prospective students and their potential employers. They include masters' (both science and arts) in information, information studies, information science, information systems, library studies, as well as masters' degrees in library and information science, library and information studies, information management, communication and information studies, as well as information studies and information science and technology (the latter two both carrying the apt acronym MIST—as in cloudy, overcast, or unclear). On the schools' Web sites, the descriptions of the career opportunities for graduates of these programs are overlapping and inconsistent. For instance, preparation for work as a so-called information architect is advertised for graduates of MS information studies and master of information management programs, as well as masters of library and information science programs. Consultants and analysts of various descriptions, as well as database managers, knowledge managers, Webmasters and Web developers are also to be produced from programs with names that range from library science to information management. Furthermore, the curricula embedded in the old (library) and new (information) programs in the I-schools are also variable in content and frequently overlapping. In fact, if one looks closely, it appears that much of content of the new programs involves, essentially, a repackaging of the traditional curriculum of librarianship, and that many of the highly touted work opportunities in the new I-world are applications of the renamed skills of librarians. Indeed, it may well be that jobs such as internet content organizer, taxonomist, information consultant, chief knowledge officer, and ontologist may be performed best by people who are well prepared in the fundamentals of what some of us would still call librarianship.

KNOWLEDGE DOMAINS AND PROFESSIONAL IDENTITIES

The rush by the I-schools to develop new programs and proclaim new professional titles for graduates runs absolutely counter to practices used in more successful (and secure) professional disciplines. In medical schools, for example, despite shifts in curricula as technologies change and the knowledge base shifts, one sees continuity in the preparation of a variety of specialists, some of whom will work primarily as clinicians, while others may combine clinical work and research as academics, but all of whom are, first and foremost, physicians. Similarly, in psychology where there is a wide range of subspecialties or areas ranging from industrial/organizational to cognitive neuroscience, graduate programs prepare entrants for professional practice or the academy, all of whom, despite their particular subject emphasis, are known to the world, and each other, as psychologists. Michael Gorman (2000) has been particularly scathing in his commentary about the actions taken by some of the former library schools. Arguing that librarians "do good work and should not be afraid to proclaim it" (p. 67), he describes library education in the United States as a "train wreck" and claims that dropping *library* from the schools' names is "symbolic of the deep ill, the existential crisis, that has gripped our profession" (p. 67). Sadly, as I noted at the outset of the chapter, this angst or identity crisis does not go unnoticed by library patrons. According to Gorman, one of the serious consequences of the "L word" wars is that "many library school graduates lack basic education in the central processes of librarianship" and "do not understand the architecture of bibliographic control and, therefore, cannot function properly as reference librarians, collection development librarians or any other kind of librarian" (p. 68). This is particularly worrying since "most of the renamed schools produce graduates who seek employment in libraries" (p. 67). Indeed, an examination of some of the new curricula in these schools reveals a disturbing lack of concentration on the basics, that is, a lack of solid grounding in what I would argue are the foundational skills of librarianship, including a rigorous preparation in the fundamentals of the complex schemes for organizing and classifying knowledge, a solid grounding in the technologies that facilitate retrieval of that knowledge, and a thorough understanding of ethical practice in the service of patrons, clients, or users. The absence of this material in the preparation of librarians or masters-prepared I-school graduates, no matter what their intended future specialties or the actual sites of their work, has serious implications, not only for the graduates themselves, who may find themselves poorly prepared for their intended work, but for those who rely on their services.

Describing the impact of ICTs on the professional domain of medical practitioners, Nettleton and Burrows (2003) explained that "medical knowledge is no longer exclusive to the medical school and the medical text; it has 'escaped' into the networks of contemporary infoscapes where it can be accessed, assessed and reappropriated" (p. 179). One might argue that similar forces are at work in librarianship in that the information or material once controlled in the domain of the library has escaped to be accessed, assessed, and reappropriated by e-connected members of the broader community. Ton de Bruyn (2007) argues, for instance, that librarians (and archivists) have become "endangered species," in part because of the digital "emancipation of information" (p. 113). While this emancipation may enable contemporary information seekers to bypass libraries, it bears remembering that there were always producers and users of information who chose to operate without the benefit of the library resources that might have been available to them. However, in the future, libraries' historic role as important sites for information storage and retrieval will remain of value as librarians continue to purchase and lease materials on behalf of library users, thereby providing access to information that users might not be able to afford, and of which they might have been otherwise unaware. In fact, Gorman (2000) suggests that regardless of the ready access to information afforded by the Internet, libraries will continue to have not only a viable but an important future because while "electronic resources are valuable, they are, in most instances, enhancements, not replacements, of other [library] collections and services" (p. 31). He argues that the traditional library "is one that selects, collects, and gives access to all the forms of recorded knowledge and information that are relevant to its mission and to the needs of the community it services, and assists and instructs in the use of those resources," including electronic resources (p. 32).

With respect to future work roles, the challenges of dealing with information will remain, no matter its format, fluidity, or the settings in which it is used. How can it be identified, collected, gathered, or tagged in some organized and replicable fashion? How can its potential users be connected to it and supported in sifting through it to locate that which has value to them? So-called information work continues to incorporate these elements, but as we've seen in the case of the I-schools, descriptions of this work and those who perform it are often spun as though they constitute something different or novel. Regardless of the spin, even though technology may have enabled information to escape the library, there is still much to be done in support of users' needs, whether in libraries or elsewhere, and for which, presumably, librarians (or their I-clones) will continue to be required. Given the apparently growing need for information architects, knowledge managers, ontologists, taxonomists, and information consultants (aka librarians), why have the library schools tried to hide their origins and why do some extremely successful librarians abandon their own professional identities?

I return again to the gender/technology relation that underpins the perception that library work is women's work and that women's work is not technical and, therefore, work related to ICTs cannot be performed properly by librarians and must be done by some other occupational group, presumably one that attracts more men. If library practitioners and academics believe that the status and compensation they (quite reasonably) desire is not available to them because of the leaden freight attached to librarianship, it isn't surprising that some choose to adopt identities that seem more easily to fit within the technology/skill rubric and which they perceive to be less tainted by feminization. However, as understandable as it may be to want to unpack or lose the negative trappings of the so-called L word, the folly in this tactic is that it is undermines a field of endeavor with a recognizable history and identity and leaves the public completely in the dark about exactly who the I-experts are and what they should actually be able to do. As a result, unlike the engineers and accountants who move onto new turf as it becomes available and proclaim their expertise to remind the public that they remain valuable and indispensable, the new information experts can't claim or proclaim their successes because no one knows or agrees about who and what they are. Forgive me for suggesting that the I-people have created a serious classification problem.

SELF-SERVICE TECHNOLOGIES AND THE DEMOTION OF CARE

So why should we care? At a minimum, the disappearing of librarians is a problem for the profession. If respect for the skills and abilities of librarians continues to erode, it will be difficult to persuade those who fund libraries to provide the necessary resources to recruit and retain professional staff when less expensive employees, that is, those without the educational qualifications of professional librarians, can arguably be used as substitutes. And, if the expertise of librarians continues to disappear from the front lines of library workplaces, a practice Victoria Marshall and I described as "a giant step back from the front" (Harris & Marshall, 1998, p. 579), the quality of public services will drop, as will the expectations of library users, and the invisibility of librarians and their skills will intensify in an unpleasant and prophetic cycle. Current management practice in some North American libraries favors the replacement of professional librarians at centralized service points with less-qualified staff and the substitution of paid labor with do-it-yourself technologies for users. This arrangement was very much in evidence in our U.K. study where interviews with public library managers, staff members, and patrons revealed uneasiness over the role of library staff. This uneasiness was related, at least in part, to the presence of ICTs, particularly public Internet access in the library, which was connected, in turn, to the self-service model that has been adopted by the library's management. As the following passages reveal, the comments of the managers, staff members, and library users can tell us a great deal about how technology intersects with different stakeholders' views of the positioning of library work, workers and relations with users.

When asked about the library's self-service strategy, one of the managers explained,

> We are trying to empower the users . . . to give people choices of what they want to do. So if they don't want to talk to a member of staff then they can come in and they can return their books, issue their books, collect their reservations on a PC without necessarily having to queue up . . . There isn't much time for enquiry desk staff to do more research-intensive questions. I think we would normally say a maximum of ten minutes for enquiry and if they can deal with them in less time then so much the better. It's . . . giving the means for the person to be able to find out the answer, referring to some books and websites, or materials that can be used . . . At the enquiry desk we might provide sort of short answers to questions but then we would normally channel people to the resources that they can find out themselves.

Several of the patrons in our study had clearly accepted this idea and expected to look after their own needs in the library. As one man told the interviewer, "If you had a problem you should try and sort it out yourself before you go and start asking for help from other people." Others patrons, however, appear to have adapted to the self service model out of necessity, in order to avoid long line-ups at the inquiry desk or because they aren't sure what kind of a reaction they'll receive from the staff. Some described their frustration when they've waited for over-worked staff members to pay attention to their needs. Others felt snubbed as a result of the limited time staff spent with them. One woman said about an interaction with a library staff member, "I left there thinking . . . she doesn't really care. I think she gave me about eight minutes of her time."

The value patrons place on meaningful connections with library staff, especially librarians, ought not to be underestimated. As one woman explained,

> I would assume it would be the case if I came in and said to someone who worked in the library, "I'm looking for information on such and such" they can certainly tell me where the information is and they . . . may be able to recommend something. What's more important is that you feel that they're genuinely helping you, rather than pointing over their shoulder toward a particular aisle. It's all to do with that moment with interaction, which is what gives you your final opinion on the librarians.

Members of the staff are quite aware of this desire by some of the library's patrons for more access to their time and for better quality interactions at the inquiry desk. Several of them described their frustration in trying to meet users' needs within the constraints imposed by the library's policy to limit the time spent in response to reference inquiries:

> I suppose we have a responsibility, but I don't know if it's an official responsibility, it's kind of a moral responsibility, to find the information for somebody and make sure it's trustworthy. But when you're that rushed and other people are in the queue, jumping up and down, and the phones are ringing it's very hard . . . it's not our fault, we do the best we can and I know we're not nearly meeting the needs of people.
>
> People want you to spend time . . . they want to tell you a bit about it, so you need to be able to listen, I think, and spend that time. But sometimes you're conscious that obviously there's a queue of people and you can't spend the time. . . . It's all to do with time, isn't it? Being able to give each person that time.

Some staff members also contest the boundaries of the library's self-service orientation and commented on the impact of the self-service model in terms of its value to users. One librarian remarked,

> The organization wants new ways of working that the public don't like, and we've been developing. I think that perhaps we went too far . . . all this emphasis on self-service . . . we have expectations of ourselves that are not the expectations that the user base in general has.

Furthermore, as the following comments reveal, some librarians are painfully aware of what the positioning of technology within the library's self-service model implies for their own work roles:

> I personally think they've thrown the baby out with the bathwater . . . they've actually forgotten what libraries are about . . . I mean with people in it, physical human beings who as well as helping people with technology, who actually know what they're talking about can give that sort of advice across a whole range of subjects . . . *there's no need for us, IT services replaced it all.*
>
> We are spending less time on the enquiry desk and I think that is the nature of where public libraries are going, in general . . . it is not about clarity and depth and precision of the information anymore. It is about point and facilitating, rather than gatekeeping and providing. I think that is the difference. *I think that is why librarians, especially in public libraries, feel that their little bit of ground is slowly being squashed into nothing.* (emphasis added)

If the ultimate expression of the gender/technology relation in librarianship is to remove librarians almost completely from the front-end of library service, it would be a very sad thing indeed. It seems quite clear in the comments from library users and staff in our U.K. work—and I've no reason to believe that it is otherwise in North America—that there is a desire for more rather than less relationship, that is, supportive mutuality in the information search and use process in the library. Banishing librarians from this role seems unfair to users and undermining of what, at least in my mind, is one of the core missions of the library. Why would we write out of the script this care role of librarians? Again, one can look to the role of gender in the valuing of work. Care work is generally seen to be women's work and, because women's work (yes, even when it's performed by men) is not seen to be particularly skilled, it is, as a result, accorded little value. There is great pressure on managers, especially in public sector organizations, to reduce the costs of service by bringing down or eliminating labor costs, particularly labor that seems over-priced relative to the value it adds. The time that librarians (and other library staff) spend interacting with library patrons in what may seem, on occasion, to amount to little more than meandering chat, is, in fact, part of the relational work that builds trust and often brings to the fore what users need. Replacing such opportunities for exchange with self-service technologies will indeed reduce costs and enable patrons to perform routine library work themselves, such as checking out and renewing books. Pushing patrons to the Internet, essentially to perform their own reference transactions, will also keep costs down, as this work, too, is offloaded from library staff to end users. Such strategies are often justified by claims that they will empower users and free up staff time for real professional work. However, in many cases, the end result is simply that patrons look after themselves, do not see library staff as having much to offer, and that fewer librarians have jobs in these settings. In other words, librarians are disappearing while, just as they might at home, patrons rely on keyword searching in popular search engines, which yields results that are sometimes disappointing, often overwhelming, and frequently full of material from dodgy, unreliable sources.

CONCLUSION

To step out of this downward spiral, the profession's members must work together to (re)claim librarianship's rightful position as a leader in the information sector and proclaim (to themselves and their publics) the ongoing significance of the profession and the important skills its members have to offer. Awareness of the fundamental sexism that drives the denigration of the field and its members should, I hope, fuel a little gumption by librarians to push back against those who are, with little thought, disappearing them. I agree with Michael Gorman (2000), who writes that "librarianship has a structure and a history, and it behooves librarians to recognize and celebrate their unique identity and mission" (p. 14). During a recent visit to the University of Wisconsin–Milwaukee's School of Information Studies, I was very much impressed by the graduating students who presented reports at a research seminar. These students are sophisticated, knowledgeable, and confident users of technology, and several of them were completing dual degree programs, master's of library science in combination with master's programs in other disciplines, such as geography and public history. Their entrance to the profession is a positive indication that librarianship continues to attract gifted individuals who have what it takes to make significant contributions to the field. This is good news indeed, given the persistent failure within the profession to promote the skills and expertise of its own members, which is one of librarianship's most significant challenges and seems inconceivable in the face of the obvious talents of its newest entrants. To rebuttress the discipline, we need, in addition to greater public recognition of the skilled members of the profession, a serious rethinking among educators in the field about what it is we're doing. Reclaiming, with pride, the labels of library, librarian, and librarianship as the core identity of the profession is an obvious first step. Just as important, however, is a renewed commitment to prepare graduates who share the fundamental knowledge base of librarianship on which they can build specializations that will enable them to serve well, regardless of whether they are situated in libraries or other sectors. Knowledge of technology is, of course, part of this mix. However, such knowledge, set atop a void in the basics of L-skills, is not a very likely recipe for success.

NOTE

1. Accountants, for example, are often perceived to be dull, while engineers are sometimes regarded as socially inept nerds.

REFERENCES

The Alberta Library. (2007). *Welcome to the Alberta Library.* Retrieved July 23, 2007, from http://www.thealbertalibrary.ab.ca.

Audunson, R. (2007). Library and information science education—Discipline, profession, vocation? *Journal of Education for Library and Information Science, 48*(2), 94–107.

Ayers, E. L., & Grisham, C. M. (2003). Why IT has not paid off as we hoped (yet). *EducauseReview, 38*(6), 40–51.

British Library. (2008). Dame Lynne J. Brindley, DBE. Retrieved July 21, 2008, from www.bl.uk/aboutus/governance/blboard/memberslist/brindley/.

Chartered Accountants of Canada. (2007). *Canada's CAs symbolized by new logo.* Retrieved July 23, 2007, from http://www.cica.ca/3/8/2/9/3/index1.shtml.

de Bruyn, T. (2007). Questioning the focus of LIS education. *Journal of Education for Library and Information Science, 48*(2), 108–115.

Detroit Medical Centre. (2008). DMC Detroit Medical Centre. Retrieved July 21, 2008, from http://www.dmc.org.

Gill, R., & Grint, K. (1995). Introduction. The gender-technology relation: contemporary theory and research. In K. Grint & R. Gill (Eds.), *The gender-technology relation: Contemporary theory and research* (pp. 1–28). London: Taylor & Francis.

Gorman, M. (2000). *Our enduring values. Librarianship in the 21st century.* Chicago: American Library Association.

Harris, R., Henwood, F., Burdett, S., & Marshall, A. (2007). *Layers of uncertainty: Conflicting expectations over consumer health information service in the public library*. Unpublished manuscript.

Harris, R. M., & Marshall, V. (1998). Reorganizing Canadian libraries: A giant step back from the front. *Library Trends, 46*(3), 564–580.

Harris, R., & Wilkinson, M. A. (2004). Situating gender: Students' perceptions of information work. *Information Technology & People, 17*(1), 71–86.

House of Commons, Culture, Media and Sport Committee. (2005, March 10). *Public libraries. Third report of session 2004–2005*. 1, HC 81.

I-Schools Project. (2008). What are iSchools? Retrieved July 21, 2008, from http://www.ischools.org/oc/field.html.

Mayo Clinic. (2008). About our Web Sites. Retrieved July 21, 2008, from http://www.mayoclinic.org/about-web.

Nettleton, S., & Burrows, R. (2003). E-scaped medicine? Information, reflexivity and health. *Critical Social Policy, 23*(2), 165–185.

Nilsen, K., & McKechnie, E. F. (2002). Behind closed doors: An exploratory study of the perceptions of librarians and the hidden intellectual work of collection development in Canadian public libraries. *Library Quarterly, 72*(3), 294–325.

Ohio State University. (2008). Academic plan. Retrieved July 21, 2008, from http://www.osu.edu/academicplan/exec.php.

Online Computer Library Center. (2008). About OCLC. Retrieved July 21, 2008, from http://www.oclc.org/about/default.htm.

Ontario Council of University Libraries. (2005). Welcome to scholars portal. Retrieved July 21, 2008, from http://www.scholarsportal.infoUniversity Affairs. (2001). *Software engineering dispute reaches an impasse*. Retrieved July 23, 2007, from http://www.affairesuniversitaires.ca/issues/2001/oct/pg42.pdf.

University of Washington Libraries. (2008). UW Resources. Retrieved July 21, 2008, from http://www.lib.washington.edu/types.

9

CHILDREN AND INFORMATION TECHNOLOGY

Andrew Large

The rapid penetration of information technology (IT) into schools, libraries, and homes since the early 1990s has opened many opportunities for children to enrich their educational, leisure, and social activities. The children represent the first generation to grow up in the so-called digital age. At the same time, IT has raised a plethora of concerns, including fears about uncontrolled access to inappropriate content on the Web, an encouragement to plagiarism through the ease of cut and paste operations, personal insecurity as a result of adult Web predators, reduced time devoted to book reading, a widening of the gulf between the digital haves and have-nots, and even the rise of child obesity as a result of hours spent in front of computer monitors. This chapter will explore IT for child users and provide some critical commentary on the research findings discussed.

Given the breadth of the topic under consideration, some boundaries must be drawn. First, as far as possible the focus will be children up to the age of around 12 years (a few exceptions will be made when adolescents have been included alongside children within the same research study). At the lower end of this age scale, children are now using computers from their parents' knees by their second year, and by their third year are able to control a mouse, and can point and click (Calvert, Rideout, Woolard, Barr, & Strouse, 2005). The upper age marks both the end of child development (Kail, 2004) and in many educational jurisdictions the termination of elementary school studies. Second, it will draw heavily on research studies conducted with North American children, and only to a much lesser extent with those in other parts of the world. Third, it will concentrate heavily on one information technology—the Web—and have less to say about other technologies such as CD-ROM as well as communication technologies like e-mail, chat rooms, and instant messaging, although younger and younger children are using those as well. Finally, it will not consider the expanding area of social networking, despite the growing popularity among young people of services such as Facebook and YouTube as well as the virtual environment offered by Second Life. Researchers are now turning their attention to such phenomena, but as yet it is premature to evaluate their use by young children and the role they play in children's educational, leisure, and social activities.

Children's encounters with IT can be traced back to the 1980s, and it is in the second half of that decade that the early research studies on their information behavior in digital environments began to appear. Nevertheless, interest in children as a specific user community was relatively slow to emerge. For example, the *Journal of the American Society for Information Science and Technology* (under this and its earlier names), a leading information science journal, published its first article of any kind on children (or teenagers) as primary research subjects in 1985, but it was only in 1994 that an entire volume of the journal included as many as two articles devoted to them (Rothbauer & Gooden, 2006). The growth of interest in children and IT in the late 1990s can be ascribed in part to the emergence of the Web and the consequent large-scale introduction of IT into elementary schools. It can also be explained by developmental theories that remind us that children are not merely short adults but a user community (or in reality a series of communities) with different cognitive and affective capabilities from their adult counterparts when it comes to using and exploiting IT.

INFORMATION TECHNOLOGY AT HOME AND IN SCHOOL

A growing number of studies in North America and Europe attest to the ubiquitous roll of IT in young people's lives. Very young children spend most time at the computer playing games (Calvert et al., 2005). Game playing continues as they get older, but the Internet as a broader resource becomes an alternative attraction both at home and in school as development continues. Several surveys of Internet use have concerned themselves with the kinds of Internet activities engaged in by children. In Canada, a Media Awareness Network survey found that in 2000 the most popular Internet activity among students aged 9 to 17 was playing and downloading music, followed by e-mail, surfing for fun, playing and downloading games, instant messaging, chat rooms, and, only in last place, homework (Media Awareness Network, 2001). When asked about the greatest benefits from using the Internet, the respondents placed easier access to information in second place, below communicating with people but above entertainment or enjoyment; nevertheless, educational benefits were placed at the end of the list. A survey of parents (Media Awareness Network, 2000), however, had them placing much more weight on the educational advantages of the Internet for their children rather than its entertainment benefits (61% compared with just 11%). There is, therefore, a disconnect between what children actually are doing online and what their parents think they are doing!

Do leisure-based Internet activities adversely affect children's mental and physical well-being? Attewell, Suazo-Garcia, and Battle (2003) found little evidence in the United States that children's use of computers for a moderate amount of time (up to eight hours per week) is associated with less time spent on reading, sports, or outdoor activities, but heavier usage can be associated with less time for sports and outdoor activities and, in a small but worrying number of children, with obesity and consequent health problems (though they concede that this could be explained by obese children preferring to play with computers, rather than computer use causing obesity).

In the classroom, research studies demonstrate ambivalence as to the benefits derived from IT. One perspective is that it can act as a powerful motivator in school and can encourage creative thinking (Waite, 2004). In their review of the literature on the Web as an information resource for students in elementary and high schools, however, Kuiper, Volman and Terwel (2005) point out that the Web does not support the learning process as a matter of course but is a tool that, in certain conditions, can play a role in students' learning processes. Wallace, Kupperman and Krajcik, (2000) share this view. In studying grade-six students carrying out an assignment on the Web, they found the students to be engaged and involved in their work but remained skeptical about the Web as a learning resource. The authors say that Web tools are not yet designed to support learning and give almost no support for finding content based on meaning and no means for using information once it has been found. They raise a number of crucial questions, including how tasks and tools can be defined to take advantage of the unique features of the Web, and what comprise the real information needs of students that can be satisfied by the Web.

Some teachers have found that technological innovations can help level the playing field for special needs students by expanding the learning environment beyond the classroom. Hasselbring and Glaser (2000) think, however, that the Internet becomes a powerful tool for learning only if it offers students opportunities not only to gather a wide variety of resources and information but also to exchange their thoughts and ideas with others in collaborative learning environments—they say that this is especially beneficial for students with learning disabilities as it can actively engage them in the learning process. Waite, Wheeler, and Bromfield (2007) agree that lower achievers may improve their performance by using IT but only if carefully planned in the context of their learning styles. In general Waite, Wheeler, and Bromfield say that it is the able students who appear to best adapt IT to their purpose and achieve the greatest improvements in attainment. Hyperlinks are especially helpful for students with mild learning disabilities, although they also can overwhelm them, and multimedia can help by providing alternative ways to present information. Planning Web activities for students with mild disabilities has to consider the structure of the learning, the amount of guidance the learner will receive, the kinds of activities that emphasize higher order thinking skills, and the interactivity of the sites selected (a key principle behind meaningful learning on the Web).

Williams (1999) found in his visits to an elementary school that teachers themselves expressed concerns about their own abilities to incorporate the Internet into their work in a way that would maximize its potential; formal, structured training for teachers appears to be needed. Sutherland-Smith (2002) says that teachers as well as students must be comfortable and competent with the Web if they are to use it successfully. She argues that special teaching techniques are required to teach students how to read Web-based text, including developing mechanisms to overcome frustration with technology and search guidelines to avoid random text scanning. Wallace et al. (2000) also believe that teachers need strategies to help students learn from the Web. A Pew study conducted in the United States during 2001 and 2002 found that many teachers had not yet recognized the new ways in which students access information, identified wide variation in teacher policies on Internet use by students, and concluded that professional development and technical assistance for teachers is crucial for the effective integration of the Web into curricula (Levin & Arafeh, 2002). In the context of digital library use, Abbas (2005) argues for better instruction of children in schools in such matters as term selection and information seeking more generally. The incorporation of information literacy into the elementary school curriculum would likely pay dividends throughout not only the remainder of their education but also into adulthood.

LIBRARIES, INFORMATION TECHNOLOGY, AND CHILDREN

Surprisingly little research has been published about young people's use of the Web within public or school libraries. Dresang, Gross, and Holt (2003) comment on the irony that so much importance is given to networked digital resources for children and yet it was not until 2001 and 2002 that the first efforts were made to collect or analyze data to evaluate children's use of them. These authors have developed an outcome-based research evaluation model to guide them in a study of children aged 9 to 13 who were using resources and services in the St. Louis Public Library. In the study, four critical questions were raised: To what extent are resources invested in technology in public libraries reducing the digital divide for children? What level of knowledge, skills, behaviors, and attitudes do children have with networked technology, as evidenced by public library use? What effect does children's use of technology have on library policies and service responses? What is the impact of children's use of technology in various public libraries over time? These questions await clear answers, though Gross, Dresang, and Holt (2004) have themselves made a start. For example, regarding the first question, they report that the public library is playing an important role in reducing the gap between the technical elite and the technical poor in low-income communities. In the case of other questions (such as the attitude of library staff towards young computer users and the effects this may have on repeat use), however, the authors call for more research. Overall, they conclude that public libraries need to know more about how children use the technology being provided for them.

Silverstein (2005) argues that digital reference services can play an important role for children. Such services can help them find information for school projects but also for broader purposes such as enabling sick children to identify chat rooms where they could talk to others with the same problems. In this way, these services can support self-initiated learning. Silverstein believes that children should receive training in school about the use of digital reference services. A number of AskA services also have been created for children (these work outside formal libraries and provide answers, often from experts, to questions submitted on specific themes such as science, volcanoes, or art). Lankes (2003) provides an interesting discussion of both library-based and AskA services. He offers data to suggest that all levels of education, including elementary, use digital reference services, and that students' education questions, while covering a broad range of topics, concentrate most heavily on science. He also argues that the library community has many contributions to make to the digital reference research agenda specifically with respect to education.

Librarians serving youth in public and school libraries have been early and active adopters of IT of all kinds (Walter, 1997). Kafai and Bates (1997) believe there are abundant opportunities for school library media specialists to be involved in Internet instruction in schools. Schofield and Davidson (2002) found that school librarians took a leading role in devising and managing Internet activities in the school district they investigated: they introduced the Internet to students and teachers who did not have classroom access, shared resources from the Internet with teachers, and helped with curricular activities. Shantz-Keresztes (2000) summarizes a conversation between Canadian teacher-librarians in the Calgary (Alberta) Board of Education who discuss, among other topics, how teacher-librarians sell their role as information literacy specialists to teachers, and what strategies can be used by teacher-librarians in their cooperative planning with teachers to ensure students have the necessary background to evaluate Web sites.

Children have not been ignored in the provision of digital libraries of various kinds. The International Children's Digital Library (ICDL) can be accessed via the Web to find the full text of 1630 children's books in 38 languages (as of spring 2007). Its innovative interface, which allows books to be retrieved by their cover's color, their length (short, medium, and long), target age group and genre (make belief or true), and characters (kids, real animals, imaginary creatures) as well as by a more traditional keyword subject search (http://www.icdlbooks.org), was designed by an intergenerational team including children alongside adults. Its originator, Allison Druin, says that "when it comes to libraries, adults generally talk about children but rarely talk to them"; she decided to change this (Druin, 2005, p. 21; see also Druin et al., 2003). The ARTEMIS digital library was designed for middle and high school students to help them find information about science topics in order to support inquiry-based learning. It was organized by topic, included a scavenger hunt practice area, and incorporated scaffolding to support and structure users' thinking (Abbas, 2003). ARTEMIS has been used to support research into children's information-seeking behavior (Abbas, 2005). Also available on the Web is StoryPlace, a digital library for children from the Public Library of Charlotte and Mecklenburg County (http://www.storyplace.org). It offers a series of bilingual (English and Spanish) services to its young readers.

In terms of library catalogs, CD-ROMs, and other electronic sources of information typically found in libraries, there is a substantial research literature on children's use of such resources, which will be covered in the following section.

INFORMATION-SEEKING BEHAVIOR

The early studies of information-seeking behavior in digital environments mainly looked at how children retrieved information from CD-ROMs. By the early 1990s, a wide variety of multimedia information resources targeted specifically at children were available in this medium. Many were children's encyclopedias, designed to facilitate rapid retrieval of discrete information chunks, and often multimedia versions of an original print title. These CD-ROMs could offer an engaging, interactive experience for the young student. Although students were willing to explore and experiment with interfaces (Large, Beheshti, & Breuleux, 1998; Large, Beheshti, Breuleux, & Renaud, 1994), they were not necessarily effective at retrieving information from these CD-ROM titles (Marchionini, 1989; Oliver, 1996). In any event, regardless of its strengths and weaknesses as a classroom resource, CD-ROM technology proved transient and has been largely superseded by the expansion of the Internet and the rise of the Web.

With the introduction of Online Public Access Catalogs (OPACs) into public and school libraries, interest was stimulated in how children used these tools to find bibliographic information and what implications their behavior had for OPAC design. Edmonds, Moore, and Balcom (1990) had compared children's use of a card catalog with an OPAC in the context of a public library. They found that the children preferred the card catalog and were more successful when using it, perhaps because the OPAC required users to navigate through multiple screens, at each of which errors could be committed. Borgman and her colleagues sought a solution to such problems by building a prototype that featured direct manipulation and browsing (Borgman, Hirsh, Walter, & Gallagher, 1995). They reported that this approach overcame problems relating to several difficulties typically encountered when children use traditional OPACs to search for information: typing and spelling keywords, selecting appropriate keywords to answer an information need, and linking keywords with the appropriate Boolean operators. Solomon (1993) looked at children in grades one through six as they used their school OPAC throughout an academic year. He was surprised to find that even the youngest children could be successful but nevertheless suggested the incorporation into OPACs of specific tools that ranged from spell checkers to interactive interfaces that could adapt to users' competencies. Abbas (2005) cites several studies to argue that children benefit from metadata schemes developed specifically for them and with their unique needs in mind, but she adds that few have been developed. She also proposes that children should be involved in metadata creation alongside adult experts in order to get the best results.

Riba (2007) criticized the help screens offered by children's OPACs as being written in a language that was simply inaccessible to its potential users. More generally, she comments that OPACs were designed on the assumption that users know how to search, whereas young users have not honed such skills through practice. To be fair, a number of commercial OPACs from companies like DRA (DRA Kids) and Innovative Interfaces (Kids Online) have tried to respond to the special needs of children (Abbas, 2005).

Turning to the Web, a useful overview of early Web-based information-seeking studies can be found in Hsieh-Yee (2001), who includes research with children as well as adults, while Abbas (2003) summarizes several relevant studies of children's information-seeking behavior on the Web as well as in other digital environments such as OPACs and CD-ROMs. Large (2005) reviews the literature on children in the context of the Web in general but includes information-seeking behavior among his topics. Kuhlthau's (1991) elaboration of the information-seeking process, while neither confined to children nor targeted at the Web, nevertheless is also useful preliminary reading for any consideration of this topic.

Children in the later grades of elementary school have received more attention from researchers than have younger children, in part because they were the first to make use of IT in their school work. In contrast, relatively little attention has been directed at information seeking by very young users. Cooper (2005) emphasizes that the developmental level of children affects their ability to use IT and that "responsible and well-considered design and content choices in keeping with a child's developmental needs provide the basis of positive digital environments for children" (p. 299). Kafai and Bates (1997), when looking at students in all six elementary grades, found that the children were able to use Web sites to advantage in their learning and could scroll and use hypertext links. Only the older children, however, could effectively use search engines and the rudiments of Boolean logic. Even then children generally encounter problems in selecting appropriate search terms and orienting themselves when browsing. There is a tendency to fly from page to page with little time spent reading and digesting information, and relevance judgments about retrieved pages are difficult to make. Information seeking does not appear to be intuitive, and practice alone does not make perfect! All too often children fail to answer their information needs from the Web even though they—and in many cases also their teachers—are optimistic about their success. Children find it hard to express their information needs in the kind of query formulations required by Web-based search engines and encounter problems in revising unsuccessful strategies. Schacter, Chung, and Dorr (1998) observed fifth- and sixth-grade students as they searched for information to solve two complex problems, one well-defined and the other ill-defined. Their findings confirmed previous research (Borgman et al., 1995; Hirsh, 1999; Kuhlthau, 1991; Large et al., 1994; Marchionini, 1989) that children are reactive searchers rather than planners, do not exploit the advanced search features available to them, and perform better on ill-defined tasks than well-defined ones. Bilal (2000, 2001, 2002a) examined how seventh-grade students used a Web portal designed for children, Yahooligans!, to find information for an assigned, fact-based search task, an assigned research search task, and a fully self-generated search task. Overall she found that the students tended to query the system in natural language (despite the fact that Yahooligans! only expects keywords), generated their queries using either too broad or too specific concepts, initiated new searches when confronting an error in spelling rather than attempting to correct the spelling mistake, ignored next links when examining the search result pages, and skimmed the search result pages, usually exploring only the first links appearing at the top of the list. Bilal attributed the children's limited degree of success to the complexity of the task, their inadequate level of research skills, their tendency to seek specific answers, their inadequate knowledge of how to use the Yahooligans! search engine, poor navigational skills, and inadequacies in the design of Yahooligans!

Large, Beheshti, and Moukdad (1999) collected data from a series of searches conducted over several weeks by 53 sixth-grade students working in groups of two or three on a class project. The students made little use of Boolean operators or other advanced search features. They had difficulties generating search terms to articulate their information need in a manner that would retrieve relevant information from the Web. The students expressed frustration at the difficulty in finding a few highly relevant pages and at determining relevance from the information displayed in their hits

(Large & Beheshti, 2000). Bowler, Large, and Rejskind (2001) looked at the captured search data and interview transcripts from just one of these student groups. The authors report in some detail on the problems encountered by the one girl and two boys in searching, interpreting and using the retrieved information. They conclude that the search engines used were unsuitable for children and the retrieved Web pages in the main also unsuitable in content and vocabulary. For the most part, students' searches were unplanned, demonstrating a lack of strategic thinking. Students' information-seeking skills improved, however, with experience (see also Lawless, Mills, & Brown, 2002).

Hirsh (1999) examined the search strategies and relevance criteria employed by elementary school students when seeking information on the Web for a class project. She found them to be very impatient (often aborting a potentially useful search if a Web site took too long to download) and negligent in keeping track of how they searched for information. This meant that they spent a great deal of time attempting (often unsuccessfully) to recreate an earlier successful search. Wallace et al. (2000) also conducted a study of sixth-grade children searching the Web for information for a classroom assignment. The study found that the students used simple and repetitive keywords and, despite the exploratory nature of the Web, did not stray far from their latest list of search results. They seemed to prefer to find immediate answers to their questions rather than explore more generally a topic, and they were unable to improve their strategies in the light of earlier experience.

An alternative to the keyword search is browsing subject hierarchies or following hyperlinks. Many studies (Bilal, 2000, 2001, 2002a; Large & Beheshti, 2000; Large et al., 1999; Schacter et al., 1998; Watson, 1998) report that children seem to prefer browsing strategies to searching strategies, probably because the former require less cognitive effort on their part, recognition being easier than recall. Furthermore, they may be more successful when employing browsing techniques than when using keyword searching. Browsing, however, is not free from problems. In particular, children can encounter navigational problems when following links and may quickly become disoriented. For example, Bilal (2000, 2001, 2002a) in her work with seventh-grade students attributes the many looped searches and hyperlink paths (indicative of difficulties with memory recall) to disorientation and cognitive overload caused by the nature of the Internet environment. Furthermore, Large, Beheshti, Nesset, and Bowler (2006) found that browsing is the preferred student strategy only when it is straightforward to select the top-level entry point into the taxonomic structure, and then again at each succeeding level through the hierarchy to identify the appropriate entry (term).

Hirsh (1999) focused her attention on the important question of relevance: how do children make relevance judgments about information retrieved from print materials and CD-ROMs as well as the Web? She concluded that children had problems in evaluating the authority and accuracy of information, and that their opinions were mixed about the Web as an information resource. Enochsson (2001) also was interested in how students (in her case Swedish children aged 9 to 11) make relevance judgments. Although she was able to categorize some students as reflective in performing this task, she found many to be credulous or unreflective.

Considerable interest has been focused on gender differences in children's attitudes towards and perceptions of computers in general, but research results are not consistent. Some studies suggest that males show greater interest than females in and knowledge about computers (for example, Teasdale & Lupart, 2001; Young, 2000) or that females perceive them as being difficult to use or less interesting than do males (Teasdale & Lupart, 2001; Wolters, 1989). Others (for example, Bain & Rice, 2006; Calvert et al., 2005) found that gender differences were not significant, especially at younger ages. In the more specific context of information retrieval, however, gender appears to influence certain searching and browsing behaviors on the Web (Schacter et al., 1998; Mumtaz, 2001; Orleans & Laney, 2000; Siann, Durdell, Macleod, & Glissov, 1988). In particular, boys scan pages more rapidly and click on more hyperlinks than girls (Large, Beheshti, & Rahman, 2002b). In terms of search success, however, it remains unclear as to whether gender plays a significant role.

Surprisingly, Bilal and Kirby (2002) are the only authors explicitly to examine the similarities and differences between children (in their case from seventh grade) and adults (graduate students in information science) as they looked for information on the Web using a children's portal (all were novices). The latter were more successful than the former in finding answers to a factual question, although the researchers do identify many similarities in the behavior of these two very different age groups. As regards comparisons between young people and adults, a major problem lies with the adult research literature: it has focused very heavily on university students who may not be the most appropriate group to compare with children—it would be interesting to see how children compare with less well-educated adult populations whose language manipulation skills, for example, may be different from those in the university community.

What do children themselves have to say about the Web as an information and learning resource? Surprisingly few researchers have focused attention on the students' own perceptions of the Web despite the stress, at least in library and information science, on a user-centered approach to the design and deployment of information systems. As a consequence, data are piecemeal as well as being scattered across various age groups.

Large and Beheshti (2000) interviewed 53 students from two sixth-grade classes in a Canadian elementary school to ascertain their reaction to using the Web to find information for a school project. On the basis of their responses, the students were categorized by the researchers as technophiles who strongly favored the Web as an information resource, traditionalists who favored print materials, and pragmatists who used whichever best suited the kind of information they needed to find. Many of the students appreciated the amount of relevant information they could find on the Web compared with books in their school or public library, and found it a good place for current or obscure information. However, they also reported frustrations with the difficulty they encountered in finding a few highly relevant articles. Although the study was undertaken some years ago, there is little to suggest that matters have greatly changed, and children continue to consult printed sources alongside their digital counterparts. Information overload (the moment when the amount of available information exceeds a user's ability to process it) was the focus of a study undertaken in a Texan elementary school (Akin, 1998). The majority of students said they had experienced information overload, and it was more marked in the younger than the older students.

CHILDREN AND INFORMATION TECHNOLOGY DESIGN

Several of the information-seeking studies reported above commented specifically on the problems typically encountered by children and teenagers when using Web portals, whether these portals are specifically designed for that age group (as in the case, for example, of AskJeeves for Kids [now known as Ask For Kids, http:www.askkids.com], KidsClick, or Yahooligans!) or not. They suggest that searching and browsing could be improved by designing more appropriate portals.

The first steps in improving portal design for young users were taken when adults began to evaluate systematically Web portals that had been designed with children in mind. Broch (2000), for example, examined Yahooligans! and AskJeeves for Kids in terms of children's cognitive and mechanical skills (see also Stevenson, 2001). McDermott (2002) reviewed a variety of specialized subject portals that are relevant to students with homework assignments, while Haycock, Dobor, and Edwards (2003) provided detailed evaluations of 20 most highly recommended and popular portals designed explicitly for children's use on the Web, as well as short annotations on 11 others. Kuntz (2000), the manager of one children's portal, identified five broad criteria that can be applied to evaluate children's search tools. The first criterion is the size of the database, though Kuntz says this is not too important because a children's portal is likely to be highly selective in terms of the sites to which it provides access. The second criterion is the level of content accountability: What is the site selection policy and who does the selecting? Third, does the portal offer added benefits such as evaluative reviews of sites, site ratings of some kind, and site categorization based on factors such as readability, age, grade, or presence of multimedia? Kuntz's fourth criterion relates to the kinds of search access methods provided—keyword searches of indexed records, subject directories, alphabetical lists, grade level/curricular listings, and so on. The final criterion deals with the availability of additional features such as help, spell checking (which he argues should be a feature in any children's search tool supporting keyword searching), URL searching, links to other search services, absence of advertising, privacy policy (regarding information about users), layout, and design. Overall Kuntz argues that children's portals should be attractive but not so as to distract from a primary focus on searching: there is a trade-off in making a site engaging without making it diffused.

Several researchers have looked at how children organize concepts into categories that can then be organized into a hierarchical taxonomy (Bar-Ilan & Belous, 2007; Bilal & Wang, 2005; Large, Beheshti, Nesset, & Bowler, 2007a). Large, Beheshti, and Rahman (2002a) organized several focus groups whose members were between 10 and 13 years of age to evaluate four children's Web portals. The children were asked to say what they liked and disliked, as well as any changes they would make to the portals in order to improve their effectiveness and attractiveness for children. Through this process useful ideas emerged from the children concerning both the presentation features (such as color, layout, graphics, and animation) and the functionality (in terms searching, browsing, and displaying information) of Web portals intended for young users.

Nielsen (2002) argues that most Web site designs are based on pure folklore about how children supposedly behave or at best are insights from designers' observations of their own children. To counter this, he conducted usability studies in the United States and Israel with children between the ages of 6 and 12. He found that the children often had the greatest success when using Web sites intended for adults rather than children, so long as such sites had been designed very simply and in compliance with Web design conventions. Too many of the children's sites had not followed such guidelines, being sufficiently complex and convoluted as to stump the test users. Kafai and Bates (1997) found that Web sites for children in grades one through six in general were not child friendly as they incorporated too much text with difficult vocabulary. In their opinion, children prefer Web sites with high visual content and short, simple texts, they like animation and interactivity, and they have a low tolerance for download delays. Large and Beheshti (2000) agree on intolerance for slow downloads but conclude that children in practice will only exploit Web-based video and sound sequences (in contrast to text and still images) if this makes sense in terms of their task. It is difficult, for example, to incorporate such multimedia content into a traditional school assignment that asks for a written report to be submitted to the teacher. Enochsson (2001) found that fourth-grade children's judgments of Web pages were based on criteria such as content, currency, layout, usability, and interactivity. Loh and Williams (2002) agree that children are sophisticated enough to see beyond color, sound, and animation as novelty artifacts, though these may initially draw children to a Web site. After this novelty effect erodes it is interesting and captivating content rather than presentation features that motivates children to return to the site.

Other researchers have taken children's involvement in the design process further by arguing that it is insufficient to design interfaces with children in mind or even to include children in usability studies: they want children to be actively involved in the entire design process (Large & Beheshti, 2005). Druin and her colleagues in human-computer interaction explored the design of interfaces through intergenerational teams including children alongside adults, leading to the International Children's Digital Library referred to previously (Druin, 2005; Druin et al., 2003). Two research teams have been influenced by Druin's approach in the context of children's Web portal design. Bilal (2002b, 2003) asked a group of seventh-grade students individually to draw an initial Web portal interface and then to modify the designs, if they so chose, after looking at two existing children's Web portals; she concluded that children can be effective design partners in such a task. Large and his colleagues organized two intergenerational teams comprising the researchers and students from a sixth-grade and a third-grade class, respectively. Each team worked over a number of sessions using a method the researchers have now named bonded design to design a Web portal suitable for elementary school students, starting with simple drawings and working towards a low-tech prototype. They subsequently converted these designs into operational portals that were enthusiastically endorsed by elementary school children in experimental and operational evaluations; the children appreciated both the interface designs and the retrieval functionalities (Large, Beheshti, Nesset, & Bowler, 2004; Large et al., 2006). One of these portals is now available on the Web (http://www.historytrek.ca) for anyone to use.

DIGITAL CONTENT AND PERSONAL SAFETY ISSUES

Access to digital information and the skills to find it are of little avail if suitable content is sparse. Minkel (2000), based on his work as a children's librarian in a public library, was able to suggest Web sites suitable for young children, but in general he considers CD-ROMs more successful than the Web for children under seven years' of age (because CD-ROMs rely heavily on point and click graphics, reducing the need to read text, while maintaining the fast response time that children demand). Pearman and Lefever-Davis (2006) add that CD-ROM storybooks can include sound and animation that make the books come alive as well as providing pronunciation and phonics games that may help reading. Harbeck and Sherman (1999) share Minkel's doubts about the efficacy of Web sites for children aged seven and under. They do not subscribe to the strong and pervasive faith that younger and younger children benefit at home and school from the marvels of electronic communication technologies, and are critical of the vast majority of Web sites they reviewed that had been designed for young children.

Children's use of the Web for both educational and recreational purposes has not gained positive reactions from all adults. The availability of text and images considered pornographic in particular has provoked widespread discussion regarding the pros and cons of content control. As Wartella and Jennings (2000) have commented, the Web is no exception here; each new mass media innovation has prompted debate on its harmful effect, especially as concerns young people. Proponents of media innovation generally have argued that new technology benefits children by opening new worlds, while opponents have warned that new media can undermine children's morality, causing them to engage in illicit sexual and criminal behavior. The latter perception does have some factual grounding. There is evidence that adults are not necessarily aware of how much time children are spending online and what exactly they are doing there. In one Dutch study (Soeters & van Schaik, 2006), 62 percent of the children (between 8 and 12 years old) admitted to using the computer secretly at home, school, friends' homes, or in the library; 50 percent of the students reported a disturbing experience of some kind while online.

Much has been said about filters, including reviews and assessments of individual products. Curry and Haycock (2001) conducted a survey among a sample of subscribers to *School Library Journal* to find out how widespread is their use in North American schools and libraries. Of the respondents, 53 percent of school libraries and 21 percent of public libraries were using filters. The researchers were surprised that so many respondents in both types of libraries understood little about how filtering software actually works. A survey of public libraries in the state of Indiana reported that 66 percent of the libraries used filters, with a further 22 percent planning to install them. For juvenile users (younger than 18 years) 90 percent imposed Internet restrictions of some kind (Comer, 2005). In the United States, the Children's Internet Protection Act (CIPA), which came into effect in 2004 and mandates schools and libraries to install filtering software if they are to be eligible for federal funding, has influenced such decisions (for a fuller discussion, see Dresang, 2006). In Australia, a survey of public libraries conducted in 2005 found that around 30 percent used filtering software. Furthermore, 71 percent required parental consent for children to use the Internet in the library, and some libraries also required a parent or caregiver to be present (Australian Library and Information Association, 2006). In Canada, McKechnie (2001) examined policies applied to services for children by a sample of public libraries; filtering software was prescribed by 21 percent, and a larger percentage required written parental permission or parental presence for Internet use by their children. These kinds of policies, of course, risk deterring unaccompanied children from visiting the library altogether (Arrighetti, 2000).

Many librarians, in contrast to politicians and parents, remain skeptical about filters and the censorship that they impose. For example, Diaz (1998) believes that such solutions have proven to be less than effective and are often chosen by libraries only to placate boards and communities or provide some stopgap measure to limit offensive materials appearing on their work stations. As an alternative to filters, she suggests software such as the Library Channel, which provides guided access to the Web through a subject directory with three access levels: preselected sites accessed via menus; any URL; or sites not blocked by domain name or word in the domain name, which are added individually by the library. Diaz concedes, however, that this is labor-intensive for librarians to build and maintain. Web portals designed specifically for children (discussed above), which provide access only to sites selected as appropriate in content and language for young users, in effect also filter out all other sites even though their primary intention may not be to impose censorship as such. The tension between access and control, especially with young users in mind, preceded the emergence of digital content, of course, but untrammeled access to Web content has undoubtedly heightened it.

CRITICAL PERSPECTIVES

The issues surrounding children's use of IT are multifaceted and complex, although some trends can be discerned in relative confidence. Information technology is likely to play an ever larger role in the lives of children both when learning and when playing. It is increasingly being used to support social intercourse, whether through e-mail and chat rooms, by swapping images, or entering virtual worlds like Second Life. Although teenagers may be more engaged than younger children in these activities, the age of participation is likely to decrease. One current obstacle is the need for typing, and therefore spelling; improved voice recognition systems could dramatically improve access for the young. It is also likely that information technology will become even more important in the classroom where every child may before too long expect to have a computer on the desk (or representing the desk). New generations of teachers who are IT-savvy will only further accelerate such developments.

For young children, one barrier to the greater use of information technology for learning is a relative dearth of content, especially on the Web, that is presented in a child-friendly way, using appropriate vocabulary and simple syntax. Large and Beheshti (2000) found that students often had to translate the content into their own syntax and vocabulary because it was not written with a young audience in mind. Furthermore, in many cases the Web provided too detailed information, or else required the students to select and merge data from several different sites. Children's books still tend to be more successfully packaged for their target audience in this respect, but as more young users exploit the Web it is probable that appropriate content will increasingly become available.

Young users need a retrieval system with tools and mechanisms that not only offer contextual support but also encourage them to continue using that system. To prevent children from experiencing anxiety through perceived information overload or lack of control, an information retrieval system should empower the young user by offering features such as visual aesthetics (as seen through children's eyes) conceptual and linguistic clarity, compatibility with the task, comprehensibility, consistency, controllability, familiarity, flexibility, predictability, simplicity, and responsiveness. In order to engage the young user, the information system may also include some fun aspects (Shneiderman, 2004). One suggestion to accomplish this is a Search Pal, which provides context-sensitive help while displaying appropriate emotions (Beheshti, Bowler, Large, & Nesset, 2005). Another might be to provide children with a measure of control over the system's interface through personalization; for example, in the children's Web portal, History Trek (http://www.historytrek.ca), users can personalize the mascot that is used to request help (Large, Beheshti, Nesset, & Bowler, 2007b).

Virtual reality systems that encourage browsing may also provide an alternative to conventional search engines. Since virtual reality environments have been shown to be a highly effective means of teaching and transferring knowledge and can have a strong motivational impact (Bricken, 1991), and since browsing is a visual activity, familiar metaphors may be utilized and presented in three-dimensional virtual reality systems to increase their value. One experimental system is the VLibrary, which represents children's Web sites about Canadian history as books stored on shelves in a library. Users can walk around the library, browse the shelves, select virtual books from the shelves, open them to see their content (that is, access the actual site on the Web), and keep any interesting books for future consultation (Beheshti, Large, Clement, & Tabatabaei, 2007).

Alongside attempts to simplify information retrieval for children goes the need to induce a sense of information literacy even in the very young. One popular approach to the provision of information literacy skills for students is the Big6 program developed by Eisenburg and Berkowitz. This series of six steps—task definition, information seeking strategies, location and access, use of information, synthesis, and evaluation—emphasizes the importance of information literacy skills in problem solving and decision making (The Big6 Associates, 2006). Abbas (2005) is one observer who argues that children should be taught more about information retrieval (IR) techniques; as she puts it, we need not only smart systems but smart children!

The world of children no less than that of adults has been transformed by IT, whether in the home or in school, whether at play or at work. The library as a physical institution has not been left unaffected by this transformation. School and public libraries themselves have embraced information technology through their online catalogs, digital libraries, and access points to the wider Web itself. They have also experienced a reduced need on the part of children, as of adults, to visit the library building in order to find information for their school work. In a wider context, printed books in the library and the home remain an important source of entertainment as well as information for children but face increased competition from computer games and digital communication for children's limited time. The challenge posed by IT to the library is every bit as real where children are concerned as with their seniors. The technology itself is likely to become easier to use, smaller to accommodate, more portable—with a shift towards hand-held devices—and ever more powerful in its multimedia capabilities. Whether ultimately this enhances or effaces the library as a source of pleasure and learning, only time will tell.

This review makes it clear that researchers from a variety of disciplines are focusing attention on a series of important issues relating to children's interactions with IT. Research studies are trying to answer critical questions relating to the role of IT in the learning process: Under what conditions, if at all, does the Web enhance learning? How can teachers effectively integrate the Web's resources into their teaching? Is the Web an important tool for students with physical and learning disabilities, and what role can school librarians and media specialists play? Should information literacy be a component within the curriculum even at the elementary level, and if so what should it encompass? A start has been made in answering these questions, but to date the results are too fragmented and in some cases contradictory to formulate with confidence policies for school administrators, teachers, and librarians. It is hard to dispute the conclusion drawn by Schofield and Davidson (2002) that without teacher interest in using the Internet in their classrooms, efforts to link schools to it are likely to be pointless. They say that teachers suffer from twin obstacles: widespread lack of knowledge about computers and the Internet, and limited time in the classroom to use the Internet, and they believe there is little solid evidence about the impact of Internet use on either teachers or students. With a new generation of IT-savvy teachers as well as teacher-librarians and media specialists entering the schools, it is to be hoped and expected that this situation will change for the better.

More research is needed to determine the current role and future potential of public libraries not only as places from which children can access IT resources and gain guidance or instruction where necessary and appropriate but also as institutions that can help to reduce the digital divide between children from IT-rich home and school environments contrasted with those from more deprived environments. More generally, what roles can children play in the design and development of children's IT resources? Are certain researchers right in their assertion that in order to design effective technologies for children, the children themselves should be involved in that design process?

Parents, librarians, and teachers are well aware of the potential dangers that can befall children as they surf the Web, whether these dangers arise from Web content or other Web users. Yet these same adults often are equally aware of the educational and social benefits that the Web brings to children. Beyond such practical concerns are the philosophical issues relating to freedom of access to information and the limits that should be set on censorship even when young information users are involved.

Information technology is but a tool whose ultimate value depends upon the user and the use. There can be no doubt that children now are enthusiastic and frequent users, whether for leisure or educational purposes, whether to sit in isolation at the computer or to utilize the computer to communicate within extended social networks. This reality will not be reversed. The role of information professionals, educators, policy makers and parents, in collaboration with children themselves, is to facilitate the exploitation of IT so as to maximize its potential to enrich the lives of young people while minimizing any harmful effects for this population that remains vulnerable to IT misuse. That remains the challenge for researchers and practitioners alike.

REFERENCES

Abbas, J. (2003). Finding science resources online with the ARTEMIS Digital Library. *Knowledge Quest, 31*(3), 12–14.

Abbas, J. (2005). Out of the mouths of middle school children: 1. Developing user-defined controlled vocabularies for subject access in a digital library. *Journal of the American Society for Information Science and Technology, 56*(14), 1512–1524.

Akin, L. (1998). Information overload and children: A survey of Texas elementary school students. *School Library Media Quarterly Online, 1.* Retrieved July 8, 2008, fromhttp://www.ala.org/ala/aasl/aaslpubsandjournals/slmrb/slmrcontents/volume11998slmqo/akin.cfm.

Arrighetti, J. (2000). The challenge of unattended children in the public library. *Reference Services Review, 29*(1), 65–71.

Attewell, P., Suazo-Garcia, B., & Battle, J. (2003). Computers and young children: Social benefit or social problem? *Social Forces, 82*(1), 277–296.

Australian Library and Information Association. (2006). *Internet Access in Public Libraries Survey 2005.* Retrieved July 8, 2008, from http://www.alia.org.au/advocacy/internet.access/summary.report.2005.pdf.

Bain, C. D., & Rice, M. L. (2006). The influence of gender on attitudes, perceptions, and uses of technology. *Journal of Research on Technology in Education*, *39*(2), 119–132.

Bar-Ilan, J., & Belous, Y. (2007). Children as architects of Web directories: An exploratory study. *Journal of the American Society of Information Science and Technology, 58*(6), 895–907.

Beheshti, J., Bowler, L., Large, A., & Nesset, V. (2005). Towards an alternative information retrieval system for children. In A. Spink & C. Cole (Eds.), *New directions in cognitive information retrieval* (pp. 139–165). Dordrecht, Netherlands: Springer Verlag.

Beheshti, J., Large, A., Clement, I., & Tabatabaei, N. (2007). *Evaluating the usability of a virtual reality information system for children.* Proceedings of the Annual Conference of the Canadian Association for Information Science, Montreal, May 10–12, 2007. Retrieved July 8, 2008, from http://www.cais-acsi.ca/proceedings/2007/beheshti_2007.pdf.

Big6 Associates. (2006). *The Big Six: Information skills for student achievement.* Retrieved July 8, 2008, from http://www.big6.com/.

Bilal, D. (2000). Children's use of the Yahooligans! Web search engine: I. Cognitive, physical, and affective behaviors of fact-based search tasks. *Journal of the American Society for Information Science, 51*(7), 646–665.

Bilal, D. (2001). Children's use of the Yahooligans! Web search engine: II. Cognitive and physical behaviors on research tasks. *Journal of the American Society of Information Science and Technology, 52*(2), 118–136.

Bilal, D. (2002a). Children's use of the Yahooligans! Web search engine. III. Cognitive and physical behaviors on fully self-generated search tasks. *Journal of the American Society for Information Science and Technology, 53*(13), 1170–1183.

Bilal, D. (2002b). *Children design their interfaces for Web search engines: A participatory approach.* Proceedings of the 30th Annual Conference of the Canadian Association for Information Science, Toronto, May 2002 (pp. 204–214). Toronto: CAIS.

Bilal, D. (2003). *Draw and tell: Children as designers of Web interfaces. Humanizing information technology: From ideas to bits and back.* ASIST 2003. Proceedings of the 66th ASIST Annual Meeting (pp. 135–141). Medford, NJ: Information Today.

Bilal, D., & Kirby, J. (2002). Differences and similarities in information seeking: Children and adults as Web users. *Information Processing & Management, 38*(5), 649–670.

Bilal, D., & Wang, P. (2005). Children's conceptual structures of science categories and the design of Web directories. *Journal of the American Society for Information Science and Technology, 56,* 1303–1313.

Borgman, C., Hirsh, S., Walter, V., & Gallagher, A. L. (1995). Children's searching behavior on browsing and keyword online catalogs: The Science Library Catalog project. *Journal of the American Society for Information Science, 46*(9), 663–684.

Bowler, L., Large, A., & Rejskind, G. (2001). Primary school students, information literacy and the Web. *Education for Information, 19*(3), 201–223.

Bricken, M. (1991). *No interface to design. Cyberspace: The first steps.* Cambridge, MA: MIT Press.

Broch, E. (2000). Children's search engines from an information search process perspective. *School Library Media Research, 3.* Retrieved July 8, 2008, from http://www.ala.org/ala/aasl/aaslpubsandjournals/slmrb/slmrcontents/volume32000/childrens.cfm.

Calvert, S. L., Rideout, V. J., Woolard, J. L., Barr, R. F., & Strouse, G. A. (2005). Age, ethnicity, and socioeconomic patterns in early computer use. *American Behavioral Scientist, 48*(5), 590–607.

Comer, A. D. (2005). Studying Indiana Public Libraries' usage of Internet filters. *Computers in Libraries, 25*(6), 10–15.

Cooper, L. Z. (2005). Developmentally appropriate digital environments for young children. *Library Trends, 54*(2), 286–302.

Curry, A., & Haycock, K. (2001). Filtered or unfiltered? *School Library Journal, 47*(1), 42–47.

Diaz, K. (1998). Filtering, selection, and guided access. *Reference & User Services Quarterly, 38*(2), 147–150.

Dresang, E. T. (2006). Intellectual freedom and libraries: Complexity and change in the twenty-first-century digital environment. *Library Quarterly, 76*(2), 169–192.

Dresang, E. T., Gross, M., & Holt, L. E. (2003). Project CATE. Using outcome measures to assess school-age children's use of technology in urban public libraries: A collaborative research process. *Library and Information Science Research, 25*(1), 19–42.

Druin, A. (2005). What children can teach us: Developing digital libraries for children with children. *Library Quarterly, 75*(1), 20–41.

Druin, A., Bederson, B. B., Weeks, A., Farber, A., Grosjean, J., Guha, M. L., et al. (2003). The International Children's Digital Library: Description and analysis of first use. *First Monday, 8*(5). Retrieved July 8, 2008, from http://www.firstmonday.dk/issues/issue8_5/druin/index.html.

Edmonds, L., Moore, P., & Balcom, K. M. (1990). The effectiveness of an online catalog. *School Library Journal, 36,* 28–32.

Enochsson, A. (2001). Children choosing Web pages. *The New Review of Information Behaviour Research, 2,* 151–166.

Gross, M., Dresang, E. T., & Holt, L. E. (2004). Children's in-library use of computers in an urban public library. *Library & Information Science Research, 26,* 311–337.

Harbeck, J. D., & Sherman, T. M. (1999). Seven principles for designing developmentally appropriate Web sites for young children. *Educational Technology, 39*(4), 39–44.

Hasselbring, T. S., & Glaser, C. H. W. (2000). Use of computer technology to help students with special needs. *Children and Computer Technology, 10*(2), 102–122.

Haycock, K., Dobor, M., & Edwards, B. (2003). *The Neal-Schuman authoritative guide to kids' search engines, subject directories, and portals.* New York: Neal-Schuman.

Hirsh, S. G. (1999). Children's relevance criteria and information seeking on electronic resources. *Journal of the American Society for Information Science, 50*(14), 1265–1283.

Hsieh-Yee, I. (2001). Research on Web search behavior. *Library and Information Science Research, 23*(2), 167–185.

Kafai, Y., & Bates, M. (1997). Internet Web-searching instruction in the elementary classroom: Building a foundation for information literacy. *School Library Media Quarterly, 25*(2), 103–111.

Kail, R. V. (2004). *Children and their development* (3rd ed.). Upper Saddle River, NJ: Pearson Education.

Kuhlthau, C. C. (1991). Inside the search process: Information seeking from the user's perspective. *Journal of the American Society of Information Science, 42*(5), 361–371.

Kuiper, E., Volman, M., & Terwel, J. (2005). The Web as an information resource in K-12 education: Strategies for supporting students in searching and processing information. *Review of Educational Research, 75*(3), 285–328.

Kuntz, J. (2000). Criteria for comparing children's Web search tools. *Library Computing, 18*(3), 203–207.

Lankes, R. D. (2003). Current state of digital reference in primary and secondary education. *D-Lib Magazine, 9*(2). Retrieved July 8, 2008, from http://www.dlib.org/dlib/february03/lankes/02lankes.html.

Large, A. (2005). Children, teenagers, and the Web. *Annual Review of Information Science and Technology, 39,* 347–392.

Large, A., & Beheshti, J. (2000). The Web as a classroom resource: Reactions from the users. *Journal of the American Society for Information Science, 51*(12), 1069–1080.

Large, A., & Beheshti, J. (2005). Interface design, Web portals and children. *Library Trends, 54*(2), 318–342.

Large, A., Beheshti, J., & Breuleux, A. (1998). Information seeking in a multimedia environment by primary school students. *Library & Information Science Research, 20*(4), 343–376.

Large, A., Beheshti, J., Breuleux A., & Renaud, A. (1994). A comparison of information retrieval from print and CD-ROM versions of an encyclopedia by elementary school students. *Information Processing and Management, 30*(4), 499–513.

Large, A., Beheshti, J., & Moukdad, H. (1999). *Information seeking on the Web: Navigational skills of grade-six primary school students.* Knowledge: Creation, Organization and Use: Proceedings of the 62nd ASIS Annual Meeting, Washington DC, October 1999 (pp. 84–97). Medford, NJ: Information Today.

Large, A., Beheshti, J., Nesset, V., & Bowler, L. (2004). Designing Web portals in intergenerational teams: Two prototype portals for elementary school students. *Journal of the American Society for Information Science, 55*(13), 1140–1154.

Large, A., Beheshti, J., Nesset, V., & Bowler, L. (2006). *Web portal design guidelines as identified by children through the processes of design and evaluation.* ASIST 2006: Proceedings of the 69th ASIS&T Annual Meeting. Information Realities: Shaping the Digital Future for All, Austin, Texas, November 3–8, 2006. Silver Springs, MD: American Society for Information Science and Technology. Retrieved July 8, 2008, from http://eprints.rclis.org/archive/00008034.

Large, A., Beheshti, J., Nesset, V., & Bowler, L. (2007a). *Children's representations of taxonomic categories for application in a Web portal: An exploratory study.* Proceedings of the Annual Conference of the Canadian Association for Information Science, Montreal, May 10–12, 2007. Retrieved July 8, 2008, from http://www.cais-acsi.ca/proceedings/2007/large_2007.pdf.

Large, A., Beheshti, J., Nesset, V., & Bowler, L. (2007b). Children's Web portals: Can an intergenerational design team deliver the goods? In M. K. Chelton & C. Cool (Eds.), *Youth information-seeking behavior* (Vol. 2, pp. 279–311). Lanham, MD: Scarecrow Press.

Large, A., Beheshti, J., & Rahman, T. (2002a). Design criteria for children's Web portals: The users speak out. *Journal of the American Society for Information Science and Technology, 53*(2), 79–94.

Large, A., Beheshti, J., & Rahman, T. (2002b). Gender differences in collaborative Web searching behavior: An elementary school study. *Information Processing and Management, 38*(3), 427–443.

Lawless, K. A., Mills, R., & Brown, S. W. (2002). Children's hypertext navigation strategies. *Journal of Research on Technology in Education, 34*(3), 274–284.

Levin, D., & Arafeh, S. (2002). *The digital disconnect: The widening gap between Internet savvy students and their schools.* Pew Internet and American Life Project. Retrieved July 8, 2008, from http://www.pewinternet.org/pdfs/PIP_Schools_Internet_Report.pdf.

Loh, C. S., & Williams, M. D. (2002). What's in a Web site? Student perceptions. *Journal of Research on Technology in Education, 34*(3), 351–363.

Marchionini, G. (1989). Information-seeking strategies of novices using a full-text electronic encyclopedia. *Journal of the American Society for Information Science, 40*(1), 54–66.

McDermott, I. E. (2002). Homework help on the Web. *Searcher, 10*(4), 10–18.

McKechnie, L. (2001). Children's access to services in Canadian public libraries. *Canadian Journal of Information and Library Science, 26*(4), 37–55.

Media Awareness Network. (2000). *Young Canadians in a wired world. An investigation of Internet content and online safety issues: A literature review*. Retrieved July 8, 2008, from http://www.media-awareness.ca/eng/webaware/netsurvey/resources/litreviewfull.htm.

Media Awareness Network. (2001). *Young Canadians in a wired world: The students' view*. Ottawa: Author. Retrieved July 8, 2008, from http://www.media-awareness.ca/english/research/YCWW/phaseI/students.cfm.

Minkel, W. (2000). Young children AND the Web: a Boolean match, or NOT? *Library Journal, 125*(1), 10–11.

Mumtaz, S. (2001). Children's enjoyment and perception of computer use in the home and the school. *Computers and Education, 36*(4), 347–362.

Nielsen, J. (2002). *Kids' corner: Website usability for children*. Retrieved July 9, 2008, from http://www.useit.com/alertbox/20020414.html.

Oliver, R. (1996). The influence of instruction and activity on the development of skills in the usage of interactive information systems. *Education for Information, 14*, 7–17.

Orleans, M., & Laney, M. C. (2000). Children's computer use in the home: Isolation or sociation? *Social Science Computer Review, 18*(1), 56–72.

Pearman, C. J., & Lefever-Davis, S. (2006). Supporting the essential elements with CD-ROM storybooks. *Reading Horizons Journal, 46*(4), 301–313.

Riba, E. A. (2007). *Children's issues in online catalog design*. Retrieved from http://www.osmond-riba.org/lis/KSR.htm.

Rothbauer, P. M., & Gooden, R. (2006). *Representations of young people in information science: The case of the Journal of the American Society for Information Science (and Technology), 1985–2005*. Proceedings of the Canadian Association for Information Science, York University, June 1–3, 2006. Retrieved July 9, 2008, from http://www.cais-acsi.ca/proceedings/2006/rothbauer_2006.pdf.

Schacter, J., Chung, G., & Dorr, A. (1998). Children's Internet searching on complex problems: Performance and process analysis. *Journal of the American Society for Information Science, 49*(9), 840–849.

Schofield, J. W., & Davidson, A. L. (2002). *Bringing the Internet to school: Lessons from an urban district*. San Francisco: Jossey-Bass.

Shantz-Keresztes, L. (2000). "In conversation": Students as Internet users in school libraries. *School Libraries in Canada, 20*(2), 13–16.

Shneiderman, B. (2004). Designing for fun: How can we design user interfaces to be more fun? *Interaction, 11*(5), 48–50.

Siann, G., Durdell, A., Macleod, A., & Glissov, P. (1988). Stereotyping in relation to the gender gap in computing. *Education Research, 30*, 98–103.

Silverstein, J. (2005). Just curious: Children's use of digital reference for unimposed queries. *Library Trends, 54*(2), 228–244.

Soeters, K. E., & van Schaik, K. (2006). Children's experiences on the Internet. *New Library World, 107*(1220/1221), 31–36.

Solomon, P. (1993). Children's information retrieval behavior: A case analysis of an OPAC. *Journal of the American Society for Information Science, 44*(5), 245–64.

Stevenson, S. (2001). K-12 education portals on the Internet. *Multimedia Schools, 8*(5), 40–44.

Sutherland-Smith, W. (2002). Weaving the literacy web: Changes in reading from page to screen. *The Reading Teacher, 55*(7), 662–669.

Teasdale, S., & Lupart, J. L. (2001, May). Gender differences in computer attitudes, skills, and perceived ability. Proceedings of the *Canadian Society for Studies in Education,* Quebeec, Canada.

Waite, S. J. (2004). Tools for the job: A report of two surveys of ICT use for literacy in primary schools in the West of England. *Computer Assisted Learning, 20*(1), 11–20.

Waite, S. J., Wheeler, S., & Bromfield, C. (2007). Our flexible friend: The implications of individual differences for information technology teaching. *Computers & Education, 48,* 80–99.

Wallace, R. M., Kupperman, J., & Krajcik, J. (2000). Science on the Web: Students online in a sixth-grade classroom. *Journal of the Learning Sciences, 9*(1), 75–104.

Walter, V. A. (1997). Becoming digital: Policy implications for library youth services. *Library Trends, 45*(4), 585–601.

Wartella, E., & Jennings, N. (2000). Children and computers: New technology—old concerns. *The Future of Children, 10*(2), 31–43.

Watson, J. S. (1998). "If you don't have it, you can't find it." A close look at students' perceptions of using technology. *Journal of the American Society for Information Science, 49*(11), 1024–1036.

Williams, P. (1999). The net generation: The experiences, attitudes and behaviour of children using the Internet for their own purposes. *Aslib Proceedings, 51*(9), 315–322.

Wolters, F. K. (1989). A PATT study among 10 to 12-year old students in the Netherlands. *Journal of Technology Education, 1*(1). Retrieved July 9, 2008, from http://scholar.lib.vt.edu/ejournals/JTE/v1n1/falco.jte-v1n1.html.

Young, B. J. (2000). Gender differences in student attitudes toward computers. *Journal of Research on Computing in Education, 33*(2), 204–216.

10

OPEN SOURCE SOFTWARE AND LIBRARIES

Ajit Pyati

OPEN SOURCE AND ITS DEMOCRATIC PROMISE?

Faced with the increased commodification of information resources and services and the encroaching dominant logics of business/corporate culture, today's libraries are in search of innovative technological solutions to protect the free flow of ideas. In response to this situation, a growing segment of the library profession is promoting open source software (OSS). OSS, both as a movement and as a form of software development, offers a challenge to dominant proprietary models of software development. The basic idea behind OSS rests in its inverted logic of property, in which value is derived in the distribution and freely available nature of software code (the building block of software), rather than in exclusive ownership over code (Weber, 2004).

OSS presents a more community-driven model of software development, with distributed developers creating code under various norms, informal and semiformal regulations, and licenses. The success of OSS can be seen in its penetration into various levels of society, through the Linux operating system, the popular Apache Web server application, and the Mozilla/Firefox Web browser, to name just a few prominent open source projects (Weber, 2004). Thus, while providing an alternative to commercial software development, OSS intersects comfortably with the proprietary software world and is also utilized by the for-profit sector. OSS and free software, however, are also associated with a sustained grassroots technology movement with an international following and community, and are often linked to alternative, community-driven visions of an information commons (Bollier, 2003). Open source seems to be implicitly linked to a wider democratic technology movement in the world, with the idea that enhanced participation in technological decisions challenges dominant societal logics of commodification (Benkler, 2003).

Two large and successful open source projects that provide a glimpse into the power of open source software are Apache and Linux. Apache dominates the Web server market, and Linux is the major open source operating system, with nearly 40 percent of large American companies using Linux in some form (Weber, 2004). The success of these projects depends on a large pool of developers distributed across the world, with many developers contributing code on a volunteer basis. However, the administrative structures of these projects ensure their financial sustainability.

The Apache Software Foundation was incorporated as a nonprofit corporation in 1999, and now serves as an organizational umbrella for a range of Web-relevant open source projects (Weber, 2004). An Apace Software Foundation board of directors is responsible for the overall direction, coordination among the different projects, legal issues, and other kinds of central services that benefit the individual projects (Weber, 2004). The Apache Foundation thus manages and guides the development of the project. On a financial level, Apache development can be described in terms of a cost-sharing mechanism. For instance, Apache development conforms to a model in which competing software users find it to their advantage to cooperatively fund open source development because doing so gets them a better product at a lower cost (Raymond, 2001). A network of Webmasters has been able to pool their resources for a large project with wide benefits, rather than to compete against each other.

Linux, on the other hand, has a more semiformal organization for decision making about code, and the last word on Linux's code management structure rests with Linus Torvalds, the project's founder (Weber, 2004). Raymond (2001) describes Torvalds's style of development as, "release early and often, delegate everything you can, be open to the point of promiscuity" (p. 21). He further argues that the success of Linux, while owed in large part to Torvalds's vision, is sustained through the effective construction of voluntary communities of interest (Raymond, 2001).

The basic premise of the open source movement is the chance for more developers to have access to software code, which will allow for more successful and bug-free software to be developed (Raymond, 2001). This approach to open source development often has a more *practical* and applied ideological orientation. The open source movement, however, is also part of a larger political movement addressing more democratic and noncommercial forms of technology development. In *Free Software, Free Society: Selected Essays of Richard M. Stallman* (Stallman, 2002), the notion of free software is juxtaposed with open source software. Richard Stallman, a computer programmer who began his work at MIT, is the main founder of the free software movement. The main distinction he makes between the free software movement and the open source movement is in the value differences between the two movements—he states that for the open source movement, the issue of whether software should be open source is a practical question and not an ethical one, whereas for the free software movement, open source is more of an ethical question and is part of a broader social movement (Stallman, 2002).

Given these divergent strands in the objectives of the open source and free software communities, how do libraries fit into this discourse? Libraries around the world have also begun utilizing OSS to help develop some of their services, and some have suggested that the gift culture of the open source programming community complements traditional library service values. Gift cultures are, according to Raymond, "adaptations not to scarcity but to abundance. They arise in populations that do not have significant material-scarcity problems with material goods" (2001, p. 81). He justifies this analogy by stating that there is no serious shortage of disk space, network bandwidth, and computing power, and software is freely shared. In a gift culture, social status is determined not by what you control but by what you give away—in the case of OSS, abundance creates a situation in which the only available measure of competitive success is reputation among one's peers (Raymond, 2001). In the case of libraries, a gift culture exists in the sense that wide distribution and access to information is at the core of library functions. Also, the collaborative nature of OSS mirrors the many resource-sharing activities of libraries (Clarke, 2000).

The benefits of OSS can potentially reduce costs, give users more control, and increase software performance (Courant & Griffiths, 2006). OSS certainly appears to give libraries more control over technological choices and an ability to bring library values to software (Frumkin, 2002); however, the technological, institutional, and social dimensions of this phenomenon need to be explored in further detail. In addition, successful OSS projects often depend on visionary leadership and the development of a large user and codeveloper community (Raymond, 2001), issues that need to be addressed in the context of library open source projects.

A growing and diverse open source development community in libraries exists, but little research has focused on understanding how or whether OSS can enhance library service ethics and goals. It is important to keep in mind, however, that open source products are as commonplace as Web server applications (e.g., Apache), databases, programming languages, and operating systems such as Linux (Weber, 2004). Libraries thus interact and use many of these products and are thus open source users on a Web infrastructure level. In addition, some commercial library vendor products utilize some open source tools and applications (Chudnov, 2006).

This chapter is a first step in contextualizing the terrain of the library open source world within the larger open source/free software debates. I identify some key library open source examples, and explore challenges in the development of library open source projects, along with future lines of action and best practices research. Articulating a political angle to the library open source debate—particularly given the rise of a techno-corporate culture in the library world (Apostle & Raymond, 1997)—remains a task of growing importance and concern.

LIBRARIES AND OSS: EXPLORING THE TERRAIN

An active open source library community exists, with groups such as OSS-4Lib and Code4Lib serving as clearinghouses for various library open source projects (Oss4Lib, n.d.). OSS is now being considered as a viable alternative to the often expensive proprietary library automation systems. For instance, a major OSS suite available for libraries is Koha. Koha is the first open source integrated library system (Koha, 2005) allowing libraries to have access to library automation software. The software is free and follows the guidelines of the open source general public license (GPL). Developed in New Zealand by a company called Katipo Communications, the software now has been adopted in several libraries around the world. For instance, in New Zealand, the Horowhenua Library Trust has implemented the Koha OSS, as well as other libraries in North America and the rest of the world.

The open source community within libraries is growing, with various applications developed for both academic and public libraries, as well as the presence of library-based groups dedicated to the promotion of OSS (e.g., Code4Lib; Oss4Lib). The size of the library open source community is seen in a growing list of publications focusing on library-based OSS developments (Chawner, 2006), and it appears that the library open source community is approaching a level of critical mass in its development. In fact, some argue that the concept of OSS has become increasingly popular in the library field, with many librarians often discouraged with commercial integrated library systems (Breeding, 2007).

Why would libraries be interested in utilizing OSS? Many of the purported advantages—such as cost, customization, a rapid development cycle, more bug-free software—certainly apply. In addition, the context of the largely commercial library automation and vendor market has played a role in pushing libraries to consider OSS. A consolidation of major library automation vendors over the years has reduced the number of choices libraries have for their automation needs (Breeding, 2006), while a changing information environment dominated by Internet technologies has given libraries new choices in meeting the information needs of their users (Pace, 2004). Thus, different models of development such as OSS can be appealing to libraries, which, like much of the IT world, are moving toward the greater adoption of OSS (Dietz & Grant, 2005). Moreover, on an ideological level, OSS, as a purportedly democratic and grassroots technology movement, has symbolic and practical appeal for libraries trying to wrest control away from commercial vendors. Libraries are taking up OSS as a way to reduce the costs of expensive commercial products and to take ownership over their own technology development. In addition, it has been argued that the library profession's values line up with those of OSS (Frumkin, 2002).

OSS potentially allows libraries to contribute to software development, which can empower libraries and bring library values to software (Frumkin, 2002). The March 2002 issue of *Information Technology and Libraries,* in fact, is dedicated to examining the possibilities for OSS in libraries. One of the major themes in this issue is that OSS offers opportunities for resource sharing and for libraries to take more control of their technology situations (Frumkin, 2002). In addition, the open source movement allows for libraries to contribute to technology development, pool resources, and save time and money (Frumkin, 2002).

Library Open Source Communities and Challenges

Active communities focused on library open source projects also exist—as mentioned earlier, Oss4Lib and Code4Lib are two major Web sites serving as clearinghouses for library-based open source projects. Dan Chudnov, a prominent library open source leader, started Oss4Lib in 1999 and maintains it. The stated mission of Oss4Lib is to build "better and free systems for use in libraries," and the site maintains a listing of free software designed for libraries and tracks news about related issues of interest (Oss4Lib, n.d.). The Oss4Lib mailing list and Web site, dedicated to OSS in libraries, examines these issues in more detail and is an active community dedicated to finding open source solutions for libraries. In terms of library-specific open source products, over 100 of these have been announced on the Oss4Lib Web site (http://oss4lib.org), but all fall into these basic categories:

- metadata tools
- protocols
- OPAC/ILS (integrated library systems)
- repositories
- public services tools (e.g., library reserves applications)
- bibliographic management
- information retrieval (Chudnov, 2006).

Code4Lib is a related Web site, and a Code4Lib annual conference now takes place, described as a "loosely structured conference for library technologists to commune, gather/create/share ideas and software, be inspired, and forge collaborations" (Code4Lib, n.d.).

Despite the promise of OSS in libraries and some of its successes, some important challenges remain. One major challenge is the lack of technical skills among staff members in many libraries (Clarke, 2000). Larger libraries with skilled systems staff may have the requisite technical expertise; however, many smaller and less financially robust libraries face daunting technical challenges. In addition, the development of a significant library community around open source projects remains a concern, especially since the development of a user and programmer community remains central to the success of open source projects (Clarke, 2000).

While communities such as Oss4Lib and Code4Lib exist, it is still an open question if enough skilled and committed programmers exist in the library community to sustain larger library-specific open source projects. On another note, a main challenge and key to the future success of open source in the library community depends on a shift in budgeting priorities (Clarke, 2000). Specifically, much of the financial resources expended on commercial vendors would have to be reallocated for investment in staff. More technical staff members could be hired, or this investment could take the form of technical competency building for existing staff.

Some of the advantages for libraries in adopting OSS are little or no upfront costs; however, proper expertise is needed to modify the code to meet local practices or requirements (Muir, 2005). In addition, open source products can develop faster because there are multiple sites working on enhancements, developers are usually closer to the end user, and troubleshooting is spread across a large number of sites (Muir, 2005). However, potential drawbacks to OSS include the issue of who actually provides support, needs for technical expertise, and the hidden costs that go into having staff spend time supporting, tailoring, and enhancing software (Muir, 2005). Regardless, OSS can benefit libraries by lowering initial and ongoing costs, eliminating vendor lock-in, and allowing for greater flexibility (Corrado, 2005).

OSS, in conjunction with open access (OA) and open standards movements, can be beneficial to libraries in the long run. For instance, open source and open standards can help libraries provide patrons with easier access to OA materials and other resources, as open standards make it possible to create interoperable systems to access the literature in various OA journals seamlessly (Corrado, 2005). Though there may be no reason to fear open source for libraries, the choice of open source software depends on whether or not the product meets a library's automation needs as well as its support needs (Balas, 2005).

OA can take many forms, and OA electronic publishing is often cited as an example. Internet technologies have allowed the wide dissemination of scholarly research—allowing libraries, scholars, and publishers alike to re-envision models of scholarly publication. OA literature is digital, online, free of charge, and free of most copyright and licensing restrictions, and what makes it possible is the Internet and the consent of the author or copyright holder (Suber, 2004). OA is compatible with peer review and is not free to produce—it is not focused on whether scholarly literature can be made costless but whether there are better ways to pay the bills than by charging readers and creating access barriers (Suber, 2004). The two most common forms of OA are OA repositories and OA journals. While it is a topic that has been gaining momentum in recent years, OA represents a growing consciousness around the need to make knowledge and information as widely accessible as possible (Willinsky, 2006). In fact, the very possibility for OA has been greatly enhanced by the presence of digital technologies (Willinsky, 2006). *Open standards* refers to protocols such as those proposed by the Open Archives Initiative (OAI), which provide for greater interoperability in standards to facilitate enhanced retrieval of OA and online materials.

Library Open Source Projects

With a sense of the open source terrain in the library community, it is useful to take a more in-depth look at a few prominent projects. This section will highlight the important institutional, technical, and economic factors that maintain these projects. Also, to analyze and compare different library open source projects, several factors will be considered, including: (1) software application, (2) funding/economic structure, and (3) management/development structure.

In terms of software application, the open source movement has the potential to make great changes in libraries if it could produce an integrated library system (ILS) that earns a level of acceptance on the same order that Apache did in the Web server market (Breeding, 2002). The ILS is an essential component of library operations, and a viable open source system will go a long way towards making OSS a more realistic option in library software development. Libraries could potentially play a more active role in the development of technology services to the public if more ILS software is open source. The Koha ILS software (Koha, 2005) is one of the major ILS open source projects currently existing, but is yet to have wide acceptance. I will discuss shortly some of the specifics about another prominent ILS open source project, Evergreen. A company called LibLime, whose stated mission is to make OSS available to libraries (LibLime, 2006), provides support services for libraries planning to use the Koha and Evergreen open source ILS software. This example illustrates the "give away the recipe, open a restaurant" model (Raymond, 2001, p. 136) and shows just one possible adaptation of an open source management style for libraries.

The role of library institutions in the development of software varies from minimal to active. While all projects are nominally open source, it is not always the case that development takes place as part of a larger development community, as it is often limited to a small, localized core of developers. In addition, basic challenges exist surrounding the nature of the technical support structure of library-based OSS projects. For instance, will support take place mainly through library-managed listservs and bug reporting Web sites, or will other spin-off entities provide support? However, despite these challenges, basic open source philosophical viewpoints and development realities tie many of these projects together.

I will look briefly at three library open source projects in more detail: Evergreen, MyLibrary, and Simon Fraser University Library's reSearcher and PKP projects. These projects have been chosen because of their prominence in the library open source community. In addition, the wide variety of these projects illustrates the different types of applications, economic structures, and management/development structures present in library open source projects. Evergreen is an open source ILS developed by the Georgia Library PINES consortium. MyLibrary developed originally out of the North Carolina State University Libraries and is focused on creating library-specific Web portals. Simon Fraser University Library's open source projects deal with both library-specific applications, as well as one of the world's leading open source journal publishing platforms.

Evergreen—Georgia Library PINES Program

The Evergreen project is one of the more ambitious open source ILS projects, and for this reason it has garnered attention in the library community. The Georgia Public Library Service is developing this open source ILS for use by the Georgia Library Public Information Network for Electronic Services (PINES) Program, a consortium of 251 public libraries (LaJeunesse, 2006). The goal for this project is to have a statewide integrated library system for the wide variety of public and academic libraries in Georgia. According to Brad LaJeunesse (personal communication, September 25, 2006), one of the leading figures in this project and a PINES system administrator, Evergreen was conceived because no product in the marketplace existed that fit the needs of PINES. The major requirement for PINES is having software that not only enforces uniformity but also allows for a certain level of local control and administration (LaJeunesse, 2006). This type of flexibility allows the software to be used across the diverse types of libraries in Georgia.

LaJeunesse (personal communication, September 25, 2006) also comments that the software meets the needs of PINES because it is designed by PINES system administrators and librarians. This statement relates to the issue of enhanced customization of OSS. He adds that the development process has included focus groups and discussions with librarians. In an e-mail correspondence, LaJeunesse explained to the author how the librarians decided on the functionality of the software, and how the entire development process has incorporated feedback from librarians (LaJeunesse, personal communication, September 25, 2006). LaJeunesse (personal communication, September 25, 2006) believes that internal support and management have been key to the project's success. In addition, he points to the presence of a "wonderful and motivated staff" and a "top-notch software development team" as important factors in sustaining the project (LaJeunesse, 2006). The Evergreen project, while at an early development stage and dealing with a large and complicated application of an ILS, nonetheless has had its successes. LaJeunesse, in fact, believes that no major setbacks have occurred with the project, but the greatest challenge will be adoption on a larger scale. As other users outside the PINES consortium begin using Evergreen, more opportunities for outside code development and feedback can occur.

Returning to our three categories for analyzing library open source projects—software application, funding/economic structure, and management/development structure—Evergreen presents an interesting case. The ILS application of *Evergreen* is ambitious—many in the library community remain skeptical over the development of an open source ILS. This skepticism is fueled by the fact that the complexity of library automation systems often exceeds the pool of programmers, and many volunteer programmers often do not have the time allotment, project management infrastructure, and other resources needed for the concerted development efforts required to build and maintain an ILS (Breeding, 2002). However, Georgia PINES has been able to release Evergreen, and this points to two major factors in its apparent success—its funding structure and management structure. A consortium is funding its development, and it enjoys the full support of management. While outside developers are not contributing much code yet (LaJeunesse, personal communication, September 25, 2006), the project appears to have a viable management and economic structure for meeting the needs of its member libraries.

MyLibrary

The MyLibrary project is a Web portal designed especially for libraries. MyLibrary is a user-driven, customizable interface for collections of Internet resources, and its purpose is to reduce information overload by allowing patrons to select as little or as much information as they desire for their personal pages (MyLibrary, 2005). The idea of customization for the user drives this project, and the project was first conceived in 1997 at the North Carolina State University (NCSU) Libraries. A driving force behind this project is Eric Lease Morgan, with whom I corresponded via e-mail. As a librarian and also the lead programmer in this project, Morgan and two other librarians at NCSU saw the emergence of personalized services such as MyYahoo during the peak of the dot-com boom and decided to extend this idea to the library realm (E. L. Morgan, personal communication, October 3, 2006). Morgan was part of the Digital Library Initiatives Department at the library, and believes the "forward thinking" nature of the library allowed them to develop MyLibrary primarily as a set of services for users (Morgan, personal communication, October 3, 2006). Thus, rather than focusing on developing collections, this project is primarily geared towards user services.

The success of the project is seen in a number of libraries that are using the software—some notable examples include Cornell University, Los Alamos National Laboratory, and Open University. Morgan (personal communication, October 3, 2006) also discusses that a fair number of MyLibrary "imitators" exists, and that imitation is the "sincerest form of flattery." The development of the product is continuing apace, with new versions being released on a regular basis. However, Morgan no longer works at NCSU Libraries and is now based at the University of Notre Dame. When he left NCSU Libraries, it was decided that the copyright for the software would remain with NCSU (Morgan, personal communication, October 3, 2006). Morgan remains the lead programmer on the project, and primary development is now based at the University Libraries of Notre Dame.

Despite the successes of the MyLibrary project, certain challenges are notable and ongoing. According to Morgan (personal communication, October 3, 2006), the lack of computer programming expertise in the library community is a pressing concern. MyLibrary is not an easy piece of software to download and install without adequate programming skills, and technical support is maintained through a mailing list Morgan oversees (Morgan, personal communication, October 3, 2006). Morgan believes MyLibrary allows librarians to take greater control over their computing environments, but he does not think enough librarians understand these technologies and are thus unable to fully take advantage of them. The time needed for ongoing development of the software remains a challenge—Morgan, as the main programmer, has to divide his time spent on MyLibrary with his other responsibilities at the University Libraries of Notre Dame.

In my correspondence with Morgan, he did not specifically mention growing the outside developer community as a major challenge, but it appears that a wider development community could result in a faster development cycle. The MyLibrary experience also points to an important fact about much of OSS development—programming time is often given on a volunteer basis, and challenges exist in balancing this volunteer work with other job demands. The initial management structure of MyLibrary at NCSU Libraries, however, gave the project an official status beyond a volunteer project, but sustaining this project beyond the original development team would require other library-based programmers to dedicate their time and expertise to the project. Although, as Morgan discusses, the level of programming skills within the library community remains fairly low.

Simon Fraser University Library: reSearcher and PKP

Simon Fraser University (SFU) Library in British Columbia, Canada has been developing OSS for several years. SFU Library has been an active developer and advocate for OSS solutions for libraries since the mid-1990s, and the library develops, supports, and coordinates the development of two software suites, the reSearcher suite and PKP suite (SFU, 2005). Central to both of these projects has been the support and leadership of key administrators. SFU Library developed and implemented the reSearcher suite, an award-winning integrated set of open source tools for locating and managing electronic information resources, designed for use by students and researchers in academic libraries (SFU, 2005). The components of reSearcher are Citation Manager, CUFTS, GODOT, dbWiz, and the CUFTS Knowledgebase, and they were developed with the support of the Council of Prairie and Pacific University Libraries (COPPUL) and the British Columbia Electronic Library Network (BC ELN; SFU, 2005).

The PKP software suite, on the other hand, is OSS that supports scholarly publishing and communication. In contrast to the reSearcher suite, the PKP suite is a development partnership with the Public Knowledge Project (PKP) at the University of British Columbia (SFU-UBC). The PKP suite components are Open Journal Systems, Open Conference Systems, and the PKP Open Archives Harvester. Open Journal Systems (OJS) has been adopted worldwide as an online publishing platform by hundreds of scholarly online journals (SFU, 2005). OJS has been recently recognized as a Scholarly Publishing and Academic Resources Coalition (SPARC) Leading Edge Project, and has received funding from Canada's Social Sciences and Humanities Research Council (SSHRC), the Max Bell Foundation, the Soros Foundation, the International Network for the Advancement of Scientific Publishing (INASP), and the MacArthur Foundation (Synergies Project, 2006).

The Public Knowledge Project (PKP) at the University of British Columbia is the original developer of this software package, but a memorandum of understanding signed on January 14, 2005 made SFU Library the home for future PKP software development. This memorandum of understanding affirms the "SFU-UBC Partnership for Open Source Publishing Software Development." In this agreement, the SFU Library and SFU's Canadian Centre for Studies in Publishing (CCSP) agreed to enter into a partnership with UBC's PKP to support the maintenance and ongoing development of Open Journal Systems (OJS), Open Conference Systems (OCS), and the PKP Harvester (PKPH; SFU-UBC, 2005). This joint venture will involve providing a permanent home for this suite of OSS in the SFU Library (SFU-UBC, 2005). A major portion of SFU Library's activities is in managing the development of the OJS, OCS, and PKPH software, with SFU Library Systems staff taking on this responsibility. SFU Library is committing Can $21,000 annually to provide ongoing systems management and support for the software suite and will work both with PKP and CCSP to coordinate and support efforts to apply for research and development grants to ensure continuing support and development of PKP software (SFU-UBC, 2005).

The PKP is a leading voice in open source and OA models in scholarly publishing. The PKP is a project funded by the Canadian federal government, which is committed to expanding the realm of public education by improving social science's contribution to public knowledge (PKP, 2007a). PKP is involved with many activities, including major grant-funded activities related to increasing the research capacities of developing nations, as well as the development of prototype Web sites in collaboration with partners, with a focus on integrating research resources with more public information sources and more interactive environments (PKP, 2007a).

The OJS software has the potential to reduce the time and energy devoted to the clerical and managerial tasks associated with editing a journal while improving the record-keeping and efficiency of editorial processes (Willinsky, 2005). In addition, while not necessarily promoting OA publishing, OJS has the ability to facilitate OA to scholarly information. The community of journals deploying OJS continues to grow, with over 140 registered users on the PKP Support Forum worldwide (Willinsky, 2005).

OJS has been a successful open source product, with several hundred journals using this software (PKP, n.d.). Much of the user base for OJS, in fact, comes from the developing world, with over 200 journals in Africa using the OJS software through the African Journals Online program (PKP, n.d.). This large amount of uptake in the developing world is not surprising given the economic challenges of accessing commercially controlled scholarly information in that part of the world. The open source nature of the product (free to download) certainly makes it an attractive product for users, as traditional corporate models of scholarly publishing can be bypassed.

The management of the reSearcher and PKP software projects differ—most reSearcher products rely on some level of support from consortia. PKP, on the other hand, depends on research grants and will benefit from a nationwide grant of $5.8 million (Can) for the Synergies Project, funded by the Canada Foundation for Innovation (PKP, 2007b). SFU Library presents the case of two successful open source projects with quite different applications—one a regional, library-based set of applications, the other being an internationally well-regarded open source journal publishing application. The continued growth of these projects will depend on the growth of the developer communities for these projects and the long-term sustainability of funding models. However, the OJS project is starting to develop wider acceptance and growth as the major open source journal publishing software. For instance, the First International PKP Scholarly Publishing Conference took place in July 2007 in Vancouver, bringing together a range of international participants with an interest in OJS, as well as a concern for improving access to research and scholarship on a global scale (PKP, 2007c).

BEST PRACTICES IN LIBRARY OPEN SOURCE PROJECTS?

This review of a few prominent library open source projects has outlined some of the challenges these projects have in common, and some important differences. Are there lessons we can begin to draw out in order to understand library open source best practices? For instance, a common theme that arises in these projects is leadership, both on an individual and organizational level. As Eric Raymond (2001) correctly observes, the initial development of an open source project often depends on the vision of an individual, but it will only be successful through sustained effort at community development. Community building is thus an important theme in developing a set of best practices for library open source projects.

Building community includes both users and code contributors—thus far, it appears for the projects I have discussed that code contribution is not occurring beyond the initial development group. However, user communities appear to be growing, especially in the case of SFU Library's OJS project. It remains an open question if, as user communities continue to grow, developer communities will grow along with them. Developing a strong community of users and developers can help ensure the technical sustainability of open source projects.

On the theme of sustainability, the financial viability of projects remains important. Different models of sustainability are presented in these examples, from consortium-funding models to foundation support, individual library support, and international agency support. Financial sustainability is also linked to the management structure of the projects. Developing financially sustainable library open source projects may require one of these models or a combination of them. Finally, establishing the means for technical support is also an important issue. For instance, will an outside company (as in the case of LibLime) provide technical support, or will project coders do it? In addition, it needs to be determined which services will be free and which services will have a fee associated with them.

Any set of best practices will thus need to include the various issues of funding and management structure, leadership, code development, community building, and technical and financial sustainability. These issues are not necessarily particular to libraries and affect other service institutions seeking to utilize OSS, but nonetheless they need to be resolved if libraries are to be successful in developing and maintaining OSS projects.

OSS IN LIBRARIES: A POLITICAL AND ACTIVIST MOVEMENT?

With a discussion of a range of technical, management, and economic issues surrounding OSS in libraries, I end with some reflections about the political and activist nature of this movement in libraries. As I mentioned earlier in this chapter, it is useful to ask how the library open source movement is tied into larger grassroots struggles in favor of an information commons and against the increasing commodification of information. A useful framework to begin addressing these questions is to look at the various levels at which advocacy and activism can take place, including: (1) policy, (2) individuals and communities, and (3) systems and institutions (Pyati, 2007).

On the policy level, it is important to understand the progressive and democratic orientations of the open source movement. For instance, is the open source movement in libraries linked to larger advocacy agendas for greater library-based control of technology? Does a consciousness of the political and grassroots democratic aspects of the open source movement exist in libraries, or are more practical reasons driving the movement? Are policies being enacted at institution- and profession-wide levels to promote open source in core functionalities, such as integrated library systems?

On the individual and community level, one has to question the participatory and community-oriented aspects of the movement. Specifically, does open source create a more participatory technology development process in libraries? Does technical expertise become more democratized, or do new technical hierarchies develop? Finally, on the systems and institution level, it is useful to explore how open and collaborative the open source process in libraries is. Does open source build on existing library strengths of resource sharing and cooperation? Does it challenge hierarchical models of technology development?

Applying these questions to the library open source context remains crucial to moving beyond the discourse of open source as a merely practical and cost-effective alternative to proprietary software development. The examples I have shown in this chapter offer a range of successes for libraries in terms of reduced cost, and increased customization, and control, but the ideological underpinnings for many of these projects, with the exception of OJS, do not appear to be activist or political in character. Strong links to *radical,* grassroots conceptions of open source and free software are generally lacking in these examples and in the wider library open source community as well. Is this fact important? Perhaps not. OSS, in fact, may not be quite the democratizing technology that many of its fervent advocates claim it is. However, OSS and the free software movement provide an opportunity and opening for libraries to re-envision alternatives to the dominance of corporate, capitalist modes of software development. Libraries are taking part in these movements, but more work needs to be done in understanding how to sustain these projects and in theorizing a larger political voice for libraries in debates about technological democratization.

REFERENCES

Apostle, R., & Raymond, B. (1997). *Librarianship and the information paradigm.* Lanham, MD: Scarecrow Press.

Balas, J. L. (2005). There's no need to fear open source. *Information Today.* Retrieved October 5, 2007, from http://www.infotoday.com/cilmag/may05/balas.shtml.

Benkler, Y. (2003). The political economy of commons. [Electronic version]. *Upgrade, 4*(3), 6.

Bollier, D. (2003). The rediscovery of the commons. [Electronic version]. *Upgrade, 4*(3), 10.

Breeding, M. (2002). The open source ILS: Still only a distant possibility. *Information Technology and Libraries, 21*(1), 16–18.

Breeding, M. (2006). Reshuffling the deck. *Library Journal, 131*(6), 40–54.

Breeding, M. (2007). An update on open source ILS. *Computers in Libraries, 27*(3), 27–29.

Chawner, B. (2006). *Open source software and libraries bibliography.* Retrieved December 18, 2006, from http://www.vuw.ac.nz/staff/brenda_chawner/biblio.html.

Chudnov, D. (2006). *The future of FLOSS in libraries.* Unpublished book chapter manuscript.

Clarke, K. S. (2000). *Open source software and the library community.* Unpublished master's thesis, University of North Carolina at Chapel Hill.

Corrado, E. M. (2005). The importance of open access, open source, and open standards for libraries. *Issues in Science and Technology Librarianship* (Spring 2005). Retrieved May 10, 2006, from http://www.istl.org/05-spring/article2.html.

Courant, P. N., & Griffiths, R. J. (2006). *Software and collaboration in higher education: A study of open source software.* Ithaca, NY: Organization for Open Source Software Study. Retrieved July 24, 2008, from http://www.ithaka.org/strategic-services/oss/OOSS_Report_FINAL.pdf.

Dietz, R., & Grant, C. (2005). The dis-integrating world of library automation. *Library Journal, 130*(11), 38–40.

Frumkin, J. (2002). Guest editorial: Balancing the playing field. *Information Technology and Libraries, 21*(1), 2.

Koha. (2005). *About Koha.* Retrieved December 5, 2005, from http://www.koha.org.

LaJeunesse, B. (2006). Evergreen: Built for a consortium. *Library Journal.com.* Retrieved October 5, 2007, from http://www.libraryjournal.com/article/CA515806.html.

LibLime. (2006). *Our mission—LibLime.* Retrieved December 27, 2006, from http://liblime.com.

Muir, S. P. (2005). An introduction to the open source software issue. *Library Hi Tech, 23*(4), 465–468.

MyLibrary. (2005). *MyLibrary@NCState.* Retrieved December 21, 2006, from http://my.lib.ncsu.edu/.

Oss4Lib. (n.d.). *Oss4lib: Open source systems for libraries.* Retrieved November 10, 2006, from http://www.oss4lib.org.

Pace, A. K. (2004). Dismantling integrated library systems. *Library Journal, 129*(2), 34–36.

Public Knowledge Project. (2007a). *About the Public Knowledge Project.* Retrieved October 5, 2007, from http://pkp.sfu.ca/node/4.

Public Knowledge Project. (2007b). *Major Canadian initiative for PKP.* Retrieved October 5, 2007, from http://pkp.sfu.ca/node/695.

Public Knowledge Project. (2007c). *PKP Scholarly Publishing Conference 2007.* Retrieved July 23, 2008, from http://ocs.sfu.ca/pkp2007/index.php.

Public Knowledge Project. (n.d.). *Open Journal Systems—publications.* Retrieved October 5, 2007, from http://pkp.sfu.ca/pkp_publications.

Pyati, A. K. (2007). *Re-envisioning libraries in the information society: A critical theory of library technology.* Unpublished dissertation, University of California, Los Angeles.

Raymond, E. S. (2001). *The cathedral and the bazaar.* Sebastopol, CA: O'Reilly.

Simon Fraser University. (2005). *Software@SFU library.* Retrieved November 30, 2005, from http://www.software.lib.sfu.ca.

Simon Fraser University, University of British Columbia. (2005). *Memorandum of understanding: SFU-UBC partnership for open source publishing software development.* Unpublished manuscript.

Stallman, R. (2002). *Free software, free society: Selected essays of Richard M. Stallman.* Boston: GNU Press.

Suber, P. (2004). *A very brief introduction to open access.* Retrieved September 29, 2006, from http://www.earlham.edu/~peters/fos/brief.htm.

Synergies Project. (2006). *Synergies—CFI application—project 12112.* Unpublished report.

Weber, S. (2004). *The success of open source.* Cambridge, MA: Harvard University Press.

Willinsky, J. (2005). Open journal systems: An example of open source software for journal management and publishing. *Library Hi Tech, 23*(4), 504–519.

Willinsky, J. (2006). *The access principle.* Cambridge, MA: MIT Press.

11

TECHNOLOGIES OF SOCIAL REGULATION: AN EXAMINATION OF LIBRARY OPACs AND WEB PORTALS

Gloria J. Leckie, Lisa Given, and Grant Campbell

In this chapter, we will address the longstanding difficulties with library catalogs (and, more recently, Web portals) as information-related search and discovery tools and the ongoing problems that users experience in understanding the role and features of such tools and retrieving relevant information with them, despite persistent advances in information technologies (IT).[1] There is a vast literature in library and information science (LIS) that has long explored these issues from the perspectives of human-computer interaction and information retrieval. Here, we will use regulation theory to argue that library catalogs and Web portals should be viewed as information technologies that are, first and foremost, commercial entities within the production system of advanced capitalism. The fact that library catalog and Web-management systems are designed, sold, and purchased for purposes deemed to be a social good sometimes obscures the fact that such technologies are not necessarily socially neutral or benign but operate very much within the capitalistic marketplace and framework. In the library realm, the production-consumption system that results in the online publicly accessible catalog (OPAC) and the library portal is relatively invisible yet has real implications for both the character and functionality of such tools and the success of information searchers who must use them to meet their information-related needs.

While the relationship between libraries and IT has been longstanding and endemic, there is no relationship more intimate or integral than that of the library and its automated or integrated library system (ILS). The ILS that the library uses represents a large and often opaque commitment of money, time, and labor (Fischer & Lugg, 2006) and encompasses a wide variety of library functions from acquisitions, cataloging, and circulation to specialized management data analyses. Currently, even relatively small libraries rely on some sort of centralized software package and requisite computer hardware to perform the myriad of housekeeping and information display tasks that are routine in most libraries.

The most familiar public face of the library's ILS is its primary access mechanism, the OPAC. This deceptively simple interface facilitates access to the library's holdings (and increasingly to resources beyond the library's walls) through a variety of avenues such as subject headings, keywords, authorship, call numbers, and so forth. Also, in the current Web-based IT environment, the OPAC (or, in its Web format, the WebPAC), appears alongside a wealth of other information access mechanisms, through the library's Web portal.

The OPAC and Web portal have been revolutionary information technologies in many respects. Together, they provide a ubiquitous and essential network of information services: displaying information from an array of different bibliographic sources, as well as allowing users to access online tutorials, pathfinders, and other learning materials, customize their searching and monitor their borrowing. Despite these benefits, as with all IT applications, the OPAC and the Web portal contain certain intrinsic difficulties. As we shall discuss later in this chapter, library users find the OPAC difficult to understand and use, with unintelligible descriptors and complex organizational concepts, resulting in confusing search experiences with problematic results. Library Web portals multiply the confusion by integrating resources from numerous sources, creating an illusion of uniform control and access that is not borne out by reality. Regulation theory enables us to explore these difficulties by placing them within a context of larger economic and social activity.

OVERVIEW OF REGULATION THEORY

Regulation theory is usually traced back to the work of Michel Aglietta (1976), who took issue with the established idea that capitalist economies display uniform features. While there may be relatively long periods in which a capitalist formation is quite stable, Aglietta argued that such economies regularly transform and change over time based on a variety of regulatory factors specific to each economy/society. Within much of the developed world, the stage of capitalism that is regarded as being one of the longest and most stable is referred to as Fordism, and is considered to have been in ascendance from about 1945 to 1973, when "a sharp recession and the shock of sudden large-scale oil price rises [brought about] an awareness that developments were taking place that meant the Fordist regime was no longer sustainable" (Webster, 2006, p. 69). Regulation theorists maintain that the Fordist regime changed noticeably and considerably since the 1970s, giving rise to a new stage of capitalism often referred to as post-Fordism.[2]

Since Aglietta's original treatise, numerous scholars (a representative sample of which are presented in Boyer & Saillard, 2002) have contributed to the body of literature identified as regulation theory. As a result, regulation theory today is not so much a unified theoretical stance but rather an ongoing approach or "research program" (Friedman, 2000, p. 60) to examine the various faces/stages of capitalist production and the changes that occur within them over time. Not all capitalist formations that exist simultaneously are the same: for instance, Boyer (2005) notes that there are "at least four forms of capitalism that exist in OECD [Organization for Economic Co-operation and Development] countries" (p. 510). Given this variability, regulationist approaches focus on (1) describing the elements of production and the accumulation regime in a particular stage or form of capitalism and (2) examining the mode of social regulation (MSR; including political and social processes, institutional arrangements, assumptions, and behaviors of social actors, etc.) that works together with the accumulation regime to support and perpetuate each stage/form of capitalist production.[3]

The literature describing various modes of production and accumulation regimes is very extensive, so we will give only the briefest glimpse into that body of work here. According to Friedman (2000) and Webster (2006), the characteristics of the Fordist production system were large oligopolistic and vertically integrated firms that mass-produced longstanding product items (such as cars or refrigerators), relying on continual improvements in mass technology and factory floor workers who required little or limited training. The Fordist economies of scale enabled such firms to constantly reinvest in their production systems and accumulate both more capital and material resources for further production. Accompanying this type of production/accumulation cycle was a continual growth in the desire for consumer goods, as well as state-supported Keynesian fiscal and social regulatory policies, including certain welfare measures, which guaranteed social stability and enabled everyone to participate more fully in mass consumption.

Post-Fordism, on the other hand, is characterized by "small batch production of differentiated products with short, hard to predict life cycles, produced using multi-purpose machines and multi-skilled workers working in small teams" (Friedman, 2000, p. 60). This gives rise to the well-known just in time mode of production, which is supported by extensive computerized information systems and a flattened management hierarchy. Firms are global in both production and accumulation activities and take advantage of global conditions to attain the most advantageous position for producing and distributing their products or services. Post-Fordism, then, has caused radical shifts in the economic base of both developed and developing economies. In the developed economies, there has been a decline in so-called smokestack industries and a rise in service, financial, and other information-related activities, much of which is done (such as for call-centers and software production) in the developing economies for a fraction of the labor costs. Also, post-Fordism in the developed economies is often accompanied by neoliberal governmental regulatory policies that seek to dismantle or undermine the welfare state of the previous Fordist economy. These trends have caused unprecedented job loss, layoffs, corporate restructuring, downsizing, and firm relocation, all of which are still ongoing.

While very detailed descriptions of all of the complex elements of production and accumulation regimes are plentiful, analyses of the MSR are relatively less common (Tickell & Peck, 1995, p. 361). The MSR is defined as a

> set of social relations which have the effect of guiding and sustaining the accumulation process. Comprised of a complex ensemble of social norms and habits; state forms, structures and practices; customs and networks; and institutional compromises, rules of conduct and enforceable laws, the MSR defines the social context in which expanded economic reproduction occurs. (Tickell & Peck, 1995, p. 360–361)

In other words, the MSR is dynamic and integral to production and accumulation regimes. The MSR enables particular capitalist formations to be sustained and to limit the effects of unforeseen crises and threats by inserting "markets into a series of institutional arrangements that socialize both information and behaviour" (Boyer & Saillard, 2002, p. 41).

This chapter will concentrate on revealing and deconstructing certain modes of social regulation within post-Fordism that we think, ultimately, account for the ongoing difficulties with the OPAC and library Web portal as search and discovery tools and are implicated in the ways in which users experience and understand library interfaces. As Webster (2006) notes, regulationist analyses are frequently used to examine the ways in which IT has become assimilated into institutional settings/practices in advanced capitalism, and so it is highly appropriate to use such a perspective to examine the evolution, role, and use of IT in library environments. Accordingly, as an alternate explanation as to why library interfaces continue to be difficult to use and why change has been slow to come despite repeated calls for it, it is our contention that certain MSRs work in concert to frame the development of library access mechanisms and their accompanying interfaces and that they constrain the types of interfaces and interface features that it is possible to provide for library users. The MSRs that we intend to explore in detail include:

- the complex standards (and their theoretical foundations) that have developed over time to regulate information display that are now embedded within commercial products (e.g., MARC, AACR2, LCSH, LCC and DDC, Z39.2, etc.);
- the professional attitudes and practices of librarians regarding the catalog production system, the intellectual content of the catalog and Web portal, and the view of the library user;
- the rise of, and dependence on, commercial library system vendors to build the kinds of systems and interfaces that they think libraries should have; and
- paradigms of information literacy and library interface development through usability testing.

However, before turning to our analysis of the MSR, we shall provide an overview of the development of the current catalog production and accumulation regime that has evolved throughout the twentieth century and has intensified in the post-World War II period.

CATALOGING AS PRODUCTION

For much of human history, cataloging of library collections was a haphazard and idiosyncratic activity carried out by workers (historically mainly monks/clergy, scholars, or government officials) in individual libraries around the world. Prior to the nineteenth century, there was no agreement on what a catalog should look like, what it should contain, or how the items listed within it should be organized. Most catalogs were prepared in a book format, which severely limited how current the catalog could be. After the French Revolution, however, the idea that a catalog could be produced on cards took hold, and by the mid- and late-nineteenth century, library catalogs were being converted to a card format and housed in drawers, thus enabling the catalog to be kept up to date much more easily by inserting new cards and removing old ones.

The movement to card catalogs, and the accompanying development of documented thought regarding how library collections should be cataloged, marked the beginning of cataloging as what could be argued to be a Fordist or quasi-Fordist production activity. By the mid-1800s, scholar-librarians (such as Charles Cutter of the Boston Athenaeum, Charles Jewitt of the Smithsonian Institute, and Sir Anthony Panizzi of the British Museum) were putting forth ideas about how cataloging could be done more effectively and cheaply, to benefit all libraries. The key and ultimately most influential ideas were that (1) cataloging should be done by agreed-upon standards (Cutter, 1876 Panizzi, 1841) and (2) catalog cards, which had been created at a central location, could be reproduced indefinitely and distributed internationally to any library who owned the same items (Jewitt, 1853). Together these two ideas would mean that all catalogs had the same information, organized and presented the same way, and that the cost of having library workers in every library catalog the same items repeatedly would be eliminated through technologies of card reproduction and distribution. This kind of centralized and cost-effective production by the few for consumption by the many is at the heart of the Fordist production model.

Cutter, Jewitt, and Panizzi turned out to be prescient, as these two fundamental ideas rapidly took hold in the late 1800s and early 1900s. By 1901, the Library of Congress (LC) was the main institution producing and selling catalog cards (Chan, 2007, p. 23) to thousands of libraries internationally, and the LC Catalog Card Service, as it came to be known, became the major way that libraries of all sizes obtained cataloging data for their card catalogs well into the twentieth century. In 1916, nine years after the Library of Congress had moved to its new building, the library's annual report referred to its burgeoning business of selling catalog records: "the card catalog of the Library . . . , owing to the sale of the printed cards, is a matter of general concern to libraries" (cited in Chan, 1999). While the report decorously worded this as a commitment to the needs of libraries, the sale of catalog cards clearly generated revenue for the Library of Congress, and the mix of public motive and private profit anticipates the curious rhetoric surrounding the rise of bibliographic utilities in the late 1960s.[4] Utilities such as OCLC, RLIN and WLN (as well as national agencies such as the Library of Congress and the National Library of Canada)[5] all touted the virtues of universal bibliographic control and the sharing of cataloging expertise: a sharing process that made it possible for small libraries to have decent catalogs, while at the same time generating healthy revenue through subscription fees.[6]

In the ensuing decades, the Library of Congress saw not only its catalog but also its subject authority file and classification system become de facto standards in the Anglo-American cataloging community. Tools originally planned for internal use only were sold to other libraries so that the Library of Congress Subject Headings (LCSH) and the Library of Congress Classification Schedules quickly became part of the library infrastructure, until other, arguably better tools—Bliss's Bibliographic Classification, the Sears Subject Headings, and PRECIS—were gradually abandoned or consigned to marginal status (Williamson, 1996, p. 163).

The rise of de facto standards was accompanied by a number of formal regulatory standards that had started to appear in different countries regarding how the information on catalog cards should be conceptualized, organized, and presented. In addition to the cataloging standards published by the Library of Congress, other bodies, such as the American Library Association, the Vatican, and the British Library, also put forward cataloging standards documents (Chan, 2007, pp. 53–56). Ultimately, the promulgation of numerous, sometimes conflicting, standards led to a historic international conference in 1961, resulting in the first edition of the Anglo-American Cataloging Rules (AACR) in 1967 and eventually the creation of the International Standard Bibliographic Description or ISBD (Chan, 2007, pp. 49–51). Catalog cards, then, became even more standardized and more acceptable internationally as a product to be purchased.

The creation of the ISBD and the AACR resulted in a mild schizophrenia in cataloging practice and education. On the one hand, regular invocations of Cutter's influential 1904 edition of the *Rules for a Dictionary Catalog* admonished catalogers to consider their users and their "habitual way of looking at things," however eccentric (as quoted in Carpenter & Svenonius, 1985, p. 65). On the other hand, the ideal of universal bibliographic control, together with the fact that most libraries could not afford to do original cataloging on their collections, combined to create the impression that there was one way to catalog, and one ideal record for a document, that would be the same across the globe.

The drive for global consistency gathered momentum in the 1950s and 1960s, as the potential of electronic data transfer became clear. The Library of Congress was proactive in moving its sale of catalog records into this new area, and machine-readable cataloging (MARC) first appeared in the mid-1960s, becoming a national standard, and then an international standard, in 1971 and 1973, respectively (Chan, 2007, p. 448).

The impact of MARC on library cataloging took place in two stages. First, MARC introduced computerization into the cataloging workflow, and the perspectives of computerization rapidly infiltrated the intellectual and economic practices of bibliographic control. Electronic distribution greatly enhanced the spread of catalog cards from central agencies like the Library of Congress. Despite Cutter's admonishment to consider the "convenience of the public before the ease of the cataloger" (Cutter, 1904, p. 6), this widespread distribution of records based on LC practices created new layers of de facto standards, such as the Library of Congress Rule Interpretations, which catalogers had to follow if they were to produce consistent records. Libraries that could not afford MARC-compliant equipment and technology quickly became marginalized. The work of cataloging itself fell under the quantifying spirit of measurement, manifested in through-put models of catalog record production that monitored how many books would be catalogued per day and how many subject headings would be applied per record. If, as Webster (2006) suggests, the mode of social regulation frequently manifests itself in the assimilation of information technologies into institutional settings and practices, MARC quickly emerged as a crucial vehicle for an MSR based on the widespread adoption of cataloging procedures, customs, and de facto standards in the name of resource sharing.

The second stage of MARC's impact took place in the early 1980s, when most large public and academic libraries were automating their catalogs. Some of the early automation projects included the development of in-house systems, which utilized the MARC framework to receive and store electronic catalog records. However, at the same time, corporate vendors of library automation systems (such as GEAC, one of the earliest) began to appear in the marketplace to sell off-the-shelf commercial integrated systems to library customers. Gradually, as the complexity of the typical ILS grew and as the programming expertise needed to create such systems became more specialized, libraries got out of the business of developing in-house library systems and came to rely almost exclusively on commercial products (Breeding, 2007b). The result now is that there are a limited number of commercial vendors (Breeding, 2005) developing and selling large integrated library systems, and another handful selling systems for small libraries. Breeding (2007b, p. 35) comments that "when looking at the recent evolution of the library automation industry, we see major consolidation among the commercial competitors resulting in a smaller group of vendors and a troubling narrowing of options." The annual vendor survey in the April issue of *Library Journal* provides an overview of current ILS vendors and their products, with the 2006 edition aptly titled "Reshuffling the Deck" (Breeding, 2006). In the most recent examination of ILS vendors and their products, Breeding (2007a) comments that there was a rash of mergers and acquisitions, with some giants emerging from this consolidation, thus reducing competition significantly. He also notes that "the industry grew at a healthy pace in 2006, with overall revenues expanding from an estimated $535 million in 2005 to about $570 million in 2006" (p. 40). Thus there is no doubt that commercial development of integrated library systems is the norm, and while there are examples of working open-source integrated library systems and growing interest in them (Breeding, 2007b, 2007d; also discussed by Ajit Pyati in chapter 10 of this volume), such systems are not yet widely implemented.

A similar contraction has occurred in the production of catalog records. During the era when libraries purchased centrally produced catalog cards, most moderate-sized libraries had cataloging departments and did a great deal or at least some of their own cataloging. Now, however, virtually all moderate-to-large sized libraries in the developed economies rely heavily on bibliographic utilities that have various sorts of packages for purchase to provide bulk electronic catalog records and other services to library customers. Also within the playing field are commercial interests such as book vendors (e.g., Baker and Taylor, Blackwell North America, and Coutts Library Service) that not only provide shelf-ready books for their library customers but also related electronic catalog records and other enhancements for the OPAC. The overall result of the greater reliance on institutional/commercial cataloging sources is that numerous libraries have radically downsized or completely divested themselves of their internal cataloging departments, preferring to rely on outsourced cataloging records (Anyomi, 1999; Ayers, 2003; Libby & Caudle, 1997; Martin et al., 2000). Also, much of the cataloging that is still done by libraries has been deprofessionalized: so-called copy cataloging is now routinely done by library assistants and clerks rather than the more-expensive librarians.

The MARC standard has been all the more pervasive for the fact that the standard explicitly refrains from dictating specific cataloging rules. As a coding standard that theoretically supports multiple cataloging approaches, MARC exists beneath the cataloging rules, and its modest objectives to provide a standard means of encoding bibliographic data disguise the degree to which it has become an integral part of the infrastructure of library operations. To use Stewart Brand's (1997, p. 13) concept of pace layering, MARC works at a slower layer of change: just as it is easier to move chairs in a room than to move the walls, so it is easier to change cataloging rules than it is to change the way they're encoded. MARC occupies the hegemonic position of infrastructure in library systems: a standard so thoroughly integrated into our systems and our thinking that it can only be dislodged with great difficulty.

Over time, MARC has given cataloging a distinctly Fordist quality: the large-scale production of bibliographic records in an environment that values adherence to consistent standards over the exercise of options based on specific user communities. Within the past decade, however, post-Fordist cracks have appeared in the catalog production system, particularly the trends towards increasingly complex automated systems, vendor concentration and market control, outsourcing of cataloging records and services, deprofessionalization of labor, and the globalization of cataloging data. How, then, is the MARC-based library catalogue faring in an age when new trends in IT create an interest in integrated portals, metadata harvesting, and semantic Web innovations?

MARC AND THE OPAC TODAY: AN UNEASY FIT

The library community can justly claim MARC as one of its greatest technological successes, as indicated both by its early adoption and by its surprising longevity. As early as the late 1950s (Chan, 2007, p. 447), the Library of Congress began work on the MARC program, and the early success and widespread adoption of MARC in the 1960s and 1970s justify the proud claim of Marcia Bates that librarians, very early on, acquired experience working with large databases (Bates, 2002). Even today, MARC has weathered the advent of SGML, HTML, XML, XHTML, and RDF to remain the uncontested standard for coding and transferring bibliographic data in libraries. Nicholson Baker documents the events surrounding the great retrospective conversion to MARC that took place in the 1970s and 1980s: confident that they had crossed over into a new digital age, libraries openly embraced the demise of the card catalog. For the Health Sciences Library at the University of Maryland at Baltimore, MARC and the OPAC represented an unabashed celebration of the new at the expense of the old:

> Chancellor Edward N. Brandt Jr., wearing a red T-shirt that said "The Great Discard," chose a drawer of the catalog and pulled it from the cabinet. With the help of a beaming Cyril Feng, who was then director of the library, he drew the retaining rod from the chosen drawer and let its several hundred cards ceremonially spill into a trash can decorated with colored paper. (Baker, 1994, p. 64)

However, the vision of MARC as the way of the future has since faded. In a world dominated by Web information systems, search engines, online databases, social software, and user tagging, MARC's longevity owes more to its entrenched patterns of social regulation than it does to its enduring relevance, either to catalogers or to users. Because the standard was adopted so early, MARC preserves procedures and decisions that have long since lost their relevance. The widespread adoption of MARC, its current status as the standard for encoding bibliographic records, and its current visibility in many library catalog interfaces can prevent us from remembering that MARC was originally designed not for OPACs but for card catalogs. This card-centered design appears in the order of the MARC fields, which place numbers like call numbers at the beginning of the record and the tracings (i.e., additional access points beyond the main entry) at the end. It also appears in the division between main entry and added entry, with the main entry appearing towards the top of the record (as it would in a card catalog environment) and the added entries appearing in the tracings section, which would represent the bottom of the card, indicating the additional cards that would need to be printed for filing as access points throughout the catalog drawers. In addition, the indicator values for the 245 field require the cataloger to specify whether the title is an added entry: a requirement that only makes sense if that decision entails the printing of another card and makes no sense at all in an online environment.

MARC, then, has for many years required OPAC catalogers to step around the anachronisms in its design and to think back to previous catalog formats to guide them through the process (Coyle, 2005). These anachronisms have also prevented the library community from adapting to changing circumstances, such as the call to abandon the principle of main entry. The entrenched status of the MARC record, and the demands of backward compatibility, require libraries to avoid disruptions to their catalog designs that would hinder access to existing archives of records. Furthermore, MARC has perpetuated a massive fiscal investment in catalog databases: after decades of creating, purchasing, and fine-tuning MARC-based records for their OPACs, libraries around the world are now virtually forced to continue on with the same processes by virtue of the fact that a huge amount of money is already tied up in the cataloging production system. At the same time, the constant reproduction of the catalog results in concomitant consumption, as libraries in turn must buy more electronic records to maintain the currency of their OPACs. The regime of accumulation thus continues, with the investment in bibliographic, fiscal, and social capital continually growing and reproducing.

CATALOGING THEORY AS PART OF THE MSR

The extraordinary resistance of catalogs and cataloging to change comes from two levels of regulation: regulation that sustains accumulation in terms of bibliographic and economic wealth, and that rests on entrenched procedures and customs. Furthermore, this regulation often relies on appeals to the broader ideals of librarianship.

At the level of cataloging procedure, library practice appeals to the historic role of the librarian as information mediator and to the ideals of universal bibliographic control. Universal bibliographic control, an ideal encouraged by the International Federation of Library Associations (IFLA) and its series of ISBDs, aims to make all catalogs consistent in underlying structure, so that a user from Kansas can use a catalog in Berlin or Karachi. This appeal to universal standards of consistency, while admirable in theory, has pulled us even further away from Cutter's notion of catering to the demands of the local user. Cataloging rules are magisterial in their tone and legalistic in their detail, and students emerge from cataloging courses convinced that cataloging is an intricate network of regulatory practices that involve constant scrutiny and that tolerate neither error nor deviation from the norm.

Many of these intricate procedures rest on the vision of the librarian as an information mediator, who takes the eccentric nature of documents and the eccentric nature of patrons and tries to bring them together. Such a process, Lancaster suggests, involves analysis and translation into "the language of the system" (Lancaster, 1986, p. 2): this involves the painstaking use of cataloging tools such as rules for bibliographic description and subject access. With respect to bibliographic description, the companion regulatory mechanism to MARC is the AACR, which is now in its second revised edition, is used globally and has been adapted for use in non-English-speaking countries. Like MARC coding, AACR embeds a set of theoretical and practical procedures that arose from the requirements of a card catalog but make less and less sense in a computerized OPAC environment. Karen Coyle (2005) aptly illustrates the difficulties with this premise, noting that two authors who share the title page will be relegated to different parts of the catalog record and that the practice of inverting authors' names is still the norm, despite the lack of rationale for this practice in the online environment. She remarks that "it will take a willful act of amnesia for us to contemplate the possibilities for a library catalog as if the last 200 years of librarianship had not taken place" (Coyle, 2005, p. 61).

While over the years there has been ongoing discussion of AACR and numerous revisions to it, nonetheless, the current rules are not significantly different from their manifestation as AACR2 in 1978. A new set of bibliographic description rules has been proposed (RDA, or Resource Description and Access; see Chapman, 2006). RDA is based on FRBR (Functional Requirements for Bibliographic Records), which resulted from a study done by IFLA (1998) and purports to be a new way to consider bibliographic relationships for cataloging records. However, there has been widespread concern that RDA is just as problematic as AACR2, or even more so—that it is mired in the past and is not far-reaching enough (Tennant, 2007), that it is still overly complex and dense (Intner, 2006), and that it is theoretically confused and misguided (Gorman, 2007). In a rather devastating critique, Coyle and Hillmann (2007) note that RDA is failing libraries and that

> If libraries are to avoid further marginalization, they need to make a fundamental change in their approach to user services. The library's signature service, its catalog,

uses rules for cataloging that are remnants of a long departed technology: the card catalog. Modifications to the rules, such as those proposed by the Resource Description and Access (RDA) development effort, can only keep us rooted firmly in the 20th, if not the 19th century. A more radical change is required that will contribute to the library of the future, re-imagined and integrated with the chosen workflow of its users.

It seems debatable, therefore, whether RDA on its own will be a significant enough departure from the current regulatory practices within cataloging to truly make a difference in how library catalogs are constructed and thus experienced by users.

The other major cataloging tool that is widely used and is also embedded into catalog records around the world are the Library of Congress Subject Headings. Although many subject headings do not stand up to close scrutiny in terms of either theoretical coherence or measured utility for the users (Dykstra, 1988, p. 43), nonetheless, subject catalogers take great pains to render complex, precoordinate headings that will order documents in a useful display. A catalog's subject index for Lithium, for instance, should show a complex display of a primary heading, its relevant subdivisions, and then more specific aspects of the topic, which often have the primary heading as an adjective:

Lithium (primary heading)

Lithium—Isotopes (primary heading with subdivided aspects)

Lithium—Isotopes—Spectra

Lithium—Spectra

Lithium alloys (a more specific heading)

Lithium cells (another more specific heading)

Whether all of these intricate rules and procedures do any good is clouded by the library community's adherence to the ideals that their implementation supposedly manifests. In the words of Dillon and Jul, libraries provide "intellectual access" to information through "a widespread application of library standards and practices," manifested in a "matrix of schemes that facilitate the expression and discovery of content" (1996, pp. 198–199). Cataloging produces records that are universally consistent and intricately structured, and the regulatory practices that insist on this consistency and complexity serve to justify the existence of librarians: universal mediators who add value to the chaotic world of information through their loving and conscientious labor.

However, even if these procedures are useful, they frequently go for naught once they collide with a second level of regulation. In addition to the library community with its intrepid procedures, we find a community of vendors with its captive customers, all of whom are committed to a MARC standard. Unfortunately, vendors of MARC-based systems can by no means be relied on to do justice to the work that catalogers do. For instance, many systems organize the 5XX note fields in ascending order, regardless of the fact that AACR2 order stipulates a specific order that the field numbers do not reflect. Furthermore, the painful work of a subject cataloger goes for naught when the OPAC software strips headings of their subdivision indicators and orders them alphabetically, such as:

Lithium
Lithium alloys
Lithium cells
Lithium—Isotopes
Lithium—Isotopes—Spectra
Lithium—Spectra

The alphabetical machine reordering of complex and logically-structured hierarchical knowledge is very problematic in many instances, but it is particularly noticeable in many OPACs where chronological historical headings and periods are reorganized into a nonsensical alphabetical order placing, for example, Canada—History—Confederation, 1867 before Canada—History—War of 1812 in an alphabetical list before the War of 1812. This misplacement of the chronological historical sequence is incorrect, unhelpful, and completely confusing for catalog users. The fact that such egregious problems fail to be solved speaks to the peripheral nature of the issue and the limited options available to the library. Most catalog users have always found subject headings unsatisfactory in online catalogs (Drabenstott, 1996, p. 107), and a Library of Congress–commissioned report went so far as to recommend that LCSH be abandoned (Calhoun, 2006, p. 18). With the advent of keyword searching, a declining number of catalog searchers use subject headings extensively (Larson, 1991; also see an excellent overview of the literature by Villen-Rueda, Senso, & Moya-Anegon, 2007) and even if they did, libraries have very limited means of taking their business elsewhere to achieve a better interface, and extensive customization of commercial OPAC interfaces is prohibitively expensive.

Thus, while the theoretically complex critique of MARC and cataloging standards such as AACR is ongoing, it is a critique that is completely impenetrable to most users of the OPAC, who only understand that the catalog is challenging to conceptualize and use. The limitation of this discussion to the professional library community thus results in an OPAC that remains a retrieval tool largely for experts, which is yet another regulatory element preventing necessary change from occurring.

To summarize, in the preceding sections, we have discussed a number of disparate yet interconnected factors in the MSR that have worked in concert to shape the main technological tool that the library offers to the public, namely the OPAC. The regulatory factors we have noted include

- the continuing production and consumption of electronic cataloging records on an international scale as a for-profit or cost-recovery venture;
- the entrenchment of the MARC format as the current established framework for the dissemination of electronic catalog records;
- the embedding of certain standards of bibliographic description and presentation (which have well-known limitations) into cataloging records;
- the embedding of the MARC format and cataloging standards into commercial OPAC systems and interfaces; and
- the involvement of a relatively small number of commercial vendors and organizations in the sale and promulgation of cataloging data, associated cataloging tools, and integrated library systems.

These regulatory features have resulted in OPACs and the records that they contain that are remarkably consistent from library to library, whether the environment is an academic, public, or special library. While, on the one hand, this uniformity can be regarded as a good thing for access to, and the transfer of, information internationally, there is a down side. The very entrenchment of such regulatory mechanisms into the OPAC means (1) that information seekers must learn the conventions regarding how library items are cataloged and displayed if they are to find materials successfully and (2) that the problems library users encounter in searching the OPAC are constantly perpetuated and even exacerbated within the current production-consumption system.

INFORMATION SEEKERS AND THE OPAC

For more than two decades, evidence has been mounting that for OPAC users, finding materials successfully is frequently not the case. In 1986, Christine Borgman published an article asking the key question "Why are online catalogs hard to use?" Ten years later, seeing that not much had changed in the intervening years, Borgman published a second article (1996) posing the question as "Why are online catalogs *still* hard to use?" In these two articles, Borgman notes the lack of change in the functionality of library OPACs and the serious and ongoing problems that users have in trying to conduct successful searches using a typical OPAC interface, a few of which include:

- OPAC query systems that are designed more for skilled searchers, such as librarians;
- an overall structure to the catalog that is less apparent to users in an electronic environment;
- the assumption that seekers can describe what it is they are seeking;
- the assumption that seekers know at least something to start with as an access point;
- the fact that information seekers formulate questions in stages, not as a one-stop-shopping query approach;

- the inability of many seekers to understand what a subject heading is, and to be able to convert their own thoughts into a controlled vocabulary language; and
- a lack of awareness as to the nature of Boolean operators and query syntax.

In addition to these issues, as previously noted, there has been ongoing criticism of specific tools such as the LCSH, which have problems with inconsistent vocabulary, long strings of descriptors that are difficult to understand (Drabenstott, Simcox, & Fenton, 1999), and a filing logic that often does not transfer well into the electronic environment. Furthermore, various authors have pointed out that most OPACs use confusing library-related jargon, which further compounds the difficulties that users have in navigating and understanding the OPAC interface (Cherry, 1998). The problems/issues noted above have meant that for many OPAC users, the experience of searching the library catalog is frustrating and time consuming and often does not result in the desired information. In their review of the literature on OPACs, Large and Beheshti (1997) note many of the same issues as Borgman and other scholars, remarking that "improved interfaces, ranked lists of retrieved output and enhanced browsing features now appearing in third generation OPACs are all in line with recommendations from many research studies . . . Despite such advances, however, the fundamental problems of OPAC use, and indeed of IR systems in general, still remain" (Large & Beheshti, 1997, p. 128).

A brief look at more current research confirms that information seekers are still having problems with OPAC searching and that recent generations of OPAC interfaces have not ameliorated ongoing difficulties. For instance, Slone's study of OPAC users in a public library (2000) revealed that searchers frequently made errors in spelling, which affected retrieval results, and had difficulty in generating appropriate terms for topical searches. The author remarked that "users often had such little knowledge of what they sought, many were unable to generate even closely related terms to initiate a search. Thus, they guessed." (Slone, 2000, p. 764). In their study of Web catalog use, Halcoussis Halverson, Lowenberg, and Lowenberg (2002) also noted that subject searching was problematic for the participants they studied, and that participants who performed subject searches were more likely to report navigational problems within the catalog (Halcoussis et al., 2002, p. 154). Krueger, Ray, and Knight found that while participants in their study could use the catalog to find a book, most could not locate a journal title (2004, p. 290), a finding also noted by Valentine and Nolan (2002). Valentine and Nolan discovered that many students in their study did not distinguish between title and subject searches in the OPAC (Valentine & Nolan, 2002, p. 57), and, likewise, Turner (2002, p. 76) found that participants in her study did not distinguish between keyword and subject searches. Novotny (2004) found that even for experienced users of a Web-based OPAC, "Keyword searching remained the favorite option, even for known items. There was minimal use of Boolean and no demonstrated understanding of LC Subject

Headings" (Novotny, 2004, p. 530). Furthermore, Novotny observed that searchers "demonstrated minimal knowledge of how information is structured in a library catalog and how that underlying structure affects their searches . . . [and] showed no curiosity about how the catalog worked, nor did they feel they should" (Novotny, 2004, p. 533).

Two further complicating elements in the ongoing OPAC searching debate are (1) the tendency for libraries to add free URLs to their catalogs and (2) the popularity of Web search engines with information seekers. With respect to the former, Burke, Germain, and Van Ullen (2003) were concerned about whether the widespread practice of adding URLs to the catalogs of research libraries in particular inserted unreliability into the bibliographic database due to the well-known problem that URLs either change or become defunct. They found that "A large percentage of the researched library catalogs, linking to free URL resources, had a significant number of errors" with half of the libraries having an error greater than that for missing books (Burke et al., 2003, p. 295). The authors wonder whether this is a "tolerable rate of failure" (p. 295) and suggest that the addition of URLs may be diluting the credibility of the OPAC and thus alienating users further. Given that the practice of adding URLs to catalogs is continuing apace, these concerns are still very valid and point to yet another way in which users may fail to find appropriate information through an OPAC search.

Regarding point (2), the rapid rise of Google and other similar Web search engines has revealed a large disparity between the perceived ease of use of such search engines and the perceived difficulty in using library catalogs. Holly Yu and Margo Young (2004) remark that

> In spite of many studies and articles on Online Public Access Catalogs (OPAC) over the last twenty-five years, many of the original ideas about improving user success in searching library catalogs have yet to be implemented. Ironically, many of these techniques are now found in Web search engines. The popularity of the Web appears to have influenced users' mental models and thus their expectations and behavior when using a Web-based OPAC interface. (Yu & Young, 2004, p. 168)

In their research, Yu and Young found that Web-catalog searchers had many of the same problems previously cited by other authors, including ongoing difficulties with subject searching, retrieval results that yielded far too much information, and the use of highly ineffective search strategies such as trial-and-error and screen browsing. The authors suggest that OPACs should incorporate more of the features of Web search engines to facilitate greater user searching success. The relative ease of searching the Web using Google also came through in the study by Fast and Campbell (2004), whose participants felt that "the OPAC took longer to search and required more effort" (p. 143) without necessarily giving a good result. Despite admiring a perceived level of organization in the OPAC, the study participants found the catalog to be complex, intimidating, and confusing, and they preferred to search the Web using Google for their information-related needs.

THE NEXT GENERATION OPAC

Critical analyses that contextualize library OPACs, integrated library systems, and the rather invisible production-consumption regime that reproduces them as part of a larger, evolving, capitalist market-based system are still relatively rare. However, given the ongoing difficulties with the OPAC as an information-retrieval tool, some librarians and scholars are beginning to talk openly about both the OPAC and the ILS as failing or declining products. For instance, in a recent study commissioned by the Library of Congress, Karen Calhoun (2006) uses a very market-oriented analogy when describing the state of contemporary OPACs. She comments that

> The online library catalog has been a successful product. Like other products, it has passed through a life cycle. . . . Fortunately, there are ways to use the knowledge that today's catalog has reached the end of its life cycle. (Calhoun, 2006, p. 10)

Calhoun then reviews some of the business literature for revitalizing products and dealing with declining product demand (Calhoun, 2006, pp. 10–11). She quite rightly points out that the production of local catalogs in research libraries is big business, stating that "in 2004, ARL [Association of Research Libraries] libraries spent an estimated $239 million on technical services labour alone" (Calhoun, 2006, p. 11).[7] This figure does not account for the considerable additional money spent to purchase bulk electronic catalog records and upgrade integrated library systems nor does it include the same types of outlays made by public and special libraries. Yet despite ongoing challenges to the notion that the OPAC is a user-friendly search tool for everyday information seekers, and despite the immense outlay of monies needed to perpetuate the OPAC as a search mechanism of debatable utility (at least in some circles), Calhoun notes that "Libraries are unlikely to divest themselves of their catalogs . . . [deeming] such a course of action unthinkable" (Calhoun, 2006, p. 12).

As testament to that fact, reaction to Calhoun's report was swift and vociferous. Mann (2006), for instance, points out major flaws in Calhoun's argument, citing a misrepresentation of a business model that is inappropriate to begin with. As Mann notes, there are very good reasons for libraries to maintain catalogs of their collections, which have a different organizational basis than what is typically found on the Web. He makes a compelling argument that controlled vocabulary is far superior to keyword searching and that to lose a tool like the OPAC, which has controlled vocabulary features built into it, would be a major setback for scholarship on many levels.

Nonetheless, despite various defenses of the online catalog and its underlying structure, problems with the OPAC and the regulatory standards embedded within it (such as the LCSH, AACR2, and the MARC format) continue, at least in the short run, resulting in calls for urgently needed improvements that have been voiced since the 1990s (Byrum, 2006; Hildreth, 1995; Sleeman & Bluh, 2005; Yee & Layne, 1998). Along these lines, well-known technology commentator Marshall Breeding (2007b, 2007c) suggests that the problems with OPACs and the integrated library systems are a result of an era when libraries were more concerned with inventory control than user searching success and thus are based on an outmoded approach. Similarly, Balas (2007) asks "Will the ILS soon be as obsolete as the card catalog?" Some libraries are taking their dissatisfaction even further. Antelman, Lynema, and Pace (2006) describe the efforts of North Carolina State University Libraries to implement Endeca's IAP software, used for the Web sites of Wal-Mart, Barnes and Nobel, and Home Depot, among others. The authors comment that

> The promise of online catalogs has never been realized. For more than a decade, the profession either turned a blind eye to problems with the catalog or accepted that it is powerless to fix them. . . Libraries cannot force users into those "closed", "rigid" and "intricate" online catalogs. . . . Coupled with the relative paucity of current literature on next-generation catalogs is a scarcity of library industry interfaces from which to draw inspiration, RLG's Red Light Green and OCLC's FictionFinder being notable exceptions. (Antelman et al., 2006, pp. 128–129)

Change has been very slow, but many library IT commentators are hopeful that the next generation of OPAC interfaces will solve many of the searching and use problems currently evident in what is now called the legacy catalogs of today. Features such as enriched content (images, book jackets, summaries, reviews), faceted navigation, relevancy ranking, RSS feeds of new items received, and detection of common spelling errors are all examples of enhancements that many IT analysts believe may help users find the information they want and need. As to who will provide such enhancements, Breeding suggests that it will be a combination of libraries using open source components and commercial vendors with new products. He comments that with the increasing amount of open source software now available, it is:

> quite a bit easier for library staffers to get back into the process of creating their own software. And we're seeing a resurgence of in-house software projects that place librarians back into a more visible role as technology innovators. I don't see a radical shift taking place anytime soon that takes commercial companies out of the picture but competition is heating up. The automation companies, it seems to me, have quite a bit of an advantage over the competition to deliver this new generation of library interfaces. They have significant experience creating products to meet our automation needs, have vast resources available and have deep expertise in the complex processes of professional software development. (Breeding, 2007b, p. 36)

Breeding and others may be right, and the enhancements of the next generation OPAC may go some way to resolving the user searching difficulties that we have outlined. Nonetheless, despite this optimistic view, most of the regulatory elements of the catalog production and accumulation regime that we have already discussed still remain intact, leaving us to wonder if the next generation OPACs will be truly revolutionary or if it will manifest many of the same constraints that are evident in current legacy catalogs. Without accompanying changes to the underlying MSR, the implementation of new and more powerful technologies can only go a certain way to the eradication of entrenched problems for users. The most recent technological innovation, library Web portals, amply illustrates this very point, and so we shall now turn to a consideration of that technology.

WEB PORTALS: THE SEARCH GOES ON

As the cracks within the OPAC (re)production and accumulation system continue to widen, the ongoing issues related to user searching success and the elements of the MSR that perpetuate those problems have spilled over to the latest search and discovery tool, the library Web portal. There are varying definitions of the word *portal*, from a generic term used to describe the library's Web site, to a more complex definition that emphasizes federated searching and the ability for users to customize their access (Maloney & Bracke, 2005). Here we will use the term *portal* in the broadest sense, to describe the library's Web site, providing a gateway to collections, other resources, and services, with or without a federated searching approach and customization options. As Maloney and Bracke (2005) note, the portal is not a single technology but rather a "combination of several systems, standards and protocols that interoperate to create a unified experience for the user" (p. 87).

Librarians have been actively involved in the creation of library portals and information repositories, particularly in the last few years. Library portals contain a wide array of resources, including commercial databases, disciplinary guides and links to academic Web sites, writing resources, community links, institutional newsletters, feedback mechanisms, and items/areas for specific user groups, such as youth or seniors. In addition, as a complement to traditional digital library collections, clearinghouses of organizations' internal documents and related external materials (such as university's institutional repositories) are becoming increasingly popular, allowing various stakeholders to examine and add to a body of resources that have been identified as relevant to an identified user group. Recent projects include: the My Chicago Library project, developed by librarians at the University of Illinois at Chicago to streamline user access to library resources (Brantley, Armstrong, & Lewis, 2006); the UNESCO Libraries Portal project, which provides access to Web sites of library institutions around the world (UNESCO, 2005);

the development of a global information portal used by 65,000 employees at Aventis Pharmaceuticals (Srodin & Strupczewski, 2002); and the Common Knowledge Database project at Rutgers University, which allows reference librarians to share resources and strategies for serving academic library patrons (Jantz, 2001).

Portal technologies go beyond the traditional point-and-click Web site. In some cases, individuals can customize the look and feel of a site, include or exclude particular resources from their personal portal page, and receive personalized information (e.g., RSS feeds) that reflect their own interests and information requirements. As access to articles, links to experts, lists of ready-reference sources, and other information objects are what keep people coming back to a Web site of this type, user-friendly design is vital for success. For those sites designed to foster the development of communities of interest through the sharing of information and knowledge (e.g., through the use of chat forums or areas where individuals can add new materials), portal technologies highlight the value of design features such as clear labels, intuitive navigation, and quick download times. Given the potential that portals have, Byrum (2005) suggests that even though portal technologies, especially federated searching, are still limited, it is the library portal, and not the OPAC, that will

> serve as the user's principal Web gateway to digital resources and services, providing a high level of seamless integration and including a feature-rich toolkit for cross-resource searching according to the personalized needs of the users. (Byrum, 2005, p. 151)

Unfortunately, the rush to implement portal technologies and the widespread production of library portals has resulted in a new but interrelated set of use and searching problems for information seekers. First, there are no clear guidelines about what a library portal should contain, how the resources and services on it should be presented, or the level of complexity that can be tolerated by users. While there are general guidelines about good Web site and portal design (e.g., Johnson, 2003; Nielsen, 2000, 2004) and guidelines about various types of library Web sites/portals in particular (e.g. Jackson, 2004), there is no clear consensus about how libraries should operationalize such guidelines or even what guidelines should apply for particular libraries. Illustrating that point, after their extensive review of the literature and of library web sites, Nichols and Mellinger (2007, p. 483) found that "no single site included all of the features and qualities" that their task force identified as desirable.

Furthermore, there is often contradictory evidence about what users seem to prefer on library portals: for example, Wegener, Goh-Ong Ai Moi, and Lim Mei Li (2004) found that some of their users used information sources presented in the middle of the portal interface while others preferred information presented on the sides rather than the middle, making it challenging to discern the best layout option to meet the needs of the majority of portal users. Opinions also differ on what the portal should contain for various specific user groups such as students (Nichols & Mellinger, 2007) or seniors (Aula & Kaki, 2005), or for particular types of resources (Vaughan & Dillon, 2006). Such variability in findings makes it difficult for library portal designers to take concrete guidance from the research literature. As a result, portal construction practices vary widely, and even a cursory browse through a sample of library portals will demonstrate that some are incredibly complex and cluttered, while others are extremely sparse.

Second, studies of information seeking on library portals reveal many of the same problems for users as in searching the OPAC. Labeling of the various resources on the portal is problematic, often still using library-centric jargon, which is opaque to users (Benjes & Brown, 2001; Brantley et al., 2006; Cockerell & Jayne, 2002; Feeney & Newby, 2005). With the complexity of resources and services provided on a typical library portal, users experience navigational problems, becoming lost within the myriad of options, some of which they do not understand (Benjes & Brown, 2001; Cockerell & Jayne, 2002). Robins and Kelsey (2002) also found that participants in their study had difficulty finding known-item links on their Web site, thus making more moves or clicks than necessary. Valentine and Nolan noted that the participants in their study

> generally searched pages superficially; they tended to follow only a layer or two of links before abandoning that path. . . . Although scrolling was the most popular way to scan a page for information, most did not scroll beyond a certain point. They also spent a brief time on the pages. . . . Most students did not use help screens. They seemed to operate on the assumption that the navigational structures of a web site would take them to all they needed without explanation. (Valentine & Nolan, 2002, p. 56)

Sometimes the portal design obscures even the most basic resource, the OPAC, so that users cannot find it or cannot tell the difference between the OPAC and other resources (Ward & Hiller, 2005; Wegener et al., 2004). In other cases, the portal presents far too many options so that users become confused about what will best meet their needs or miss crucial information because it is presented "in a sea of words" (Valentine & Nolan, 2002, p. 58). Federated searching has been touted as a way to solve such problems by providing a common interface that will search many different information resources seamlessly. However, there are limitations to federating searching (Breeding, 2007d, p. 8), with some expressing doubts that federated searching is the panacea that it is purported to be (Balas, 2006) or that federated searching will be used by the population for which it was intended (Nichols & Mellinger, 2007).

Third, research has repeatedly shown that very few users will customize a portal site even though customization features are available. For example, two different studies of undergraduate students revealed that very few of them customized the library's Web site, and many complained that customization took too long and/or wasn't that useful (Nichols & Mellinger, 2007; Ward & Hiller, 2005). In another study, where 2,700 users registered with a myLibrary service, only 15 user profiles were created, a finding that was "particularly worrying" to the designers, who believed that this would be a popular feature providing a great deal of flexibility for user searching (Groenewegen & Huggard, 2003, p. 456). Ward and Hiller (2005) cite Nielsen's statement that "web personalization is much over-rated and mainly used as a poor excuse for not designing a navigable website" (p. 170). Although customization might be helpful in some cases, information seekers tend to use the quick and superficial searching strategies that they have used in the past, including trial-and-error, and they do not have a very good sense of overall portal organization (Brantley et al., 2006; Nichols & Mellinger, 2007). Further, users may conceive of portals as extensions of the institution's Web site rather than that of the library itself, leading them to request that university-level resources be integrated into the library's Web portal (Brantley et al., 2006). In other cases, users may believe that the library portal provides free access to databases, journal articles, and other resources, without realizing that these Web-based materials are part of the library's cost-based services, with restrictions on their use (Zemon, 2001).

Given the relative entrenchment of the OPAC as the library's primary access tool and the rapid implementation of Web portals, what is being done to ameliorate the longstanding difficulties that users have in searching such library interfaces? There are two regulatory practices that librarians have actively used to circumvent the current searching and retrieval difficulties of information seekers, those being information literacy instruction and Web usability testing. We shall examine these two sets of interrelated practices in turn.

THE INFORMATION LITERACY TRAIN—ALL ABOARD!

Librarians have been very aware of the ongoing difficulties that information seekers have in understanding and using OPACs and Web portals. Indeed, a great deal of the literature examining what information searchers do and why they do it when using OPACs and Web portals has been written by librarians. Nonetheless, the belief, widely held by librarians, that the best way to overcome users' difficulties when using commercial catalog interfaces and portals is to train or condition them to think about and search for information in particular ways has become yet another element in the social relations of OPAC/portal technology and serves to perpetuate the very problems that are presently occurring.

In the post-WWII period, there has always been a certain amount of user education in libraries, academic libraries in particular. However, since the advent of online catalogs and the obvious difficulties users were experiencing with them, there has been an explosion of user education activity (previously known as bibliographic instruction and more recently as information literacy instruction), which has moved beyond the realm of academic libraries into public and other types of libraries (Julien, 2005; Julien & Breu, 2005; O'Beirne, 2006; Skov, 2004; Tosa & Long, 2003). The literature is now full of descriptions of information literacy programs, with extensive commentary on the need for such instruction, suggestions for appropriate content, and pedagogical approaches.

The premise of information literacy is that to be a productive citizen in the new knowledge economy, a person ought to be able to find, evaluate, and use information from a variety of sources (Association of College & Research Libraries [ACRL], 2000). In the library context, this means that the user must learn how to conceptualize the array of information sources found on library interfaces and translate them into a mental model of how to search those sources most effectively and when to use them. Unfortunately for most users, the array of information resources presented to them have already been conceptualized by librarians and organized in ways that seem unimaginable to the layperson. So, for instance, to have success with an OPAC search on a topic that is rather hazy in his/her mind, the searcher would have to know either what authors had written on the topic, what keywords represent the topic, and/or what controlled vocabulary terms (i.e., LCSH or other subject headings) would be appropriate. Searchers also would have to know that the OPAC gives them different information than a periodical database, and they would have to make a decision about which is the best route for information on their topic. Since many searchers typically do not know any of these things, information literacy instruction is deemed to be a necessity. However, as part of the MSR, such instruction, while well-intentioned, is insidious and self-perpetuating, tied as it is to commercial products that already have problematic regulatory mechanisms built into them. Because the difficulties with searching the OPAC (and to a certain extent the portal) do not change, because the OPAC and its underlying bibliographic database is continually produced and reproduced, therefore information literacy instruction completes the endlessly revolving circuit.

One could understand the appeal of information literacy instruction if it were done as a form of resistance to the hegemonic tendencies of the catalog/portal production system, working to liberate information seekers from their reliance on information retrieval systems that fail to help them find what they need. However, information literacy instruction is not done for this reason but is, instead, purported to be a way to aid unknowledgeable searchers in understanding and navigating the universe of information sources and using existing library systems/interfaces to find needed information. Within this framework, information seekers are constructed as having no, or a very limited, understanding of the OPAC and other resources on the Web portal, no understanding of the differences among various kinds of materials, weak research skills, and generally low information literacy skills as defined by standards such as the ACRL's statement on information literacy (ACRL, 2000). The assumption and belief by librarians that information seekers appear to lack information literacy skills because they are naïve, unaware, or uneducated (rather than because library systems are not helpful) is another aspect of the MSR that only serves to reinforce the current situation.

Does information literacy accomplish the task of helping information seekers find, evaluate, and use information from a variety of sources? The jury is out on that question. Of the evaluation research that does exist, some indicates that information literacy instruction may make a difference as to whether users search more effectively, understand the catalog better and/or cite more appropriate materials for their assignments (e.g., Julien & Boon, 2004; Novotny, Cahoy, & Stern, 2006; Spackman, 2007). The study by Novotny et al. (2006) examined whether user search strategies would improve immediately after instruction. They found the evidence inconclusive: while some students did seem to improve their searching abilities with new techniques, "a powerful gravitation toward keyword searching persisted. Even those who began by using the browse search tended to abandon it in favor of keyword searching" (Novotny et al., 2006, pp. 158–159). A recent review of the literature by Crawford and Feldt (2007) suggests that there is limited evidence of the efficacy of instructional efforts, causing the authors to remark that "with the increasing importance that college and university libraries have been placing on library instruction and information literacy, there is a definite need for articles researching the efficacy of the efforts of librarians in these areas" (Crawford & Feldt, 2007, p. 87). However, as Crawford and Feldt demonstrate, only a very small proportion (1.5%) of the information literacy articles they reviewed are about evaluation of instructional efforts, suggesting that either writing about instructional outcomes is not a high priority or that evaluation is not routinely done. Despite this, the belief that information literacy is good and necessary is a widespread aspect of the MSR, subtly working to reinforce the problematic aspects of OPACs and Web portals as primary access mechanisms.

WEB USABILITY: THE FIX IS IN?

As instructional librarians work to mediate the user's engagement with the system and change his/her conceptual model of the organization of library resources, others look to ways to fix systems design to resolve access and searching issues. Although existing research in the areas of information behavior and user-centered design point to Web usability theory as a useful mechanism for empowering users in system design and solving common access issues, current design practices—often couched in the language of Web usability—have become yet another element of the MSR.

Information literacy instruction and Web usability are intertwined regulatory elements that shape the way in which information access is constructed and practiced. As libraries implement customizable portal options for users, usability testing sessions are used to investigate the appropriateness of their Web designs. This context has lead to a number of missteps in the attempt to empower users, all of which reinforce the current MSR, including:

1. Web usability testing (if done, at all), is often limited in scope and conducted after a site has been launched, resulting in surface changes to existing sites, rather than large-scale systems redesign that would best meet users' needs;
2. participatory systems design, where users are involved from system conception through launch, is rarely used; and
3. usability testing is based on a confused notion of the user.

Together, these missteps bring us back to information literacy instruction as the default solution for addressing entrenched systems problems, including those vendor-developed Web sites that are neither user-friendly nor customizable. We shall address these three concerns in turn, with commentary upon how such practices/beliefs serve to reinforce current difficulties that users experience with library portals.

USABILITY: THE SURFACE TWEAK

Over the past decade, Web usability and user-centered design of portals and repositories have gained in importance and profile in the LIS literature. Usability theory outlines principles that place users' needs at the forefront of Web design (Nielsen, 2000, 2004; Rosenfeld & Morville, 2002). Here, information architecture must fulfill three main goals: (1) to organize information in a logical, usable fashion; (2) to build simple, effective sites grounded in users' needs; and (3) to create flexible designs that evolve over time as users' needs change. To achieve these goals, Web design must focus on content and functionality, from the user's perspective, including quality writing, consistency, utility, simplicity, and other elements that privilege function over form. Aesthetics are important but not to the point that the look (e.g., flash-enabled splash pages) subsumes the informational focus of a site.

Studies of Web usability in academic and other library contexts are increasingly prevalent and inform professional practice. This trend has been pushed forward, in part, by a rise in information behavior research, which places individuals' needs and the ways that individuals search for information, at the forefront of systems design (see Case, 2007). These studies illuminate users' behaviors in seeking digital resources, by assessing the ways that users navigate a site's layout or otherwise make sense of its physical design (e.g., Allen, 2002; Graham, Poe, & Weatherford, 2003; Gullikson, Blades, & Bragdon, 1999; Palmquist, 2001; Saumure & Given, 2004; Travis & Norlin, 2002).

Users are easily frustrated when they cannot find needed information and will abandon useful resources when a site is difficult to navigate, relies on gratuitous graphics, or uses inappropriate language (Ahuja & Webster, 2001; Gullikson et al., 1999; Schuyler, 2000).

In this context, building usable library Web sites is realized through minor tweaking for those small, surface-level problems (such as relabeling terms, where library jargon is confusing to users) and relying on Web site instruction to solve more extensive (and expensive) Web design problems. Rather than solving existing Web site issues, and designing new sites according to the published research (which outlines common pitfalls), libraries often focuses on fixing (i.e., retraining) users rather than systems.

Portal technologies themselves often compound the usability conundrum. Where vendors offer inexpensive and ubiquitous portal packages for library use, many problems are replicated from system to system and become deeply entrenched in library practice. Often, we are replicating systems designed for print materials rather than creating unique Web (i.e., hypertext) environments, despite research that explores differences in how individuals search for, interact with, and read digital resources (e.g., Hodkinson & Kiel, 2003; Hsieh-Yee, 2001; Kari, 2004). Users are expected to learn the language of these systems (such as *truncation* or *RSS feed*), rather than being presented with the intuitive, user-focused language advocated by usability standards. Familiarity of language, look, and feel across systems (i.e., where users might be confused by a new or different design), is often touted as a reason to retain the status quo. Such paternalism does little to satisfy users' needs in Web design; however, this approach does further entrench systems design as an MSR, with librarians—often, inadvertently—working against users' best interests by reinforcing problematic, unusable Web designs. Although researchers and designers outside of LIS are moving to participatory design as a more effective approach to systems design, with users truly at the center of the design process (and the resulting product), libraries lag behind. We have not yet established our own standards for effective, user-friendly Web portal design, nor do we demand that system vendors provide users with features and tools that follow usable Web design principles.

Many sites, therefore, may be launched under the guise of having been user tested (with the implication that they are user approved), while structural and organizational changes may never be addressed. In other cases, users may be provided with options developed by designers only, leaving them to choose the best design from two or more problematic options, leaving users' true preferences and needs at the margins of system design. Unfortunately, today's system design often reinforces, rather than fixes, a systems-driven approach to design—where Web designers are keen to integrate new technologies (such as RSS feeds or social networking tools), without knowing if or how users might make use of these options. In the case of institutional repositories, the drive to gather and store materials that reflect the corporate memory and activities of an organization (such as the intellectual property of university faculty) may often be pushed by designers and administrators before questions of information ownership, copyright, or implementation may be addressed with the users themselves (Wust, 2006).

THE ILLUSION OF PARTICIPATORY DESIGN

In examining the ways that people use digital sources of information, and how people interact with Web-based libraries and portals, there are many resulting principles that can inform the development of digital collections for the purposes of knowledge management. The challenge, then, for designers of Web-based collections, is to make information accessible for future use—to people who have yet to look for it and may not yet know why they need it—while recognizing that no single collection can possibly serve everyone's information needs all of the time. Usability theory does seem to provide a useful framework for this type of anticipatory design, in a way that best suits users' information-seeking strategies.

Yet while usability studies have gained in prominence, many interfaces are still designed by computer programmers or graphic designers, with users' needs marginalized in the design process. Usability testing is not ubiquitous; where testing does occur, individuals are often asked to assess existing sites so that designers may tweak final designs, as noted previously. As librarians, Web designers, and other information specialists embrace the tenets of usability theory, users themselves—ironically—are being pushed further to the edges of appropriate systems design. Where usability theory and testing was intended to identify and address users' concerns with poor, unusable Web design, users continue to be disenfranchised and distanced from much systems design. Users are rarely included as participants in the early design phases of library Web projects. Where usability testing is conducted, this is typically during the postdesign phase, when designers and administrators may be hesitant to spend additional money on a project or delay the launch of a long-anticipated design project. Although some small fixes (such as moving a search box or relabeling a Web tool) may be possible at this stage in the design process, other user concerns may never be addressed, as the changes would substantively alter the design of the information system.

Thus in the rush to personalize individual access to Web resources, and to provide access to a range of new technologies, one of the central tenets of usability theory is often violated—that is, grounding systems design in users' own perspectives of what information they need, when they need it, and how they need it. In its current form, the practice of usability testing constructs an unknowing and ineffective user. Here, while we might be able to fix some small problems with Web sites, more extensive issues are dealt with via so-called user education. In this way, usability testing has devolved from a continuous process of user engagement into a post hoc testing situation, where findings may or may not be addressed; here, users learn the system and internalize strategies to find what they can within that system.

Participatory user design, although common in visual design and other fields, has not yet been embraced in LIS practice. While it is true that some studies explore individuals' use of Web interfaces in the context of information behaviors and with implications for design (e.g., Saumure & Given, 2004; Vaughan & Dillon, 2006), projects that involve users at the conceptual design phase and account for users' specific needs are in the minority (e.g., Beyer & Holtzblatt, 1999; Bilal, 2002; Given, Ruecker, Simpson, Sadler, & Ruskin, 2007; Large, Nesset, Beheshti, & Bowler, 2006; Trigg & Anderson, 1996). One recent example is a project currently underway in Canada, which uses a participatory design approach for the development of a health information and medication management tool for health consumers (Given et al., 2007). This project involves the exploration of online browsing environments, which are situated within the design of new digital affordances (e.g., Gibson, 1979; Ruecker, 2003; Sadler and Given, 2007; Vicente, 2002) and which use simple, effective design to craft Web sites that meet users' needs (e.g., Cockrell & Jayne, 2002; Krueger, Ray, & Knight, 2004).

The rise of participatory design in the last decade points to flaws in the usability testing system—and the need for a new model of design—if we are ever to break through the current usability design impasse. A new model also demands that the LIS community break ties with its current, regulated system of design, where proprietary packages are ubiquitous, despite ongoing frustrations for users. Librarians need to opt for customizable vendor options, where available, and focus on open source interface solutions for long-term change. We need to work with users to create our own portals that solve, rather than replicate, existing problems. We also need a critical reassessment of information literacy practices, which are currently designed to help users navigate impenetrable systems design.

WHO IS THE USER?

Given librarianship's seemingly clear focus on understanding and meeting user needs and enhancing user access to resources, why does the situation described above recur? First, librarians have a confused conception of the user. While some librarians see users as customers or clients who will demand the systems and features they want and need, other librarians construct users as ignorant individuals who need librarians to make choices on their behalf and provide instruction on how best to interact with library Web sites (Hedemark, Hedman, & Sundin, 2005; Hoffman & Polkinghorne, 2007; Tuominen, 1997). In effect, there is no common view of users and users' needs to shape the design of systems to actually give users what they want and need. Second, in this environment, systems design is then based on an existing design is good design model (i.e., what seems to work elsewhere will work in our library), combined with trial-and-error, small-scale redesign in the local context. Here, systems design elements may be touted as reflecting best practices when, in fact, these may be completely divorced from local users' real experiences and needs. Further, without effective assessment, these systems may simply replicate unusable features across library contexts, even when these are known to be problematic for users. Third, instruction becomes the solution for problematic design. Many existing information literacy programs are concerned with database and catalogue searching, Web searching, strategies for using customizable alert services, and other systems and special features.

Here, the ignorant customer concept rules, where librarians construct users as demanding these systems while not understanding the range of uses of these tools. Users become caught in a library-imposed view of systems use and design, where new systems, new features, and additional resources are constructed as improvements to library service, with little critical examination of whether users want these tools or whether they meet the intended goals of user-centered design, as articulated in the published research literature. As Sanna Talja (1997) noted more than a decade ago, this stance is highly problematic; if users are "seen as uncertain people who need help, there is a risk that the objective of helping the user is implicitly grounded on a faith in objective expert knowledge existing outside history, social relations and contradictory interests" (p. 77). This approach feeds into the regime of accumulation, with library Web sites, and instruction in their use, controlling and shaping users' access to the information they need.

CONCLUSION

This chapter has attempted to examine the ongoing difficulties with library information access interfaces by using the lens of regulation theory to cast new light on the current situation. As we have shown, the construction of access mechanisms, such as OPACs and Web portals and the infrastructure that supports them, can be viewed as a particular production/consumption system within the changing capitalist context often referred to as post-Fordism. Regulation theory posits that, in the face of economic change and instability, there will be institutional arrangements and other social relations (the MSR) that work to prop up or reinforce the existing capitalistic mode. The MSR, then, can be viewed as a set of practices and social relations that work in concert to either maintain the status quo or at least put up barriers to the pace of change within the capitalistic environment. Accordingly, our quest here has been to try to disentangle and reveal the elements of the MSR that have been at work over the past 30–40 years that may account for the relative lack of change to, and persistent problems with, library OPACs. As we have also noted, some of these longstanding problems are now being imported into library Web portals despite their promise as a new and possibly better access technology.

The elements of the MSR that have been identified in this chapter are a complex and interwoven combination of regulatory mechanisms, including formal and informal standards for the organization of information, cataloging practices, professional values and assumptions, information technologies, and institutional and corporate ideologies and actions. In the case of library OPACs and portals, the MSR has contributed to the protection of a number of crucial and ongoing large-scale investments by commercial vendors, institutional stakeholders, and the library community, including:

- Intellectual investments: in cataloging standards such as AACR, ISBD, MARC formats, and controlled vocabularies;
- Disciplinary investments: in LIS education, professional norms, practices, beliefs, and rhetoric;
- Material/infrastructure investments: in computer hardware, networks and other software, integrated library systems, and Web-management systems;
- Capital investments: in the development and marketing of vendor-based integrated library systems and portal management systems;
- Labor investments: in the production of catalog records, development and implementation of integrated library systems, information literacy instruction, and usability testing; and
- Institutional investments: in the growth of bibliographic utilities and the development and production of content for the OPAC and Web portal, evaluation mechanisms, and various types of user assistance and education.

As the library community struggles to adapt to new Web environments, particularly those made possible by the Web 2.0 and the semantic Web, it must avoid such investments from sealing the catalog off from fresh influences that could give it a new lease on life. Web 2.0 tools can do more than offer libraries new means of organizing groups and facilitating social interaction; they can also provide means of user tagging and user commentary that could integrate the catalog with other features such as Facebook. Furthermore, the advent of social networking, bookmarking, and commentary sites has made Web interaction significantly easier, drastically altering the user's expectations about a minimally usable system.

New innovations in cataloging theory have opened up the potential for a richer interaction between catalogs and XML. Tentative efforts have been made in the past to separate MARC from cataloging by providing an XML definition based solely on AACR rather than on the MARC encodings of AACR (Fiander & Campbell, 2003, p. 29). These efforts could gather momentum alongside the FRBR paradigm of treating bibliographic entities in a hierarchical fashion (IFLA, 1998), which is very similar to the structures of XML: a work receives one or more expressions, each of which undergoes one or more manifestations, each of which is duplicated into one or more items. This hierarchical rigor could make our catalogs more amenable to inventive and useful mutations of our bibliographic records.

Even without FRBR, catalogs have an enormous potential to participate in a broader metadata community. The Open Archives Initiative (see http://www.openarchives.org) has developed a metadata harvesting protocol that enables library catalogs to export their records in Dublin Core metadata, for inclusion in search services based on metadata systems of varying types (Fast & Campbell, 2001, p. 5). Furthermore, semantic Web technologies have the potential to do the reverse: to enable us to drag semantically tagged data from reliable Web sites into bibliographic records (Campbell & Fast, 2004, p. 382).

All of these possibilities depend, to some extent, on being able to break up our catalogs and bibliographic records so that we can integrate that data with data drawn from elsewhere, thereby making our bibliographic heritage more flexible and more embedded in the context of a modern information environment. Unfortunately, such activities threaten the intellectual, disciplinary, material, capital, labor, and institutional investments we have listed above.

Coyle and Hillmann (2007) have commented that "users have spoken with their keyboards, overwhelmingly preferring non-traditional and non-library sources of information and methods of discovery." While librarians cannot control users' needs or the ways that users choose to search for information, our systems nonetheless need to respond to those needs and actions. However, we can control and evaluate our belief that we are locked in to the systems that we have, with instruction being our only avenue for change. We can build intuitive systems that meet users' needs; we can lobby vendors to redesign systems that are problematic for users; we can assess and deconstruct our current approach to information literacy instruction; and we can involve users in participatory design, where they are empowered and enabled to help us to craft systems that suit their intentions.

Librarians also need to engage in open dialogue with users to see if they want Web 2.0 technologies (e.g., a reference desk in Second Life? A library page on Facebook?), to assess these tools, and to know if these are the best ways to engage with users and provide services to meet their needs. At present, we do not know the answers to these questions, and yet we feel driven to go down these paths; often, we are pulled by the very vendors who have provided us (and our users) with problematic systems that are anything but usable. If we see our users as customers and the library as competing with the existing marketplace, then, yes, we would want and need to give users these tools. However, we have very little critical research to date on these issues, despite the dollars being spent on system design. We may find that these technological paths are exactly the right for our users—or not. We may find ways to design more appropriate systems as well. However, this will remain elusive if we are not in dialogue with our users in a meaningful way, working with them more collaboratively to build better, more intuitive systems, and looking beyond the regulatory practices that we have engaged in to date.

NOTES

1. For the purposes of this chapter, we are defining information technologies to include computer hardware, companion devices such as printers, scanners, and so forth, and the necessary operating systems, software, protocols, and operability standards.

2. There is disagreement about the term *post-Fordism,* as some authors prefer to describe it as *neo-Fordism,* while others insist it is primarily just another variant of Fordism (see discussion in Webster, 2006, pp. 85–93).

3. The accumulation regime is described by Webster (2006, p. 64) as "the prevailing organization of production, ways in which income is distributed, how different sectors of the economy are calibrated and how consumption is arranged."

4. Bibliographic utilities are consortiumlike organizations that coordinate the production and processing of electronic catalog records for sale and redistribution to member libraries. The bibliographic databases of the utilities are enormous, far beyond the size of their member libraries' local catalogs.

5. OCLC originally stood for Ohio College Library Center, then Online Computer Library Center, and now is simply known by the acronym OCLC. RLIN is the Research Libraries Information Network, and WLN is the Western Library Network.

6. It must be noted, however, that some of the fees collected by bibliographic utilities (unlike fees charged by commercial vendors) are often channeled into advocacy, education, and library community building, in the form of scholarships, training, and efforts to raise the visibility and profile of libraries in the broader community; see, for instance, the current statement by OCLC on their Web site (OCLC, 2008).

7. Calhoun's estimate was based on an informal survey of directors of large research libraries, indicating that about 20 percent of staff work in technical services. This percentage was taken as a proxy for labor costs (Calhoun, 2006, p. 49). Using this method with the current ARL statistics on salaries and wages (Association of Research Libraries, 2008) technical services expenditures would have increased slightly.

REFERENCES

Aglietta, M. (1976). *A theory of capitalist regulation: The US experience* (D. Fernbach, Trans). London: NLB Publishers.

Ahuja, J. S., & Webster, J. (2001). Perceived disorientation: An examination of a new measure to assess Web design effectiveness. *Interacting with Computers, 14*(1), 15–29.

Allen, M. (2002). A case study of the usability testing of the University of South Florida's virtual library interface design. *Online Information Review, 26*(1), 40–53.

Antelman, K., Lynema, E., & Pace, A. K. (2006). Toward a twenty-first century catalog. *Information Technology and Libraries, 25*(3), 128–139.

Anyomi, M. E. (1999). Outsourcing cataloging functions in South Carolina public libraries. *The Bottom Line, 12*(10), 29–33.

Association of College & Research Libraries. (2000). *The information literacy competency standards for higher education*. Chicago: American Library Association. Retrieved July 17, 2008, from http://www.ala.org/acrl/ilcomstan.html.

Association of Research Libraries. (2008). ARL statistics 2005–06: A compilation of statistics from the one hundred and twenty-three members of the Association of Research Libraries. Compiled and edited by Martha Kyrillidou and Mark Young. Retrieved July 23, 2008, from http://www.arl.org/stats/annualsurveys/arlstats/arlstats06.shtml.

Aula, A., & Kaki, M. (2005). Less is more in Web search interfaces for older adults. *First Monday, 10*. Retrieved February 15, 2008, from http://firstmonday.org/issues/issue10_7/aula/index.html.

Ayers, S. (2003). The outsourcing of cataloging: The effect on libraries. *Current Studies in Librarianship, 27*(1/2), 17–28.

Baker, N. (1994, April 4). Discards. *New Yorker*, pp. 64–70.

Balas, J. L. (2006). Does one-stop searching really serve all? *Computers in Libraries, 26*(9), 42–44.

Balas, J. L. (2007). Will the ILS soon be as obsolete as the card catalog? *Computers in Libraries, 27*(9), 41–43.

Bates, M. (2002). After the dot-bomb: Getting Web information retrieval right this time. *First Monday, 7*(7). Retrieved February 15, 2008, from http://firstmonday.org/issues/issue7_7/bates/index.html.

Benjes, C., & Brown, J. F. (2001). Test, revise, retest: Usability testing and library Web sites. *Internet Reference Services Quarterly, 5*(4), 37–54.

Beyer, H., & Holtzblatt, K. (1999). Contextual design. *ACM Interactions, 6*, 32–42.

Bilal, D. (2002). Children design their interfaces for Web search engines: A participatory approach. In L. C. Howarth, C. Cronin, & A. T. Slawek (Eds.), *Advancing knowledge: Expanding horizons for information science—Proceedings of the 30th Annual Conference of the Canadian Association for Information Science* (pp. 204–214). Toronto: Canadian Association for Information Science.

Borgman, C. (1986). Why are online catalogs hard to use? Lessons learned from information retrieval studies. *Journal of the American Society for Information Science, 37*(6), 387–400.

Borgman, C. (1996). Why are online catalogs *still* hard to use? *Journal of the American Society for Information Science, 47*(7), 493–503.

Boyer, R. (2005). How and why capitalisms differ. *Economy and Society, 34*(4), 509–557.

Boyer, R., & Saillard, Y. (2002). *Regulation theory: The state of the art*. London: Routledge.

Brand, S. (1997). *How buildings learn: What happens after they're built* (Rev. ed.). London: Phoenix Illustrated.

Brantley, S., Armstrong, A., & Lewis, K. M. (2006). Usability testing of a customizable library Web portal. *College and Research Libraries, 67*(2), 146–163.

Breeding, M. (2005). The new landscape of the automation business. *Computers in Libraries, 25*(8), 40–42.

Breeding, M. (2006). Automation system marketplace 2006: Reshuffling the deck. *Library Journal, 131*(6), 40–46, 48, 50, 52, 54.

Breeding, M. (2007a). Automation system marketplace 2007: An industry redefined. *Library Journal, 132*(6), 36–44, 46, 48.

Breeding, M. (2007b). The birth of a new generation of library interfaces. *Computers in Libraries, 27*(9), 34–37.

Breeding, M. (2007c). It's time to break the mold of the original ILS. *Computers in Libraries, 27*(10), 39–41.

Breeding, M. (2007d). Next generation library catalogs. *Library Technology Reports, 43*(4), 5–42.

Burke, G., Germain, C. A., & Van Ullen, M. K. (2003). URLs in the OPAC: Integrating or disintegrating research libraries' catalogs. *Journal of Academic Librarianship, 29*(5), 290–297.

Byrum, J. D. (2005). Online catalogs and library portals in today's information environment. *Journal of Library Administration, 43*(1/2), 135–154.

Byrum, J. D. (2006). Recommendations for urgently needed improvements of OPAC and the role of the national bibliographic agency in achieving it. *International Cataloging and Bibliographic Control, 35*(4), 75–81.

Calhoun, K. (2006). *The changing nature of the catalog and its integration with other discovery tools. Final report, March 17, 2006.* Prepared for the Library of Congress. Retrieved July 17, 2008, from http://www.loc.gov/catdir/calhoun-report-final.pdf.

Carpenter, M., & Svenonius, E. (1985). *Foundations of descriptive cataloging: A sourcebook.* Littleton, CO: Libraries Unlimited.

Case, D. O. (2007). *Looking for information: A survey of research on information seeking, needs and behavior* (2nd ed). San Diego, CA: Academic Press.

Chan, L. M. (1999). *A guide to the Library of Congress classification.* Englewood, NJ: Libraries Unlimited.

Chan, L. M. (2007). *Cataloging and classification: An introduction* (3rd ed.). Lanham, MD: Scarecrow Press.

Chapman, A. (2006). RDA: A new international standard. *Ariadne, 49*(October). Retrieved February 18, 2008, from http://www.ariadne.ac.uk/issue49/chapman/.

Cherry, J. M. (1998). Bibliographic displays in OPACs and Web catalogs: How well do they comply with display guidelines? *Information Technology and Libraries, 17*(3), 124–137.

Cockrell, B. J., & Jayne, E. A. (2002). How do I find an article? Insights from a Web usability study. *Journal of Academic Librarianship, 28*(3), 122–132.

Coyle, K. (2005). Catalogs, card—and other anachronisms. *Journal of Academic Librarianship, 31*(1), 60–62.

Coyle, K., & Hillmann, D. (2007). Resource description and access (RDA). *D-Lib Magazine, 113*(1/2). Retrieved February 18, 2007, from http://www.dlib.org/dlib/january07/coyle/01coyle.html.

Crawford, G. A., & Feldt, J. (2007). An Analysis of the literature on instruction in academic libraries. *Reference & User Services Quarterly, 46*(3), 77–88.

Cutter, C. A. (1876). Rules for a dictionary catalogue. Reprinted in *Public Libraries in the United States of America: Their history, condition and management.* Washington, DC: Government Printing Office.

Cutter, C. A. (1904). *Rules for a dictionary catalogue* (4th ed.). Washington, DC: Government Printing Office.

Dillon, M., & Jul, E. (1996). Cataloging Internet resources: The convergence of libraries and Internet resources. *Cataloging & Classification Quarterly, 22*(3/4), 197–238.

Drabenstott, K. M. (1996). Classification to the rescue: Handling the problems of too many and too few retrievals. *Advances in Knowledge Organization, 5,* 107–118.

Drabenstott, K. M., Simcox, S., & Fenton, E. G. (1999). End-user understanding of subject headings in library catalogs. *Library Resources & Technical Services, 43*(3), 140–160.

Dykstra, M. (1988, March 1). LC Subject Headings disguised as a thesaurus. *Library Journal, 113*(4), 42–46.

Fast, K. V., & Campbell, D. G. (2001). The ontological perspectives of the Semantic Web and the Metadata Harvesting Protocol: Applications of metadata for improving web search. *Canadian Journal of Information and Library Science, 26*(4), 5–19.

Fast, K., & Campbell, G. (2004). "I still like Google": University student perceptions of searching OPACs and the Web. *Proceedings of the 67th Annual Meeting of ASIST, Providence, RI, Nov. 2004,* 138–146.

Feeney, M., & Newby, J. (2005). Model for presenting resources in Scholar's Portal. *Portal: Libraries and the Academy, 5*(2), 195–211.

Fiander, D. J., & Campbell, D. G. (2003). An XML definition for an ISBD-based encoding scheme. *Journal of Internet Cataloging, 6*(4), 29–58.

Fischer, R., & Lugg, R. (2006). The real cost of ILS ownership. *The Bottom Line, 119*(3), 111–123.

Friedman, A. L. (2000). Microregulation and post-Fordism: Critique and development of regulation theory. *New Political Economy, 5*(1), 59–76.

Gibson, J. J. (1979). *The ecological approach to visual perception.* Boston: Houghton-Mifflin.

Given, L. M., Ruecker, S., Simpson, H., Sadler, E., & Ruskin, A. (2007). Inclusive interface design for seniors: Image-browsing for a health information context. *Journal of the American Society for Information Science and Technology, 58*(11), 1610–1617.

Gorman, M. (2007). RDA: Imminent debacle. *American Libraries, 38*(11), 64–65.

Graham, J-B., Poe, J., & Weatherford, K. (2003). Functional by design: A comparative study to determine the usability and functionality of one library's Web site. *Technical Services Quarterly, 21*(2), 33–49.

Groenewegen, D., & Huggard, S. (2003). The answer to all our problems? Trialling a library portal. *Library Review, 52*(9), 452–459.

Gullikson, S., Blades, R., Bragdon, M., McKibbon, S., Sparling, M., & Toms, E. (1999). The impact of information architecture on academic Web site usability. *The Electronic Library, 17*(5), 293–304.

Halcoussis, D., Halverson, A. L., Lowenberg, A. D., & Lowenberg, S. (2002). An empirical analysis of Web catalog user experiences. *Information Technology and Libraries, 21*(4), 148–157.

Hedemark, A., Hedman, J., & Sundin, O. (2005). Speaking of users: On user discourses in the field of public libraries. *Information Research, 10*(2). Retrieved February 15, 2008, from http://informationr.net/ir/10-2/paper218.html.

Hildreth, C. R. (1995). *Online catalog design models: Are we moving in the right directions?* Washington, DC: Council on Library Resources. Retrieved July 17, 2008, from http://myweb.cwpost.liu.edu/childret/clr-opac.html.

Hodkinson, C., & Kiel, G. (2003). Understanding Web information search behavior: An exploratory model. *Journal of End User Computing, 15*(4), 27–49.

Hoffman, C., & Polkinghorne, S. (2007, August). *Launching infolit 2.0? What is being said about the social web and information literacy?* Presentation for the Pacific Northwest Library Association Annual Conference, Edmonton, Alberta, Canada.

Hsieh-Yee, I. (2001). Research on Web search behavior. *Library and Information Science Research, 23*(2), 167–185.

International Federation of Library Associations. Study Group on the Functional Requirements for Bibliographic Records. (1998). *Functional requirements for bibliographic records: Final report.* Retrieved February 16, 2008, from http://www.ifla.org/VII/s13/frbr/frbr.pdf.

Intner, S. (2006). RDA: Will it be cataloger's judgment or cataloger's Judgment Day? *Technicalities, 26*(2), 1, 10–12.

Jackson, M. E. (2004). *Current status of portal applications in ARL libraries: Results of a survey conducted by the ARL Portal Applications Working Group.* Washington, DC: Association of Research Libraries.

Jantz, R. C. (2001). Knowledge management in academic libraries: Special tools and processes to support information professionals. *Reference Services Review, 29*(1), 33–39.

Jewitt, C. C. (1853). *Smithsonian report on the construction of catalogs of libraries, and their publication by means of separate, stereotyped titles, with rules and examples* (2nd ed.) Washington, DC: Smithsonian Institution. Reprinted Ann Arbor, MI: University Microfilms, 1961.

Johnson, J. (2003). *Web bloopers: 60 common Web design mistakes and how to avoid them.* San Francisco: Morgan Kaufmann.

Julien, H. (2005). A longitudinal analysis of information literacy instruction in Canadian libraries. *Canadian Journal of Information and Library Science, 29*(3), 289–313.

Julien, H., & Boon, S. (2004). Assessing instructional outcomes in Canadian academic libraries. *Library & Information Science Research, 26,* 121–139.

Julien, H., & Breu, R. (2005). Instructional practices in Canadian public libraries. *Library & Information Science Research, 27*(3), 281–301.

Kari, J. (2004). Web information seeking by pages: An observational study of moving and stopping. *Information Research, 9*(4). Retrieved January 27, 2008, from http://informationr.net/ir/9-4/paper183.html.

Krueger, J., Ray, R. L., & Knight, L. (2004). Applying Web usability techniques to assess student awareness of library Web resources. *Journal of Academic Librarianship, 30*(4), 285–293.

Lancaster, F. W. (1986). *Vocabulary control for information retrieval* (2nd ed.). Arlington, VA: Information Resources Press.

Large, A., & Beheshti, J. (1997). OPACs: A research review. *Library & Information Science Research, 19*(2), 111–133.

Large, A., Nesset, V., Beheshti, J., & Bowler, L. (2006). "Bonded design": A novel approach to intergenerational information technology design. *Library and Information Science Research, 28*(1), 64–82.

Larson, R. R. (1991). The decline of subject searching: Long-term trends and patterns of index use in an online catalog. *Journal of the American Society for Information Science, 42*(April), 197–215.

Libby, K. A., & Caudle, D. M. (1997). A survey on the outsourcing of cataloguing in academic libraries. *College & Research Libraries, 58*(6), 550–560.

Maloney, K., & Bracke, P. J. (2005). Library portal technologies. *Journal of Library Administration, 43*(1/2), 87–112.

Mann, T. (2006). *The changing nature of the catalog and its integration with other discovery tools. Final report, March 17, 2006: A critical review.* Retrieved July 17, 2008, from http://www.guild2910.org/AFSCMECalhounReviewREV.pdf.

Martin, R. S., et al. (2000). *The impact of outsourcing and privatization on library services and management: A study for the American Library Association.* Denton: Texas Woman's University, School of Library and Information Studies.

Nichols, J., & Mellinger, M. (2007). Portals for undergraduate subject searching: Are they worth it? *Portal: Libraries and the Academy, 7*(4), 481–490.

Nielsen, J. (2000). *Designing Web usability: The practice of simplicity.* Indianapolis, IN: New Riders Publishing.

Nielsen, J. (2004). *Usable information technology.* Retrieved January 27, 2008, from http://www.useit.com.

Novotny, E. (2004). I don't think I click: A protocol analysis study of use of a library online catalog in the Internet age. *College & Research Libraries, 65*(6), 525–537.

Novotny, E., Cahoy, E. S., & Stern, E. (2006). If we teach, do they learn? The impact of instruction on online catalog search strategies. *Portal: Libraries & the Academy, 6*(2), 155–167.

O'Beirne, R. (2006). Raising the profile of information literacy in public libraries. *Library & Information Update, 5*(1/2), 44–45.

OCLC. (2008). Advocacy, education and sharing. Retrieved July 23, 2008, from http://www.oclc.org/community/default.htm.

Palmquist, R. A. (2001). An overview of usability for the study of users' Web-based information retrieval behavior. *Journal of Education for Library and Information Science, 42*(2), 123–136.

Panizzi, A. (1841). Rules for the compilation of the catalogue. In *Catalogue of printed books in the British Museum* (Vol. 1, pp. v–ix). London: British Museum.

Robins, D., & Kelsey. S. (2002). Analysis of Web-based information architecture in a university library: Navigating for known items. *Information Technology and Libraries, 21*(4), 158–169.

Rosenfeld, L., & Morville, P. (2002). *Information architecture for the World Wide Web* (2nd ed.). Sebastopol, CA: O'Reilly.

Ruecker, S. (2003). *Affordances of prospect for academic users of interpretively-tagged text collections.* Doctoral dissertation, University of Alberta, Edmonton, 2003.

Sadler, E., & Given, L. M. (2007). Affordance theory: A framework for graduate students' information behaviors. *Journal of Documentation, 63*(1), 115–141.

Saumure, K., & Given, L. M. (2004). Digitally enhanced? An examination of the information behaviours of visually impaired postsecondary students. *Canadian Journal of Information and Library Science, 28*(2), 25–42.

Schuyler, M. (2000). The future of Web design. *Computers in Libraries, 20*(1), 50–53.

Skov, A. (2004). Information literacy and the role of public libraries. *Scandinavian Public Library Quarterly, 37*(3), 4–7.

Sleeman, B., & Bluh, P. (Eds.) (2005). *From catalog to gateway: Charting a course for future access.* Chicago: Association for Library Collections and Technical Services, American Library Association.

Slone, D. J. (2000). Encounters with the OPAC: On-line searching in public libraries. *Journal of the American Society for Information Science, 51*(8), 757–773.

Spackman, E. (2007). Utilizing focus groups to evaluate an information literacy program in a general biology course. *Science and Technology Libraries, 27*(3), 3–28.

Srodin, S., & Strupczewski, J. (2002). Creating a global information portal: Our 9-month odyssey. *Computers in Libraries, 22*(2), 14–19.

Talja, S. (1997). Constituting "information" and "user" as research objects: A theory of knowledge formations as an alternative to the information man theory. In P. Vakkari, R. Savolainen, & B. Dervin (Eds.), *Information seeking in context—Proceedings of an International Conference on Research in Information Needs, Seeking and Use in Different Contexts* (pp. 67–80). August 14–16, 1996, Tampere, Finland.

Tennant, R. (2007). Will RDA be DOA? *Library Journal, 132*(5), 25.

Tickell, A., & Peck, J. A. (1995). Social regulation after Fordism: Regulation theory, neo-liberalism and the global-local nexus. *Economy and Society, 4*(3), 357–386.

Tosa, Y., & Long, T. (2003). Teaching library research skills: Online and at the library. *PNLA Quarterly, 68*(1), 14–15.

Travis, T. A., & Norlin, E. (2002). Testing the competition: Usability of commercial information sites compared with academic library Web sites. *College and Research Libraries, 63*(5), 433–448.

Trigg, R. H., & Anderson, S. I. (1996). Introduction to this special issue on current perspectives on participatory design. *Human-Computer Interaction, 11*(3), 181–185.

Tuominen, K. (1997). User-centred discourse: An analysis of the subject positions of the user and the librarian. *Library Quarterly, 67*(4), 350–371.

Turner, N. B. (2002). Baffled, befuddled or bemused: Testing students' use of the online catalog. *College & Undergraduate Libraries, 9*(1), 71–79.

UNESCO. (2005). *UNESCO libraries portal: An international gateway to information for librarians and library users.* Retrieved January 27, 2008, from http://www.unesco.org/cgi-bin/webworld/portal_bib2/cgi/page.cgi?d=1.

Valentine, B., & Nolan, S. (2002). Putting students in the driver's seat: Web usability testing on a shoestring. *Public Services Quarterly, 1*(2), 43–66.

Vaughan, M. W., & Dillon, A. (2006). Why structure and genre matter for users of digital information: A longitudinal experiment with readers of a Web-based newspaper. *International Journal of Human-Computer Studies, 64*(6), 502–526.

Vicente, K. J. (2002). Ecological interface design: Progress and challenges. *Human Factors, 44*(1), 62–78.

Villen-Rueda, L., Senso, J. A., & Moya-Anegon, F. (2007). The use of OPAC in a large academic library: A transactional log analysis study of subject searching. *Journal of Academic Librarianship, 33*(3), 327–337.

Ward, J. L., & Hiller, S. (2005). Usability testing, interface design, and portals. *Journal of Library Administration, 43*(1/2), 155–171.

Webster, F. (2006). *Theories of the information society* (3rd ed.). London: Routledge.

Wegener, D. R., Goh-Ong Ai Moi, M., & Lim Mei Li, M. (2004). Web usability testing in a polytechnic library. *Australian Library Journal, 53*(2), 173–179.

Williamson, N. (1996). Standards and rules for subject access. *Cataloging & Classification Quarterly, 21*(3/4), 155–176.

Wust, M. (2006). *Attitudes of university researchers in the field of education towards institutional repositories.* Masters thesis, University of Alberta, Edmonton, 2006.

Yee, M. M., & Layne, S. S. (1998). *Improving online public access catalogs.* Chicago: American Library Association.

Yu, H., & Young, M. (2004). The impact of Web search engines on subject seaching in OPAC. *Information Technology & Libraries, 23*(4), 168–180.

Zemon, M. (2001). The librarian's role in portal development. *College & Research Libraries News, 62*(7), 710–712.

12

LIBRARIES, ARCHIVES, AND DIGITAL PRESERVATION: A CRITICAL OVERVIEW

Dorothy A. Warner

The decision process as to whether or not to digitize a document, information, or an object remains a prudent and necessary exercise if for no other reason than there is no turning back now that born-digital information exists. While much research is underway, much of it takes as a given starting point that digitization is both inevitable and that the primary concerns are technical/technological in nature: "Libraries have to accept that the future is now. [W]e have adopted the digital mindset and have seized many of the opportunities new technology offers to inspire our users to learn, discover, and innovate" (British Library Press Release, 2008; see also Huwe, 2006). And, within this research (as this chapter will show), many of the crucial problems are aired, but there is no *critical* approach that attempts to assess the overall impact of the lack of agreed-on standards or digitization methods or the enormous institutional expenses being faced, and the real possibility of lost or inaccessible information is dramatically underrepresented.

DEFINITIONAL ISSUES

Are you digitizing for access only and preserving the original, physical item, or has the original decayed? Or are you digitizing for access and preservation because the cost to remobilize and redigitize is too great (Lytle, 2006, p. 27)? Coyle (2006) summarizes the issues, explaining that "to say that you

---

This chapter is a revision and update of a previous article, (2002) "'Why Do We Need to Keep This in Print? It's on the Web. . .': A Review of Electronic Archiving Issues and Problems." *Progressive Librarian* (19/20), 47–64.

are planning to digitize some items, or that you will create a digital library, is somewhat like saying that you will buy your daughter a mammal for her birthday. Is it a hamster, or a Bengal tiger? Is your digital object an e-book or a set of statistical data? Is it optimized for long-term preservation, for machine processing, or for viewing in a Web browser?" (p. 205). She describes several purposes for digitizing, including preservation, discovery, delivery, reading, research, or machine manipulation, and she notes that, although these distinctions can be applied to born-digital objects, it would not be "without some difficulty," wrapped up as it is in the issue of the purpose of the born digital object, which "might be determined based on the programs that created them and the formats in which they are produced." Some are very "program-specific," and, she notes there are "dozens, if not hundreds, of different formats. In addition, the people using these programs exercise varying degrees of creativity in producing their outcomes" (p. 207). For instance, Microsoft Excel files may hold a meeting agenda or a geometrical drawing. She points out that born-digital files "will be the hardest to characterize based on their file format, and provide the greatest challenge for long-term preservation" (p. 207).

Duranti and Thibodeau (2006) remind us that "the term, 'record' comes from the Latin, *recordari,* to remember. The essential function of a record is to serve as a bridge over time, to carry information about an action, event, or state of affairs forward for when it is needed in subsequent actions or for reference about what happened or was described or said in the past. . . . Defining the concept of record in the context of interactive, experiential and dynamic systems is a very tall order," (p. 47) and they recognize that the discussions about this have only just begun. The concept of a record as articulated by the InterPARES (International Research on Permanent Authentic Records in Electronic Systems) projects "needs to be tested in other environments. The practical possibilities of preserving such records needs to be explored. . . . There is an undoubted need to explore the great practical implications and legal consequences for all the parties directly involved, and all the stakeholders" (Duranti & Thibodeau, 2006, pp. 67–68).

CHALLENGES/THREATS

O'Mahony's (1998) early concerns about electronic government information remain true today:

> Each day that the problems of electronic preservation and permanent public access go unresolved, alarming amounts of government information continue to be lost as databases come and go from agency websites, files are deleted from government computer servers, digital storage media deteriorate, and hardware and software become obsolete. The continuous and cumulative effects of this ongoing catastrophe are to deny taxpayers access to information they already paid for, to impair the public's ability to use government information already collected and compiled, to waste public and private resources in having to duplicate efforts to retrieve information previously

available but now lost, and to allow the historical record of the nation to literally vanish before our eyes. Moreover, it severely undermines the potential promise and usefulness of new electronic technologies when the long-term consequence of their use is an ever-widening breach in our collected knowledge and information bank. (p. 114)

Sharpe (2007) offers the illustration of "The Domesday Book," William the Conqueror's survey of England in 1086, which may be read at the U.K. National Archives at Kew, London. In 1986, in celebration of the 900th anniversary of the original, a digital version was created and stored on the "latest technology," 12-inch laser discs—"to guard against obsolescence." In only 15 years, "serious action had to be taken to save these records from being lost" because a few laser disc readers still existed. "The files were extracted in binary format onto more modern media. The next challenge was to interpret this so that it was not just a meaningless string of 1s and 0s, as the digital files could not be interpreted by any modern software. Solving this problem was not a trivial exercise, but was completed successfully after considerable effort including experience and input from the original record creators" (para. 4). Are these records now safe? Perhaps for another 15 years. The movie industry is struggling with its own similar digital dilemma, recognizing that digital film is not as durable as 35-millimeter film. The rate at which DVDs degrade is ensuring their future for no more than 15 years (Cieply, 2007).

There is also the issue of how to begin to preserve digital Web-based material, which has been labeled a moving target. Consider, for example the claim on the banner on the BBC Web site "that the site is updated every minute of every day," or a short-term Web site for an election, or that the "average lifespan of a Web page . . . is forty-four days" or that "entire Web sites disappear at an alarming rate," according to Guenther and Myrick (2006, pp. 142–143). They summarize the unique challenges of preserving these materials when they ask "How do we collect it before it changes or disappears? How do we manage these hundreds or thousands of snapshots of a single site (times however many sites we are curating)? How do we manage the huge variety of MIME types captured in a single snapshot? How do we provide effective, sufficient metadata for management and discovery? And finally how do we guarantee that this material can be preserved in order to make it available for the foreseeable future to a community of users?" (p. 162).

The National Archives and Records Administration (NARA) faces unique challenges in regard to records of the federal government of the United States. The issue of diversity of data formats is compounded because "not only does the government use practically all products sold on the market, but it even produces technology that is not sold on the market" (Thibodeau, 2004, p. 635). In order to preserve digital information for at least 20 years, "the architecture of the preservation system must allow easy replacement of any or all components of hardware or software. Otherwise, the system itself will actually compound the problems of preservation, rather than solve them"

(Thibodeau, 2004, p. 636). Thibodeau (2007) again provides several illustrations of the "daunting" challenges to NARA, including

> one example [that] illustrates the challenge of complex digital formats. Traditionally the National Archives preserves a complete set of ship's drawings at least for every class of Navy ship, and such records are requested fairly frequently. Today, there are no ship's drawings. They have been replaced by computer-assisted design, engineering and manufacturing records, amounting to at least 100,000 digital files per ship. The problem of preserving such records is one [NARA] share[s] with the Navy. The Navy keeps ships in operation for many decades. These ships are, in effect, floating cities. Like cities, they are not static entities. Over time, they need to be repaired and changed. They change their mechanical system, computer systems, kitchens, laundries, and so on. What does the Navy, or anyone, know about computer-assisted design, engineering or manufacturing systems 25 years from now? The only thing they can count on is that such systems will be different. There is no way of guaranteeing that today's data can be used in future systems, either to modify or repair a ship or even to show what its design was. Initial research that [NARA has] done with the Navy, other government agencies, and computer scientists and engineers around the country, has shown that solving these problems is not only beyond the state of the art in technology. It is beyond the state of computer science. ("The Challenge of Records" section, para. 6–7)

In addition, NARA faces the obligation to preserve an overwhelming amount of e-government information, including the 38 million e-mail messages received from the Clinton administration, annual transfers of approximately 1 million messages from the State Department's worldwide diplomatic correspondence, the scanned images of the 2000 Census of Population, amounting to "600 to 800 million images," and military personnel files (frequently requested by military personnel who need to obtain veterans' benefits, employment, and insurance). NARA faces the "need to ingest, preserve, and provide access to between 50 and 90 million Tagged Image File (tif) images in that one series." These examples illustrate the problem of the open-ended growth of digital information, and "no one has good data on the amount of information that is being created by the government in digital form" (Thibodeau, 2004, p. 636).

The digital preservation dilemma not only remains the same as it has since the conceptualization of digitization but is becoming increasingly complex as professionals grapple with the ever-growing issues. Teper (2007) recognizes that "preservation of materials existing in digital formats is the greatest preservation challenge currently facing research libraries" (p. 10). Rosenthal, Robertson, Lipkis, Reich, and Morabit (2005) present a "taxonomy of threats" ("Threats" section, para. 2) in concurrence with recommendations by the National Research Council to the National Archives "that the designers of a digital preservation system need a clear vision of the threats against which they are being asked to protect their system's contents, and those threats under which it is acceptable for preservation to fail" ("Threats" section, para. 1). They recommend that a threat model include these threats: media failure, hardware failure, software failure, communication errors, failure of network services, media and hardware obsolescence, software obsolescence, operator error, natural disaster, external attack, internal attack, economic failure, and organizational failure.

AN OVERVIEW OF THE PROBLEMS

Although there are groups working at the state, national, and global levels to determine the best practices for digital archiving, the problems are complex and the stakeholders are many. Understanding the issue of digital archiving is important for librarians at all levels as local collection development and preservation decisions are being made. There are no agreed-on standards and no agreed-on solutions. One must know whom the stakeholders are, the technological problems involved in archiving and retrieving digital information, the current recommendations for archiving digital information, the costs involved, and some of the groups working for a solution.

The problems are not all technological, though the technological problems are many. Feeney (1999, p. 108) describes the relevant stakeholders as authors, publishers, libraries, archive centers, distributors, networked information service providers, IT suppliers, legal depositories, consortia, universities, and research funders. He also suggests considering the relationship of the stakeholder to the digital material: "initiators, who are involved in collection development; regulators, such as those bodies involved in the legal deposit system or copyright legislation; creators of digital records; rights owners; fund holders, who manage the funds available for preservation activity; providers of electronic publications and new or repackaged editions; readers, who require access to digital material; and archivists, who are concerned with conserving digital material and maintaining its integrity." Each stakeholder is involved at a different stage of the life-cycle of the digital resource and may not be considering the effect on a stakeholder at another stage, thus requiring a more coordinated effort on the part of the stakeholders. Feeney (1999, pp. 112–113) summarized the main stages in the life-cycle concept developed by the Arts and Humanities Data Service (AHDS) as: (1) data creation; (2) data management and preservation (including acquisition, retention, or disposal; data structure; data description and documentation; data storage; and data preservation); (3) data use; and (4) rights management.

Abundant recommendations have emanated from groups struggling with digital preservation problems at all levels. At the national level, the U.S. National Commission on Libraries and Information Science (NCLIS) recognized problems regarding the preservation of government information that were compounded by technological developments. Included in the problems was the lack of an overall organized plan for preserving digital government resources. A narrative description of the legislative proposal by NCLIS, the Public Information Resources Reform Act of 2001, was prepared. The proposed legislation advocated reforming the federal government's public information structure to bring together "in a systematic fashion all of the key elements necessary for a comprehensive public information resources management program and to elevate the importance of federal government public information resources to the status of a strategic national asset" (NCLIS, 2001, p. 2–3). NCLIS recommended harmonizing the information resources management policies, programs, and practices at each stage of the information life-cycle because of the inseparable interrelationship of government agencies. This harmonization or collaboration directly relates to the technological issues described here because of the need for government agencies to provide uniform effectiveness across agencies within all of the digital resource life-cycle stages. Included in this detailed report were recommendations for surveying preferred user formats for data (including bibliographic, graphical, numerical, sound, spatial, textual, video, and multimedia data types); for surveying patterns of user preference for format types (including database, spreadsheet, tagged markup, image, audio, video, text, and word processing formats); and for tracking online approaches to information (user interfaces supported, Web design approaches, bulletin board systems). NCLIS suggested that both the opportunities and the challenges of technological developments needed to be approached from an interbranch, intergovernmental, and interagency direction in order to ensure future interconnectivity (NCLIS, 2001).

Issues that are unique to large-scale digitization projects were recently addressed by a conference of representatives of statewide and large regional collaborative digitization programs in the United States. The issues included, but were not limited to, metadata, harvesting, interoperability, storage, business planning, training, strengthening of collaborative digitization projects, funding goals, selection priorities, and the immediate risk of born-digital objects (Lytle, 2006). There were many questions, but few answers. For example:

- Sustainability—digital preservation is a black box of unknown costs—how can I sustain it if I don't know what it is?
- Expertise—there is not enough expertise in digital preservation to spread around all collaboratives. How do we manage this?
- Collaborative digital preservation—given limited resources and big unknowns . . . are there ways to divide the work and collaborate? (Lytle, 2006, p. 27)

The issue of the multiple formats of objects to be digitized becomes magnified by the increasing number of ways that information can be stored (Coyle, 2006). Sharpe's (2007) concern is with the storage of archival records and the need to retain the necessary links between records. He notes the difference between the metadata (which can change) and the actual digital files (which remain the same). One way to resolve this issue is to store the metadata and files separately (e.g. in an XML-enabled database and a separate file store respectively). This means that the responsibility of keeping the links between the two must be performed by the archive. The alternative is to store the metadata and the files together as one object, in order to ensure that they cannot become separated and to simplify backup issues. However, this can lead to the creation of unwieldy large objects, and it makes the editing of these records a potentially complicated process. ("Storage Is an Essential Component" section, para. 1)

He notes a second issue, which is the necessity to back up everything and to store it off site. Next, there must be active management to "ensure that every file held is appropriately cared for with an automated programme of checks. This includes, for example, exercising tapes to prevent them from sticking and ensuring regular maintenance occurs before there is a problem" ("Storage Is an Essential Component" section, para. 3).

STANDARDS

There is still a substantial standards debate since "no computer technical standards have yet shown any likelihood of lasting forever" (Bearman, 1999). However, those recommending an adherence to standards use the rationale that standards "can assist by facilitating the transfer of information between hardware and software platforms as technologies evolve" and "resources which are encoded using open standards have a greater chance of remaining accessible after an extended period than resources encoded with proprietary standards" (PADI, 2001c). Descriptive metadata has no agreed-on standard. "Commonly known as 'data about data', [metadata] is the data describing context, content and structure of records and their management through time" (University of Lethbridge, n.d.). Research continues in the attempt to develop a uniform standard (see OCLC/RLG Working Group on Preservation Metadata, 2001), which Bearman (1999) states must exist for any of the electronic preservation models to succeed. "Serious proposals for metadata encapsulation strategies need to address how the required metadata will be identified, created or captured at the time of the creation of the records; by what means it will be stored in inviolable conjunction with the record contents; how it will support the use of the record by authorized users over time; and by whom, where, and at what costs the infrastructure for record keeping will be constructed and maintained" (Bearman, 1999, p. 4).

Cantara (2005, p. 251) concurs that as the number of library digital collections of a variety of types of objects and formats continues to grow, a "metadata framework . . . is imperative to support interoperability" (p. 251), or the requirement for systems to "talk to each other" (Lytle, 2006, p. 22). Types of interoperability include "technical (operating systems and communication protocols), organizational, and content related interoperability, which are addressed by metadata" (Lytle, 2006, p. 22). Those involved with collaborative projects realize "that issues regarding the quality of metadata are compounded in collaborative projects" (Lytle, 2006, p. 22).

Knight (2005), of the National Library of New Zealand, describes the dilemma that libraries find themselves in.

> The lack of international consensus on preservation metadata is a key inhibitor to full implementation of a preservation metadata strategy at the Library. This lack of consensus reflects to some degree a catch-22 implicit in the notion of preservation metadata. There is no way to test the effectiveness and efficiency of the metadata approach to digital preservation without suffering some catastrophic loss of digital objects against which to test the metadata approach. There is a significant degree of faith involved in the development and implementation of a preservation metadata program (which might also explain, at least partially, why it is that the library community has been at the forefront of developments in preservation metadata—metadata is a natural and integral component of our normal business practice). In making any decision on whether to implement a preservation metadata process, organizations must bear in mind the potential costs of data recovery. The risks and associated costs of data loss are as yet unknown. In a recent publication on preservation, Wendy Duff from the University of Toronto states that "reliable authentic digital objects will not be preserved across time without adequate preservation metadata" (as cited in Duff, 2004, p. 27). Yet, what is there in our experience of the digital environment that makes this so? . . . Our legacy to the future is minimal loss of our digital heritage. To that end the cost of preservation metadata today can be considered negligible compared with cost associated with a catastrophic loss of digital material in the future that might have been mitigated had preservation metadata been available. (Knight, 2005, p. 96)

Cantara (2005) gives the background of the Metadata Encoding and Transmission Standard (METS): "a data communication standard for encoding descriptive, administrative, and structural metadata regarding objects within a digital library, expressed using the Extensible Markup Language Schema (XSD) of the World Wide Web Consortium" (pp. 238–239). She notes that METS has many so-called parents in the form of the Digital Library Federation (DLF), an international editorial board, and that it is maintained in the Network Development and MARC Standards Office of the Library of Congress:

> METS is a direct successor to the Making of America II (MOA2) Project, a multi-institutional library effort to create a standard for encoding descriptive, administrative, and structural metadata. . . . The primary goal of the project was to develop a standard that would promote interoperability, scalability, and digital preservation of digital library objects. . . . Around the same time, the International Organization for Standardization (ISO) and the Consultative Committee for Space Data Systems (CCSDS) of the National Aeronautics and Space Administration (NASA) issued the first draft of its *Reference Model for an Open Archival Information System* (OASIS), "a framework for understanding and applying concepts needed for long-term digital information preservation" [which] define[d] a model for archiving digital (and nondigital) objects

> and describe[d] the composition of three types of "information packages" for a digital repository: submission information packages for transmission and/or exchange of digital objects to and from a digital repository (SIP), archival information packages to archive digital objects for long-term preservation and access (AIP), and dissemination information packages to publish digital objects via the web to end users (DIP). METS can be used to create any or all of these information packages. (Cantara 2005, pp. 238–239)

However, there are problems with METS: "While METS provides a flexible mechanism for encoding digital library objects, flexibility is often the enemy of interoperability, and METS is no exception to this rule. The potential range of variation in METS documents is extraordinarily high, and the challenges this presents to software developers are considerable. Given METS' flexibility, METS documents created at two different institutions, even for two similar (or identical) objects can be very different. Very basic software operations such as indexing, retrieval and display can be difficult to code when the exact nature of the metadata and content to be processed are left as ambiguous as they are in the METS format" (McDonough, 2006, pp. 151–152).

OCLC and the Research Libraries Group (RLG) coestablished an "international working group to develop a common, implementable core set of metadata elements for digital preservation. . . . PREMIS (Preservation Metadata: Implementation Strategies) was charged to define a set of semantic units that are implementation independent, practically oriented, and likely to be needed by most preservation repositories" (Caplan & Guenther, 2005, p. 111). This group found that there is scant experience with digital preservation and among those attempting it, they

> still lack a common vocabulary and, to a large extent, a common conceptual framework. Although most . . . claimed to have been informed by the OAIS reference model and to be at least partly compliant with it, there was substantial difference of opinion as to the meaning of . . . compliance. . . . [M]ost [OAIS] terms have not been widely adopted in the community, at least not in informal communications such as survey responses [and users] were recording several different types of metadata, and more than half were recording metadata in all of these categories: rights, provenance, technical, administrative, descriptive, and structural. Repositories appear to draw metadata elements from various schemes to suit their purposes. . . . Overall, thirty-three different metadata element sets or rule sets were mentioned by at least one repository. In general, the survey shows a picture of a community trying to take advantage of prior work but not at the point of developing or settling on dominant standards. (Caplan & Guenther, 2005, p. 115)

Conclusions from recent conference attendees include the recognition that this is a "complex and labor-intensive task. There is need for more tools to automate processes for metadata creation, revision, and harvesting [which would] provide benefits in terms of consistency, interoperability, and long-term viability of meaningful metadata" (Lytle, 2006, p. 27), offsetting some of the current costs of creating and sustaining meaningful metadata. Currently, "the initial expense and difficulty of creating high-quality metadata is compounded by the need for constant revision to correct mistakes and incorporate revisions to subject terms, taxonomies, and controlled vocabularies, along with revisions to meet the continually evolving patron research needs" (Lytle, 2006, p. 26). Metadata creation problems include inconsistency (both structurally and semantically), and data that is either missing, incorrect, confusing or insufficient. Poor quality records exist because they are "often created by people who are not catalogers, are created based on local practice that does not facilitate interoperability, or are based on curatorial traditions that do not translate well for managing digital objects" (Lytle, 2006, pp. 21–22).

COSTS

There is an operating assumption that "we are all faced with an unknown but big preservation per-unit cost" (Lytle, 2006, p. 27). Cost considerations include but are not limited to: selection, metadata creation (technical and descriptive), management, storage (including backup copies), training, and legal issues (including intellectual property rights). The human costs alone are extensive. The selection process of what should be digitally preserved is very expensive to do manually and, although it has been suggested that tools will be developed to assist with this selection, "records tend to be hierarchical in nature" and the logical structure for records to be archived should be determined by archivists (Sharpe, 2007, "The Structure of Records" section, para. 1). Appropriate metadata must then be assigned by archivists, "but the sheer quantity of these records (and the fact that it is necessary to use appropriate application software, operating systems and hardware to view them) means that this is potentially a bottleneck in the process" (Sharpe, 2007, "Bringing in the Metadata" section, para. 3). Sharpe offers possible solutions but recognizes the imperfections of those solutions.

Management issues include the need for off-site backup and storage noted earlier by Sharpe (2007), but he goes on: there must be an automated program to check storage media that includes "exercising tapes to prevent them from sticking and ensuring regular maintenance occurs before there is a problem . . . [and] a way to guarantee that files have not been changed during storage can be achieved by the creation (and subsequent verification) of checksums for each file. . . . A key requirement of an archive should be to ensure that a single bit is never lost—and, in any case, there should always be another backup copy of every file if the system needs to be restored" (para. 4, 5). Training is another much-overlooked cost: not merely the personnel costs for the trainers, but, for online courses, the infrastructure and staff required for technological issues and for hands-on workshops, which require appropriate space and equipment. Sustainable funding for training is another cost consideration closely related to training. Bradley (2007) notes that "digital sustainability" now includes funding and the context of the economic health of the digital-preserving institution as another consideration.

Feeney (1999, pp. 116–120) gives a breakdown of cost considerations based on one of the studies commissioned by the Digital Archiving Working Group (DAWG): "One clear message that has emerged is that a great deal of money can be wasted if digitization projects are undertaken without due regard to long-term preservation. It is now relatively easy to produce digital versions of texts or images. However, if there is no plan in place for archiving the digital files, long-term preservation will be expensive, or may even result in the work having to be repeated" (Feeney, 1999, p. 120). As it is difficult to isolate preservation costs within the life-cycle of a digital resource, costs associated with all elements in the life-cycle of the digital resource are considered. The following cost model summary defines seven key areas: data creation; data selection and evaluation; data management, including data documentation, validation, structure, and storage; resource disclosure; data use; data preservation; and rights management.

Cost Model Summary

Data creation costs: A key to this stage is providing adequate documentation of the digital resource.

Data selection and evaluation: Acquisition decisions include how easily a digital resource can be managed, catalogued, accessed, and preserved.

Data management including data documentation, validation, structure, and storage: Documentation, the description of the "structure, contents, provenance and history" (Feeney, 1999, p. 117), must be checked, edited, added to if necessary, made available to users, and kept up-to-date. Validation involves the periodic assessment of the resource and the copying and refreshing necessary for preservation. The structure refers to the original format of the resource and will determine the costs involved for providing future storage and access. Available resources determine storage, by data volume and by the choice of preservation and use. (Feeney, 1999, pp. 118–120, also describes in detail the high costs of rescuing data, or "digital archaeology.")

Resource disclosure: These costs, though not necessarily involved with preservation, involve "discovering, extracting and preparing the object for use" (Feeney, 1999, p. 117).

Data use: The structure of the digital resource will determine the costs of delivering the resource to end users.

Data preservation: The main costs include "agreeing on the preferred standard formats; testing the conversion for a specific category of resource; running the conversion as a batch process; testing a sample of converted resources; deleting the old versions if required; copying the resulting files" (Feeney, 1999, p. 118).

Rights management: Consideration must be given to intellectual property rights and the legal issues of data protection and confidentiality, which determine issues of access, use, and legal preservation. These potentially substantial costs can actually be the highest cost of digital archiving.

One cost model is the Yale University Libraries Project Open Book, designed to study the costs of converting the printed text and accompanying materials in 10,000 brittle books to digital image (Butler, 1997, pp. 73–74). One of the realities that became clear following this analysis of digital storage costs is that "the digital world not only makes collaboration possible, it may make it economically imperative . . . [forcing us] to think about the economics of digital libraries not as single institutions, each trying to build the digital mega collection, but as a system of digital libraries and archives that works collaboratively to acquire, describe, disseminate, preserve and store information resources which may be individually or jointly owned" (p. 74):

> Project Open Book investigators expected to find that both digital storage and access costs would be cheaper than the costs of storage and access in a traditional paper-based library. However, the results of the study showed that unit costs for storage were more than 12 times higher, and for access 50% higher in the digital archive than in the traditional library. These results were true in the first year of operation and continued to be true for storage costs, though to a lesser degree projected over ten years, even when staff and overhead costs for the traditional library were taken into consideration. Clearly this economic analysis favors the traditional library. On the other hand, if we think about the digital library as a fundamentally different kind of organization which needs to be structured, organized, and managed in a different way, a different picture begins to appear.
>
> When Yale modeled the costs for a distributed network-based system of archives rather than for a single institutional model, the cost comparisons begin to improve significantly. Access costs per volume evened out in the 4th year and favored the digital archive by 57% in year 10. Even then, however, the digital archive began to be less expensive than the traditional library for storage costs only in the 7th year. (p. 74)

While funded research is underway on several levels, including awards provided by The National Science Foundation (NSF) and the Library of Congress through their Digital Archiving and Long-term Preservation program (DIGARCH), what happens when the grant funding ends? It will be imperative for organizations to develop a business plan that "helps link digital programs to the host institutions' overall strategic plans and goals" (Lytle, 2006, p. 23). It is always an option to do nothing and leave most of the work of digital archaeology to our descendents. "'Digital archaeology' reminds us that extra work today for preservation is not always essential—merely cost-effective. It leaves rescuing content to (agents for) whoever wants what it conveys. This might be done as a matter of policy, or simply because we cannot persuade people to prepare works for preservation . . . [or because one is not] willing to expend money and effort on behalf of unknown future beneficiaries" (Gladney & Lorie, 2005, p. 306). The movie industry has realized that the cost of storing a digital master record is nearly 12 times the cost of storing a conventional film master. "Much worse, to keep the enormous swarm of data produced when a picture is 'born digital'—that is, produced using all-electronic processes, rather than relying wholly or partially on film—pushes the cost of preservation to $208,569 a year, vastly higher than the $486 it costs to toss the equivalent camera negatives, audio recording, on-set photographs and annotated scripts of an all-film production into the cold-storage vault" (Cieply, 2007, para. 7). However, "movie companies rely on their libraries for about one-third of their $36 billion in annual revenue" so the business model in this case includes a substantial return on investment that libraries cannot rely on (Cieply, 2007, para. 15).

Digital Preservation Strategies

The U.S. National Archives and Records Administration

Deserving of special attention in the discussion of standards and digital preservation strategies is the particular challenge faced by the U.S. National Archives and Records Administration (NARA) because of its responsibility to "preserve and deliver authentic records to subsequent generations of users" (Thibodeau, 2001, p. 1).

> What differentiates records from documentary materials in general is not their form, but their connection to the activities in which they are made and received. If this link is broken, corrupted, or even obscured, the information in the record may be preserved, but the record itself is lost. This fundamental difference between records and documents can be readily illustrated empirically. For example, a map of Sarajevo is a document, but a map of Sarajevo known to have been used in making a targeting decision that led to the bombing of the Chinese Embassy is an essential record of that action. The key difference between the document and the record is the specification of the context of action in which the record was involved. To preserve authentic records entails preserving the documents themselves and also their connections to the activities in which they were used. . . . To preserve records means to preserve them in their original order. To extend the National Archives of the United States into the digital era, then, entails being able to preserve the content, structure and context of the records. When any of these elements can only be expressed in digital form, the records must be preserved in that form. For NARA, as for other archival institutions, the difficulty of doing so is compounded by the commitment to preserve records permanently. . . . The wholesale absence of proven methods for digital preservation presses acutely on NARA. But NARA is not only responsible for preserving unique historical materials, but also for guiding all other federal agencies in creating and managing all of the records they need in performing their functions. The requirements for managing active records in support of the specific needs of ongoing activities are significantly different from those entailed by the objective of preserving and delivering authentic records to future users whose interests, objectives, methods and tools are essentially unknowable. (Thibodeau, 2001, pp. 1–2)

Migration

Hunter (2000) notes that in international discussions regarding archiving issues there is a presumption that for online journals, migration will be the methodology of choice. However, a great number of questions still need to be answered, and she suggests that "until those questions are resolved, libraries will be understandably reluctant to make a permanent switch from paper to electronic collections. What should be archived? In what format? How many copies of the archive are needed? Who holds those copies? What is the access to the archive and who controls that access? How does licensing affect archive building? What can the scholarly community afford?" (Hunter, 2000, para. 3).

Keeping those questions in mind, migration is defined as the "periodic transfer of digital materials from one hardware/software configuration to another, or from one generation of computer technology to a subsequent generation" (PADI, 2001b). For example, the information on a floppy disk may be transferred to a CD-ROM format, offering only a temporary preservation since the CD-ROM format must then be migrated when the technology changes again. The digital information must be refreshed without changing it, and in a new operating environment the copy is not exactly the same as the original, requiring decisions about the aspects that need to be preserved. Metadata can assist here in providing information about migrations and the effect on the digital object. In some cases, software that is backwards compatible can simplify the migration process (the most recent version of the software having the capability of decoding the files created in the earlier version). And systems that are interoperable will also help. However, there is no guarantee as to the compatibility over time as technological developments become increasingly complex and/or it is no longer financially worthwhile for a software manufacturer to support such compatibilities. Some question the practicality of migration while some point out that each new format will require a unique solution.

Migration discussions include the most basic strategy of changing media and transferring from the digital mode to a more stable, controlled environment, the most extreme version being the preservation on paper or preservation-quality microfilm. Although an archival quality paper or microfilm record can last up to 500 years (Lyons, 2001), the advantage of preserving a digital record is that the print or microfilm record may not be able to adequately represent the original object as the digital functionality of the resource can be destroyed. Feeney (1999, p. 114) mentions the computation capabilities, graphic display, or indexing that can be lost, citing the equations embedded in a spreadsheet and the impossibility of printing out an interactive full motion video or preserving a multimedia document as a flat file. Concerns over data loss and the loss of functionality or the look and feel of the original platform are still of a concern regarding the migration method. "The idea of *transformative migration* (a.k.a. *active migration*) is to transform saved data to a new encoding with replacement technology whenever the imminent demise of some technology threatens its interpretability. If programming technology continues to change as quickly as has been the case in the most recent two decades, this could be needed roughly every 5 years" (Gladney & Lorie, 2005, p. 307).

Emulation

Those concerned about the drawbacks to migration view emulation as the alternative, superior method. "The essential idea behind emulation is to be able to access or run original data/software on a new/current platform by running software on a new/current platform that emulates the original platform" (Granger, 2000, para. 2). Granger (2000) and Bearman (1999) provide thorough reviews of the emulation option, which is championed by Jeff Rothenberg (1998).

Encapsulation

This technique has been proposed as a strategy to be used in conjunction with other methods in order to interpret content using new systems over time. "Encapsulation can be achieved by using physical or logical structures called 'containers' or 'wrappers' to provide a relationship between all information components, such as the digital object and other supporting information such as a persistent identifier, metadata, software specifications for emulation" (PADI, 2001a).

Durable Encoding

The debates about the most effective strategies "have not resolved the issues. To help us choose a course of action, it is sufficient to note that neither method [migration nor emulation] has been demonstrated to permit a sure way of avoiding syntactic errors. What they fail to provide is sure conversion to future interpretable languages for computer programs or for other information for which broadly accepted data standards are insufficiently reliable. . . . Both try to preserve obsolete technical environments—information that is both difficult to capture correctly and also irrelevant to authors' objectives" (Gladney & Lorie, 2005, pp. 307, 306). In response to the debate about transformative migration versus preservation emulation, Gladney and Lorie (2005) suggest durable encoding using "current hardware and software information in rewrite routines whose outputs exclude irrelevant information from preservation bit strings. This is accomplished by creating universal virtual computer (UVC) programs that accompany today's content to render it for our descendants. The UVC definition is simple enough that a complete specification can be written to be correctly understood whenever needed. Every step of creating and emulating UVC programs can be executed by programmers of ordinary competence. Part of each preservation package can be today's bit-strings. No bit need be discarded. No detail should be altered. Durable encoding will not interfere with any invention for exploiting the saved information in new ways (repurposing), because all essential details about today's context can be saved" (pp. 321–322). Gladney and Lorie address the need for the stored object to be intelligible to the future researcher by identifying the problem as "the kind of language problem that has been central to computer science since it emerged as a discipline in the 1960s" (p. 300). However, this recommendation "treats only relatively simple digital objects—static data files and the class of programs called filters. Static data files and filters are sufficient for a large fraction of the resources at risk. If it is truly urgent, as other authors have suggested, to start preservation activities because significant cultural losses would otherwise occur, our method is practical for the implementation of early large-scale repositories" (Gladney & Lorie, 2005, p. 317).

CONCLUSION

Digital preservation is a well-intended response to the proliferation of formats and the radical extension of access that networked technology offers. However, even this brief review of the shop talk among librarians dealing with these projects and their problems highlights three related overarching problems: even after 10 years of work, there are still no standards clearly emerging; the simultaneous proliferation and then obsolescence of formats, reading mechanisms, and software continues to be a staggering problem; the costs to address the issues just noted on top of doing what libraries traditionally do with materials (including digital ones) are unsupportable. Soete (1997) suggests stepping back, considering the organizational mission and "how it might best be served through digital preservation programs; to recall and understand what is known already in the organization about digital preservation—the experiences everyone has had, for example, with migrating digital data from one system to another; to consider analogous experiences with preserving the print heritage—what are the lessons to be learned?" (p. 15). Solutions to the problems of digital archiving are still years away. Beware of the promises of electronic publishers, and, yes, unfashionable as it may be to note, for preservation purposes, print is still unrivalled.

REFERENCES

Bearman, D. (1999). Reality and chimeras in the preservation of electronic records. *D-Lib Magazine, 5*(4). Retrieved February 6, 2008, from http://www.dlib.org/dlib/april99/bearman/04bearman.html.

Bradley, K. (2007). Defining digital sustainability. *Library Trends, 56*(1), 148–163.

British Library (2008, January 16). Press release: Pioneering research shows "Google generation" is a myth. Retrieved February 8, 2008, from http://www.bl.uk/cgi-bin/print.cgi?url=/news/2008pressrelease20080116.html.

Butler, M. (1997). Issues and challenges of archiving and storing digital information: Preserving the past for future scholars. *Journal of Library Administration, 24*(4), 61–79.

Cantara, L. (2005). METS: The Metadata Encoding and Transmission Standard. *Cataloging & Classification Quarterly, 40*(3/4), 237–253.

Caplan, P., & Guenther, R. (2005). Digital preservation: Finding balance. *Library Trends, 54*(1), 111–124.

Cieply, M. (2007, December 23). Scene stealer: The afterlife is expensive for digital movies. *The New York Times.* Retrieved January 2, 2008, from http://www.nytimes.com/2007/12/23/business/media/23steal.html?

Coyle, K. (2006). Managing technology: One word: Digital. *The Journal of Academic Librarianship, 32*(2), 205–207.

Duff, W. (2004). Metadata in digital preservation: Foundations, functions, issues. In F. M. Bischoff, H. Hofman, & S. Ross (Eds.), *Metadata in preservation: Selected papers from an ERPANET seminar at the Archives School Marburg* (pp. 27–38). September 3–5, 2003 (Veroffentlichungen der Archivschule Marburg, Institute fur Archivwissenschaft, Nr. 40), Marburg: Archivschule.

Duranti, L., & Thibodeau, K. (2006). The concept of record in interactive, experiential and dynamic environments: The view of InterPARES. *Archival Science, 6,* 13–68.

Feeney, M. (1999). Towards a national strategy for archiving digital materials. *Alexandria, 11*(2), 107–122.

Gladney, H. M., & Lorie, R. A. (2005). Trustworthy 100-year digital objects: Durable encoding for when it's too late to ask. *ACM Transactions on Information Systems, 23*(3), 299–324.

Granger, S. (2000, October). Emulation as a digital preservation strategy. *D-Lib Magazine, 6*(10) Retrieved February 6, 2008, from http://www.dlib.org/dlib/october00/granger/10granger.html.

Guenther, R., & Myrick, L. (2006). Archiving Web sites for preservation and access: MODS, METS and MINERVA. *Journal of Archival Organization, 4*(1/2), 141–166.

Hunter, K. (2000). Digital archiving. *Serials Review, 26*(3), 62–64.

Huwe, T. K. (2006). From librarian to digital communicator: following the media to new organizational roles. *Online,* 30(5), 21–26.

Knight, S. (2005). Preservation metadata: National Library of New Zealand experience. *Library Trends, 54*(1), 91–110.

Lyons, S. (Ed.) (2001). *Staying digital: Recommendations on preserving New Jersey government information in the digital age.* Report of the State Documents Interest Group of the Documents Association of New Jersey. Retrieved February 6, 2008, from http://www.danj.org/.

Lytle, A. (2006). Statewide digitization planners conference summary report. *Microform & Imaging Review, 35*(1), 19–30.

McDonough, J. P. (2006). METS: Standardized encoding for digital library objects. *International Journal on Digital Libraries, 6*(2), 148–158.

National Commission on Libraries and Information Science (NCLIS). (2001). *A comprehensive assessment of public information dissemination.* vol. 2, containing Appendices 11 and 12, the Legislative and Regulatory Proposals: Available in print and in electronic form. Washington, DC: U.S. National Commission on Libraries and Information Science. Retrieved February 4, 2008, from http://www.nclis.gov/govt/assess/assess.vol2.pdf.

OCLC/RLG Working Group on Preservation Metadata. (2001, January 31). *Preservation metadata for digital objects: A review of the state of the art.* Retrieved February 6, 2008, from http://www.oclc.org/research/projects/pmwg/presmeta_wp.pdf.

O'Mahony, D. P. (1998). Here today, gone tomorrow: What can be done to assure permanent public access to electronic information? *Advances in Librarianship, 22,* 107–121.

Preserving Access to Digital Information. (2001a). *Encapsulation.* Retrieved February 4, 2008, from http://www.nla.gov.au/padi/topics/20.html.

Preserving Access to Digital Information. (2001b). *Migration.* Retrieved February 4, 2008, from http://www.nla.gov.au/padi/topics/21.html.

Preserving Access to Digital Information. (2001c). *Standards.* Retrieved February 4, 2008, from http://www.nla.gov.au/padi/topics/43.html.

Rosenthal, D. S. H., Robertson, T., Lipkis, T., Reich, V., & Morabit, S. (2005). Requirements for digital preservation systems. *D-Lib Magazine, 11*(11). Retrieved December 7, 2007, from http://www.dlib.org/dlib/november05/rosenthal/11rosenthal.html.

Rothenberg, J. (1998). *Avoiding technological quicksand: Finding a viable technical foundation for digital preservation.* The Council on Library and Information Reports. Retrieved February 6, 2008, from http://www.clir.org/pubs/reports/rothenberg/contents.html.

Sharpe, R. (2007). Digital preservation: Solving archive challenges. *Research Information, 30*(June/July). Retrieved December 10, 2007, from http://www.researchinformation.info/features/feature.php?feature_id=134.

Soete, G. (1997). *Transforming libraries: Issues and innovations in preserving digital information. Systems and Procedures Exchange Center SPEC Kit 228.* Washington, DC: Association of Research Libraries.

Teper, T. (2007). The future of preservation in ARL libraries. *ARL, 251,* 9–11.

Thibodeau, K. (2001). Building the archives of the future: Advances in preserving electronic records at the National Archives and Records Administration. *D-Lib Magazine, 7*(2). Retrieved February 6, 2008, from http://www.dlib.org/dlib/february01/thibodeau/02thibodeau.html.

Thibodeau, K. (2004). NARA's electronic records archives program. *Law Library Journal, 96*(4), 633–642.

Thibodeau, K. (2007). The Electronic Records Program at the National Archives and Records Administration. *First Monday, 12*(7). Retrieved December 7, 2007, from http://www.uic.edu/htbin/cgiwrap/bin/ojs/index.php/fm/article/viewArticle/1922/1804.

University of Lethbridge. (n.d.). Library. *Records management terms.* Retrieved February 6, 2008, from http://www.uleth.ca/lib/archives/records_management/glossary.asp.

Additional Works Consulted

Academy of Motion Picture Arts and Sciences, Science and Technology Council. (2007, November). *The digital dilemma* [report]. Beverly Hills, CA: Academy of Motion Picture Arts and Sciences.

ARL Task Force on the Future of Preservation in ARL Libraries. *Research libraries' enduring responsibility for preservation.* Association of Research Libraries, http://www.arl.org/bm~doc/preservation_responsibility_24july07.pdf.

CAMiLEON (Creative Archiving at Michigan and Leeds Emulating the Old on the New), http://www.si.umich.edu/CAMILEON/.

Caplan, P. (2003). *Metadata fundamentals for all librarians.* Chicago: American Library Association.

CEDARS (Curl Exemplars in Digital Archives), http://www.leeds.ac.uk/cedars.

CLIR & the Library of Congress. *Building a national strategy for preservation: Issues in digital media archiving.* Commissioned for and sponsored by the National Digital Information Infrastructure and Preservation Program, Library of Congress. Retrieved from http://www.clir.org/pubs/reports/pub106/pub106.pdf.

CLOCKSS (Collecting Lots of Copies Keeps Stuff Safe), http://www.clockss.org.

Commission on Preservation and Access (CPA) & the Research Libraries Group (RLG). (1996). *Preserving digital information: Report of the Task Force on Archiving of Digital Information.* Washington, DC: Commission on Preservation and Access.

Council on Library and Information Resources (CLIR), http://www.clir.org.

Cunningham, A., & Phillips, M. (2005). Accountability and accessibility: Ensuring the evidence of e-governance in Australia. *Aslib Proceedings, 57*(4), 301–317.

Digital Opportunity Investment Trust (DO IT), http://www.digitalpromise.org/newsite/about/What_Is.html (for text of legislation and to identify the latest major action on this pending legislation, see http://thomas.loc.gov/cgi-bin/query/z?c108:S.1854:).

Electronic Records Archives System (NARA), http://www.archives.gov/era.

Florida Center for Library Automation (FCLA) Digital Archive (FDA), http://www.fcla.edu/digitalArchive/index.htm.

Future Digital System (FDsys), http://www.gpo.gov/projects/pdfs/FDsys_RD_v2.1.pdf.

Institute of Museum and Library Services (IMLS), http://www.imls.gov.

International Internet Preservation Consortium (IIPC), http://www.netpreserve.org/about/index.php.

International Research on Permanent Authentic Records in Electronic Systems Project (InterPARES), (2 phases, 1999–2001, 2002–2006), http://www.interpares.org/book/index.cfm.

LOCKSS (Lots of Copies Keep Stuff Safe), http://www.lockss.org.

Metadata Object Description Schema (MODS), http://www/loc.gov/standards/mods.

MINERVA Web Archiving and Preservation Project (Library of Congress), http://lcweb2.loc.gov/cocoon/minerva/html/minerva-home.html.

NARA (National Archives and Records Administration), Project (NARA: Persistent Archives and Electronic Records Management), http://www.sdsc.edu/NARA.

National Digital Information Infrastructure and Preservation Program (NDIIPP), http://www.digitalpreservation.gov.

NEDCC (Northeast Document Conservation Center), http://www.nedec.org/home.php.

Open Archival Information System (OAIS) Reference Model, http://public.ccsds.org/publications/archive/650xOb1.pdf.

Open Archives Information-Protocol for Metadata Harvesting (OAI-PMH),

PANDORA: Australia's Web Archive (National Library of Australia), http://pandora.nla.gov.au/about.html.

Preservation Metadata: Implementation Strategies (PREMIS), http://www.oclc.org/research/projects/pmwg. For updates of implementation, consult Preservation Metadata Maintenance Activity, http://www.loc.gov/standards/premis. For Data Dictionary for Preservation Metadata, http://www.oclc.org/research/projects/pmwg/premis-final.pdf.

CONCLUSION: JUST HOW CRITICAL SHOULD LIBRARIANSHIP BE OF TECHNOLOGY?

John E. Buschman

In 1998, James O'Donnell wrote a "deliberately associative and informal" book, *Avatars of the Word: From Papyrus to Cyberspace,* meant as a "series of meditations approaching the issues and experiences of our own time" (p. x). The book was widely reviewed (including some in the library press), was issued in paperback, and has attained an afterlife as a continuing source of commentary and debate. It is notable for our purposes here because of two interwoven themes of the book: the prominence in the analysis of historical shifts in technologies of writing (from the scroll to the codex to the printed book to current electronic manifestations of "text", and the related prominence of libraries and librarians in all of this). Another notable point is that O'Donnell was fortunate enough to alight then on what is now a Web 2.0/Second Life buzzword in his choice of title: *Avatar.* By this he means a "'manifestation'—the form in which some abstract and powerful force takes palpable shape for human perception" (p. xi) and not a digital character inhabiting digital real estate on a digital island. *Avatars* (the book) is still instructive for our purposes not because of a choice of a now-hip word but because of the ways in which O'Donnell is importantly right and, perhaps more importantly, wrong. He interweaves his analysis of the transition from orality to writing, then print, beginning in Latin late antiquity (his scholarly area and a continuing touchstone), the achievement of the building of libraries, teaching, learning, and scholarship in what became modern higher education, and the meaning of digitized resources for the future. In the process, O'Donnell articulates (sometimes explicitly, mostly implicitly) the question suggested by the subtitle of this conclusion, which speaks to many of the motivations driving developments in librarianship and deserves an answer: given the extremely large role of technology in librarianship, just how critical should we actually be of this new Leviathan? Reviewing O'Donnell and the relevant issues he raised 10 years ago gives us a chance to answer that question.

IMPORTANTLY RIGHT

First and foremost, O'Donnell notes that the book is *not* dead: "zealots foolishly proclaim [it], and utopians and dystopians croon and keen over the futures their fantasies allow them" (p. 9). Time and again, he takes the longer view that there are "no simple changes, . . . all changes will bring both costs and benefits, loss and gain" (p. 9). He demonstrates this by noting the various resistances to printed books during the late Middle Ages (pp. 77–81), noting that such objectors were not mere Luddites or foot-draggers but rather rationally preferred the beauty of script, or wished only to copy out shorter portions of various books to bind together, or rightly objected that printing reproduces the same error in all copies. More importantly, printed books "undermin[ed] the ethos of the monastery and its scriptorium" with all the attendant religious and cultural fallout (p. 81). In other words, even early on, technologies of communication were a form of power, especially illustrated in the new reach of the papacy (through writing and the codex) to codify (and thus control) the Mass and bureaucratize the operations of Rome (pp. 35–37). O'Donnell is making the point that our choices of technology embody long-range consequences of import beyond the immediate, that technologies do not simply supplant their predecessors but rather join an existing ensemble, and that critiques of technology are not mere anachronisms.

Culturally, O'Donnell is dead-on when he notes just how tenuous our constructions of the texts of the "classics" and our religio-cultural "fathers" are. Saint Jerome, Thomas More, Erasmus, Saint Augustine, the Bible, and re-rediscovered interest in Greek "origins" are all the products of a shaping, reading, and (sometimes convenient) rereading backward from present to the past (pp. 1–13, 51–53, 99–105, 124–143). Furthermore, he gleans from this not a program of deconstruction (though he comes close) but rather an intellectual globalism: the notion that learning and absorbing other languages will damage cultural unity is "preposterous *chutzpah*" and "just who we exclude and include in our cultural legend-making has lasting political effects," like the deeming of Islam as "Eastern" and not "Western" (pp. 114–116). Some of our "classic" authors like Erasmus and More consciously shaped their images, and the British appropriation of classical antiquity was consciously adopted as an implicit justification for empire and pre-Christian values. Greece thus has a heritage of importance rooted as much in the nineteenth century as the fourth century bc. Some texts were enormously advantaged by their technology: "if you were a very farsighted text of the second century and you wanted to be read a thousand or more years later, the thing you most wanted was to be copied into a codex format" (p. 52). O'Donnell goes on to outline the considerable technical and preservation advantages of the codex, and the consequence that "in the age of writing . . . it is possible to know things without committing them to memory, and that is a very great revolution indeed" (pp. 54–55). In other words, we have reified a series of readings, constructions, and technological accidents and privileges into a legend we call Western culture at our peril, and the book (as we have conceived it) is at the core of much of this.

Finally, O'Donnell gives librarians and libraries their due:

- Responding to the electronic network–induced potential that there may soon "be as many publishers as readers," he responds that the value of the "traditional library [is] suddenly obvious[:] not its inclusivity but its exclusivity; its discerning judgment" (p. 43).
- Open stacks, indices, iterations of catalogs, the flexibility of forms of access, and "chronologically diverse" collections are all indications of the "flexibility, the diversity, and the subtlety of the machine we have created." Librarians have been among the busiest and most productive (if overlooked—actually a measure of their success) adapters of technology for sensible, coherent uses (pp. 64–70).
- The "assault on the legally defined concept of 'fair use' . . . threaten[s] our public and research libraries as nothing has in decades" (p. 95).
- In an era of unlimited information (both dependable and otherwise), the crucial decision about what is worth paying for and not, ownership versus access, and so forth, raises the provocative question "Can we imagine a time in our universities when librarians are the well-paid principals and teachers their mere acolytes?" (p. 90).
- He notes that the "virtual library" is a not-so-updated version of the very old dream of the universal library, which continues to "seem so current [and] enthrall" us. In the end, it is a "very conservative dream" (p. 42). Though O'Donnell does not necessarily mean this in a purely positive light (in terms of *conceptions* of libraries, not a reflection on the current profession or institution), *conservative* is taken here to mean *conserve,* and much of what librarians have achieved has been, in the most literal sense of the term, positively culturally conservative. Having done so, libraries enable some grounding of a rational dialogue with the past—a fundamental point O'Donnell implicitly and explicitly states time and again throughout the book.
- Technologically however, O'Donnell notes that "an electronic text subjected to the same degree of neglect" as, for instance, a book that has lain around for many (or hundreds) of years, "is unlikely to survive for five years." Library users have come to expect the latest, best, fastest, *and* "permanence and reliability as well. We can't have both" (pp. 48–49).
- Finally, in the bibliographic notes, O'Donnell states flatly that the fashionable assumption that virtual resources will do away with library buildings is a "wrong-headed expectation" (p. 199).

IMPORTANTLY WRONG

Where *Avatars* is importantly wrong is a case that builds throughout the volume. First, after declaring the foolishness of declaring the end of the book, O'Donnell goes on to state that the nature of the "media on which the word relies are changing their nature and extending their range to an extent not seen since the invention of movable type." And while there is not a pure technological supplanting, the times are "exciting [and] we will be put on our mettle to find ways to adapt technologies to our lives and our lives to technologies" (p. 9). The fixity of words and their resulting durability (that is, their worth—we are speaking of print now) is equated with "authoritative discourse [and] a single monologic voice," which cannot really be defended. That printed words cannot be in flux is their great drawback, and that "forms of organization of knowledge in electronic media do not resemble those of the traditional codex book" is their great strength. In sum, what we communicate now is, essentially, not worth preserving—the speed and trajectory of society and technology making those words "obsolete" very fast (pp. 40–43). We leap backwards in time to the lesson of the failed experiment of Cassiodorus in the sixth century to instill monastic scribal culture. Though Cassiodorus has mistakenly been seen as a direct "link" to this development, O'Donnell still sees value in his endeavor now: he "had the right idea. He did not despise the new; he used it wholeheartedly. He did not reject old social institutions, but rather found new ways to adapt them. . . . Most of all, he *did* things" (pp. 86–88).

Avatars then goes on to the observation that "education is not just downloading information" (p. 155) and a simultaneously amusing and dispiriting précis on higher education ("for professors only") and why "we're not an industry a reasonable person would invest money in by any conventional criterion" (pp. 168–172). What he takes from all this is, in sum: (1) that technology's effect has consistently been the "attenuation of social linkages"; (2) thus there are corollary expansions of virtual connections scattered across a wide geographic range; (3) which means an embracing of some (but only some) forms of distance and virtual learning for efficacy's and efficiency's sake; (4) in turn there should be a productive emphasis on forms of community in higher education and a conscious further blurring of the boundaries between "school" and "life"; (5) higher education should adopt a sensible institutionalization of a form of lifelong/continuous learning within the structure of degrees (e.g., a "lifetime warranty") enabled now by technology; (6) there should also be a frankness about the "youth camp" and competitive/consumerist aspects of current academic life (pp. 175–189); and (7) finally there is the related need to disassociate new *intellectual* media and discourse from the vast profits and lawsuits "over [pirated] punk-rock CDs and *Lion King* videos" to preserve/rescue the underpinnings of libraries and humanistic research (p. 98).

To start off most simply, while O'Donnell nods toward loss and gain with every "technological advance" (p. ix), the exemplars of gains rhetorically outweigh the losses considerably throughout—as the word *advance* in the prior phrase implies. In combination with other language noted above (test our mettle, exciting times, historical epoch, etc.), it is clear that the burden of proof lies, as he has constructed the issue, on the negative case against technological change. Then there is the dual problem of his lack of overarching concern/worry about the fixity of words/content/data combined with analysis that digital resources will require an entirely new universe of knowledge organization. To tackle the second issue first, O'Donnell himself notes that alphabetization, indexes, concordances, and mere compilations of reference information in a book all enable nonlinear access, and have done so since the medieval codex. Moving between texts using the Gospel canon tables was, in his view, just an early form of hyperlinking. In other words, it is resolutely not a new issue, but where does it necessarily follow now (as he indicates) that we will end up in the "ultimate postmodern authorless creation"? (pp. 57–63). And how does this square with the role of research and scholarship to humanize the past and "de-dignify" it? Further, how does he square the disregard for fixity with the need to read the past to "engage . . . our commitments and our opportunities in the present" (pp. 138–143)? Where is that past of the future to come from with so little concern for fixity or casting it as the enemy of new, nonlinear developments?

O'Donnell's perch is high (and he acknowledges this), but surely someone in his position knows full well that "anyone who has used a word-processing system . . . knows how easy it is to transform information in a digital context. . . . The alternation of digitally stored photographs . . . is also quite practical. . . . [T]his represents a major problem in terms of the integrity of historical documents" (Provenzo, quoted in Buschman, 1993, p. 143). The lack of regard comes off as curious at best—especially given that many of the issues he outlines concerning preservation and access (varying digital formats/codes, and obsolescent reading devices) remain of vexingly current and large-scale concern. Finally, *Avatars* nods approvingly toward Richard Lanham's work (1993) but critically notes that because Lanham concluded that communication skills and rhetoric are foundational in an electronic age, and because "rhetoric is indeed a very old discipline," therefore a "magically benign cultural continuity emerges." (O'Donnell, 1998, p. 149) However, that is precisely where O'Donnell ends up—albeit with more recognition that we will have our mettle tested in the mean time—in his discussions of what the technology is driving us to do with libraries and higher education. The effect is to seriously raise the concern of just how critical should we actually be in taking on the Leviathan of technology—particularly *librarianship* doing so. He thus undercuts the basis of critique from the start: we must transform ourselves and our practices, adapt, or die and go the way of the elevator man or the buggy whip maker. This backdrop clearly underlies much of the management thinking in librarianship today (Buschman, 2003). It explicitly discourages and marginalizes productive critique

Avatars comes very close to casting technologies as neutral and apolitical, whereas any more-than-casual examination indicates they are resolutely not so: tomato picking machinery assumes the need to develop the hybrid of a tougher tomato that can be machine-handled; overpasses built too low to accommodate public transportation (buses) privilege the automobile and those who can afford to operate one (Winner, 1986, pp. 19–39). One can legitimately ask: Are we creating the educational/intellectual/library technological equivalents of inedible tomatoes or unnavigable paths for our conveyances? Are we privileging other things with these choices? What are they? Are those things being privileged best for society or democracy? Furthermore, there is a strong streak of narrowing essentialism here "which privileges one attribute of technical artifacts—function—over all the others" (Feenberg, 2000b, p. 305). Altogether these approaches in *Avatars* cast technologies as an autonomous, rationalizing force. Alternately, if we take O'Donnell at his word that what will become of our digital communication technologies will be what we make of them in our daily struggles (constructivism), then the focus narrows and ignores the "larger question of how particular . . . choices are made over other choices which . . . is an inherently political question" (Veak, 2000, pp. 227–228). If technology is neutral, if it is a fact on the ground we must deal with, if it will simply be what it is going to be shaped through intelligent individual struggle, *then we really do have no business critiquing technologies, especially in librarianship.* However, there would be significant issues overlooked in such a case.

Feenberg (2000b) observes that technologies reproduce hierarchies, and they are embedded in economic disparities. There is further a deep symbiosis between technologies, inequalities, the control of technologies and technological choices, and the embedding of technologies in our daily lives through marketing (Power, 2000; Veak, 2000, pp. 230–235). Borgmann (quoted in Higgs, Light, & Strong, 2000, p. 13) argues that there is a "central vacuity" about our technologies: they have not delivered fuller, richer lives, and we are in fact losing an essential, grounding element of the good life in their pervasiveness (see also Borgmann, 2000; Power, 2000). Elsewhere, he makes another crucial link: "engaging and changing the public sphere must remain our goal" (Borgmann, 2000, p. 343). That is radically difficult to do in an inauthentic environment that (technologically) privileges individual gratification, minimizes collective action, conceals complexity, and frames life and work within regimes of consumption (Borgmann, 2000; Winner, 2004). Hopes for networked communications to reinvigorate the democratic public sphere will not be realized without a critical approach to technologies and networked information resources, and librarianship will/can play no positive role in democratic consequences of information technologies without critique. *That* is the overarching message behind the variety of chapters in this book. Finally, there is the even more fundamental issue of playing our part in the "survival of agency in technocratic societies," that is, critically enabling people "to act as agents in the technical sphere from which technocracy draws its force" (Feenberg, 2000a, p. 241). In other words, as a learned profession that claims a broad swath of public and cultural responsibilities, not to engage and further the critical interrogations of technology would be a fundamental abdication of responsibilities we loudly claim. *Avatars of the Word* acknowledges the achievements of librarians and libraries vis-à-vis technologies, it has productively highlighted relevant issues (not the least of which is the long historical tail of them), and it has instructed via its avenues of insight and (sometimes) blithe assumptions and essentialist constructions of technology. In turn, this volume has, like its first iteration, opened many paths to potential critique but has not exhausted them. So, in answer to the question posed in the title of this chapter, yes, librarianship *must* question and critique technologies (library-related ones and the larger socioeconomic technical structures in which we are embedded).

REFERENCES

Borgmann, A. (2000). Reply to my critics. In E. Higgs, A. Light, & D. Strong (Eds.), *Technology and the good life?* (pp. 341–370). Chicago: University of Chicago Press.

Buschman, J. (1993). Issues in censorship and information technology. In J. Buschman (Ed.), *Critical approaches to information technology in librarianship: Foundations and applications* (pp. 125–149). Westport, CT: Greenwood Press.

Buschman, J. (2003). *Dismantling the public sphere: Situating and sustaining librarianship in the age of the new public philosophy.* Westport, CT: Libraries Unlimited/Greenwood.

Feenberg, A. (2000a). Do we need a critical theory of technology? Reply to Tyler Veak. *Science, Technology & Human Values, 25*, 238–242.

Feenberg, A. (2000b). From essentialism to constructivism: Philosophy of technology at the crossroads. In E. Higgs, A. Light, & D. Strong (Eds.), *Technology and the good life?* (pp. 294–315). Chicago: University of Chicago Press.

Higgs, E., Light, A., & Strong, D. (2000). Introduction. In E. Higgs, A. Light, & D. Strong (Eds.), *Technology and the good life?* (pp. 1–16). Chicago: University of Chicago Press.

Lanham, R. A. (1993). *The electronic word: Democracy, technology, and the arts.* Chicago: University of Chicago Press.

O'Donnell, J. (1998). *Avatars of the word: from papyrus to cyberspace.* Cambridge, MA: Harvard University Press.

Power, T. M. (2000). Trapped in consumption: Modern social structure and the entrenchment of the device. In E. Higgs, A. Light, & D. Strong (Eds.), *Technology and the good life?* (pp. 271–293). Chicago: University of Chicago Press.

Veak, T. (2000). Whose technology? Whose modernity? Questioning Feenberg's *Questioning technology. Science, Technology & Human Values, 25,* 226–237.

Winner, L. (1986). *The whale and the reactor: A search for limits in an age of high technology.* Chicago: University of Chicago Press.

Winner, L. (2004). Who will we be in cyberspace? In F. Webster (Ed.), *The information society reader* (pp. 45–54). New York: Routledge.

INDEX

ABOUT THE EDITORS AND CONTRIBUTORS

MICHAEL W. APPLE is John Bascom Professor of Curriculum and Instruction and Educational Policy Studies at the University of Wisconsin–Madison. He teaches courses in curriculum theory and research and in the sociology of curriculum. His major interests lie in the relationship between culture and power in education and his current research centers on the limits and possibilities of critical educational policy and practice in a time of conservative restoration. He is the author and editor of numerous books, among them *Ideology and Curriculum,* 25th Anniversary 3rd edition (2004), *The State and Politics of Education* (2003), *Educating the "Right" Way: Markets, Standards, God and Inequality* (2001), *Official Knowledge: Democratic Knowledge in a Conservative Age* (2000), *Cultural Politics and Education* (1996), and *Education and Power,* 2nd edition (1995). His EdD is from Columbia University.

SANDRA BRAMAN has been doing research on the macro-level effects of the use of new information technologies and their policy implications since the mid-1980s. Recent work related to her chapter in this volume includes *Change of State: Information, Policy and Power* (2006) and the edited volumes *The Emergent Global Information Policy Regime* (2004) and *Communication Researchers and Policy-Making* (2003). She is former chair of the Communication Law and Policy Division of the International Communication Association, and sits on the editorial boards of 10 scholarly journals. Her research has been supported by the Ford and Rockefeller foundations. Braman is currently professor of communication, University of Wisconsin–Milwaukee, and previously served as Freedom of Expression Professor, University of Bergen, Norway;

fellow, EDUCAUSE Center for Applied Research; director and visiting professor, Telecommunications and Information Policy Programme, University of South Africa; Reese Phifer Professor of Telecommunication, University of Alabama; research assistant professor, University of Illinois-Urbana; and Henry Rutgers Research Fellow and Assistant Professor, Rutgers University. Braman earned her PhD in 1988 from the University of Minnesota.

JOHN M. BUDD is a professor and associate director with the School of Information Science and Learning Technologies at the University of Missouri. He is the author of a number of journal articles and several books, including *Knowledge and Knowing in Library and Information Science* (2001), winner of the 2002 Highsmith Award, and *Self-Examination* (Libraries Unlimited, 2007).

JOHN E. BUSCHMAN is Associate University Librarian for Scholarly Resources and Services at Georgetown University Library. Immediately prior to this he was department chair and head of Collection Development at the rank of professor-librarian at Rider University Library in Lawrenceville, New Jersey for 19 years. He has published three previous books before this volume: *Critical Approaches to Information Technology in Librarianship: Foundations and Applications* (1993, editor and author of three chapters), *Dismantling the Public Sphere: Situating and Sustaining Libraries in the Age of the New Public Philosophy* (2003), and *Library as Place: History, Community and Culture* (2006, coeditor with Gloria J. Leckie and coauthor of the introductory chapter with Leckie)—all from Libraries Unlimited/Greenwood Publishing Group. *Dismantling the Public Sphere* was the recipient of the American Library Association's Futas Award and the New Jersey Library Association's Research Award—both in 2004. He is a coeditor of the journal *Progressive Librarian,* is on the Progressive Librarians Guild Coordinating Committee, and served for three years on the National Council of the American Association of University Professors (AAUP). Recent publications include articles on Habermas and LIS theory and another on Foucault and LIS theory (both in *Library Quarterly*), a piece on democratic theory and LIS in *JASIST,* and an article on the ALA Code of Ethics in *Library Philosophy and Practice.* He holds a BS in history and sociology and an MLS, both from Ball State University, an MA in American Studies from St. Joseph's University, and is a doctoral candidate in the Liberal Studies Program at Georgetown University.

GRANT CAMPBELL completed his PhD in English at Queen's University in 1990 and his master of information studies at University of Toronto in 1997. He has taught at Dalhousie University and currently teaches in the Faculty of Information and Media Studies at University of Western Ontario. His research interests include information organization, metadata, classification, and electronic text design in the humanities.

ROSS COLLIN is a PhD student in curricular theory and literacy studies in the department of Curriculum and Instruction at the University of Wisconsin–Madison, with a minor in composition and rhetoric. Prior to beginning work in graduate school, Ross taught language arts, humanities and media studies for three years at West Chicago Community High School in West Chicago, Illinois. Ross currently works with preservice teachers in the University of Wisconsin–Madison's School of Education. His research interests are in comparing and contrasting dominant literacies sponsored in contemporary schools and certain digital literacies of increasing value in emerging informational socioeconomic orders in order to understand how powerful literacies can be developed among all students as part of democratic projects to construct more just social, economic, and political orders. He received an MS in curriculum and instruction at the University of Wisconsin–Madison and received a BS in secondary English education at the University of Iowa, Iowa City.

NICK DYER-WITHEFORD is associate dean and associate professor in the Faculty of Information and Media Studies at the University of Western Ontario. He is the author of *Cyber-Marx: Cycles and Circuits of Struggle in High Technology Capitalism* (1999); coauthor with Stephen Kline and Greig de Peuter of *Digital Play: Culture, Markets and Technology* (2003); and with Greig de Peuter of *Games of Empire: Virtual Play and Global Capitalism* (forthcoming).

ANDREW FEENBERG is Canada Research Chair in Philosophy of Technology in the School of Communication, Simon Fraser University. He has also taught for many years in the Philosophy Department at San Diego State University. He is the author of *Critical Theory of Technology* (1991), *Alternative Modernity* (1995), *Questioning Technology* (1999), and *Heidegger, Marcuse and Technology: The Catastrophe and Redemption of Enlightenment* (2004). A second edition of *Critical Theory of Technology* appeared with 2002 under the title *Transforming Technology.* Dr. Feenberg is also coeditor of *Technology and the Politics of Knowledge* (1995), *Modernity and Technology* (2003), and *Community in the Digital Age* (2004). He holds a BA in philosophy from the Johns Hopkins University, and an MA and PhD in philosophy from the University of California, San Diego.

LISA GIVEN, PhD, is associate professor, School of Library and Information Studies, director, International Institute for Qualitative Methodology, and an associate adjunct professor in Humanities Computing at the University of Alberta. Her research interests include individuals' information behaviors, the social construction of knowledge, Web usability, spatial analysis, information literacy, research methods, and information issues in the context of higher education. Her current research project is funded by Canada's Social Sciences and Humanities Research Council and is titled "Participatory Design for a Visually-Based Drug Information Interface: Web Usability in the Context of Consumers' Health Information Behaviours."

ROMA HARRIS is a professor in the Faculty of Information and Media Studies at the University of Western Ontario. Known for her work on gender relations and technology in librarianship and for her studies of abused women's search for information, Harris is the author of *Librarianship: The Erosion of a Woman's Profession* and, with coauthor Patricia Dewdney, *Barriers to Information: How Formal Help Systems Fail Battered Women.* Currently, Harris's work focuses on health help seeking in rural communities and she is leading the Rural HIV/AIDS Information Networks Project funded by the Canadian Institutes of Health Research. She is also coeditor with Nadine Wathen and Sally Wyatt of the forthcoming book, *Mediating Health Information: The Go-Betweens in a Changing Socio-Technical Landscape.*

ANDREW LARGE holds the CN-Pratt-Grinstad Chair in Information Studies at the School of Information Studies, McGill University, and was the school's director from 1989 until 1998. His recent research and publications have focused on the information-seeking behavior of children and information technology that can support this behavior. He is currently investigating the role of information visualization in Web portals intended for young users. His latest coauthored book is *Digital Libraries: Principles and Practice in a Global Environment* (2005).

GLORIA J. LECKIE graduated with her MLIS in 1974 and worked for a decade as a librarian in academic and research libraries. After completing her PhD in geography from the University of Western Ontario in 1991, she accepted a position with the Graduate School of Library and Information Science (now a component of the larger Faculty of Information and Media Studies) at Western. Leckie's primary areas of teaching and research include cataloging, academic librarianship, information-seeking practices, and library as place. She is the coeditor (with John Buschman) of *Library as Place: History, Community and Culture* (Libraries Unlimited, 2007).

GARY T. MARX is professor emeritus from M.I.T., and is currently the Hixon-Riggs Professor of Science, Technology and Society at Harvey Mudd College, Claremont, California. He is the author (with Doug McAdam) of *Protest and Prejudice, Undercover: Police Surveillance in America, Collective Behavior and Social Movements*, editor (with C. Fijnaut) of *Racial Conflict, Muckraking Sociology, Undercover: Police Surveillance in Comparative*

Perspective, and other books. With Norman Goodman, he edited *Sociology: Popular and Classical Approaches.* Marx was named the American Sociological Association's Jensen Lecturer for 1989–1990. He received the Distinguished Scholar Award from its section on Crime, Law and Deviance, the Silver Gavel Award from the American Bar Association, and the Bruce C. Smith Award for research achievement. In 1992 he was the inaugural Stice Memorial Lecturer in residence at the University of Washington, and he has been a UC Irvine Chancellor's Distinguished Fellow and the A. D. Carlson Visiting Distinguished Professor in the Social Sciences at West Virginia University. He received his PhD from the University of California at Berkeley.

AJIT PYATI is an assistant professor in the Faculty of Information and Media Studies at the University of Western Ontario. His MLIS and PhD degrees are from the University of California, Los Angeles. His research interests at present cover these following major areas: international library development; information society and policy; globalization, migration, and ICTs; and critical information studies.

DOROTHY A. WARNER is assistant preservation librarian at Georgetown University Library and, immediately prior to this appointment, was professor–librarian, coordinator of the Library Instruction Program, and government documents librarian at Rider University Library for 14 years. She has published two books, most recently *A Disciplinary Blueprint for the Assessment of Information Literacy* (Libraries Unlimited, 2008) and *Knowing Good Schools: A Guide to Rating Public High Schools* (coauthored with W. Guthrie, Greenwood Publishing, 2001). She holds a BA from the University of Arizona and an MLS and an MPS (in art therapy), both from the Pratt Institute.

MICHAEL F. WINTER is social and behavioral sciences librarian at the University of California, Davis Library, where he has been since 1985. He is the author of *The Culture and Control of Expertise: Toward a Sociological Understanding of Librarianship* (Greenwood Publishing, 1988), and coeditor of *Crime and Deviance: Essays and Innovations of Edwin M. Lemert* (2000), as well as "Specialization, Territoriality, and Jurisdiction: Librarianship and the Political Economy of Knowledge," in *Library Trends, 45* (Fall 1996), "Umberto Eco on Libraries: A Discussion of 'De Bibliotheca,'" in *Library Quarterly, 64* (April 1994), and "Garlic, Vodka, and the Politics of Gender: Anti-Intellectualism in American Librarianship," in *Progressive Librarian,* (14, Spring 1998). Winter holds a BA from Kalamazoo College, an MA and PhD from Northwestern University, and an MLS from the University of Minnesota.